THE SOCIAL IMPERATIVE

FOR MY TWO Es, MOTHER, AND FATHER

The Social Imperative
Architecture and the City in China

First edition 2017

Published by: Actar Publishers,
New York, Barcelona, www.actar.com
Graphic Design: Lam Lai Shun
Translation: H. Koon Wee

Distribution:
Actar D, Inc. New York
440 Park Avenue South, 17th Floor
10016 New York NY
T +1 212 966 2207
F +1 212 966 2214
salesnewyork@actar-d.com

Actar D, Inc. Barcelona
Roca i Batlle, 2-4
08023 Barcelona, Spain
salesbarcelona@actar-d.com

Printing:
Tiger Printing, Hong Kong
Printed in Shenzhen, China

ISBN 978-0989331791

Library of Congress Cataloging-in-Publication Data
Library of Congress Control No.: 2016953801
1. China – Architecture – Design Theory   2. Social
Mobility – Labor   3. Socialism – Architecture
4. Urbanization   5. Urban Planning – Renewal –
Heritage   6. Habitation – Housing   7. Aesthetics
– Rationalization   8. Identity – Tradition –
Resistance – Culture

AA
ASIA

Publication of this book was made possible by a grant
from AA Asia.

Frontispiece: Photographs of the word *chai*
(demolish) written over properties slated for
demolition in Beijing. First published in "City of
Walls," *AA Asia Monograph 8*, 2008. Images courtesy
of Colin Choo.

THE
SOCIAL
IMPERATIVE

ARCHITECTURE AND THE CITY IN CHINA

edited by
H. KOON WEE

CONTENTS

04   CONTROLLING   130

05   RESISTING   162

Residents in Shanghai protest against urban renewal, hoisting
banners at the entrance of their *xiaoqu* with slogans such
as "*shaogao zhengji menmian gongcheng, duo jiejue baixing
kunnan*" ("reduce the political rhetoric of improvement,
and solve the hardship of the masses"). Image courtesy of
Lam Lai Shun, 2014

FOREWORD

WILLIAM S.W. LIM

To write about China's social and urban challenges, we first need to have a broad understanding of three critical issues about the nation. Firstly, the urban population has exploded, mainly due to the inflow of migrants from the rural areas. This will continue for two or more decades until China's urban-rural ratio is stabilized. This condition will have a great impact on the country's old age dependency and necessitate a substantial increase of the retirement age. Secondly, China has to close the wide gaps between rural and urban developments, between the coastal regions and the rest of the country, as well as between the rich and poor. Corrective measures are being taken in recent years, but it will be a slow and painful process. Thirdly, there is an urgent need to restructure the relationships between the industrial and service sectors. With a per capita income of only approximately USD10,000, strong political commitment and progressive policies are beginning to achieve this transformation. There has to be vigorous support from the citizenry in order to make better choices for the society and environment. This is seen particularly with the reduction of energy-oriented and polluting industries and the substantial growth of the service sector, coupled with a sustainable, affordable, and responsible lifestyle. It is in this context that I wish to identify five critical areas of interrelated complexities.

De-Haussmannization

The present state of many Chinese cities can be accounted for by an urban process known as *Haussmannization*—a systemic destruction and modernization of a city by a centralized authority in order to achieve a particular form of urban renewal. This is based on an obsession with greed and economic growth, which would tip the balance towards those with power and wealth. The chasing of higher economic returns has created market forces that would eradicate an existing urban fabric with the process of gentrification, where the poor are displaced from the urban centers without affordable housing options. Led by global capitalism, planetary urbanization has arrived in major urbanized regions in China, as theorized by Neil Brenner and Christian Schmid. Measures must be urgently taken to correct the process of *Haussmannization* of Chinese cities and prevent further destruction of their historic and traditional character. Civil society and communities in China are gaining support in their fight to conserve their neighborhoods from polluting industries and unnecessary destruction. There is a growing appreciation for urban heritage and places with intrinsic historic value.

Rethinking History and Tradition

The basis of modernity is fundamentally grounded in our perspectives of history. There is no denying that China will redefine the premises of what it means to be modern on its own terms. In China, we have the potential to expand or shrink our consciousness of the past and, consequently, our capacities to chart a way from the present to the future. This outlook towards history and historiography will gain traction in many societies today, because many chronologies in non-Western countries had been carefully constructed by those in power to establish their political legitimacy and legacy. History tends to be written by the victors. The present Euro-American interpretation of history has its roots in colonialism, slavery, and indentured labor, which distances and alienates local and traditional cultures, and disregards their voices in history. Enlightened historians and policymakers in China have produced alternative narratives, in contrast with officially sanctioned versions. In recent decades, the re-imagination of a New Silk Road allows China to reestablish her long and heterogeneous cultural history. Drawing complex lessons and multiple transcendental ties to the past will ensure that their present frameworks for progress are enriched, inclusive, and consistently reevaluated. According to Li Shiqiao in his publication entitled *Understanding the Chinese City*, only when our historical perspectives are correctly set up can we construct different forms of Chinese modernity. Our histories must manifest themselves physically in order to influence the developmental model.

Reforming *Hukou* with Urban Agriculture

The concept of urban agriculture has gathered traction internationally, and it should be introduced in China's existing urban areas and their adjoining rural land. Intensive high-productivity agriculture, including vertical and rooftop farming, would moderate food cost and dependency in urban areas. It would provide employment opportunities for millions of urban workers affected by structural unemployment as China shifts towards new technologies and digitalization in the coming decades. Extensive implementation of urban farming would blur the present urban-rural divide, especially in the large metropolitan areas of China with an emerging economy. This can reduce the huge income gap between urban residents and rural migrants brought about by the unequal *hukou* household registration system. The number of rural migrants moving to the city increased substantially over the past few decades in order to fill the demand for labor. Making up a third of China's workforce, there are over 250 million rural migrant workers with no *hukou* residency rights as the urban residents, and they are restricted from accessing education, healthcare, social welfare, and public services in the city. Authorizing the same range of rights to these migrants would be a serious challenge to the Chinese government, but urgent socio-urban policy reforms are needed. Urban agriculture can potentially add to the economic and social benefits arising from a newly merged urban-rural sector in the city, and rural migrants may begin to enjoy greater social and income equality, as well as an improved quality of life.

New Energy and Creative Sustainability

It is inevitable, if not mandatory, for China to embark on a journey towards a true form of sustainability, because the threat of the present climate crisis will have a worldwide effect. Creative sustainability is a multidimensional process of transformation with many socioeconomic, environmental, and cultural interactions that are evolving in unexpected directions. Middle-income countries like China would have to restructure its priority of growth, constrained within the boundaries of sustainability. China has done well not to blindly follow solutions used by other high-income nations, evident in its global leadership in technical advances in renewable energy, from wind and solar energy to hydropower. Increasingly attractive and affordable, such clean energy sources can compete with the existing ones. China must combine its global dominance in renewable energy with a more progressive and socially oriented form of sustainability, especially in its understanding of urbanization. China must look for the intrinsic value in its people and move beyond the same culture of wasteful consumption suffered by many advanced nations. However, such action would not be easy in a globalized consumerist culture, and China would need to decide its own path for change, unique to its particular set of social, political, and economic circumstances.

Social and Urban Sustainability

Recent discourse strongly indicates the importance of each city to have its own developmental strategy in tackling the multiple complexities of urban sustainability. This is particularly relevant to large cities with an emerging economy such as cities in China. Apart from de-*Haussmannization* and minimization of urban destruction, having fewer roads and fewer cars would improve the traffic gridlock in many cities. This is no longer an empty slogan; global trends suggest, especially with ground-up support, that improved public transport, better traffic flow, pollution reduction, usage of electric cars, and environmental improvements all lead to a better quality of life. Pedestrianization and cycling would positively engage the young and benefit the lower-income. It is a welcome departure from the dominance of automobiles, and its major negative impact in discouraging social interaction. These technical measures are working towards a holistic carbon-free energy environment, but they need to be combined with other socially sustainable practices, such as the recycling of garbage, food waste, and water, intensive urban agriculture, construction with fair labor practices, minimal use of resources, and the provision of community-oriented public spaces. With rapid technical development, many of these processes would become affordable and easily applicable. With increased employment options, there would greater interests and awareness to work in non-profit and socially-oriented environments serving the young and old, and providing services and improvements in the quality of life for the city.

In recent years, China has greatly enhanced the impact of cultural activities in both traditional and contemporary arenas. Much emphasis and freedom has been given to multicultural characteristics of popular culture, in particular the culture of the minorities. All forms of the arts have benefited from an increased patronage. What appears missing is a better understanding of the criticality of arts as a positive change agent, as shown in the case of Chinese patriots such as Ai Wei Wei. Art stimulates and sharpens our sensitivity towards the society and the broader environment. Art questions our assumptions with a flexible mindset and provocative attitude. Art thinks the unthinkable and imagines the unimaginable. Artists and creative talents should remain independent and effective, as they produce novel ways to understand and contribute to society as change agents.

01
SPATIAL LIMITS OF SOCIALIST CHINA | H. KOON WEE

The organization of the following chapters takes advantage of the core social actions occurring since the beginning of socialist thought, especially in the form of socialism in the twentieth century. Ideas in social action tend to begin with economic reactions against the mistreatment of the laboring class, and they often seek to liberate them and provide upward social mobility. They also call attention to the political engineering and control of society. Forces of discontent and discord are always assembled or self-organized in such a way that they are able to devise different modes of resistance and retaliation. Propaganda is central to the communication and mediation with the masses, who are increasingly seen as abled and networked bodies in society. The rationalization of the economy and labor would eventually be taken towards the rationalizing of production, ownership, education, and even aesthetics. Social movements are always political and ideological by nature, but the ways in which they manifest themselves tend to be less well understood within the spatial disciplines. This introduction not only situates the operative nature of each social action but also draws upon parallel histories in the production of social spaces in China.

Construction hoarding in Shenzhen, with socially-minded messages, such as *shehui zhuyi hao* (socialism is good) and *ziyou, pingdeng, gongzheng, fazhi* (freedom, equality, justice, rule of law). Image courtesy of H. Koon Wee, 2016

INTRODUCTION

SPATIAL LIMITS OF SOCIALIST CHINA

The urgency of this study on China can be described in three ways. Firstly, as a large nation playing an increasingly enlarged role in the world today, the contemporary Chinese society has emerged from strong socialist and communist roots since the middle of the twentieth century. It remains difficult to predict just how a society with such strong civilizational history and such dominant political ideology is transforming with the neoliberal global economy of the twenty-first century. Secondly, the rampant process of urbanization in China seems to follow the same logic of modernization experienced during the industrial revolution that permanently altered the societies in Europe and the United States. In China, there would be an expected upheaval in its society and a backlash on its damaged environment, yet the regime appears to be managing discontent. The emergent forms are deviating from established narratives of social histories around the world. Architects, urbanists, and professionals of the built environment are not as ideological compared to the predecessors of socialism, yet they are strong accomplices to this accelerated process of rapid growth and equally rapid decay. They are playing a more mainstream role compared to the socially-grounded European avant-gardes who blended art, architecture and literature together with social and political ideology to great effect. Thirdly, with newfound wealth and development potential coming alongside one of the worst income inequality in the world,[1] where is the Chinese society heading? Would there be interest in a reformulation of a Chinese society, much like the Ebenezer Howards and Lewis Mumfords of the twentieth century in Europe and America? Would intellectuals and professionals be harboring ambitions of improving society with new visions? Would they muster the courage to dream of a fairer society? Given a discernible complacency and lack of revolutionary tendencies, can the Chinese society comprehend or tolerate another Utopia?

---

1   Yu Xie and Xiang Zhou, "Income Inequality in Today's China," *Proceedings of the National Academy of Sciences of the United States*, Vol.111, No.19, May 13, 2014.

Social Upheaval and the Advent of Social Science

As Andrew G. Walder examines the profound impact politics, economics, and cultural production had on sociology in his study of the revolutionary periods of China, he could not help but reflect on what he claims to be the birth of modern social science. He suggests that social science was formed through urgent efforts to understand the complex upheavals in Western Europe during the periods of industrialization beginning from the eighteenth century.[2] This book has the benefit of highly original formulations of suppressed or concealed social issues from architects, urbanists, theorists, critics and academics operating from within China, or invested in China for long periods. This concern for social issues grew from the vantage point of architecture, the city, and other spatial practices. The book openly explores the broader histories of social change across different cultures and geographies, in order to situate the histories of social reform and revolutions in China itself. Why are the social questions posed within the politics of spatial practices worth studying? Or how are they yielding new ways of looking at familiar problems? In the thrust towards the geopolitics of a globalized economy, is China becoming more like the United States? As China deregulates its economy more, to fall in line with the global condition, it is also quickly re-regulating its labor force, and its housing markets. It may eventually privatize its social, educational, healthcare and other welfare sectors as well. After all, United States had all but abandoned any possibility for social protection for the people, where the most important pillars of a society—healthcare and education—are the most privatized and least affordable sectors. Europe was the birthplace of social action largely because of its leadership in industrialization. The formation of cities in the modern sense was inextricably tied to the industrial revolution. New forms of concentrations had brought about new formations of labor. The forty-hour urban work week, and the inculcation of punctuality and efficiency were all passed down by the well-organized factory and the urban work place. China is the latest and largest to come from such a socialist tradition, and on paper, it has yet to relinquish its strong socialist roots. The contributors in this book share a profound disbelief in the current state of affairs in China, but none are prepared to suggest that China cannot become an exemplar in the delicate balance of a globalized market economy and a set of well-honed social values.

Social Action and Production of Social Spaces

The organization of the chapters of the book takes advantage of the core social actions occurring since the beginning of socialist thought, especially in the form of socialism in the twentieth century. Ideas in social action tend to begin with economic reactions against the mistreatment of the laboring class, and they often seek to liberate them and provide upward social mobility. They also call attention to the political engineering and control of society. Forces of discontent and discord are always assembled or self-organized in such a

---

2   Andrew G. Walder, *Communist Neo-Traditionalism: Work and Authority in Chinese Industry* (Berkeley: University of California, 1984), p.10.

way that they are able to devise different modes of resistance and retaliation. Propaganda is central to the communication and mediation with the masses, who are increasingly seen as abled and networked bodies in society. The rationalization of the economy and labor would eventually be taken towards the rationalizing of production, ownership, education and even aesthetics. Social movements are always political and ideological by nature, but the ways in which they manifest themselves tend to be less well understood within the spatial disciplines. In *Spaces of Hope*, geographer David Harvey gave a full exposition of this transformative process—from utopian thought to spatial designs.[3] Not only was Harvey concerned about the spatial urban realm, he remains a strong commentator on China. He argues for an understanding of China as part of a longer time-space analysis, whether it is in the form of questions about urbanization, social justice or inequality.[4] The burden is one of translation and transformative power. The chapters in this book intentionally avoid the traditional fields in which architects and researchers of the built environment identify themselves in, whether it is in architectural, urban planning, infrastructure, landscape, geography, communication studies, or other realms of policy making. This book also avoids the typologies found in the built environment, such as housing, museums, factories, dormitories, malls, offices, and so on. Instead, the focus is on the operative nature of social action, namely, the dynamic and unstable processes of mobilizing, laboring, controlling, resisting, networking, mediating, rationalizing and aestheticizing. This introduction not only situates each of the chapters, but it draws upon parallel histories in the production of social spaces.

Defensive Social Management

One of the themes of the development of Chinese society in the past century would be the social rationalization of tradition in political rhetoric and policy making. These inflections would emerge and subside as and when tradition, especially the good virtues of Confucianism, are needed to suppress other Western values that may threaten the governance of Chinese society. On other occasions, Confucianism may be in direct conflict with the values of the Chinese Communist Party.[5] According to a 2015 Chinese Academy of Social Sciences survey, the general public described a good Chinese society as foremost a society with equality, with 47.2% indicating its importance. The top six values of a good society are democracy (43.1%), justice (40.3%), civility (39.7%), prosperity (39.3%) and harmony (37.7%). This was conducted across thirty-one provinces amongst residents from urban and rural backgrounds. Attributes such as human rights and freedom were ranked relatively lower in eighth and thirteenth places, with only 23.6% and 18.7% surveyed considered them significant. Revered humanistic and ethical qualities of

---

3   David Harvey, "The Spaces of Utopia," *Spaces of Hope* (Berkeley: University of California Press), pp.133-181.
4   David Harvey, "The Right to the City," *Social Justice and the City* (Athens: University of Georgia Press, 2009), pp.315-332.
5   Chen Duxiu, "The Constitution and Confucianism," in *The Chinese Human Rights Reader*, Stephen C. Angle and Marina Svensson, eds. (Armonk: East Gate, 2001), pp.67-74.

great importance in a Confucian society include *ren* (benevolence and humaneness), *yi* (honesty), *zhi* (knowledge), *xin* (faithfulness) and *li* (correct behavior and propriety), but they are not figuring prominently in contemporary interpretations of a virtuous society. Honesty receives 22.4%, well below the top six qualities.[6] Whether it was Mao Zedong calling upon the Confucian-inspired society of *datong* or the Great Way, or Deng Xiaoping's use of Confucian's *xiaokang* that permits the accumulation of moderate wealth and prosperity, such resurrection of tradition can lead to contradictory effects. Social development analysts and researchers in China admit that the main purpose of social research today is to "defuse social conflicts and increase harmonious factors, and in order to accomplish this core mission, it is necessary to reinforce social management."[7] Coming from social research academies involved in the innovation in social governance, it appears that the advancement is set up to be defensive, and to constantly rationalize their work to identify problem areas. The control of society is about anticipating its meltdown, suppressing dissension, and managing discontent. This represents a sharp turn from the ideological purposes for creating and mobilizing society, and channeling the energy and potential of society to achieve certain aspirational goals. There was a positive mandate for China during the height of socialism, even if China was politically unstable. Having attained Utopia, China is arguably in management mode today.[8] Critics often suggest that there can be a strong basis for the re-rationalization of Confucian thinking that is fundamentally leading to a different of liberal democracy. It is critical for China to legitimize policies on a national level, but also to push back against global pressure to adopt Western models of societal and human rights development. If China is able to participate in a principled approach towards building its civil society, then perhaps China would be able to contribute towards the "unfinished project of liberal democracy."[9]

---

6   Li Wei, "Shehui gongzhong de 'hao shehui' jiazhi biaozhun diaocha baogao," ["Survey Report on the Value Standards of a 'Good Society' held by the General Public"] in *Society of China Analysis and Forecast 2015*, Li Peilin, Chen Guangjin, Zhang Yi, Li Wei and Xu Xinxin, eds. (Beijing: Social Sciences Academic Press, 2014), p.117.

7   Jianming Zhang, ed., "Abstract," *Research Reports on China Social Development 2015: Exploring Innovation in Social Governance, Promoting Healthy Social Development* (Beijing: Renmin University of China Press, 2015), pp.1-8.

8   This notion of a managerial state of expanded bureaucracy for the management and rationalization of a state of idealism was the theoretical framework used in an earlier exploration of an advanced post-industrial, post-revolutionary state—Singapore. See H. Koon Wee, "Introduction: We Have Only Been Modern," in H. Koon Wee and Jeremy Chia, eds., *Managing Utopia: Singapore Dreaming* (Singapore: Select Books, 2016), pp.9-25.

9   Inque Tatsuo, "Liberal Democracy and Asian Orientalism," in *The East Asian Challenge for Human Rights*, Joanne R. Bauer and Daniel A. Bell, eds. (Cambridge: Cambridge University Press, 1999), p.59.

LIBERATED LABOR
AND SOCIAL MOBILITY

Participation and Upward Mobility of the Ninety-Nine Percent

The understanding of social issues in architecture can gain much from understanding how the market economy has gradually privatized many sectors that were once important within the socialist framework. The escalating cost of housing in China is one of such outcomes, and it remains an uncurbed anxiety across China today. Cooling measures had not work effectively in the past decade, as policy-makers toyed with the volatile market mechanisms undergirding housing. The ubiquity of housing was made very much part of the omnipresence of socialism in Communist China, whether it is in the modernized forms of the Soviet-influenced *xiaoqu* or *mikrorayon* (microdistrict) adjacent to other urbanized *danwei* (work units), or the collectivized production brigades of *gongshe* (communes), first planned in rural or suburbanized areas during the Great Leap Forward.[10] Even by the time China adopted a decentralized policy for housing during the period of economic reform, there was still hope of finding affordable housing in self-organized and informal *chengzhongcun* (urban village), which are resilient enough to persist in some cities even today. By citing an urgent need of thirty-six million units of affordable housing between 2011 and 2015 in China, Huang Weiwen co-organized a ground-breaking design competition for affordable housing in 2012. It was a timely idea because it took place at a time when the growth rate of housing prices was at a dizzying record high. This irrational growth is in part fueled by optimism and the exuberant expectation of the market. Researchers predict that while real estate growth has hogged the headlines for the past decade, it can only lead to new headlines of serious social

---

10 Lu Duanfang, *Remaking Chinese Urban Form: Modernity, Scarcity and Space, 1949-2005* (New York: Routledge, 2006), pp.35-46, 51-67, 104-106. Zhang Jie and Wang Tao also discussed the development of the various typologies, and organized them around three distinct periods of Soviet influences, the Great Leap Forward, and the Cultural Revolution. See Zhang and Wang, "Part Two: Housing Development in the Socialist Planned Economy from 1949 to 1978," in *Modern Urban Housing in China: 1840-2000,* Lu Junhua, Peter Rowe and Zhang Jie, eds. (Munich: Prestel, 2001), pp.120-138, 151-168, 174-186.

and economic problems in the next decade.[11] Huang goes on to identify the structural imbalance within the existing system, and suggests new ways of looking at the urban poor in China. He argues that the principles of affordability should be drawn closer to the fundamental ethics of a socially-minded and livable city, not solely based on the mechanics of a market system.

While the development of housing provision can be considered a socially-oriented norm, this issue has been widely debated during significant periods of social upheavals around the world. In a 1934 essay entitled "The Social Imperatives in Housing," Lewis Mumford protested against the greedy private developers of housing in the United States. He wrote,

> "The housing problem was insoluble in terms of free enterprise, private land speculation, and production for profit: for these institutions, unmodified by more social interests, produced the very slums, semi-slums, and super-slums that the housing reformer sought to escape... [H]uman values [could not be sustained] because capitalism puts pecuniary values first and centers attention mainly on operations that tend to foster such values. If our communities display in their structure mainly the predatory and parasitic aspects of modern society, it is because our civilization as a whole has not yet been organized economically so as to produce what one may call, with the biologist, a flourishing symbiosis, that is, a cooperative life grouping."[12]

This conclusion was recorded in the exhibition catalog, which was provocatively titled *America Can't Have Housing*. This came at a time when the United States was in the middle of the Great Depression, and the free market had failed to bring about the economic prosperity that it promised. In the often binary discourse of socialism and capitalism, most of the sociopolitical rhetoric fails to grasp that the ordinary people who struggle to afford housing on a day to day basis do not subscribe to such rhetoric. Most would be looking to preserve their wealth and seek upward mobility. Zhao Liang argues that there is nothing intrinsically wrong with housing as a commodity, as long as ownership and influences can come from a broader spectrum of participants. The problems of housing and even homelessness are not highly visible in the city;[13] hence, it is possible to underestimate its magnitude.

---

11 Yuan Pengfei, "Fangdichan zengzhang de jjngji xiaoying yu fangjia de fei lixing shangzhang," ["The economic effect of real estate growth and irrational rise in the housing prices"], *National Bureau of Statistics Research Institute*, Feb 2012, http://www.stats.gov.cn/tjzs/tjsj/tjcb/dysj/201203/t20120312_38068.html. Accessed Dec 12, 2016.

12 Lewis Mumford, "The Social Imperatives in Housing," in *America Can't Have Housing*, Carol Aronovici, ed, (New York: Museum of Modern Art, 1934), p.16.

13 The low coverage of such issues has given rise to citizen journalism, and activists such as Zhang Shihe, nicknamed Laohu Miao (Tiger Temple), have gained prominence. For other urban poor, see Wu Kaming and Zhang Jieying, *Feipin shenghuo: Lajichang de jingji, shequn yu kongjian* [*Living with Waste: Economies, Communities, and Spaces of Waste Collectors*] (Hong Kong: Chinese University Press, 2016), pp.43-46.

Racial Myths and Favoritism

In another parallel analysis on the other side of the Cold War, historians caution that housing is one of the most charged environment, and it can be used to privilege particular social groups, or construct particular identities. Beyond the social class analysis prevalent in theories of socialism, Dianne Harris makes a link between race and housing, namely the construction and privileging of white Americans that contributed to the expectation of extreme privacy and problems of racism in the ubiquitous housing of suburban America.[14] Because Han Chinese is such an overwhelmingly dominant ethnic group in China, a race analysis of Chinese housing would have to be subtle. Apart from the racial minority of the Tibetans and Uyghurs discussed in Zhang Ke and Michael Kokora's essays about specific adaptions and experimentations of cultural signifiers, and cultural erasure, respectively, racial analyses are not particularly common. The discourse of a racialized society, that means being Chinese is both a nationality and an ethnicity, allows China to build loyalty in all ethnic Han Chinese around the world. Frank Dikötter's notion of "race as nation," and in particular the concept of racial nationalism does not tell a story of racial discrimination as much as it does about racial favoritism.[15] This favoritism would be discernible from the vantage point of the early foreign investments into China, not only in the manufacturing and technology industries, but also in housing development, real estate management and even city building. More likely than not, such external expertise would turn out horribly wrong, no matter how "Chinese" they may be, and the notorious China-Singapore Suzhou Industrial Park is a case in point. Countries with significant Chinese diaspora such as Hong Kong, Taiwan, Macau, and Singapore are prominent sources of Foreign Direct Investments (FDI), totaling nearly 65% of all FDI cumulatively from 1979 onwards.[16] It is undeniable that China has favorable socioeconomic policies for overseas Chinese,[17] and conversely, these investing nations with large Chinese populations have a specific way of identifying with China.[18]

This influx of investments brought with it a transfer of design and economic planning practices in the architecture of housing, especially during the infancy periods of the early 1990s. For example, in the transmission of Hong Kong methods to China, every

---

14 Dianne Harris, *Little White Houses: How the Postwar Home Constructed Race in America* (Minneapolis: University of Minnesota Press, 2013)

15 Frank Dikötter, *The Discourse of Race in Modern China* (Stanford: Stanford University Press: 1992), pp.123-124.

16 Kevin Honglin Zhang, "Why does so much FDI from Hong Kong and Taiwan go to Mainland China?" *China Economic Review 16*, 2005, pp.293-307.
Wei Shang-Jin, "Foreign Direct Investment in China: Sources and Consequences," in Takatoshi Ito and Anne O. Krueger, eds., *Financial Deregulation and Integration in East Asia, National Bureau of Economic Research-East Asian Seminar on Economics (NBER-EASE) Volume 5* (Chicago: University of Chicago Press, 1996), p.81.

17 Shen Hsiu-hua, "'Doing Chineseness': Taiwanese Capital in China," *ARI Working Paper No. 46*, Asia Research Institute, pp.5-7.

18 Wang Gungwu, *"Chinese Identity and Loyalty in Singapore," in the National Library Prominent Speaker Series*, given on 26 July 2016. http://mothership.sg/2017/05/historian-wang-gungwus-take-on-chinese-identity-loyalty-in-spore-is-worth-reading/. Accessed Dec 12, 2016.

housing development must attain an extremely high efficiency, in terms of the percentage of saleable floor area, in order to maximize profit for the developer. Every decision is based on the marketing and selling of the property, not the delivery of good housing. A socially-engaged lifestyle is not possible within such housing conditions because there is a detrimental reduction of open and shared spaces, as well as a rigid treatment of private property and a desire for a gated compound that shields one from the city. In China, every private apartment building is marketed as "luxury" housing, just because it carries a foreign name. Critics argue that this naming of housing and addresses of exotic and faraway places[19] are embedded in the conditions of colonialism found in Hong Kong, Macau and Singapore.[20] In a belated recognition of China's need for affordable housing, CapitaLand from Singapore decided to differentiate its housing developments from the mainstream by focusing on the affordable housing segment severely lacking in the Chinese market. To gain expertise on low-cost housing, with special attention on the design of the public realm and socialization of new inhabitants, CapitaLand bought up a 40% stake in Surbana in 2011, formerly the Housing Development Board, the municipal agency responsible for designing and building public housing, and planning new towns for over three decades in Singapore. In a 2011 research report "Laboring for a Home: Establishing a sustainable market to fulfill China's Aspiration," CapitaLand clarified this new direction by borrowing the language of socialism, and combining it with the new ethos of sustainability.[21]

It is therefore not surprising that there is an existence of communities who cannot afford housing, such as the Rat Tribes of Beijing. By picking up first-hand accounts of such informal groups in their decade-long research, Robert Mangurian, Mary-Ann Ray and Max Obata are pleading for stronger empowerment of the collectives and ordinary users of housing in a more balanced claim to the production of space in the city. Many have suffered great injustice, yet they continue to show resourcefulness, and the possibility of upward mobility.[22] In another research environment, Long Ying suggests that it is about time that the bureaucrats fully grasp how tremendous yet unaccounted social support and affordable housing can still be found in Chinese cities, as data is emerging from social media rather than national census. He differentiates them as occurring in the real social sphere of cities, as opposed to the planned physical sphere. The number of migrant population, including their families in tow, is clearly underreported in formal household

19 Anthony King and Abidin Kusno, "On Be(ij)ing in the World: 'Postmodernism,' 'Globalization,' and the Making of Transnational Space in China," in Zhang Xudong, Arif Dirlik, eds., *Postmodernism and China* (Durham: Duke University Press, 2000), p.44.

20 Jason Wordie, "How Hong Kong developments gained such incongruous names," *South China Morning Post*, Mar 26, 2016.

21 Neo Poh Har and Wang Jin, "Laboring for a Home: Establishing a sustainable market to fulfill China's Aspiration," *Inside Different Geographies: An e-Publication by CapitaLand*, May 2011. http://inside.capita-land.com/investment/778-labouring-for-a-home. Accessed Dec 12, 2016.

22 Robert Mangurian and Mary-Ann Ray, *Caochangdi Beijing Inside Out: Farmers, Floaters, Taxi Drivers, Artists, and the International Art Mob Challenge and Remake the City* (Hong Kong: Timezone 8, 2009).

surveys. In the development of commodity housing, after the Chinese Communist Party had gone through years of experimenting with the restructuring of the economy and plausible models of private ownership in the 1900s,[23] it is a pity that it could not make a more coordinated effort or give stronger protection to the social ideals that were upheld before the opening up of China.

Superstructure of Architecture—Production Functions of Labor

To put things into context, in the field of architecture and the built environment, the most marginalized labor pool is the construction workers in the secondary sector of the economy, not the design professionals such as architects and planners. Zhang Ke is attentive to this division of labor in the Marxist sense, and he appeals for more ideas to come from the ordinary people in the making of architecture. He realizes that it is the *shangceng jianzhu* or superstructure of society that conceives and manages the realm of the professional bodies, cultural institutions, and political organs in an ideological capacity, without directly shaping the built environment in the role of the base that forms the actual laborers and producers of architecture and cities. However, in a more contemporary or late-modern distortion of this relationship between the superstructure and base, architects and other urban professionals have lost their ideological command over the field of architecture, and instead they become merely service providers who produce forms to suit the prevailing capitalist market of real estate. This is a fiercely contested argument, as Huang Weiwen believes that the only way to achieve social equity is to work within the mechanism of real estate production, rather than to seek an autonomous or separate ideological space for architecture. Zhao Liang also believes architects must channel their research and creative energy towards the ninety-nine percent of society. This debate does not change the fact that architecture remains a powerful tool for the shaping of society, and at the moment, it is leaning heavily towards the neoliberal and fully globalized investors who see architecture as a commodity. By first recognizing the division of labor amongst the different stakeholders, the exploiters and the exploited, Liu Jiakun, Hua Li, and other architects in this chapter seek to reempower the exploited participants in the industry of the built environment.

Architects are often intellectually oriented, conducting their work from the drafting board, visualizing a future that would more likely be utopian, communicating and transmitting ideals through highly provocative imagery and lucid arguments. Critics have suggested that there is an inherent alienation from the actual production of architecture in its construction. This structural problem reveals that "the capitalist division of labor has divorced the intellectual aspect of work from the purely physical,"[24] which means the work

---

23 Lu Junhua and Shao Lei, "Part Three: Housing Development from 1978 to 2000 after China Adopted Reform and Opening-up Policies," in Lu Junhua, Peter Rowe and Zhang Jie, eds., *Modern Urban Housing in China: 1840-2000*, p.250-255.

24 Carlo M. Buldrini and Raj Nayar, "Architecture of Socialism," *Social Scientist Journal*, vol. 1, no. 10, May 1973.

of architects is not only detached from the laborious nature of the actual construction of the architecture, but in the absence of an ideological void, it has no other choice but to serve clients with money. This means such an intellectual activity will inevitably serve the powerful—those who have the capacity to own architecture or build cities. Of course, in the multiple modes of practice of an architect, there is no easy demarcation. Ma Qingyun refers to the need to build for production, return to the true meaning of the land, and the activity of building itself was argued as the basis for social change and a genuine renaissance. Yet there is no denying that his appeal for a return to an agrarian lifestyle is not going to lead to a bourgeois lifestyle that is massively profitable. It is not surprising that many socially conscious architects would foreground the methods of construction as the most fundamental way to create positive change in the building industry, especially in Hua Li, Liu Jiakun, and Zhang Ke's analyses. With urbanization in full force since the economic reform of the late 1970s, the number of workers in the secondary sector has been growing steadily from 69 million to 226 million workers in 2015.[25] This represented 29% of workers supporting the secondary sector, contributing to 41% of the China's Gross Domestic Product. Predictably, China is gradually moving more of its workers towards the tertiary sector, even though it is still lagging well behind advanced nations such as the United States and Japan. The migrant labor force in China are usually underprovided for, yet they represent approximately 50% of all labor force since 2011.[26] While the construction industry is a smaller portion of the entire secondary sector that also includes manufacturing, the demand for construction workers is still rising, but the labor force in the manufacturing industry has experienced reduction since 2012. This in in part due to Chinese labor becoming more expensive in the global manufacturing export market. As the reliance on migrant construction workers reaches a high of 60 million in 2014,[27] the maintaining of social stability and the provision of social welfare for this floating population becomes critical. The continual neglect and lack of protection from the *hukou* system[28] threatens to undermine the entire Chinese society.

Exploitation of Labor in the Economy

A large part of the social issues emerging within architectural and urban discourses can be linked to the great rural to urban migration. From a meager 18% at the beginning

---

25 National Bureau of Statistics, "Section 4-1: Employment," *China Statistical Yearbook 2016* (Beijing: China Statistic Press, 2016)

26 National Bureau of Statistics, "2014 Nian quanguo nongmingong jiance diaochabaogao," ["Report on the Survey of Migrant Workers in China in 2014"]. http://www.stats.gov.cn/tjsj/zxfb/201504/t20150429_797821.html. Accessed Dec 12, 2016.

27 National Bureau of Statistics, *China Statistical Yearbook 2016*. See also Hudson Lockett, "China's workforce faces tough year shifting gears from manufacturing to services," *China Economic Review*, Jan 8, 2016. http://www.chinaeconomicreview.com/chinas-workforce-faces-tough-year-shifting-gears-manufacturing-ser-vices. Accessed Dec 12, 2016.

28 Jason Young, *China's Hukou System: Markets, Migrants and Institutional Change* (New York: Palgrave Macmillan, 2013), pp.67-72.

of the economic reform policy in 1978 to 55% in 2015.[29] This 37% represents the fluid population, who seems to have the capacity to accept a transient presence in the cities that exploit their labor. They were able to come to terms with being treated like outsiders in mainstream urban society, while bearing with the poor working and living conditions.[30] Since establishing their practice Urbanus in new city of Shenzhen in 1999, the work of Meng Yan, Liu Xiaodu, and Wang Hui have paralleled Shenzhen's condition of urbanization and urban-rural migration. The *chengzhongcun* or urban village quickly became one of the archetypal forms for their research. These urban villages not only cross-subsidize the other highly-formalized urban functions, but they offer a transitory social space for migrants to enter the city. Zhang Ke argues for a better recognition and provision for the shadow economy of informal laborers, who tend to be housed in such urban villages—the three-*bao*, three-*liu*, and three-*xiao*. While providing for the exploited labor, urban villages are able to demonstrate how the bottom-up vitality and density could carry the seeds of future urban solutions. Meng Yan describes a real sense of inclusivity and freedom arising out of such low-resource settlements and self-organized societies, which would prove more well-used and adaptable than the formal public squares of Shenzhen. The municipal planners must have been deceived by the messy conditions of the urban villages, and they fail to take heed of the same lessons sociologist Herbert J. Gans observed more than half a century ago in the West End neighborhood of Boston.[31] They fail to realize that the naming of slums is simply an evaluative term that legitimizes the demolition of a perfectly functioning community, with an equitable spread of wealth amongst the largest possible group of small storekeepers. After urban renewal, this equitable spread of wealth could only be channeled into the hands of a large corporation or a conglomeration of developers, fueling the income inequality that is already rampant in China.

As Chinese society matures over time, coupled with the increasingly apparent shortage of labor in key industries,[32] the migrant workers became more aware of their rights, and the real cost of their labor, and they were prepared to challenge the authorities when they sense corruption or a violation of their rights.[33] The most telling episode came a year ago, around the period running up to the October First National Holidays, when construction workers were not able to bring wages home to their families. China Labor

---

29 United Nations, Department of Economic and Social Affairs (UNDESA), "Population Divisions: World Urbanization Prospects." https://esa.un.org/unpd/wup/Country-Profiles/ and http://data.worldbank.org/indicator/SP.URB.TOTL.IN.ZS?locations=CN. Accessed Dec 12, 2016.

30 Liu Linping, Fan Changyu and Wang Kaiqing, "2014 Nongmingong diaocha baogao," [Investigation Report of Migrant Workers] in *Society of China Analysis and Forecast 2015*, p.158.

31 Herbert J. Gans, *The Urban Villagers: Group and Class in the Life of Italian-Americans* (New York: Free Press, 1962).

32 Li Peilin, "Xin changtai' beijing," ["Background of the 'New Normal'"] in *Society of China Analysis and Forecast 2015*, p.3.

33 Alexandra Harney, *The China Price: The True Cost of Chinese Competitive Advantage* (London: Penguin, 2009), p.121.

Bulletin, a labor activist and watchdog organization based in Hong Kong, captured nearly a hundred cases of construction workers protesting against wage arrears in the month of August alone, many threatening suicide or extreme means to obtain justice.[34] The Bulletin has been monitoring social media and news reports around the clock, and translating them into an interactive map of archives of strikes or protests across China since 2011.[35] In fact, this form of activism and investigative journalism starting flourishing in China from the 1980s, as many started to witness that would reveal the inequalities and exploitations found among the working class.[36] Not seen before in the Maoist era, this coincided with the formation of highly exploitative work places, often associated with the process of rapid urbanization and construction, and export-oriented industries on a tight production schedule. These new patterns of employment met with a greater interest for the welfare of the workers, because in the governing regime is still officially protective and sympathetic towards labor in the socialist sense.

Portrayal of Labor

Even though the prospects and roles of labor had very different and nuanced meaning since the economic reform of China, it is still remarkable to see how labor is foregrounded in architectural discourses. The potency of labor was visible in the 1979 China cover of the French architecture journal *L'Architecture d'Aujourd'hui*, in the symbolically red photograph taken by architect Xavier Luccioni. The photograph shows an everyday scene of six workers on a wooden scaffold repainting a wall of slogans, and the introductory text in the kick-off editorial pages was full of praise.

> "The neighborhood factory and the national enterprise have become efficient and prosperous. If the urban communes and accelerated collectivization had failed, the rural communes and their brigades were recognizable successes. The Chinese were realistic, not only did they innovate, but they also adapted to old and tested methods. The political genius of Mao Zedong was to quickly realized that it was impossible to build a new society without marrying modern concepts with the achievements of a very long and rich history. 'Putting the past at the service of the present' was not a vain slogan, but a rule of conduct which, like so many others, expressed a poetic dimension of everyday practices."[37]

34 "Construction workers become desperate in run-up to Golden Week holiday," *China Labor Bulletin: Supporting the Workers' Movement in China*. http://www.clb.org.hk/content/construction-workers-become-desperate-run-golden-week-holiday. Accessed Feb 1, 2017.

35 "Strike Map applies new fixed sampling method in 2017," *China Labor Bulletin*. http://www.clb.org.hk/content/strike-map-applies-new-fixed-sampling-method-2017 and http://maps.clb.org.hk/strikes/en. Accessed Feb 25, 2017.

36 Anita Chan, *China's Workers Under Assault: The Exploitation of Labor in a Globalizing Economy* (New York: East Gate, 2001), pp. 4-5.

37 Marc Emery, "Editorial: Architecture Et Urbanisme En Chine 1949-1979," *L'Architecture d'Aujourd'hui*, Issue 201, Feb 1979, p.1.

This issue was a comprehensive report of China, covering topics from social and geographical data, the reliance of architecture and planning on economic and social policies, modernization in habitation, and technology transfer from the Soviets. With as many as eleven investigative journalists, architects and photographers on assignment with local translators, this issue also covered traditional urban forms and Beijing, industrial modernization and its relationship to rural architecture, construction techniques, as well as Chinese pedagogy and its relationship to Russian academies.

Fast forward to the 2015 British *Architectural Review* special issue on China, the cover shows the absent worker. Instead it chooses to depict labor-intensive materials of wooden sticks stacked up and shored up against a shoddily constructed slate wall, sitting beneath the eaves of a traditional terra cotta roof. Photographer Iwan Baan carefully cropped and rendered abstract an incomplete aspect or a temporary storage space of the Wencun Village project by Wang Shu and Lu Wenyu. The introductory essay of this China issue decries the state of Chinese society today.

'LABOUR'S · MAY · DAY ·
DEDICATED · TO · THE · WORKERS · OF · THE · WORLD

Walter Crane, International Solidarity of Labor, 1889

"In the recent July 2015 crackdown, three hundred lawyers and activists were arrested, interrogated, and harassed—journalists and bloggers, lawyers and feminists. Many political prisoners have died due to torture, interrogation, and failure to provide medical treatment. Architects and architectural critics have been similarly circumspect in their criticism of the Chinese state during the building boom that has bankrolled the profession through the recession. It does not feel socially responsible to write about Chinese architecture without acknowledging that these projects were realized without due processes with regards to planning, land acquisition and public consultation. In publishing these works, we do not condone the regime that enabled them. We do support these architects striving to forge a unique Chinese identity through their work."[38]

Guest editor Austin Williams carefully selected only projects by Chinese architects, sustaining a quietly national but infinitely optimistic tone throughout the featured projects. There is a mixture of three foreign critics and two Chinese critics. Iwan Baan's abstract cover photograph is the perfect preparation for the project feature of the Wencun Village in the concluding pages of the special issue. The remaining nine photographs would capture the village in its everyday context, always juxtaposed against local residents or

---

38 Christine Murray, "Editorial: China," *The Architectural Review*, Issue 1425, Nov 2015, p.2.

construction workers. In these two unique documentary moments in history, labor seems to exist in a state of latency.

When labor became the suppressed subject, and social movements became political and ideological, one remarkable thing occurred—previously fragmented societies became cohesive in ways that it could not have. Coming full circle to the analysis of race and ethnicity at the beginning of this section, it appears that social action can give mankind the capacity to transcend the worst of his cultural and racial prejudices. This is evident in the political art of the late nineteenth century. English illustrator Walter Crane showed the possibility of uniting all workers under the "solidarity of labor," and included the equally disenfranchised workers across the continents—there were Asian, African, Australian, and American workers around the European ones. On the wings of May Queen are the words "fraternity" and "equality," and on her crown reads the word "freedom." Historian Eric Hobsbawm observed that this was a period when social movements had the audacity to bring everyday artistic production closer to the mass movements of social and political change. The artist Crane was also famous for illustrations of children books. The artistic practices of the everyday and the avant-garde served as a powerful ally for social action.[39] Artists, architects, poets, writers, and philosophers were working hand in hand with political economists, lawyers, and labor union leaders. This possibility of a multinational and multiethnic togetherness would prove to be a unique moment in history, as the relative homogeneity of Chinese society did not prevent other European nations from identifying with it.

---

39 Eric Hobsbawm, "Socialism and the Avant-Garde, 1880-1914," *Uncommon People: Resistance, Rebellion, and Jazz* (New York: New Press, 1984).

SOCIAL CONTROL
AND MODES OF RESISTANCE

Society Must Be Defended—Control and Discipline

In the series of eleven lectures by Michel Foucault between 1975 and 1976, he revealed the vulnerability of a society in terms of its racial composition, and its relationship to larger historical patterns of colonialism and war. These lectures were posthumously published in an English volume entitled *Society Must Be Defended*. China was not the subject of his inquiry, but it did not stop scholars from examining its relevance to contemporary themes of global terrorism and racial discrimination.[40] Chinese society must be noted for its relatively homogeneous and dominant Han ethnic group, forming 91.6% in a population of nearly 1.4 billion people.[41] And as noted earlier, the investment patterns of Foreign Direct Investments by the Chinese population overseas demonstrate a strong affinity between the Chinese diaspora and the Mainland Chinese. In fact, this underlying dominance has become a non-issue, as the entire nation has practically been assimilated into a single race in the project of nationalism which began over a century ago.[42] Discourse of race was suspended during the rise of Communism, and the focus was squarely on the discourse of class in a classically Marxist sense. It is therefore not surprising that the National Bureau of Statistics of China does not find it necessary to differentiate the social indices between ethnic groups, except to show the routine racial composition breakdown in one of the last chapters of its Statistical Yearbook.[43]

---

40 Bernard E. Harcourt, "Four Themes for 'Society Must be Defended'," Foucault 13/13: 13 Years at the Collège de France, 13 Seminars at Columbia, Columbia Center for Contemporary Critical Thought, and Society of Fellows in the Humanities, Columbia University. http://blogs.law.columbia.edu/foucault1313/2015/11/24/foucault-613-four-themes-for-society-must-be-defended/. Accessed Sep 1, 2016.

41 Central Intelligence Agency, "China: People and Society," *World Factbook 2015*. https://www.cia.gov/library/publications/the-world-factbook/geos/ch.html. Accessed Sep 1, 2016.

42 Frank Dikötter, "Racial Nationalism," *The Discourse of Race in Modern China* (Stanford: Stanford University Press: 1992), pp.123-125.

43 There were indicators describing the ethnic composition of China, listed under the "Geographical Distribution and Population of the Ethnic Minorities," *National Bureau of Statistics of China*, and "Principal Aggregate Indicators on National Economic and Social Development and Growth Rates," *China Statistical Yearbook 2015*. http://www.stats.gov.cn/tjsj/ndsj/2015/indexeh.htm. Accessed Sep 1, 2016.

Instead, statistics show that the Chinese government still thinks the more pressing social problems are class-based, namely rural-urban migration, labor exploitation and poverty.

No Place for the Discourse of Race and the Complex Geography of War

For race to be conflated with the nation, modern China was centered around the dominant Mandarin majority, and it gained its size by a systematic inclusion of the other Han subgroups of seven main dialect languages of Yue, Hakka, Min, Xiang, Gan, Wu, and Jin. These subgroups were, in one form or another, different kingdoms in the ancient period. The discourse of race and ethnicity is so confusing. The biological taxon method could have been used to describe the ethnic group by its biological features, appearances and geographical origin, or ethnic membership could have been determined by heritage, language and ancestry. The widely accepted version today is to organize ethnicity along the lines of nationhood, and it is easy to understand why many multi-ethnic or minority families would have been Sinicized, and would actively shed any non-Han identity and cultural practices. The unification of China through the use of Putonghua or the Beijing dialect would invariably suppress the regional characteristics of China. As one accepts the coming together of "race as class" in the form of Frank Dikötter's historicizing of race in socialist China, the main question is how does this control and suppression of "ethnic" or by extension cultural differences reveal itself in the built environment of China? To be clear, this ethnic difference is no longer the visually detectable difference exhibited by the formally recognized minorities of China, but the internally stratified regional groups that exhibit unique cultural practices and architectural forms. It is not surprising to find some of the best works of Yu Kongjian, Hua Li, and Zhang Ke in the contexts of outlying minority regions of Liupanshui Valley of Guizhou, the Gaoligong Mountain of Yunnan, and the Yaluntzangpu Grand Canyon of Tibet respectively. They stand elegantly as silent testimonies to the specter of race. In arriving at the deceptively stable global society that is assumed to be the case today, China had to undergo combinations of dictatorship and anarchy during sustained periods of revolutions and revisions to a dictatorship of the people.[44] History suggests that there is in fact a lack of uniformity in the social structure of China, even if there is an appearance of homogeneity in Han ethnicity and the rapidly urbanizing middle class. China is represented by a complex geography of colonialism and wars, from the Japanese, Manchuria, Soviet, Tibet, and other border wars to the conflicts with the European colonizers. The Chinese are familiar with the racial inequality brought about by the multiple extraterritorial districts, which were formed on the basis of concessions and unequal treaties since the nineteenth century. Modern Chinese society would therefore define itself against outsiders with superior racial and class distinctions, and the Chinese often suffer from a deep sense of injustice.[45] But this would evolve from

---

44 Joseph W. Esherick, Paul G. Pickowicz and Andrew G. Walder, eds., *The Chinese Cultural Revolution as History* (Stanford: Stanford University Press, 2006), p.27.

45 Frank Dikötter, *The Discourse of Race in Modern China* (Stanford: Stanford University Press: 1992), p.36.

a geopolitical distinction in the early twentieth century to an ideological separation in the Chinese civil war between the democratic nationalists and the communist revolutionaries.

Has the ideology of socialism unified and disciplined race to such an extent that China's identity in its architecture is secure and singular? Does the *modus operandi* of discipline and control cut right through the realm of race, class, and other identity categories in such a way that it is no longer possible to maintain a seamless and coherent mode of spatial production? The most direct expression of control can be seen in the Forbidden City in Beijing, and it is in this cosmic and urban center, where the Manchu ethnic minority ruled the Han Chinese for nearly three hundred years. Li Hu and Huang Wenjing's critique of the rational form of the Forbidden City reminds one of the inappropriateness of its form as an expression of power, because there was no possibility of a social notion of a public sphere within such an aristocratic realm. Even if the revered Le Corbusier did make a reference to its orderliness, Li and Huang argued that there should be no place for such architecture of power. Instead, power must emanate from the broadest base of society. They reject the evoking of classical Chinese works of art and literature by many contemporary Chinese architects, because many fail to realize that it is often an aristocracy and racism that underpin such exemplary work. Pritzker Prize winner Wang Shu persists in analyzing a painting of Chen Hongshou from the seventeenth century. The sociopolitical tension between Chen's belief as a Buddhist and the prevailing Confucian government, or his figuratively-charged bodily distortions and strange colors in his paintings were not emphasized.[46] Instead, Wang chooses to examine an interiority or a unique projection of space found in the landscape depicted in the painting. This analytical method demonstrates that an epistemological break is necessary in a reading of classical works. Wang ends this analysis with a juxtaposition of Lu Xun's framing of an uneasy relationship between nature and Chinese society—"shadows so dense it shadows the sun"—at the threshold of another class revolution in China in the 1940s. Wang visualizes this shaded interior composed by nature in a landscape painting as an appropriate shelter for everyday life in a city in Ningbo, not for the single scholar with social and political status. Born in the city of Ürümqi in the Xinjiang Uyghur Autonomous Region, Wang champions the everyday and spontaneity in a socially conscious way, and he shuns the professionalized and monumental. The discourse of race may indeed be veiled by a more dominant class discourse, and only the latter would have been given any space for discourse.

---

46   Tamara Heimarck Bentley, *The Figurative Works of Chen Hongshou (1599-1652): Authentic Voices / Expanding Markets* (Farmham: Ashgate, 2012), pp.165, 180-188.

Urban Governance and Surveillance

It is equally important to realize that for Foucault, the society he was referring to was none other than one borne out of a modern and democratic period. This was a socially-conscious period since the early forms of labor organized around industries and cities, and certainly after the savage mechanisms of control of the feudal and colonial periods. Alessandro Fontana and Mauro Bertani suggest that the general features of such "disciplinary power" would lead to critical explorations of "governmentality," which would be asserted through institutions and technologies of the state or the government for the good of society.[47] This formed Foucault's deep mistrust of institutional and social forms. Wu Gang and Chen Ling describe the planning and building of cities as one of the institutionalized forms of economic development, and all levels of local government from provincial, prefectural, county or township levels, are beating to the drums of urbanization. No local government leadership would want to fall short of the demands of city building and infrastructure building, even if they are thinning out China to such an extent that the new cities are too big and too empty. While technologies of control go beyond the simple notion of surveillance, the rapid growth of Chinese cities parallels the rise of Hangzhou-based CCTV and security equipment manufacturer Hikvision to become the world's top ranked supplier, as Beijing toppled London as the city with the greatest number of CCTVs. Wuhan, Chongqing, and Urumqi[48] may well be one of the top ten cities under surveillance as well. The best indication of this intention can be seen in the *National New Urbanization Plan (2014-2020)*. "Chapter Nineteen: Strengthening and Innovating Urban Social Governance" clearly outlines the plan to improve an internet-based urban information network to improve speed and management of law enforcement and urban services. Such a management system unambiguously links urbanization to an intensified coverage of surveillance and social control.[49] The plan is to fully cover the cities with digital surveillance by 2020.[50] Urban renewal is one of the twin engines of urban sprawl as discussed by Wu and Chen. Jeremy Chia and Andrew Lee examine the possibility of an emergent soft power that can be returned to Chinese society as a new resource, when it reestablishes new cultural and social functions for the once unyielding monumentality of the Beijing Shougang Steel Mill. In another essay, Zhan Yuan and Ruan Hao argue for a renewal strategy based on a weakened and reversed urban panopticon in an attempt to empower the neighborhood while arresting the fragmentation caused by spaces of capital and consumption. Such

---

47 Alessandro Fontano and Mauro Bertani, "Situating the Lectures," *Society Must Be Defended: Lectures at the College de France, 1975-76*, David Macey trans. (New York: Picador, 2003), p.273.

48 James T. Areddy, "One Legacy of Tiananmen: China's 100 Million Surveillance Cameras," *The Wall Street Journal*, Jun 5, 2014.

49 The State Council, The People's Republic of China, *Guojia xinxing chengzhen hua guihua (2014-2020)*, [*National New Urbanization Plan (2014-2020)*]. http://www.gov.cn/zhengce/2014-03/16/content_2640075. htm. Accessed Dec 12, 2016.

50 Mengjie, ed., "China to fully cover key public areas with video surveillance by 2020," *Xinhuanet News*, May 13, 2015. http://news.xinhuanet.com/english/2015-05/13/c_134236159.htm. Accessed Dec 12, 2016.

capitalist spaces have the tendency to create fantasies within itself, without relating to the exterior condition of the city. These examples of frameworks of control ought to alert architects and thinkers in the fields of the built environment to be more self-critical of the good intentions behind the design and planning of spaces, even if they are meant for the public good. Foucault warned that these intentions are already framed by certain institutional norms aimed at disciplining the public.

Ground and Resistance

The notion of resistance can be taken quite literally as the opposite side of the same coin within the regiment of control. On another technological level, Zhu Tao discusses the unsuspecting development of infrastructure for the purpose of efficient commuting in the city of Hong Kong. Unfortunately, as the underground metro system and the pedestrian linked ways get super-connected, they quickly become coopted by commercial interests. When the government-owned Mass Transit Railway was subsumed under a partially privatized MTR Corporation with unbridled real estate development and management power, the MTR Corporation gained massively unfair access to locational advantages brought about by a publically funded transportation system. Zhu sees such infrastructural conveniences as a surreal form of ungrounded reality, which alienates the street and the ground. It culminated in a poignant takeover of the ground that was once lost to automobile highways and commerce during the Umbrella Movement. The spatial distortion brought about by infrastructure and architecture cannot be underestimated, in part because they are built with an incredible amount of resources. Zhu lays down the challenge for Chinese architecture in the era of economic reform by resurrecting the strongest defender of civil society and pioneer of modern architecture—architect and Professor Feng Jizhong. Feng professed that "All architecture is civil architecture, especially in our era as such, and only civil architecture is true architecture. Other architecture, if it does not represent the citizens' interests, is not true architecture."[51] Such a statement would readily come under the banner of socialist China, except, as Zhu points out, by late 2010, the term "civil society" was paradoxically dropped by the Central Ministry of Propaganda for the fear that it may arouse sentiments of civil rights. In another comical error, coincidentally by another metro company, the Shanghai Shentong Metro, new single journey tickets in 2015 carried three slogans. These perfectly normal and unsuspecting messages described a commuter's rights to travel safely, rights to supervise public safety as a responsible commuter, and rights to serve the people in truth, written in Chinese slogans of *"shi quanli zai guidao nei yunxing"*, *"wei quanli jiandu anshang yanjing"*, *"rang quanli zhenzheng fuwu renmin"*, Unfortunately, the graphic design for the third slogan highlighted the *ren* character in white, intended to echo the *renmin* or the people, was unwittingly superimposed over one of the *quan* character, turning the whole message

---

51 Tao Zhu, "Architecture in China in the Reform Era: 1978-2010," in *A Critical History of Contemporary Architecture, 1960-2010*, Elie G. Haddad and David Rifkind, eds. (Farnham: Ashgate, 2014), p.416.

graphically to *renquan*, which means human rights. Shanghai Shentong Metro would not be remotely interested to invoke sentiments of human rights in Shanghai.

Bourgeois Human Rights and Traditional Interpretations

The traditional social structure underlying modern Chinese society cannot be underestimated.[52] Political scientists and researchers have shown that the ruling regime has continually deployed the rationalization of tradition in establishing its own limits of broadly accepted norms such as human rights and freedom. Art historian Richard Vine argues that, neither the market economy of the past thirty years, nor communism and socialism since the turn of the twentieth century has seriously altered the structure of Chinese society. Chinese society was so securely based on Confucianism and had "based social order and harmony on a system of hierarchical fealty, with youths admonished to give respect and obedience to older persons, women to men, subjects to officials, and officials to their superiors in a ladder of authority leading ultimately to the emperor."[53] While exemplary qualities of a fair society are not held in high esteem by Chinese society in general, they still represent difficult social expressions to deal with. The views rendered by the regime would also be shown to transform over time. Following in the footsteps of Marxism, the Communist Party of China rejected the demand for human rights as a bourgeois slogan in the beginning.[54] They argued that China's attention to the fundamental rights of the working class is even more protective and far-reaching than the mere rights to private property, without misusing the notion of freedom to degrade and exploit others. By the late 1980s, the regime came to realize that the younger generation was drawn to concepts of human rights, and it had to make a clear analysis of how China should view the pressure from the global community as well as from its younger population. China began to describe itself as the true defender of human rights, suggesting that it was in the constitution and laws of China to protect all basic political, economic, cultural, educational, religious, and personal rights, including protection given to children, women, the elderly and the poor, without undermining its socialist base.[55] As a powerful form of traditional ethics, Confucianism was frequently used to organize state affairs and establish the hierarchy of social control on the basis of timeless virtue of respectfulness, humility, righteousness, and so on. But critics argue that Confucianism builds in inherent social inequality, and is incompatible with modern definitions of human rights, because it subscribes to the rationale of authoritarian rule, the stratification of nobility and a class-based society. In addition, it fosters a patriarchal society and gender inequality, with the expectation of producing descendants to continue the family line, and other forms of suppressions of freedom.

---

52 Joseph C.H. Chai, *An Economic History of Modern China* (Cheltenham: Edward Elgar, 2011), pp.45-49.

53 Richard Vine, *New China New Art* (Munich: Prestel Verlag, 2011), p.11.

54 Lan Ying, "Is 'Human Rights' Always a Bourgeois Slogan? A Discussion with Comrade Xiao Weiyun and Others," *The Chinese Human Rights Reader*, pp.288-296.

55 Shi Yun, "Who are the True Defenders of Human Rights?" *The Chinese Human Rights Reader*, pp.323-329.

Public Space and Women

Critically, in an effort to build a socialist base, Mao had denounced any blind adherence to the laws of the elders in Chinese society as feudal and corrupt. In terms of the spatial implications of such a social hierarchy, Cheng Weikun argues that the Confucian doctrine that called for a differentiation of the inner and outer spheres in relation to society produced further segregation between women and men.[56] It reinforced the highly segregated and gendered character of public versus domestic spaces. Cheng identifies the progressive moments when these stereotypes were challenged in the twentieth century period of modernization and urbanization in Beijing and elsewhere in China. Women became more visible in the city when the economic plight of the nation drove women to seek work outside their traditional domestic spheres. Modernization was coupled with industrialization, and new modes of education. Women became very much part of the new workforce during the socialist era. "If poverty, dislocation, and political instability forced lower-class women to enter street occupations, the Republican ideal of gender equality, the destruction of conventional norms and restrictions by the revolution and reforms, and the flourishing of Western culture inspired middle-class women to imagine self-sufficiency and public presence."[57] Such an unplanned process of empowerment took place during various periods of social, economic and political upheavals of the twentieth century, from the economic collapse that followed the fall of the Qing Dynasty, the opening up of China to Western influences, the Chinese civil war that ensued, and the rise of social awareness at the birth of Socialism and Communism. This liberation came at a time when the city was chaotic and traditional doctrines and national policies were ineffectual and unclear.

Economic Experiments and Resistance as Heterotopia

Are the forms of resistance in spatial practices only predicated on race or class, or would the capitalist distortions of a socialist base lead to unexpected emergent forms in China? On the fringes of mainstream Han China, it is important to realize that the discourses of race or racialization were implicit in the formation of identities in the regional territories. This is especially true between north and south China. The Tang dynasty saw mass migration towards the south between the seventh and tenth century, and the southerners had a tendency to describe themselves as Tang Chinese, with a return to the Yue culture, to distinguish themselves from the Han Chinese from the north.[58] While the capital city was in Chang'an and Luoyang, in Xi'an and Henan respectively, it was the southern port region of Guangzhou (Canton) that was considered to be more transgressive by nature, because of its cosmopolitanism. Canton was wheeling and dealing with foreigners

---

56 Weikun Cheng, *City of Working Women: Life, Space, and Social Control in Early Twentieth-Century Beijing* (Berkeley: Institute of East Asian Studies, University of California, 2011), pp.9-13, 22-27.

57 Ibid., p.65.

58 Erica Fox Brindley, *Ancient China and the Yue: Preceptions and Identities on the Southern Frontier, c.400 BCE–50 CE* (Cambridge: Cambridge University Press, 2015), p.3.

since the ancient silk road and maritime trade. This Tang Chinese identity would be adopted by the Chinese diaspora, and whenever a Chinese enclave grows in a foreign city outside China, they would name it as *Tang Ren Jie* or Chinatown.[59] If foreignness was transgressive and corrupt, the cosmopolitan disposition of Canton was also the reason for selecting Guangdong province and the Pearl River Delta region as Deng Xiaoping's first Special Economic Zone. As China's experimental window for trade and global manufacturing started to grow from 1978, cities such as Shenzhen was described as an "oasis of decadence in socialist China—a capitalist playground replete with nightclubs, massage parlors, gambling halls and all manner of illicit financial dealings,"[60] merely a decade after opening up to the world. This comes back full circle to the Foucauldian notion of heterotopia and spaces of the other—alternative to the clarity of a Han ethnicity and a socialist narrative. Yet it is such heterotopic layers of meaning that reveal the most human and down to earth aspirations of material comfort and pleasure. The narratives of resistance in this book are in fact found in everyday circumstances and livelihood. Hu Yan and Li Han draw upon the most interesting of local occurrences to reveal the deepest contradictions and aspirations of Beijingers. It may be a disillusionment brought about by gentrification, or an illegal and temporary construction that became more monumental in the social lives of the commoner than grand buildings. It could also be the inconvenience of temporary construction that became more memorable and tactile than a finished city. Urban researchers Shi Jian and Daan Roggeveen both approach the everyday in order to distill a message for contemporary Chinese society. Shi is central to the effort by a number of prominent architects and developers to resist urban renewal and destruction by stipulating guidelines for protection. Roggeveen uses accessible reportage language to recount the problems and promise of China's relentless desire for bigness in the book *How the City Moved to Mr Sun*, coauthored with Michiel Hulshof in 2010. The anonymity of the everyman is central to the project of resistance.

Agency of Consumption

Perhaps it takes the man in the street to validate a nation's identity.[61] As China embraces consumerist culture and globalization, there is supposed to be a different ending to the narrative of inequality and wastefulness. Having gone through three decades of revolutionary correction, China ought to have a predisposition to prevent the self-destruction of capitalism. In fact, the concept of consumption was promoted during the nationalist years under Dr. Sun Yat-sen, because it was seen as a fairer and wide-reaching way to distribute affordable goods to everyone. As the leader of the 1911 Chinese revolution, Dr. Sun had clear socialist tendencies. Consumption was meant to allow the

---

59   Tan Koon San, *Dynastic China: An Elementary History* (Kuala Lumpur: The Other Press, 2014), p.213

60   Alexandra Harney, *The China Price: The True Cost of Chinese Competitive Advantage* (London: Penguin, 2009), p.31.

61   Prasenjit Duara, "Making the People for the End of History," *Rescuing History from the Nation: Questioning Narratives of Modern China* (Chicago: Chicago University Press), pp.90-95.

ordinary citizen to attain a modernized and decent quality of life.[62] Shopping perhaps had a more civic-minded aspect, as a social leveler, rather than the consumerist form that it is today, where it is heavily distorted to benefit the corporate sellers. Confucian thought would surface every so often throughout China's history, and in the period where the Communist Part of China borrowed the broadly accepted notion of attaining well-being in a material sense. The Confucian principle of *datong xiaokang* seems to legitimize social inequality, or it seems to suggest an accommodation of an expected inequality under the common good of society. This is a surprisingly tolerant view for the ruling regime as it experiments with its economic reform in the 1980s.[63] Whether it is the ethics of revolutionary China or Confucian China, there is no longer any disdain for extravagant accumulation of wealth and materialist behavior in an openly consumerist society of China. This is something the Communist Party is desperate to rectify today.

Borrowing of Public Resources under Duress

There is an unpredictable but dynamic acceptance of the spaces of contradiction, where boundaries between the private and public are blurred, and the limits of the legal and illicit are vague. Everything is under negotiation. This explains why the alienated worker and producer of consumer products at Foxconn did not translate to a disdain for the iPhone. It seems to have only whet the appetite for more *shanzhai* or counterfeit phones. Wang Yan and Wang Fei were not able to be moralistic about these contradictory behaviors of resistance and assimilation, except to take a documentary approach. The two opposing reactions are ultimately both wrong, or both right under different circumstances. As the separation of spaces of production from spaces of consumption become more accentuated, informal and compensatory activities would kick in. "Whether it was pool tables at the roadside or multilevel discos, entrepreneurs saw profitable niches, and the number of commercial venues where residents could relax beyond the purview of their employers and their relatives grew exponentially."[64] This proliferation of informal commerce brings about a great degree of mix use, and enriches the city in a dynamic way. As consumerist spaces seep into every conceivable function in China, ordinary users would begin to borrow any space for their socializing needs. In the same way, the artists in the inaugural self-made exhibition entitled *Zichan jieji huale de wuchan jieji (Bourgeoisified Proletariat)* would follow where there is depressed real estate and cheap rent. In other words, this tactic of resistance is itself not freed from the necessity to be centered on an economic form of survival.

The two performance art projects discussed by Darren Zhou, Eunice Seng, and the author are both predicated on the architecture of the exhibition space made available

---

62 Peter N. Stearns, *Consumerism in World History: The Global Transformation of Desire* (New York: Routledge, 2006), p.97.

63 Deborah S. Davis, "Introduction: A Revolution in Consumption," in *The Consumer Revolution in Urban China,* Davis, ed., (Berkeley: University of California Press, 2000), p.19.

64 Ibid., p.12.

at no cost by the developer Li Gang. One of them was provocatively titled *Tofu Wall* by Polit-Sheer-Form-Office (PSFO). Established in 2005 by artists Hong Hao, Xiao Yu, Song Dong, Liu Jianhua, and art critic Leng Lin, PSFO insists on collective work based on a clear critique of consumerism. Political connotations of their work would be intentionally made absent in hollow forms, so viewers can imbue it with their own consumerist identities. The site-specific *Tofu Wall* was first created in Songjiang in 2009 as a critique of the newly built space given to them for free, and the "live" performance shows half a dozen people chopping the wall down with axes. The artists describe the enclosure of architecture as fragile, alluding to its commercial lifespan. They consider such an act as an opening up of their world, and allowing others to enter. This piece was re-enacted at their solo exhibition in Queens Museum, New York, for a month from February 8, 2015, while the rest of the exhibition lasted longer.[65] Members of PSFO were all born in the mid-1960s, which means their work is an autobiographical account of China's emergence out of the Cultural Revolution into the Consumerist China that is today. The borrowed space of PFSO's art work speaks precisely to the artists' intention to exploit a surplus space in society. Now with a global art following, the artists might even be benefiting commercially from the original 2009 work. This manner of borrowing of the resources, especially from the public, was prevalent in a resource-scarce China. Civil servants, with very little incentive to excel in their work, would exploit the provisions by the Communist government, calling it *chi guojia* or feeding off the country's resources.[66] This can also apply to a segment in the Chinese population who are disenfranchised by the upward mobility promised by the new consumerism ethos of China, bringing to mind Michel de Certeau's idea of strategies and tactics in everyday spatial practices, in order to subvert the power of control over these spaces.[67] Architecture is a discipline of design in the spatial and physical realms, which tends to be very well exploited as spectacles of consumption. Because architecture tends to be produced by the powerful and wealthy, it means architecture may not be best poised to solve problems of inequality or a lack of freedom directly. But it can offer up sites of resistance, or become the host for altered spatial practices.

---

65 Shen Ruijin, "Curator's Statement," Polit-Sheer-Form! Exhibition Brochure, Nov 1, 2014 to Mar 8, 2015. http://www.queensmuseum.org/wp-content/uploads/2015/06/PolitSheerForm.pdf. Accessed Dec 12, 2016.
66 Davis, "Introduction: A Revolution in Consumption," p.130.
67 Michel de Certeau, *The Practice of Everyday Life*, trans. Steven Rendall (Berkeley: University of California Press, 1984).

MEDIATED MASSES
AND NETWORKED BODIES

Poorly Understood Consumerist Culture

Not by coincidence, there is very little direct interest in consumerist typologies in the socially-oriented works of architects in China. One rare interest in such an extreme consumerist environment can be found in the Yiwu Market, Zhejiang province. Widely recognized as the world's largest wholesale market, Li Shiqiao describes this China Commodity City as the spatial displacement of capitalism, scouring the world of all its cheap labor. It draws in traders from around the world, especially from the Middle East and North Africa, but also from parts of Europe and Asia. Many would take up temporary residency in Yiwu, making it the testbed for China's tolerance of multicultural and multiracial activities.[68] This fast-growing global community would only be augmented by the opening of the Yiwu-London freight train line in January 2017, passing through Kazakhstan, Russia, Belarus, Poland, Germany, Belgium, France to the United Kingdom. This is very much a reestablishment of the ancient Silk Road as part of China's One Belt, One Road strategy. Jiang Jun expands on the complex interdependency of such a major political and economic policy, but he also seeks to find the territorial and spatial ramifications. There is no doubt about what this Chinese-led network would do economically, politically and geographically in the world system that Li and Jiang refer to, but the social implications need to be better understood.

Seventy percent of the world's Christmas decorations are being manufactured in China and passing through Yiwu. Although the workers producing these commodities are gaining employment, they are also being alienated by the production process. This is because Christmas is not fully understood in China yet, compounded by the lowly wages, long work hours, health problems and environmental pollution. These expulsions of a throwaway consumer culture are being absorbed by Chinese workers in Yiwu. Despite the sweeping labor law reform of 2008 that required employers to provide formal contracts for every worker, the nature of small commodity manufacturing industries tends to required less skills and education, and the laborers remain easily exploited. The aim was to

---

68 Mark Jacobs, *Yiwu, China: A Study of the World's Largest Small Commodities Market* (New Jerey: Homa & Sekey, 2016).

limit the use of temporary and low wage labor, and make it harder to terminate contracts, but each year, social scientists are still reporting that the government must do more on behalf of the working class for a more equitable share of economic gains and improve collective labor rights.[69] Until the workers and producers are able to connect with the meanings and implications of their work to the wider sociocultural contexts they serve, the disaffected working class would always remain. The substandard factories serve to shore up the endless corridors of merchandize at the Yiwu Market, and Li describes them as the least stimulating of environments with no ideology, and no conception of any human experience.

Digital Networks and the Threat of Social Connectivity

China's bullish economic growth has a lot to do with its investments in mass communication and digital networks. Yet it is also the same networks that serve as the "grounds of services" for the rise of social media and mobility that threatens China's ability to control society. This McLuhanite notion of a concealed environment of services, and the fetish for innovation can be very true of China's approach to media. By virtue of its population, China is the world's largest internet market of around 632 million users. With twice as many mobile manufacturers than the United States, China is expanding its smartphone mobile market, and is the leader in producing content for its mobile phone users.[70] If affordable technology is a powerful social leveler, then China is expediently transmitting knowledge to everyone and mobilizing communities. But it is also proving to be threatening because knowledge is power. Ou Ning argues that such virtual spaces and other forms of mass media are the true civic spaces of contemporary society, more powerful than the agoras and piazzas of yesteryears. This is described as a new institutional aspect of space, and the governance of such spaces must be open and accountable. While China still has a poor reputation in overcontrolling and censoring information, with less-than-transparent surveillance bureaus such as the Golden Shield Project, critics are optimistic that the leveling effect of technology will inevitably put power back in the hands of the people.[71] However, social scientists argue that the governing solutions would have to be updated and reflexive. The notion of control in China must to be redefined, such that there is minimal policing of citizens, and the government must stop treating its

---

69 Qian Jian, "2010 Nian Zhongguo zhiye zhuangkuang: huhuan gongxiang jingji fazhan chengguo he jiti laoquan," ["The Situation of China's Working Class in 2010: Calling for the Sharing of Economic Gains and Collective Labor Rights"] in Ru Xin, Lu Xueyi, and Li Peilin, eds., *2011 Nian Zhongguo shehui xingshi fengxi yu yuce* [*Society of China Analysis and Forecast (2011)*] (Beijing: Social Science Academic Press, 2011), p.256-259.

70 Jonathan Woetzel, et.al., *China's Digital Transformation: The Internet's impact on productivity and growth*, McKinsey Global Institute, Jul 2014, p.15.

71 Chen Xiaoran, Pan Yufeng and Zhu Huaxin, "2016 Nian Zhongguo hulianwang yuqing fenxi baogao," ["2016 China Internet Public Opinion Analysis Report"] in *2017 Nian Zhongguo shehui xingshi fengxi yu yuce* [*Society of China Analysis and Forecast (2017)*], Tian Feng, Fan Lei, Li Wei, Zhang Yi, Chen Guangjin and Li Peilin, eds., (Beijing: Social Science Academic Press, 2016).

citizens as control subjects. The mechanisms of control should be attuned to society's shift towards a more materialist life, and recognize the contradictions and dynamic changes in the ideologies and value systems of the people. Authorities see their roles to "put enlightening and counseling of social mentality or spiritual values into operation" and to "resolve social contradictions,"[72] but this paternalistic approach would have to change. Instead, they would have to find novel ways to manage the newly attained freedom found in new social networks.

The analyses of Han Tao, Xu Tiantian, Lee Ambrozy, and Zhou Yi paid due attention to the spatial consequences of this network society. These four critical essays cross two chapters of the book, and they share the subject matter of art, whether it is from the vantage point of a curator, critic, historian, advocate or architect. As the architect of the Chinese Academy of Oil Painting in Gaobeidian, Beijing, Han has also become an advocate for the life of an artist. When he was leading a seminar about a new form of an "individualized collective" community in 2015, the artists living on campus, beneficiaries of his design, huddled around the classroom and participated keenly in the debates. There is a remarkable resilience about the way these artists have chosen to live in the academy, with the same sense of collectivity and solitude found in a monastery, in quiet defiance of the market economy of the art world beckoning them to join. Xu harbors the ambition that architecture can be central to both the experimentation of art and the network of an art economy. After all, the artists living in the studios in Songzhuang Art Village have their top-selling art works circulating in Documenta in Kassel, Art Basel in Hong Kong, the Affordable Art Fair in Singapore, and the various biennales and triennales of art. Xu reflects on her effort in designing a network of three buildings at different locations in Songzhuang, the biggest art colony in China. The art museum, artist studio and residence, and cultural center for the promotion of art seem to exemplify the network of consumption, production and circulation of art. Ambrozy discusses the work of four artists and art groups to reveal a deep sense of displacement within the fraternity of artists, so much so that they would take on spatial practices as a symptomatic way to distort and retaliate against the commodification of space and architecture. The "ubiquity of construction and demolition" forms the subtext of these works, as the human scale or the body contorts itself to fit back into the architecture made for capital, not for society. As the curator-client of Inside-Out Art Museum, Zhou Yi recounts his experience in the making and sustaining of the museum. The museum has a strong focus on international networks, with a residency program that invites emerging artists to react to Beijing. The program has received artists from the United States, Canada, United Kingdom, Germany, France, Switzerland, Russia, Spain, Japan, Korea, and other countries. Zhou quickly came

---

72 Zhang Jianjing and Hong Dayong, eds., "Abstract," *Zhongguo shehui fazhan yanjiu baogao 2015: Shenxun shehui zhili chuangxin he tuijin shehuijiankang fazhan* [*Research Reports on China Social Development 2015: Exploring Innovation in Social Governance and Promoting Healthy Social Development*] (Beijing: Renmin University of China, 2015), pp.3-4.

to terms with the unique opportunities in China, as there is an incredible openness and space for experimentation in such a way that the conventions of quality and permanence would have to give way to the sheer energy and cacophony of the city.

Media and Art in Service of Society

Artistic production was co-opted by Mao Zedong towards social and revolutionary goals. In his speech at the 1942 Yan'an Forum on Literature and Art, he argued that "writers and artists should study society, that is to say, should study the various classes in society, their mutual relations and respective conditions, their physiognomy and their psychology. Only when we grasp all this clearly can we have a literature and art that is rich in content and correct in orientation."[73] Fast forward to a 2014 symposium on the arts, Xi Jinping put an end to "weird architecture," and in his two-hour speech, he suggested that artistic production should serve society, "like sunshine from the blue sky and breeze in spring that will inspire minds, warm hearts, cultivate taste, and clean up undesirable work styles."[74] Every news article that reported this admonition showed Rem Koolhaas and OMA's CCTV Tower and Zaha Hadid's Galaxy Soho in Beijing as examples of "weird architecture." It was evident that the leadership in China sees the artistic production of art, literature, and by extension, the aesthetics of its built environment as the next frontier of a competition in cultural supremacy. According to Xi, "Chinese art will further develop only when we make foreign things serve China, and bring Chinese and Western art together via a thorough understanding, and artistic efforts must "disseminate contemporary Chinese values, embody traditional Chinese culture and reflect Chinese people's aesthetic pursuit."[75] The society evoked here is a culturally oriented society, tantamount to a national pride associated only with the Chinese. Even though Mao and Xi were discussing art and architecture, they are really addressing society. This resonated with Layla Dawson's reluctant account of the level of influence foreign architects have been exerting on contemporary Chinese architecture, foretelling Xi's worry about a slack cultural position of Chinese architectural design. "Modern architecture marks the transformation of the People's Republic from a controlled welfare system to a privatized and profit-based economy with explosive repercussions in the built environment."[76]

From a European avant-garde position, classical forms of architecture were rejected in favor of a more self-conscious expression of qualities and utility of its time. Ornamental forms were derided as being willful at best, and bourgeois and materialistic at its most condemned, and every effort must be made to eradicate it. This design ethic remains

73 Mao Tsetung, *Selected Readings from the Works of Mao Tsetung* (Peking: Foreign Language Press, 1971), p.256. This was also discussed by Vine in is introduction to *New China New Art*.
74 Zhang He, "Beyond the Official Report, What Else did Xi Jinping Talk About at the Symposium for the Arts?" *People's Daily*, Oct 16, 2014.
75 Austin Ramzy, "Xi Jinping Calls for Artists to Spread 'Chinese Values'," *The New York Times*, Oct 16, 2014.
76 Layla Dawson, "Towers to the People," *China's New Dawn: An Architectural Transformation* (Munich: Prestel Verlag, 2005), pp.16-33.

largely true even today, in academies of design and education, even though society has moved well beyond its socialist era. Unfortunately, modernism has also been turned into a mere style in America,[77] having lost its ideological roots from Europe. In the same way, if Xi was only advocating a superficial and decorative Chinese style, he would risk missing the opportunity to embolden Chinese artists and architects to develop a real critical agenda for society. The original avant-garde form in architecture has many roots, but three of them could shed light on this Chinese analysis, namely the Russian Constructivists led by Vladimir Tatlin, the German Werkbund led by Joseph Maria Olbrich, and the Bauhaus led by Walter Gropius. Werkbund's emphasis on *typisierung*, followed the development, identification and classification of typologies, which led to advanced conditions of industrial standardization and social equality.[78] In type, there was the element of control, argued from the vantage point of economy, quality, social harmony, responsible production, and universal correctness. On the other hand, as an organization of artists, architects, designers and industrialists, the Werkbund would inevitably champion the genius and individualism of the members' work. The contested identity between artistic authorship, the basis of production and the market place revealed problems of "citizenship" and "individualism" in a cultural sphere that is public and free for exchange of ideas and benefits, but also deemed the language of bourgeois liberalism.[79] This separation of the spaces, and ethics of production and consumption is well documented today around the world, since the cultural analyses of the Frankfurt School thinkers, and even more so in Guy Debord's notion of perfect separation or alienation of production.[80] China would enter into this global cycle of production and consumption after opening its doors to the world in the late 1970s, causing massive social inequality since. Painter-photographer László Moholy-Nagy was one of the key teachers at the Bauhaus, and he brought a form of political theory into the teaching of architecture, where there was a "link between social change and visual form."[81] Constructivism was considered the most powerful form of social art in service of the prevailing industrial productivity of the Soviets, and it was influential not only in architecture, but also in graphic design, industrial design, film, theater and fashion. This rejection of the autonomy of art was not only borrowed by Mao, and more recently by Xi, but it gave Chinese artists and architects a new decree to channel their visions towards social goals. One of the best expression of revolutionary social ideas in production and consumerism in the 1920s was the constructivist's use of graphic design in commercial advertisements, such as Alexander Rodchenko's work for Russian Dobrolet Airlines and Mossel'prom

---

77 Henry Russell Hitchcock and Philip Johnson. *The International Style* (New York City: W.W. Norton & Company, 1932).

78 Frederic J. Schwartz, *The Werkbund: Design Theory and Mass Culture before the First World War* (New Haven: Yale, 1996), pp.121-146.

79 Ibid., p.168.

80 Guy Debord, *Society of the Spectacle*, trans. Donald Nicholson-Smith (New York: Zone Books, 1994), p.8.

81 Chris Nineham, "The Two Faces of Modernism," *International Socialism Journal*, Issue 64, Autumn, 1994.

Cooking Oil Company. During that same period, China was emerging from the anti-imperialist May Fourth Movement, and leading intellectuals and national figures such as Lu Xun was dominant in disseminating sociopolitical ideas in advancing Chinese society. Though Art Deco and other consumerist orientation were prevalent in Chinese cities with cosmopolitan traits, Lu had strong affinities and admiration for Constructivist art, while advocating for a stronger Chinese identity in the modern form of woodblock art.[82] Lu's work would eventually be co-opted by Mao towards the goals of the communist revolution in China, including the establishment of the Lu Xun Academy of Fine Arts by the Communist Party of China in Yan'an four years prior to Mao's 1942 Yan'an speech.[83]

Communication and Interdisciplinarity

In the preface to his 2010 edition of the *Rise of the Network Society*, first published in 1996, Marxist sociologist Manuel Castells made numerous observations about China under the same influence of the global informational network in the context of the state and the economy. At the heart of his lifelong work, he questions how class struggles are being transformed by the availability of such mass communications and networks.[84] How do the structural changes in the "spaces of flows" he observes in the new informational city[85] going to radically improve lives? While sociologists, economists, and political scientists examine these complex organizational relationships, they are always looking for evidence in how it affects the lived reality of people. Sociologist Saskia Sassen suggests that these abstract flows remain abstract for strategic reasons. She argues that for the effects to be really understood and documented, one has to closely observe the "variety of global circuits as they hit the ground in a city and get wired into urban space."[86] In other words, as a methodological necessity, the real site of documentation for this book must be found in the physical and spatial dimensions of architecture and the city.

Architecture is a highly social field, but it has almost never been recognized as part of the social sciences in a disciplinary way. Yet social research would consistently claim the territories and issues of the city, turning a remarkably visual realm into a series of self-serving charts and graphs. Architecture and other spatial expressions of the built environment are not normally considered a socially conscious intervention, yet the act

---

82 Julia F. Andrews, *Painters and Politics in the People's Republic of China, 1949-1979* (Berkeley: University of California, 1994), pp.16-18.

83 Scott Minick and Jiao Ping, "Yan'an and the Artistic Ideal," *Chinese Graphic Design in the Twentieth Century* (London: Thames and Hudson, 1990), pp.89-99.

84 Manuel Castells, *The Rise of the Network Society, The Information Age: Economy, Society and Culture Vol. I* (Cambridge: Blackwell, 1996). Castells, *The Power of Identity, The Information Age: Economy, Society and Culture Vol. II* (Cambridge: Blackwell, 1997). Castells, *End of Millennium, The Information Age: Economy, Society and Culture Vol. III* (Cambridge: Blackwell, 1998).

85 Manuel Castells, *The Informational City: Information Technology, Economic Restructuring, and the Urban Regional Process* (Cambridge: Blackwell, 1989).

86 Saskia Sassen, "Cities in Today's Global Age," *in Connecting Cities: Networks (A Research Publication of the 9th World Congress of Metropolis)*, Metropolis Congress, 2008. p.27.

of design can end up defining a set of power relationships. It could carry the distributive power in housing, the sequencing of spaces within a building to facilitate entry for some and filtering others out, or the arrangement and situating of buildings and public spaces in a city could lead one building to have an unequal relationship to sunlight or other necessary services. In a 2008 interview with a communications journal, Castells argued that good communication scholarship would naturally span different disciplines.[87] The way the discipline of architecture builds upon the foundation of other fields shows how it can successfully mediates between the society it serves and the built space it constructs, and this analytical method is shared by Joan Leung Lye, Kengo Kuma, and Shirley Woo. Leung Lye asks for the definition of obsolescence in architecture to be reevaluated by considering the wider disciplines of biological science, ecology, and even cultural fields. She argues that the current understanding of architecture and its shelf life is being dictated by the production of wealth and a calculated interest in economic returns through private ownership of buildings. In a sense, urban economics and urban planning have been coopted by the rich and powerful to justify change. Kuma and Woo expand on the thesis of *Defeated Architecture*, first written by Kuma in 2004, to continue to develop an antithesis to monumental architecture. The hope is for the symbolism of architecture to be weakened, in order for it to foreground the users. If architecture can dissolve into the fields of the landscape or the city, then this concept of an anti-object can be a new form of mediation in architecture. The tactility and geometry of the surfaces of architecture would therefore be decisive in the creation of newly assimilated topographies, whether it is the clay tiles of a series of stepped roofs that merge with the hilly landscape, or the façades of hung bricks that allow the building to dematerialize into the textures of an industrial district.

Technical Coordination and Socially Enacted Spaces

Cities in China are very much part of a system of infrastructure and people, technically and socially coordinated in such a way that it does not implode. Reinhold Martin prefers the term *Mediators*, for the implicit role of architecture within the wider field of aesthetics and politics in the global arena.[88] He is working out a philosophy for cities today. It is useful to recall the New Babylon project by Dutch artist and visionary Constant Nieuwenhuys for the purpose of understanding how his dream of an ideal society could lead to a two decade-long project. While Constant was meditating on notions of freedom, he produced an aesthetic of super connections, a highly networked city, as well as a hybrid condition of formality and informality.[89] Apart from his artistic production of models, maps, drawings,

---

87 School of Journalism and Communication, Chinese University of Hong Kong, "Interview with Manuel Castells," *Chinese Journal of Communication*, vol. 1, no. 1, April 2008, pp.3–6.

88 Reinhold Martin, *Mediators: Aesthetics, Politics, and the City* (Minneapolis: University of Minnesota Press, 2014).

89 Rem Koolhaas and Pascal Gielen, "The Topsy-Turvy as Utopian Architecture," *Constant: New Babylon. To Us, Liberty* (Ostfildern: Hatje Cantz, 2016), p.64.

collages, and paintings, he also lectured about his work and wrote manifestos and essays about a particular kind of forerunner of the network society. Constant's disdain for the class of property owners[90] from 1958 to 1974 led him to explore a spatial language of openness and connectivity in the New Babylon project. There is an unexpected parallel in the way Dong Gong searches for the civic potential of private architecture, or for that matter, any architecture. Dong refers to a similar capacity for architecture to be absorbed into a continuous system of public amenities and leisure. The freedom to move and the social problems Constant saw in his day are important in giving impetus to such thinking. Fast forward from events of May 1968 in France, and the Civil Rights Movement between 1954 and 1968 in the United States to China today, one can expect that artists and the creative professionals are searching for what Dong describes as the tectonics and physical expressions of the public. Mark Wigley argues for an imperative role for such socially enacted spaces, which he visualizes as the architecture of hospitality. "Architecture likes to think of itself as the first host, creating the space for social life, even the possibility of social life. It is an ethical act before it is a practical act. Hospitality is genuine openness to the stranger, embracing the risk of the Other—of people, actions, and ideas that are different, unfamiliar, changing, confusing, or unknown. This risk of the Other brings the possibility of companionship, discussion, play, pleasure, affection, friendship, education, sharing and solidarity but also the possibility, even inevitability, of antagonism and violence."[91]

---

90 Mark Wigley, "Extreme Hospitality," *Constant: New Babylon. To Us, Liberty*, p.49.
91 Ibid., p.38.

RATIONALIZATION
AND SOCIAL AESTHETICS

Revisiting Techno-economic Coordination

In the introductory essay to his 1984 book on the various control methods of a communist regime, Andrew G. Walder argues that "the declining reliance on political terror and mass mobilization does not represent a fundamental change, but merely the greater refinement, 'rationalization,' and sophistication of political control."[92] In the organizational systems that were deemed important for tight social control, such as industrial and agricultural production, the Chinese Communist regime would focus on developing it more as an advanced social form of organization, rather than a normative productive or economic form. This form of social rationalization has a diametrically opposite but intricately intertwined correlation to what Herbert Marcuse observed in the United States as an advanced techno-economic regime of scientific coordination to gain profit. While the entire globe seems to have accepted that the path to prosperity is to engage in peaceful trade and consumerism, advancing with greater civility from the days of war and colonialism, it would still be important to observe how the social form is continually being invoked by the different regimes in very different ways. It is interesting to see wide acceptance of humanity being trampled on in the race for economic growth in China, where there is still a deeply seated base of social control.

In all the forms of rationalization in socialist thought, the rationalization of production, private ownership, and education have the most profound effect on architecture and the instrumentality of form. The innovation of Taylorism found in America had left Europe's methods of industrial production lagging behind, but it was precisely this shift towards a greater fragmentation and mindlessness of labor, and a replacement of labor by machines, that had created a dramatically unequal distribution of economic gains and social unrest. The rationalization of labor to reempower the disenfranchised workers instead of the entrepreneur served as the beginning of socialism.[93] It is not surprising that industrial

---

92 Andrew G. Walder, *Communist Neo-Traditionalism: Work and Authority in Chinese Industry* (Berkeley: University of California, 1984), p.3.

93 Vladimir Lenin, "A 'Scientific' System of Sweating," *Lenin Collected Works: Volume 18*, trans. Stepan Apresyan (Moscow: Progress Publishers, 1975), pp.594-595.

architecture is not a particularly fertile area for experimentation and creativity, because the production process tends to be very strictly controlled by the logic of manufacturing, not the social logic of the workers. For the purpose of appreciating how deeply entrenched the architecture of production is in the society and cities of China, it is important to note that multiple authors across different chapters in this volume are directly dealing with a rehabilitation of this architectural type. They include Meng Yan and Urbanus's OCT Loft; Darren Zhou, Eunice Seng, and SKEW Collaborative's Jia Little Exhibition Center and Ateliers; Kengo Kuma, Shirley Woo, and KKAA's Shanghai Shipyard; Joan Leung Lye, Jeremy Chia, and Andrew Lee's reflections on the Shougang Steel Mills; Liu Yichun and Atelier Deshaus's Laobaidu Coal Warehouse; and He Jianxiang and O-Office's Honghua Garment Factory. In China, the large stock of industrial buildings mean that architects and planners must fully grasp the legacy of production rationalization in China before they become complicit with the real estate developers in turning these industrial heritage or creative industry sites into a poorly veiled consumerist logic of cultural forms.

The Impossible High-rise Form

Socially-minded architectural practices in China tends to be small by default, and experimental by nature. The tendency in China is to build tall and large, and cheaply and in the shortest amount of time. With limitations dictated by an economy of scale, small and medium practices are not likely to be involved in most of such building activities. One can certainly observe very few high-rise forms in the work of architects committed to the social cause. In this volume, the majority are dealing with low density and low-rise typologies, but it is at least heartening to observe that the formal strategies and vocabulary developed by these contemporary architects continue to allow them to reflect on the social issues in China. As one examines the high-rise form, J.G. Ballard's allegorical and dark high-rise living narrative should shed light on its social implications. High-rises are purported by some to be a distortion of the built form by capital and power, while others believe it can one day build social capital.[94] In the novel *High-rise*, the tenants were unsurprisingly affluent. The critique was squarely on its social failures, as well as the technological aspects of architecture. The superficially harmonized social front did not prepare the readers for the dystopia that would follow.

> "The two thousand tenants formed a virtually homogeneous collection of well-to-do professional people—lawyers, doctors, tax consultants, senior academics and advertising executives, along with a smaller group of airline pilots, film-industry technicians and trios of air-hostesses sharing apartments. By the financial and educational yardsticks, they were probably closer to each

---

94 Edward Glaeser, "How Skyscrapers Can Save the City," *The Atlantic*, Mar 2011.

other than the members of any conceivable social mix, with the same tastes and attitudes, fads and styles—clearly reflected in the choice of automobiles in the parking lots that surrounded the high-rise."[95]

Born and raised in the International Concession in Shanghai, Ballard witnessed the charm and contradictions of a modernized city, the failed promise of technology, and the trauma of war. It is not surprising that in works such as *High-rise* he would knowingly take up the critique of modernity and social contradictions. Ballard would have been acquainted with the work of Shen Yanbing, who was similarly overwhelmed by the lack of social cohesion in modern Shanghai. Shen wrote under the pseudonym Mao Dun, which translates to contradiction.[96] The high-rise in a socially-minded framework can be problematic, according to Constantinos Doxiadis. He argued against the high-rise because it destroys nature, isolates humanity, works against society by preventing family units from coming together, and destroys past urban landscapes. Most damaging of all, high-rises redistribute resources in an intentionally unfair manner.

"A city belongs to all citizens in many senses, ranging from their common participation in daily urban life, with all its benefits and disadvantages, to their contribution to the cost of the city's development and daily operation. The obvious conclusion is that every citizen should profit from the use of all urban land and urban space. This is not true in practice, and conditions which allow a small number of landowners to benefit from the total human effort made by all citizens result in the greatest of urban crimes."[97]

There is no conceivable way to disengage with the high-rise typology in the contemporary Chinese city, nor is it possible for a full redistribution of private property rights. Hence, it is refreshing to see Rocco Yim's effort to reconnect the city by employing a high-rise architectural form that would give way to a passage of park space given over to the public. This is a different high-rise that connects horizontally to multiple parts of the city. Described as a contestation between architecture and the city, it is apparent that Yim recognizes the self-centered nature of architecture and the private ownership of buildings would be in direct opposition to the desire of the city to be more open and generous. Cui Kai describes the possibility of a shared city in the future, because he believes society has an inbuilt capacity to be ethical and magnanimous. He urges architects to be sensitive to the alienating effects of extra-large and high-rise buildings, because the more unusual they are, they appear to represent power and wealth that is unattainable and inaccessible to the ordinary citizen. Similarly, in looking for the possibility to enable the most

---

95 J.G. Ballard, *High-rise* (New York: W.W.Norton & Company, 1975), p.17.

96 Mao Dun, *Midnight*, trans. Hsu Meng-hsiung (Peking: Foreign Language Press, 1957).

97 C.A. Doxiadis, "The great urban crimes we permit by law," *Ekistics* (journal), vol.37, no.219, Feb 1974, pp.85-88.

widespread change, Jeffrey Johnson chooses to reevaluate the most pervasive megablock urbanism of China. He retheorizes the organizational logic of large urban grids, and advocate new ways to occupy and organize pedestrian passages through previously gated and underutilized spaces. Michael Kokora concludes his essay in an earlier chapter with a relatively similar quest to reclaim some of the urban spaces lost to extreme privatization. This new porosity and accessibility in the Chinese cities of megablocks is coming about because there is a willingness to work with the errors of a different regime using minimum amount of resources. The possibility for change must be approached with a combination of optimism and flexibility, but always adopting realistic and well-researched studies of the real barriers hindering Chinese society today.

Modernist by Design and the Limitation of Symbolism

In historian Perry Anderson's account of modernism, there was an unprecedented upheaval in the social and technological realms that had brought about a fair degree of disillusionment and fragmentation. In the worst cases, modern architecture was wrongly deemed to be the unequivocal solution to all social ills. This kind of dogma and judgmental belief during the period of high modernism led partially to the discrediting of modernism as a social movement. The alienating effects of modern architecture was underestimated, as much as the readiness of society in accepting such prognostic claims.

> "The 'high period' of modernism from 1900-1930 was of course a time of unmatched upheaval, in which the promises of the bourgeois revolution were finally shattered by war, slump and workers' revolt. The accelerating development of technology and the penetration of mass production techniques into every sphere of life added to a deep sense of uncertainty."[98]

It is therefore not surprising that the contemporary works discussed by the Chinese architects in this volume tend to be modernist by design, and the insular educational programs in China did not really depart from the rationalized effects of modernist thought. In the search for equality, socially-minded architects and professors in China used to look for the most utilitarian way to build, rejecting any kind of excessive ornamentation or formalism. It is to be expected that the ubiquitous and raw reinforced concrete, or the stripped down béton brut architecture of the industrial revolution was preferred, so as to project the outlook of honesty and utility since the educational curriculum of the late 1970s,[99] and it has not deviated much since.

Power and Bureaucracy of the Civil Service

Architecture is often deployed for symbolic functions, and this is where it can suffer the most. For example, architecture is charged with carrying the message of equality,

---

98 Perry Anderson, "Modernity and Revolution," *New Left Review*, I/144, Mar-Apr 1984.
99 Daniel Juillard, "China Special Issue 1949-1979," *L'Architecture D'Aujourd'Hui* (journal), Paris, February 1979.

from social housing to public spaces. While it is not short of good intentions, its design may fall short of it. It is also possible that the same architecture can mean very different things under a variety of circumstances. The famed Narkomfin Building by Moisei Ginzburg gave form to many of the socialist experiments proposed by the Constructivist *Organizatsiya Sovremmennaia Arkhitektura* (Organization of Contemporary Architects), OSA Group.[100] Described as a social condenser, each of the apartments had its dedicated kitchen removed in favor of a collective kitchen. Unfortunately, most apartments would secretly have a partitioned space as a small kitchen or pantry for the convenience of daily routines. Going against the ethics of socialism that led to the commissioning of the building in the first place, the building municipal client Nikolay Milyutin secured a penthouse on the roof level, previously planned as a shared recreation area for his personal enjoyment. Milyutin failed to live up to his own visions of a socialist linear city. When architecture becomes stylized with an appearance, it tends to fail to live up to its rhetoric. Because architecture is such a materially grounded and resource-heavy practice, it is easy to fall into a replication of a style without an embodiment of the social improvements it promised. With a longstanding history that goes back to the imperial examinations since the Han dynasty, the civil service in China was the social, political and intellectual elite that were essentially the opposite of the mercantile elites in China. The civil service enlisted talent based on intellectual capacity and knowledge, especially in the fields of the classics and literature. When the modern day civil service was tasked with the making of key municipal buildings in socialist China, they derived much of their architecture from Stalinist architecture from the Soviets, or retreated to the Chinese renaissance style derived from the Beaux-Arts.[101] Nartano Lim discusses the disappointment of such derived styles, and laments the underrepresentation of new canons in China. Surprisingly, earlier Soviet Constructivist architecture that formed part of the European Avant-garde did not gain much credibility in the transfer of ideas to China.

The social elitism of the civil service architects from the Soviet era would help to propel and sustain the heroism of modern architecture through the twentieth century, while China closed its doors to the outside world for thirty years after 1949. But such architecture would make its way to China in unexpected ways. The Soviet Constructivist architects and artists were attempting to articulate the fragmented and contradictory experiences under the influence of capitalism. Reacting against the tower form as a form that is symbolic of an American form of capitalism, Russian architect and photographer El Lissitzky went on to develop a horizontal skyscraper. He named it *Wolkenbügel*, or "cloud-irons,"[102] and contended that humans should walk, not fly, and the elevated three-story horizontal forms were meant to encourage movement across the eight towers in

---

100 Selim O. Khan-Magomedov, *Pioneers of Soviet Architecture* (London: Thames and Hudson, 1983), p.594.

101 Xuefei Ren, *Building Globalization: Transnational Architecture Production in Urban China* (Chicago: University of Chicago, 2011), p.42.

102 Khan-Magomedov, *Pioneers of Soviet Architecture*, pp.297-305.

Moscow. Modernism remains the most applicable architectural design that has a lineage to the Avant-garde, and continues to have an ideological relationship to its socialist history. To design modern architecture is to embrace the social project that, in principle, was a rejection of the attitudes of the bourgeois, including their ethics, aesthetics and other value system. In particular, Foucault anticipated this power held by bureaucracy created around administrative knowledge, and personified by the office held by the clerk. He referred to this range of knowledge of how wealth is generated and managed from the courts to the people as "a history of the displacement of wealth, of exactions, theft, sleight of hand, embezzlement, impoverishment, and ruin."[103] The contemporary clerk would be the legislator with deep knowledge about the passing and management of tolerable forms of legislation, distribution patterns, and would also thoroughly grasp gaps within the system. The fuller recognition of the influence of such civil service work was given due attention by Reinier de Graaf and Laura Baird, when AMO put out the *Public Works— Architecture by Civil Servants* exhibition in the 2012 Venice Biennale. It continues to uphold and recognize the important work of architects serving the general public under the socialist regimes of the 1950s to the 1970s. This can be considered a productive return to the socially-minded public servant in service of society. Reinier describes it as "a short-lived, fragile period of naïve optimism" in a bureaucracy that is anonymous.[104] It is not surprising that such heroic forms would find its way in the borrowed "socialist" horizontal skyscraper of the CCTV Headquarters in Beijing. Built by OMA for the state-owned China Central Television Broadcasting company, it drew unexpected resentment from the ordinary public as documented by Cui Kai in his essay in this book.

Vocationalization of Education and New Pedagogical Directions

The process of social rationalization can be applied to education. In fact, all the contributors to Chapter Eight are practitioners who are deeply involved in the design of architectural pedagogy in schools of architecture in China and elsewhere. The economic reform of Deng Xiaoping after the Cultural Revolution would not have been successful if the educational policies did not closely mirror the demands in the fields of science and technology, business, and English language as a global language, with increased levels of professionalism and specialization that spearheaded the construction industries and export-oriented manufacturing industries. In fact, the initial policy of rationalization of education literally meant greater vocationalization of education, such that graduates from high schools and universities are able to join the labor force immediately.[105] Apart from

---

103 Michel Foucault, *Society Must Be Defended: Lectures at the College de France, 1975-76*, trans. David Macey (New York: Picador, 2003), p.132.

104 Mimi Zeiger, "Celebrating the Bureaucrats: OMA's Public Works, Domus, Sep 13, 2012. http://www.domusweb.it/en/architecture/2012/09/13/celebrating-the-bureaucrat-oma-s-em-public-works-em-.html. Accessed Sep 1, 2016.

105 Stanley Rosen, "Recentralization, Decentralization, and Rationalization: Deng Xiaoping's Bifurcated Educational Policy," *Modern China*, vol.11, no.3, Jul 1985, pp.301-346.

the sheer numbers of graduates and types of specialization in university degrees associated with architecture, landscape architecture, urban design, urban planning, construction management, environmental design, interior design, civil, structural, mechanical and electrical engineering, and other related studies, it is also possible to gain insight into the level of the social awareness of architects today by examining the directions of three elite schools of Xi'an University of Architecture and Technology, South China University of Technology School of Architecture and the Peking University Graduate Center of Architecture under the respective leadership of Liu Kecheng, Sun Yimin, and Yung Ho Chang. Liu established the direction of his research and the direction of the college around the urgent need for sophisticated guidelines for preservation in China, using the ancient city of Xi'an as a laboratory. The autobiographical journey of his essay reveals the value of an intellectually grounded context to a student's understanding of history and modernity. Efforts in internationalization in Liu's program are apparent in his establishing of the China Chapter of Docomomo International, the watchdog organization for the documentation and conservation of buildings, sites and neighbourhoods of the Modern Movement. Liu also serves on the council of the China Chapter of the International Council on Monuments and Sites, and other international organizations for research and benchmarking in the areas of architectural conservation. The appreciation for the history and depth of the Chinese civilization was central in Liu's pedagogical leadership at Xi'an. Sun has another unique view of architectural education in China. He discusses the narrow focus on design creativity in an effort to elevate the role of technical rationalism and expert knowledge in place of shallow theories and esoteric concepts, in order to attain a new kind of aesthetics in architecture. Sun is the Executive Deputy Director of the prestigious nationally-funded Laboratory of Subtropical Building Science with a research capacity of around eighty researchers and PhD students, enabling him to augment design teaching with empirical research methods. Upon Chang's return from the United States, he brought a well-grounded wisdom in design culture to the Graduate Center of Architecture he established in 2001. Throughout his teaching career, he has championed the innate cultural and material context of architecture, as he transmits his early experience of teaching at the University of Michigan and Rice University to Peking University and later MIT and Tongji University. Chang's appreciation of the deep materialism of the architecture discipline itself ensures that his pedagogy would resist the temptation to bring every interdisciplinary issue or overly abstract philosophical theory into architecture, without first grasping the precise limit and role of architecture in society. He advocates the importance of discourse in architecture with the founding of the *32 Beijing / New York* Journal in 2003. The teaching and making of architecture in China would nearly always foreground social and technical issues—designing public space, producing public good through architectural design, and building rationally and responsibly with the available resources. The education of an architect would take on the long-suffering and self-sacrificial act of fighting for the common good. No good architecture students in school would propose design to privilege the developer or profit the powerful. Yet these same socially-conscious students would be confounded by the pragmatic and profit-hungry clients they serve upon leaving the schools. Architectural education favors social issues so vehemently, only for students to graduate into a world of disempowered architects, who are called to comply with the clients in a service industry. Disaffected students cannot connect the diverse socially-attuned lessons in school with the real world of rampant profiteering in an uncritical professional service and a distorted urban economy.

Aesthetics of Utopia

Most architects and professionals of the built environment are articulate about their ambitions in the making of architecture, but their work is not always intelligible to the users of their works. Most architects are not as nimble in negotiating and observing the social relations of space, which means they may be less aware or in control of the way their architecture or designs may include or exclude users.[106] This ultimately points to an awareness of a kind of citizenship that is being controlled by space. Zhu Xiaofeng laments that most architecture produced in China is done under very unfavorable conditions, where the architects have no direct contact with or understanding of the end users. Commercial projects suffer the most in this respect, because they are likely to be led by investors or developers who would dictate how ordinary people would live and work based on a profit motive. The choice given to the general consuming public then becomes a false choice, because there is no participation for end users in this architectural and urban equation. This brings the book full circle back to where the battles for society were first fought. On the territorial level, discrepancies in the modern era between social classes were first seen in the division between town and country, pitting the lowly rural working class against the corrupt urban bourgeois. In this context, it is timely to reexamine the emergence of social utopia in the spirit of Ebenezer Howard's Garden City Movement, instigated by the publication of *To-morrow: a Peaceful Path to Real Reform* in 1898. He was able to incorporate ideas of public improvement into a coherent suburban plan, inspired by Edward Bellamy on one hand, but also rigorously adapting economic recommendations by social theorist and economist Henry George in his 1879 treatise entitled *Progress and Poverty: An Inquiry into the Cause of Industrial Depressions and of Increase of Want with Increase of Wealth: The Remedy*.[107] There was a direct lineage from Garden City[108] thinking to the Soviet disurbanist school led by sociologist and town planner Mikhail Okhitovich, and architect Moisei Ginsberg,[109] and it would reach socialist China in a distorted way. While such "green" aesthetics and planning can carry with them a set of clear instructions,

---

106 Henri Lefebvre, *Production of Space*, trans. Donald Nicholson-Smith (Oxford: Wiley-Blackwell, 1991), pp.85-88. See also, David Harvey, *Rebel Cities: From the Right to the City to the Urban Revolution* (Brooklyn: Verso, 2012), pp.3-25.

107 Peter Hall and Colin Ward, *Sociable Cities: The Legacy of Ebenezer Howard* (London: Academy Press, 1999).

108 Khan-Magomedov, *Pioneers of Soviet Architecture*, pp.271-274.

109 James H. Bater, *The Soviet City* (London: Hodder & Stoughton, 1980)

the return to the morally purifying effects of the idyllic landscape may not be the only appropriate response for contemporary China. Mao's regime had taken China down the road of agrarian reform and collectivization of agricultural production in an effort to achieve socialist goals,[110] but society has not always found equality and peace in the context of *datong* or the great harmony in the countryside.[111] There is an unexpected symmetry in the social reality of the countryside, because it represented a hardworking agricultural condition of production, rather than just access to land, clean air and a fair society that was promised. The ornamental use of landscape in the creation of the first garden city of Letchworth in England is as misleading as the propaganda depictions of harmony in the *datong* communes deployed in the Chinese countryside.

Rhetoric of Tradition and Aesthetics

In Walder's notion of neo-traditionalism, he carefully situates the reinvoking of tradition within the sociopolitical rhetoric of communist China. Confucian thought emerged from time to time. In particular, the meanings ascribed to the Communist Chinese countryside was lost on the ancient Chinese countryside designed for self-cultivation, and enjoyment by the literati and aristocratic class. It is therefore important to realize the intellectual baggage that comes with contemporary explorations of the aesthetics of the highly charged genre of landscape and "nature." Historically, the Chinese landscape was the site of great cultural production and intellectual work that was equally utopian, except it was a withdrawn activity, or a communion with nature and self. There was an elitist tendency in this cultural genre. Wu Liangyong evokes the all-rounded capacity of *yiwen*, or the apex of high Chinese culture, to give contemporary architecture a clear identity. *Yiwen* can be described a pure art form that is the culmination of all forms of artistic expression, from landscape painting, calligraphy, literature, sculpture, arts and craft to architecture. Similarly, the ancient culture of *gengdu*, or the cultivation of farming work and intellectual refinement, would take place in the countryside. It represents the utopianism that Dong Yugan and Mario Gandelsonas are hinting at in their respective essays. By his own admission, Dong remains a novice in the literary field of Chinese landscape design after decades of close study, because the scholarship is so wide. Likewise, in his reflection of over a decade of study trips with Princeton students, Gandelsonas remains enthralled by the potential offered by the complexity of Chinese landscape design for contemporary Chinese urbanism. However, in both these cases, there is a necessity to transform and translate such an aesthetic tradition. Dong uses the study and experimental study of Chinese landscape as an aesthetic order system to resist the appeal of Western architectural theories and histories sweeping across Chinese architectural education over

110 Rana Mitter, *A Bitter Revolution: China's Struggle with the Modern World* (New York: Oxford University Press, 2004), pp.194-198. Frank Dikötter, *Mao's Great Famine: The History of China's Most Devastating Catastrophe, 1958–62* (London: Walker Books, 2010).

111 Hua Shiping, *Chinese Utopianism: A Comparative Study of Reformist Thought with Japan and Russia, 1898-1997* (Stanford, Stanford University Press, 2009).

a decade ago. He likens it to a moral philosophy for a Chinese practice of architecture, in the way Paul Ricoeur formulated the importance of self-knowledge, before one could relate with the outside world in the form of cultural exchange. Dong discusses the need for specificity in his looking back at the traditions of high Chinese culture, but at the same time, arriving at a commonality in the wider discourse of architecture. Gandelsonas builds in the methodical reading of the Chinese garden, but also insists on the "writing" of it, which pedagogically means a necessity to rewrite or translate into a new form of writing. He points to a circulation of ideas, and a transformation in the rewriting process that would yield aesthetics that no longer bears any resemblance to the original subject.

Instead of fleeing from the gritty and contradictory urban condition, Liu Yichun and He Jianxiang separately propose another prominent principle for the aesthetics of contemporary China. Both embrace the utilitarian and honest architecture of industry in the city, in part because the industrial legacy had left China with an incomprehensible quantity of industrial carcasses, waiting to be demolished or readapted as a modern heritage. Liu began his reinterpretation of traditional Chinese landscape design in the first decade of his practice, but gradually shifted towards an ontological focus on more profound realities discovered in industrial materialism and structures. This was prompted by a ground breaking essay[112] by Yung Ho Chang and Zhang Lufeng, which helped to establish the principles of honest and everyday architecture in modern China. In some sense, Liu discovers that his earlier fascination and oblique view of the historical promise of the Chinese landscape does not butt neatly against the grittier realities of industrialization and urbanization in China. But to his credit, he does not abandon his earlier aesthetic project of Chinese landscape, nor does he see his meditation of Chinese landscapes as escaping from the harsher realities of industrialization. The messy realities of the city and its industrial necessities continue to figure strongly in Liu's search for dignity in everyday architecture, and they inspire new ways of interacting with the high cultural forms of ancient China. He Jianxiang engages Chinese landscape through a careful differentiation of conventional scenery and the artistic *fengjing*. The latter is described as having an embedded presence of architecture. Therefore, it is necessary to use a coined term "arch-scenario" to suggest that there is always a careful choreography of an idealized architectural scale and the human body in traditional treatments of landscape in Chinese paintings, and this choreography is deployed in an industrial site in Shenzhen. Hence, there can be a commitment to revitalize the marginalized industrial heritage of China with some of the aesthetic specificities once lost to modernization and industrialization.

112 Yung Ho Chang and Zhang Lufeng, "Xiang gongye jianzhu xuexi huo ruogan jianzhu gongshi de tuidao," ["Learning from Industrial Architecture, or the Principles of Architectural"] *Zuowenben* [*Yung Ho Chang Writes*] (Taipei: Tianyuan Chengshi, 2006).

CONCLUSION

SOCIAL SCIENCE AND THE SOCIAL CONSTRUCT OF SCIENCE

The divergent motivations of the essays in this book cannot possibly add up to a single account, given the wide-ranging and complex topics. The theories, histories, and manifestos expressed here remain on the fringe of the juggernaut of urban expansion. However, they have the capacity to coalesce in such a way as to convey an extreme discontent with the social bearings of China today, in the same way Immanuel Kant found moral philosophy in the eighteenth century totally inadequate towards the necessary social and legal frameworks required in Europe. The Kantian imperative is an underlying condition of this book. This application does not stop at a mere desire to arm Chinese society with a new theoretical or even philosophical datum. It also redefines contemporary practice in China. The ideas embedded in this paradigm shift can be shown to carry the seed of social change. Kant's categorical imperative not only set the groundwork for sociopolitical and legal change in the Western world, leading to clear formulations of humanitarian laws, freedom and human rights today, but it also highlighted clear limitations of the methods of empiricism and logic. At the cusp of the big data revolution today, operating within an industry with a staunch belief in scientific, technological and quantitative methods, architects, researchers and professionals of the built environment are no closer to knowing how to make socially responsible and ethical decisions in their work. This crisis is not only found in the disciplines of the built environment, but also in the social sciences. Bruno Latour's two-year study of scientists at work at the Salk Institute for Biological Studies in 1975 dismantled the long-held belief that sociology has to lean towards empirical methods to gain credibility. This study revealed that empirical methods must begin to welcome other critical and analytical frameworks in order to advocate a more humanist and ethical outcome, and facilitate a deeper questioning of the scientific basis of science itself.[113] In Jonas Salk's reflection of Latour's work in his introduction

---

113 Bruno Latour and Steve Woolgar, *Laboratory Life: The Social Construction of Scientific Facts* (Princeton: Princeton University Press, 1986), p.243.

to *Laboratory Life: The Social Construction of Scientific Facts*, he called for the presence of philosophers, anthropologists and sociologists within the scientific community to provide non-scientific criticism of work carried out in the laboratories. This respect for multiple branches of knowledge is equally central to the ideas expounded in this volume.

History Replayed—Reconstruction of Society and Perverse Realms of Building

Part of the objective of this book is to reconnect with social questions posed for architecture and the city, and social consequences due to the actions of architects, researchers and professionals of the built environment. They serve to clarify the intentions behind spatial thought and design. Referring to the Soviet condition in 1967, Anatole Kopp recounted that the ambitions of architects of the revolutionary period was nothing short of a total reconstruction of society. If one reviews the scholarship of the city, especially the period of modernism, one would quickly come to terms with the fact that such scholarship used to rest within the discourse of architecture. However, as the scale of cities become more ambitious, architects would gradually lose control over this added complexity. The question remains whether architecture or the built environment can continue to be a revolutionary tool to bring about positive influences to society. To build is to construct, safeguard and shelter. Unfortunately, the act of building today has become a mere investment and a calculated redistribution of resources. In China, it is a rampant and careless act of wealth accumulation by private developers and private owners. It is a pragmatic act of ensuring economic advancement. With the current state of multi-disciplinarity and specialization, the visionary role of architects has been usurped. In fact, the greater accountability and statistical measures ought to be good for the discipline of architecture and the built environment, but they have often become end games in themselves. Architecture quickly becomes the end product in the broader schema of the urban machinery that generates profit for the ones who control it. Governments and large corporations are most cognizant of this potential, and have been manipulating it since. "City planners and architects, whatever their nationality, are now aware that it is primarily private ownership of the land that makes it difficult (if not impossible) to implement a rational planning and development policy, that in certain countries [...] the profit motive makes housing a rare commodity, a luxury reserved for those 'with the means.' Today, everyone knows that city planning is the key to the problems that confront the architect."[114] As an artistic and scientific field in equal measure, architecture and the built environment have always been part of the social realm, but its real ability to influence and improve lives is in jeopardy. Architects and professionals of the built environment must not risk overlooking the implications of social change in the production of space again.

---

114 Anatole Kopp, *Town and Revolution: Soviet Architecture and City Planning 1917-1935*, trans. Thomas E. Burton. (New York: George Braziller, 1970), p.33.

The upward mobility of the 99% and participation by the citizens are crucial in China's efforts in building a civil society. The understanding of social issues in architecture can gain much from understanding how the market economy had gradually privatized many sectors that were once important within the socialist framework. Housing in China is one of such critical areas that is directly involved in the formation of civil society, and today, it remains a source of anxiety across China. Other critics argue that there is nothing intrinsically wrong with housing as a commodity, as long as ownership and influences can come from a broader spectrum of participants. It is about time that the bureaucrats fully grasp how tremendous differences can be found in the real social sphere of cities, as opposed to the planned physical sphere. The number of migrant population, including their families in tow, is clearly underreported in formal household surveys. After years of experimenting with the restructuring of the economy and plausible models of private ownership since the late 1900s, it is a pity that it could not make a more coordinated effort or give stronger protection to the social ideals that were upheld before the opening up of China.

A child bikes in the open spaces of Dafen Art Village.
Image courtesy of Nartano Lim, 2013

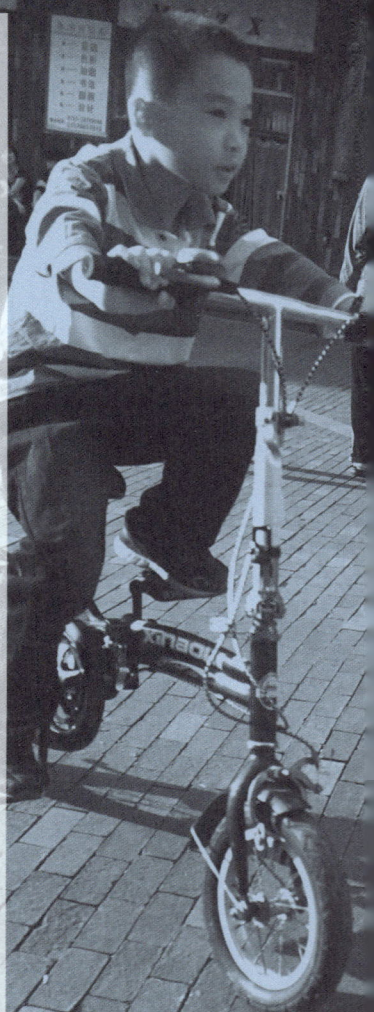

MOBILIZING

02

INTERVENTIONIST CITY

MENG YAN

In the discourse of architecture and the city—a conflicted dualism of an architectural urbanism or an urban architecture—there is a call for a deeper reflection of the role of an architect. Today, all professionals in China are described as *congyezhe*, which implies in the Chinese language a submissive position to the work at hand like a mere service provider. In such a professional climate, is it still possible for an architect to become an active agent of change or have an impact as a mediator of complex relationships? Are there possibilities for architects to practice in an expanded field? In addressing these concerns, Urbanus developed an urban strategy between 1999 and 2006 called the urban infill. A comparison between New York and Shenzhen shows the large amounts of urban voids in Shenzhen left during heydays of its rapid urbanization. These voids and residual spaces became instant opportunities for newer forms of architectural and urban practices. The voids can be redesigned for remedial actions, integrating new interventions with public spaces for a greater transformative effect on the city.

Voids and Topography as Remedial Action
Many residential neighborhoods in Shenzhen were built on hills as a result of its natural topography and urban development. One of the Urbanus' projects was at the entrance of the Cuizhu "Emerald Bamboo" Park. While the entrance sat on a parcel of land that was rightfully owned by a developer, next to a larger plot of land ripe for development, the government had requested the parcel to be surrendered as an entrance to a public park. This problem became an opportunity, where the architect was able to act as a mediator, not only between the government and the developer but also in design. The developer eventually agreed to give the entrance parcel back to the public in return for fifty underground parking lots, and the ascension to the park through this hilly gateway was designed with a public walking trail, breaking the steep incline into segments of walkable terrain. This architectural car park intervention was fully integrated with the intentions of the urban design of the park.

There were dramatic changes in the central districts of Shenzhen between 1998 and 2014. Today, these districts are forests of skyscrapers with practically no room left to build in. In the process of designing skyscrapers in such districts, it is arguably unnecessary to generate greater monumentality in each building. Instead, the programming and tactility of the built form would be of greater importance. In approaching a project of this nature, Urbanus was happy to fully relinquish the individual form of the tower because they would have become, at best, two very generic and economically-centered towers. In place of form-making, the real opportunity was in the search for shared public spaces between the two clients of the towers. The explorations led to vertically staggered public spaces alternating between interior and exterior spaces. This analytical examination of each design brief and site led to a confrontation of their banal realities, and it was up to the architect to demand a critical and reiterative mode of thinking to reveal the real potential of the project.

The Civic Center remains the biggest unoccupied piece of land in downtown Shenzhen. This 600-by-600-meter urban plot is larger than the Tiananmen Square in Beijing. It was not only large but also empty, devoid of real urban intentions. The unbearable width of Shennan Road prevented pedestrians from approaching this downtown site, which represented an enormous waste of potential. Countless proposals were created in the past decade to solve this urban problem. In 2009, Urbanus pursued a research study of this site with OMA, and the joint proposal eventually won the bid. The successful bid created a holistic system that integrated various resources of the surroundings, tackling the bigness of the site with bold gestures, and confronting the complexity of the site with complex programs. There were three primary components in the proposed urban system. Firstly, a large ring on the ground that connected all public spaces above the ground with those underground was proposed. Secondly, the sunken space in the middle that preexisted the proposal was maintained. Thirdly, a system of spaces underground was proposed to fully integrate the urban realm with the high-speed rail station of Shenzhen. Shenzhen is the only city in China that had constructed

There ought to be architects who would elect to maintain a close relationship with their hometowns and cities and improve them in small increments over time.

its high-speed rail station underground, so that it can connect to downtown Hong Kong and Guangzhou in fifteen minutes. The convenience in the future would bring vitality back to the large emptiness. A high-speed national rail station, an inter-city rail station, and four subway stations were all connected by the ring. The on-grade development was also proposed to be connected to the underground, so that people can walk in and out of the ring to get above or underground, or simply to cross Shennan Road. The sunken space in the middle also carries multiple functions—it is not only a monumental place, but it also has very public functions in the form of a library and an information center. This will be a landmark of a city, even if it is evidently not a vertical landmark. There was a conscious effort to avoid a predictable verticality, and the iconicity and success of the project was instead to be achieved through a real spatial and urban connectivity. This gave rise to the Shenzhen Eye, the project's designated name.

Infills, Contours, and the Village Scale

There would be another form of infill project in the city, flanked by the famous Lotus Hill to its left and the Beacon Hill to its right. These are the only two hills remaining in the city center after a period of dismembering the natural features and natural topography of Shenzhen. After multiple rounds of urban design and feasibility studies, the developer committed to retaining the expanse of aged warehouses between the hills and developing a large-scale mixed-use fabric. There are two bridges that connect the discontinuous urban fabric that was once separated by the two hills. The most profitable high-rises in the project were designed by SOM and a Hong Kong-based practice, and the huge shopping mall was by yet another practice. Urbanus was left with the least attractive and most difficult part of the project, which was the design of a residential component on

top of the shopping mall. Given the context of the urban reconnection of the two hills, Urbanus embraced the added challenge of reintroducing a village scale instead of the standard housing towers in the necessary housing above the mall. The return to the village scale would be an ideal reaction to the saturated commercial programs around the rest of the project, even if it is uncanny and impractical to mobilize the roof of the mall as the new urban topography for the people. It raised all forms of problems of access and privacy: can the residents gain direct access to the village from the two hills, and eventually participate in the public activities of the mall?

The initial design was to build a village with slab blocks, which served as an urban village with some of the largest buildings at its core, medium ones on the perimeter, and smallest ones in the middle. This reacquainted the site with a valley section, with a depression in the

Urban village-scale interventions by Urbanus. Image courtesy of Nartano Lim, 2013

middle. To connect the village-scale housing units, an informal network was created by weaving streets in between the housing in the sky. The loft spaces of the housing units could be adopted as either living or working spaces. The project-between-the-two-hills also included a hotel, a mini-theater, and delicate commercial streets that were relatively miniscule in size. This smallness served as a resilient form that supports everyday life and also an alternative form of urban design in China that is not big. The housing contoured as a village landscape, paradoxical to the shopping mall below.

Apart from filling in the disconnected urbanism, there were also attempts of cultural injection through program alterations in the urban fabric. Once described as a "cultural desert," Shenzhen is systematically injecting new creative industries into old urban fabric.

The Overseas China Town (OCT) has become one of the most important cultural districts in Shenzhen. It contains not only a few conventional theme parks and high-end residential areas, but there is also a series of emergent cultural and creative industries in recent years. The Museum of Contemporary Design was the first cultural landmark realized through a reconfiguration of an old laundry facility. Such alteration projects prove that spaces with new cultural sensibilities can be attained with a number of simple architectural moves.

Similar buildings have emerged all over Shenzhen in recent years. Most of them have become significant cultural landmarks despite being dilapidated at the inception. These projects ought not to be the sole genius or effort of the architects. Projects tend to be successful only when the visions and planning capacities of the architects are met with the collaboration and spontaneity of the developers. Urbanus only had the responsibility of designing the system of public spaces in the southern and northern parts of OCT, including the large murals and the consolidation of outdoor spaces, yet OCT has had the capacity to regenerate itself continuously in the past decade. Combined with a marketplace of creativity, OCT has become a cultural hotspot especially on the weekends. On the north side of OCT, Urbanus is currently working on the conversion of an antiquated factory into a contemporary art museum. It is a low-key building that blends in well with the existing fabric, but its intervention should not alter OCT substantially. It has an art exhibition hall and meeting hall, but most critically, the ground floor has to serve as a twenty-four-hour space even after the exhibition is closed.

One of the best examples of urban spaces in China that had grown from an old establishment. Shelters and artworks blend unpretentiously with the existing surroundings at an interesting scale. It creates a sense of a realistic utopia, peaceful and seemingly effortless. A great deal of sensitivity and a control of design density allow the different environments to merge. This is the urban regeneration one has always hoped to see in China, especially in a country with such cultural heritage! Caption and images courtesy of Victor Su, 2013

Messy, Filthy, and Inclusive

In recent years, there is a realization of a strong force behind the formation of urban villages. The confluence of power and capital pushes the inevitability of the making of a city within a city. Currently, urban regeneration projects in Shenzhen amount to about twelve million square meters. Many urban villages are undergoing tremendous changes, including those still under research at Urbanus. Despite the fact that every village has its distinctive morphology and character, the implementation of new development remains the same. Two case studies reveal contrasting findings.

The first case study is on the Hubei Village, which is located in the center of the old Luohu District in Shenzhen. It contains numerous historical buildings, where their structures and spaces are largely preserved in their original states. While they are not comparable to the historical buildings in Beijing or Shanghai, these historical findings

Thriving vegetable market at Baishizhou under threat of demolition. Image courtesy of Poon Yew Wai

were significant for a city with a short history of thirty years. Urbanus led a study of the district on a voluntary basis after reviewing the district's latest redevelopment plans. Without knowing who the developers might be, Urbanus proposed design solutions and economic feasibility plans to save the old village and combine it with an urban park. These plans included ideas for the local government and developer to generate profit for further improvement to the district. Finding Urbanus' research and report intriguing, the local government and developer requested that the appointed architects collaborate with Urbanus for further refinement. Through a series of workshops and field studies, as well as interviews and working groups with the government, schools, and villages, Urbanus' strong position to protect the urban village led to a positive interaction with the appointed architect, and an eventual adoption of the ideas.

The second case study is on a large urban village of Baishizhou near OCT. It represented the biggest redevelopment project in Shenzhen, sitting right next to the most luxurious villa area in OCT, with historic buildings and a central plaza. This urban village actually mediates many social and urban problems, drawing people from all walks of life to live there, including white-collar professionals, the working class, and the poor. Even new migrants are attracted to the village. To enhance the relevance of the village, especially its economic value, one could probably meet the developmental potential of the site by using the traditional and one-dimensional plot ratio in an urban renewal approach. But by doing so, the continuity of its history and context would be destroyed. There would be a failure to improve its social value alongside its spatial and economic value. Under such circumstances, a study was conducted by Urbanus, and the urban morphology of the complex village was discovered to be made of five villages, each with a different need. Urbanus proposed a preservation of some of the overlapped spaces where interactions between the five are occurring. A new spatial typology emerged as a hybrid of towers and podiums, striking a balance between the demand for a vertical city with a plot ratio of twenty and the maintenance of diversity in the village, with its urban culture and fabric kept intact.

A good city must be inclusive, which means it may be filthy and messy, with people from different backgrounds. This is the future of Shenzhen: a place where the rich and poor, the morally upright and warped, and the cultured and nouveau riche can live together harmoniously. Without clear social or cultural goals or the vision to respond to a city and its unique context and culture, the discipline of architecture will be thrown into a deep crisis. Under the universal influence of globalization, architects would travel widely to export their professional design services. There ought to be architects who would elect to maintain a close relationship with their hometowns and cities and improve them in small increments over time.

This essay is translated and adapted from an academic address by Meng Yan at the 2014 Annual Meeting of the Architectural Society of China. The original transcript was published as "Jieru chengshi: Dushi Shijian zai Shenzhen" [Interventionist City: Urbanus in Shenzhen], *Journal of Shenzhen Civil Engineering and Architecture*, Issue 2014/4, pp.37-41.

SOCIAL HOUSING AND REAL ESTATE DEVELOPMENT FOR A LIVABLE CITY

HUANG WEIWEN

The development of real estate and the growth of a city are blindsided by each other. They suffer from a lack of integration. There are countless expert forums and media commentaries on issues of real estate development and as many researchers and scholars debating about urban planning issues. Yet they seem to only have the capacity to discuss the respective topics within their own fields, failing to bring the two subjects together. The intersection of these two fields can offer a fertile ground for new research if the scholars can refocus their perspectives and interests. With approximately half of the city within their grasp, developers in China should be well aware that they are the real builders of a city. Chinese urban planners should be cognizant of the operations of real estate development, in order to appreciate how good urban planning can be realized. Only when the real motivations behind real estate development are understood can it become a constructive force behind the design and planning of cities in China.

From Self-Organized and Communal to the Commodity Market

Before the advent of modern real estate development, residential architecture was self-organized and privately built. To build a residence prior to the professionalization of the field, one needed to seek help from neighbors, friends, and relatives, or assemble a team of expert laborers and artisans. A comprehensive knowledge of the local climate, materials, and cultural practices would lead a prospective building owner to an appropriate form of architecture. These common houses would aggregate to form a compact city, within which the architecture would be tight-knit and of the same vernacular typology. Examples include the *siheyuan* courtyard houses of old Beijing, or the Naxi houses of old Lijiang. The era of self-constructed houses in Chinese cities may well have ended when the last *dingzihu* or nail house is removed. There is often a strong sense of attachment to such self-made homes, hence stories of resistance against urban redevelopment in China are not uncommon. In modern planning, big developers and real estate conglomerates have replaced the individual home builders. They organize, plan, design, and construct houses and apartments on a large scale in highly repetitive and mechanized forms. There are also constructions funded by the public sector, such as government office buildings, public institutions, infrastructure systems, and large-scale social housing. The forces that used to shape a city have shriveled from a vibrant, multi-dimensional, and participatory one to a bipolar condition of the government and private developer.

Comprehensive System and Subsidies

The issue of large-scale market and social housing must be approached in terms of policy and strategy. More studies must be conducted on land policy, funding, distribution, and circulation, such that design can be better informed. In the fields of urban planning and

A workshop with Huang Weiwen at Ascott Maillen Shenzhen. Image courtesy of Takeo Muraji

architectural design, suggestions can only be made in the context of existing standards and in terms of gradual improvements. Taking Shenzhen as an example, the housing market once had a long period of stability, where every household had a shelter because there was a comprehensive housing supply system that catered to a population with a broad range of income levels.

Resettlement areas built in the earlier stages of urban development and the coexistence of dense urban villages serve as forms of social security in terms of affordable housing for populations with low income. Even though such housing were supplied by the market, the government played a role in subsidizing them. The land on which the farmers in the urban villages had built their homes were made available cheaply.

Higher up the housing market chain, there were low-profit housing being constructed and managed by the municipal government. These homes had selling and rental prices that were lower than the market price, but higher than that of welfare housing. Welfare housing were only available to senior staff working in state-owned companies and enterprises. Such employees represent the middle-income class, and the housing security entitled to is part of a reward structure. Lastly, unsubsidized market housing is available for the general public with high income. These different tiers of housing formed a relatively comprehensive and complete housing supply system, and it gave stability to the entire housing situation in Shenzhen. Unfortunately, the housing department in Shenzhen was dissolved in 2004 due to new policies passed by the State Council of the People's Republic of China. There was a push to privatize and commodify housing at a national level, leading to imbalances in housing distribution and skyrocketing prices.

Structural Imbalance and Shortage

There are multiple reasons for the increase in housing prices. Shortage of the provision of subsidies and social housing is just one of them. Based on the total housing supply in China, the urban living space per capita is thirty square meters, which is equivalent to a moderately developed country. The living space per capita for Shenzhen is even higher at forty square meters. The "house shortage" problem is therefore an issue of structural imbalance, not that there is an actual shortage in supply or a lack of housing units. Many existing housing units remain sold but unoccupied. In order to provide a shelter for every household, policy-makers first need to ensure that housing can be maximized and occupied. The correct remedy to the problem is not to build more housing but to improve the distribution of the existing in-stock housing such that vacant housing can be occupied by those in need of housing.

Low-Income Communities

To tackle some of the housing issues in China, one has to have a vivid awareness of the lives of the low-income community. Some of them are street vendors selling goods on their mobile stalls; others may render informal services for a small community. To the urban poor, a home is not just a place to sleep but also a place to work and live. For example, the Yuanlin neighborhood in the city of Shenzhen used to be a welfare housing community with excellent architectural and neighborhood design. But as the original residents moved out over time, it evolved into a low-income neighborhood. It deteriorated from welfare housing for the middle-income to affordable housing for the low-income. Media reports suggested that the environment in Yuanlin was considered by the government to be slum-like: walls in the housing units were torn down to make storefronts, and informal street stalls were set up without permission. Multiple municipal departments were called upon to rectify these issues.

In a city undergoing constant transformation, the expectation and mentality of an orderly neighborhood with an aesthetic outlook is unrealistic, if not deeply problematic. For a community that had been transformed by newer low-income residents, the reconfigurations in the housing fabric were made in order to meet the basic daily needs of its residents. The living standards of a low-income group are bound to be different from that of the middle-income; therefore it is not appropriate to simply use urban policy to turn Yuanlin back into a tidy and clean neighborhood. Due to complex problems at the level of policy-making, planners and architects should think of the issue of large-scale housing in a broader way. For example, design solutions are still sorely needed in terms of the entire housing provision chain. Greater flexibility in design is required to cater for uncertainty in the demand and supply of housing, and for a lack of clarity of the target groups in need of social housing.

Basic Principles of Affordability and Livability

The design of good social housing is not necessarily related to a mere sense of aesthetics and artistic concerns. The greater responsibility is for architects and planners to identify and study the users, and discover a way to communicate and interact with them. Architects and planners have to reevaluate existing professional knowledge and design methods that are currently geared towards serving commercial clients and interests. Can Chinese architects return to the basic principles of good housing design? Can housing be made affordable to the general public again? While it is ideal to realize affordable housing quickly, it is necessary to be aware that the process of design cannot be reckless. It is perhaps timely to accept that patience is required to bring about improvements. The production of housing in Shenzhen can transform from a process based on speed to one based on quality. Affordable housing can be achieved in a more direct and efficient way, if design can go beyond the meeting of planning requirements stipulated by code. Design must have an impact on the formulation of policies and strategies related to funding, land use, distribution, user needs, location, amenities, unit types, materials, and green technology, in order to attain a higher standard of housing.

In China, the general public's aspiration for better living spaces and a more affordable city can only be realized through agencies such as governments and developers. Citizens' participation and leadership in the town and the community model of development can no longer exist in China. Hence it is more meaningful to reestablish the relationship between "real estate" and the city instead of "housing" and the city, because real estate development has become the primary driving force for Chinese cities today. There are five important roles that real estate in China has to play towards the creation of a more livable city.

Genuine Equality. Firstly, there has to be a better accessibility to natural resources, and an equitable sharing and enjoyment of amenities and views of landscapes in the city. To use Shanghai as an example, the early developments of the concessionary period were well planned and regulated—a street grid that connected the city with the scenery of the Bund, viewing the Huangpu River as one of the main natural landscape features of the city. Compare this to Lake Xiangmi of Shenzhen, which was one the major tourist attractions in the past. Today, public access along the eastern edge of this lake is completely blocked by two large-scale private housing sites. The real estate advertisements blatantly declared this exploitation of public resources, "Hugging Lake Xiangmi, You Own the Lakeview." Residents eastward of these two sites can no longer gain access to the views of the lake, thus reducing the livability of the city as a whole. This desire to gain exclusivity over access and views to landscape amenities and natural resources is commonplace in China.

Openness and Connectivity. Secondly, housing has to enjoy a good degree of openness in the city and ease of connectivity of the street networks. In China, the stakeholders of real estate development have a perverse enjoyment of the "big four": planners like to create big urban blocks, governments like to sell big plots of land, developers like to build on big sites, and consumers like to live in big, gated garden neighborhoods. In the Panyu District of Guangzhou, housing sites are at least hundreds of acres, fully secured and privatized with fences and security guards. Residents have to take private shuttle buses provided by the developers to do their groceries or watch a movie in the city, often taking half a day just to leave the gated neighborhood. In the beginning, the white-collar residents were enthusiastic about moving into these new "five-star homes." But as they lacked of urban vitality and connectivity, the residents promptly returned to the city for their movie theaters, ice cream parlors, herbal tea stalls, and late-night eateries. They ultimately preferred the congested but vibrant street life of a city.

A typical *xiaoqu* neighbourhood in Shenzhen. Image courtesy of Qiu Wen Hao, 2013.

Access to Public Space and Services. Public space and public service are vital to a healthy community, adding a third aspect to the livability of a city. The garden environments in private real estates in China are abundantly branded "five-stars" in advertisements, and covered in exotic plants, ponds, rocky gardens, and every luxuriant green imaginable. This green area routinely takes up 50% of a given site area, but unfortunately, the gardens often have nothing to do with the city or the public. These gated gardens repeatedly fail to even satisfy the needs of the elderly and children who reside right next to them, even when these residents only require a small open space where they can dance, exercise, bike, and play. There is also the issue of having the right membership to use the space at the right time. In fact, younger residents who stay up and wake up late would complain about the elderly for being too loud in their morning exercise routines. A gated garden or an urban park that is three bus stops away cannot solve this problem. The public needs an intelligently located public space that is close to the community: a 30-to-50-square-meter public open space or a 300-square-meter public room, taking up only 5% of developable land and 0.3% floor area ratio but adequate in satisfying the requirements for public activities and services. This shows that lush but inaccessible green public spaces do not necessarily create a harmonious relationship between the residents, the public, and the city.

Social Integration and Reduction of Class Segregation. Social integration is the fourth role in how the real estate in China can add livability to a city. Meticulous property management and services are representative characteristics of the Chinese real estate. The hallmark of a "five-star" home must have quality services from the three *baos—baojie* (janitors), *bao'an* (security guards), and *baomu* (maids). Who thinks about where these service staff might reside? They normally live in the basements, between the *pilotis*, and on the rooftops of the elaborate real estate developments they serve. How do they feel about working in "five-star homes" in the day, and sleeping in its dark basements at night? Prominent real estate developers are conscious about building up their corporate responsibility image by committing to charitable causes. However, they can add value to the discourse of affordable housing, if they do their part in providing basic housing for their service staff. It would not only fulfill their social obligation as an employer but also bring about a closer equilibrium in a society increasingly segmented by class.

Emphasis on Quality of Life over Productivity. Lastly, there has to be an appreciation of new values and a sustainable way of life. Before the implementation of the Open Door policy, China had gone through a period that emphasized production over quality of life, making no progress in the improvements in housing and building construction. By the 1990s, when China entered into an era of deregulated real estate growth, the generation who grew up in either public dormitories or commune compounds were unable to adapt to newer notions of housing. The residents in transition were overwhelmed by advertisements selling "five-star homes," "mansions," "Spanish-style living," "Parisian lifestyle," "Florida town," and so on. The Chinese way of life as depicted by these advertisements are markedly different from the actual way of life in genuinely livable cities around the world. On one hand, these lifestyles worked with the assumption of suburbanization, elitism through race and class segregation, and an over-reliance on automobile travel as a condition of modern convenience. It gave rise to materialist attitudes, a lack of awareness in the exploitation of nature, and unchecked and wasteful consumerism. On the other hand, one could take the opportunity to build up newer values in well-planned urbanization, diversity in the community, and a return to healthy and smart bike travel. This can only lead to a more humanistic attitude, a desire to protect the natural environment, and a sensitivity towards the conservation of limited resources. Even though real estate advertisements are often exaggerated and misleading, the values espoused by the slogans can be used to project effective and real changes.

> **Only when all stakeholders and agencies related to urban development have understood and accepted true and concrete ideas of livability can the city begin to move towards it.**

Real Estate Mechanism in the Making of a Livable City

It is crucial that architects and planning professionals take the chance to reflect upon this divisive schism and find ways to narrow the differences. There are voices from the real estate development sector arguing that the making of a livable city is the government's responsibility. Others lament that China is not at an advanced enough stage to tackle such an issue. While governments have an important role to play, and many cities in China have indeed set lofty goals to make their cities more livable, livability of a city is not a concept for only developed countries. China can use such a concept to speak to its latent potential in a projection towards the future, especially after decades of rapid development and utter destruction. That is to say, China is not livable at the moment—not because the nation is underdeveloped, but because the notion of "livability" was ignorantly sacrificed during the process of development. The mistakes made during the rapid construction of China are difficult to correct because of an increased awareness of property rights, and long periods of leases and master planning. Only when all stakeholders and agencies related to urban development have understood and accepted true and concrete ideas of livability can the city begin to move towards it. Without a doubt, real estate development is an integral mechanism in the making of a livable city.

This essay is translated and adapted from Huang Weiwen, "Baozhangfang sheji, women neng zuo shenme?" [Social Housing: What Can We Contribute?], *Arbitare China*, Issue 2012/01, pp.27-31, and "Dichan yu yiju chengshi" [Real Estate and Livable City], *Arbitare China*, Issue 2011/01, pp.110-113.

DISABLED PERSON, DISABLED CITY, DISABLED ARCHITECTURE

ROBERT ADAMS

A Note to the Reader

Throughout this writing, the terms disability, disabled person or *canjiren* are used to locate the gravities around a more diverse conception of any social imperative as it relates to architecture and the city. Until there are more substantive transformations within public discourse, it remains necessary to claim these terms in order to position how physical, psychological, and genetic differences contribute to defining an intersectional social body that also includes ethnicity, sexuality, and economic status. To claim the term disability and *canjiren* is to sharpen a critique of architecture to increase its operative range by incorporating disability within a more inclusive and equitable framework, and to demonstrate that the efficacy of architecture can co-locate extreme forms of social difference.

The images represent a survey of projects, interviews, and correspondence with a range of individuals and institutions in Beijing and its urban-rural environs. Their inclusion is less to illustrate the text but to provide an aperture into how the work is committed to direct social engagement. The images are part of a research project and documentary film, *Disability and Dragons: Health Infrastructure and Architecture in Urban-Rural China* directed by the author, which will debut in Beijing in 2017.

Chromo Sapiens and Heterogeneous Spaces, and Polychromatic Objects and Landscapes

Internationally renowned scholar and disability theorist Professor Tobin Siebers (1953-2015) suggested that "whenever a disabled body moves into public space, it discloses the social body implied in that space."[1] While Siebers was working within a disability studies framework, this statement not only applies to disabled human bodies, but also to a range of other, or *altérité*, bodies. The follow-up to the claim by Siebers would be

---

1   Tobin Siebers, *Disability Theory* (Ann Arbor: University of Michigan Press, 2008.)

how disability theory scales up to include other bodies—bodies of land, bodies of water, architectural bodies (object buildings), and entire urban bodies.[2] The point of Siebers' statement was that the policies, regulations, and zoning and building codes presiding over the city, including its infrastructure and architecture, are conceived within a very narrow conception of fitness and ability. The concept of the "social body" assigns value to an architecture of assimilation and normative profiles of human capacity.

Since antiquity, the formation of architectural and urban space has assumed an anthropocentric subject: a "normate" body that walks upright, possesses physical capacity for work, and is cognitively engaged.[3] These characteristics are attributes of the species of *Homo sapiens*, a binomial that literally translates into "wise man."[4] Anthropologists have gone to great lengths to establish the terms of origin for modern *Homo sapiens* with little concern for *altérité* bodies. By inscribing disability and alterity within a genealogical model, new methodologies and insights become available to reconsider architecture from a disability perspective. Disability advocates argue that, in contrast to a life of pain and suffering to be cured or ameliorated, disability is instead a creative practice. Like other practices, it produces pointedly unique types of knowledge that are insightful and useful to society.

Disability tactics destabilize architecture and force designers to confront the limits of how work is conceptualized and actuated in the city.

A new *genus* that embodies the qualities and traits of how the *Homo sapiens* species is evolving into the more hybridized, composite, sentient, or bio-techno actors of *Chromo sapiens*. *Homo sapiens* are to the epoch of the *Holocene*—9,700 BCE to the present day, a period roughly coincidental with the entire history of the city starting with Çatalhöyük in 7,500 BCE—as *Chromo sapiens* are to the emerging Anthropocene, the current epoch in which human production has influenced environmental and atmospheric climate change. *Chromo sapiens* describes a post-human condition that dissolves the binary structure produced by the use of the terms "abled" and "disabled." It offers a more suggestive description against the homogenized and sanitized term "universal," as implied by the mantras, "design for all," "access for all," and "universal design." *Chromo sapiens* have an affinity for heterogeneous spaces and polychromatic objects and landscapes. They exist in parallel states distributed across the ephemera of media seeping into the viscera of matter. *Chromo sapiens* produce equally potent digital subjects where bio-physiological bodies become fused with synthetic types of matter.

Chromo sapiens possess an aesthetic structure that, like chrome plating, is resistant to staining and oxidation, and are capable of absorbing the environment regardless of toxicity.

2   Chang Yung Ho, "City of Objects aka City of Desire," *A+U, Architecture China*, 03:12.
3   Rosemarie Garland-Thomson, "Integrating Disability, Transforming Feminist Theory," *National Women's Studies Association Journal* [NWSA], Vol. 14, No. 3, *Feminist Disability Studies*, Autumn, 2002, Johns Hopkins University Press, p.1-32. Stable URL: http://www.jstor.org/stable/4316922.
4   Carl von Linné, *Systema naturæ. Regnum animale*, 10th ed. (1758), p.18, 20. Retrieved Nov 19, 2012.

This species is distinguished by an ability to adapt to dramatic changes in atmosphere, including cultural bias and discrimination. *Chromo sapiens* are a species of super-humans: disabled figures, yet highly advanced compositions that embody artificial cognitive aptitude, genetic mutation, biomechanical dexterity, psychological neurodiversity, pharmacological enhancement, and technological advantage. *Chromo sapiens* are transitory bodies, both urban and individuated, in constant states of transformation. Though anthropologists have yet to formally recognize this emerging species, the rapid evolution of *Chromo sapiens* will likely provide the key navigation tools to chart the Anthropocene. In short, disabled persons possess the intelligence and capacity to impact a more progressive architectural and urban agenda that transcends singular and anthropocentric social imperatives.

In terms of addressing social imperatives for architecture and the city in China, disability unsettles the business-as-usual design practices that assume a normate or stable social body. By embedding a concept of disability in design methodologically, architecture can increase its capacity for a more diverse, equitable, and inclusive urban body composed of a simultaneous alterity. A key question for architecture is how disability engenders more heterogeneous forms of urbanism that support simultaneity without the collapse of difference. What incidents of architecture can be observed in China that set an example for disability to reconsider the city? Given that entirely new cities are currently under construction, China is an ideal geopolitical context to test this concept and understand to what degree disabled persons, or *canjiren*, are able to introduce more provocative spatial practices that coincide with China's high-speed urbanization in a twenty-first-century landscape of *canji jianzhu*. Disability tactics destabilize architecture and force designers to confront the limits of how work is conceptualized and actuated in the city.

Models of Engagement and Communication Infrastructure

For much of the twentieth century, disability was contained within a medical model. Disabled persons were considered an inferior sub-species that needed to be separated from a normate social body. By assigning disabled bodies with abnormal traits, these figures were categorized as medical anomalies, subjected to scientific

Meeting between You Liang, Director of the International Liaison Division at the China Disabled Persons' Federation, and the author to discuss how CDPF provides services to China's estimated eighty million individuals with a disability. You Liang was pivotal in hosting the 2008 Summer Paralympic Games in Beijing. Image courtesy of CDPF, 2013

testing. They are isolated and institutionalized, and otherwise deemed unfit to participate in civic life. However, in the post-Mao era, there was a dramatic shift in the conceptual model and status of *canjiren* in China, especially during the Cultural Revolution. In 1968,

Interview with local Beijinger who is identified as *canjiren*. He toured us through his chrome-plated three-wheeler provided by the CDPF. The combination of increased mobility and speed, coupled with the high-visibility of the reflective metallic surface profiles emerging attributes of the *Chromo sapiens*. Image courtesy of Zunheng Lai, 2013

Deng Pufang, son of Deng Xiaoping, was paralyzed, having been assaulted and thrown out a third-story window at the Peking University. Though there are conflicting reports that Deng was attempting suicide, these seem unfounded given the circumstances. This news of the great leader's son now among *canjiren* shocked Chinese society. Over the next twenty years, Deng Pufang developed robust agendas to establish a voice for *canjiren*. In 1988, he founded and chaired the China Disabled Persons' Federation (CDPF), the first governmental agency to represent the rights of disabled persons.

The efforts of the CDPF began to shift the perception of *canjiren* from a medical condition to a social group, paving the way for a host of national and international organizations to support an estimated eighty million people with disabilities within China. Non-governmental organizations such as the World Health Organization and Handicap International launched new initiatives with their Chinese partners to develop policies for disabled persons to obtain recognition, equal rights, and opportunities as non-disabled persons. One noticeable example is the Chinese government's provision of ubiquitous, stainless steel clad, three-wheeled motorized vehicles for families who required assistance to transport a disabled child or elder. With this new found mobility and speed, disabled persons are able to expand their reach within the city. But they also have to compete with a dramatic spike in car culture. Faster street speed did not equate to access for all *canjiren*, but it did for many. Those who were male heads of household were able to develop a gray-market economy and entrepreneurial spirit of distribution and speed.[5] What is notable about this phenomenon is that disabled persons were suddenly enrolled in the speed of urbanization through strangely medical-grade, stainless steel, modestly customized architectural vessels. This was a key moment for *Chromo sapiens* to exert control over a medical model of disability towards producing a sociopolitical model of greater access to the city.

In 2006, Yan Xie and Jing Lin founded One-Plus-One (Beijing) Disabled Persons' Cultural Development Center, an NGO run entirely by young disabled persons. They launched the first radio and social media platform in China dedicated exclusively to

---

5   For a comprehensive analysis of mobility relative to disability in Beijing see: Matthew Kohrman, *Bodies of Difference: Experiences of Disability And Institutional Advocacy In the Making of Modern China* (Berkeley: University of California Press, 2005).

disability issues. One-Plus-One is composed of progressive advocates for disabled persons throughout China, and represents how advocacy and access to communication and information disrupt normate practices of civic space. By fusing social media, digital technologies, and aggressive public relations campaigns, including a business model around transcription of documents for the sight impaired, One-Plus-One became an early architect of *Chromo sapiens* communication infrastructure.

At a global scale, the World Health Organization published the *World Report on Disability* with a revised language around the dichotomy between a medical model and social model. It promoted a "bio-psycho-social model" that located disability as both an individual health and environmental concern.[6] This opened up perceptions of disability to include so-called invisible disabilities, such as cognitive disorders like depression, and other types of neurodiversity. Additionally, it suggested that the environment itself—"the environmental press," or "ambient pressure"—contributed to a disability as a socially constructed framework.[7] This was striking in Chinese cities like Beijing and Shanghai, which began to monitor environmental and atmospheric qualities as they impacted public health, especially among the most vulnerable populations of children, the elderly, and the disabled. Despite the fact that Western media continue to vilify the Chinese government regarding environmental degradation, China's current Thirteenth Plan (2016–2020) focuses on balancing economic growth for all persons and addresses

The Gang of Three: Interview with Cai Cong (co-editor of *1+1* magazine), Li Yanshuang (*1+1* radio DJ, and hip-hop artist), Fu Gaoshang (co-founder *1+1*), at *One-Plus-One (Beijing) Disabled Persons' Cultural Development Center*. Coordinating efforts across Internet radio, a monthly print journal, and massive outreach via WeChat, these three represent an emerging generation of disability rights advocates in China who are making space for a critical debate around disability concerns outside governmental top-down strategies. Image courtesy of Casey Carter, 2014

---

6   Alana Officer (WHO) and Aleksandra Posarac (World Bank), "World Report on Disability," *World Health Organization and The World Bank*, 2011.

7   M. Powell Lawton, "Toward an Ecological Theory of Adaption and Aging," *EDRA 4: Fourth International EDRA Conference*, the Environmental Design Research Association, 1973, p.24-32. The Environmental Press or EP is a termed coined by the behavioral psychologist Dr. Lawton, who argued that "the model is operationalized as the outcome of the transaction or interaction between the person and the environment. Optimal fit occurs when someone's capacities are consistent with the demands and opportunities within that person's environment. However, if the demands of the environment exceed those of the person and their abilities, there is a person-environment misfit." See also, Patrick Roden, "Aging in Place and Environmental Press," Mar 9, 2013. Accessed Aug 30, 2016. http://aginginplace.com/aging-in-place-and-environmental-press/.

key environmental factors.[8] Given China's capacity to dexterously transform itself, it seems likely that it will lead the world in developing strategies to reduce environmental pressure and increase more intelligent information-intensive infrastructure.

Otherness and Alterity: Courses of Action

The questions of otherness and alterity motivated the establishment of BASEbeijing in 2006 with colleagues Robert Mangurian and Mary-Ann Ray. Given the complexity and pace of transformation in Beijing, the question was how the twenty-first-century mechanics of urbanization in China might open up spatial-material practices and new ways of working for the architect. BASEbeijing is an independent research and design studio untethered to the university or academy. It was located in Caochangdi, an urban village in northeast Beijing known for its internationally famous artists including Ai Wei Wei, Wang Qingsong, He Yunchang, He Chengyao, and many others in the allied creative industries. By working outside the contractual obligations of joint institutes formed between Chinese and American universities, BASEbeijing developed a more actionable model for architectural education that participates in the deep social structure of Chinese culture, mining its histories of innovation, documenting its current urban transformations, and seeking out a more imaginative capacity of reconsidering architecture.

BASEbeijing itself became a practice to situate a body of research and sponsored public events, as well as a site of production that worked to manage an incredibly diverse range of projects by making the work accessible to Chinese architecture students, faculty, and allies. At BASEbeijing, the curriculum are not described as classes or studios, but as *courses of action* in cooperation with others. The architects and designers at BASEbeijing are opportunistic for what is possible in China, and the work is motivated by an intense interest in what the making of things can lead to. One can engage in the

Considered one of China's *qigong* masters, Dr. Tu performed a technique to isolate pain in my lower back. Though he never physically touched my body, I felt a distinct pressure and support in my lower back about sixty seconds into the therapy. It was a disarming experience that moved me to tears. I am unable to explain in detail what had happened, but it provided a profound experience into the world of traditional Chinese medicine at Xi Yuan Traditional Chinese Medical Hospital. Image courtesy of Casey Carter, 2014

---

8   "China's 13th Five-Year Plan," *Permanent Mission of the People's Republic of China to the United Nations*, Nov 5. 2015.

production of space through direct relationships cultivated between people, especially those whose work are deeply embodied in intricate forms of making. In this context, design is not an extraneous application, nor necessarily a specific expertise resulting from years of education. It is rather a life practice of expanding human capacity to innovate within very limited resources.

Artist Lu Yang stunts a *Chromo sapiens* pose for designer Celeste Adams, who identifies as *canjiren* with Facioscapulohumeral muscular dystrophy, and BASEbeijing student Yun Yun. Outside Beijing Commune, a gallery in Dashanzi 798 arts district. Image courtesy of Robert Adams, 2014

There was a shared feeling that many architectural monuments constructed over the past decade did not possess enough diversity to accurately represent a more complex level of social engagement. At a local level, the group at BASEbeijing started to understand Caochangdi as an exciting, in-your-face, mixed-up urbanism of migrant worker's houses and taxi driver hotels, rock stars and opera singers, artist studios and maker spaces, scientists and laboratories, archivists and collectors, chefs and farmers, divas and fashionistas, low-finance developers and high-profile elites. They collectively thickened the plot for architecture. Caochangdi was and remains an extremely eclectic urban space and a field of operations to engage architecture in the midst of a living city. China continues to be a tremendous source of knowledge that confronts all preconceptions and motivates the work.

At its inception, BASEbeijing sought to correspond with numerous architects, designers, consultants, and contractors who were developing many now-famous projects in Beijing. While these engagements were incredibly insightful, it was challenging to

Detail of a government-issued chrome handrail to assist elderly farmers living in this traditional house with a *kang*—a raised masonry platform used for everyday activities. The contrast between traditional wood and masonry construction, and the reflective stainlessness of the new handrail is evidence of *Chromo sapiens* domestic practices. BASEbeijing continues working in this rural village of Shangshuiguo and several other villages in the Pearl Spring Township north of Beijing.
Image courtesy of Robert Adams, 2014

elicit a more speculative discussion of how architecture was producing new types of knowledge and practices. How did the collective project of architecture impact the social composition of the city as a blended rural-metro-politanism?[9] This was no fault of architects specifically but a symptom of how the intellectual and social terms of architecture were subsumed under the turbulent cascade of urbanization. Architects were so consumed by the sheer magnitude of production that there was little time to reflect on the consequences or after-effects of their work. By contrast, it was the artists who were theorizing and producing a critical discussion around the city as a spatial-material artifact, and, quite amicably, BASEbeijing gravitated towards these individuals. This opened up an entire world of difference. The attention shifted towards design practices that were methodologically quick, in order to keep up with the erasures—the seemingly overnight unmaking and remaking of an entire city.

When the United Nations reported in 2014 that one-half of the global population was urbanized, the ambition of architects and urbanists would seize upon the city as the way towards smart growth.[10] At BASEbeijing, this enthusiasm was shared, but there were also queries about the other half living in rural spaces. What about those who remained unaccounted for, living on the fringes of the city, and especially those whose ability to participate in civic life was in question? The work leaned into this effort, taking BASEbeijing into some of the most unlikely spaces throughout Beijing. In response, more speculative projects were developed, rather than definitive ones. For all the complexities and challenges facing the world and China in the twenty-first century, there remains an air of euphoria of what is possible for design, and how it simultaneously invents imaginative and unanticipated futures for architecture. There are consistent attempts to strike a balance between an excitement for the twenty-first-century Chinese city, and an awareness of the ethics behind the participation in some of the most volatile social conditions. Such uncertainty was prevalent at every level of engagement with China.

9   Robert Mangurian and Mary-Ann Ray, *Caochangdi Beijing Inside Out: Farmers, Floaters, Taxi Drivers, Artists, And the International Art Mob Challenge And Remake the City* (Hong Kong: Timezone 8, 2009)

10   United Nations, Department of Economic and Social Affairs, Population Division, *World Urbanization Prospects: The 2014 Revision, Highlights (ST/ESA/SER.A/352)*, 2014.

WHERE ANTS, ARTISTS, FLOATERS, AND RATS HANG OUT

ROBERT MANGURIAN AND MARY-ANN RAY

Somewhere between the countryside and the city, new forms of human habitation have emerged in early twenty-first-century China. This in-betweenness should not be understood as their physical distinctiveness, but more in terms of their differences qualitatively, atmospherically, economically, and socially. Since establishing BASEbeijing, there has been a plethora of engagements with such new environments. The immense changes in the city and countryside provided the best surroundings for an experimental laboratory for design, urbanism, and ruralism. The following are three short stories from a series of tales collected and told through the people and places encountered at BASEbeijing since 2001.

These Beijing stories include an account of Madame Yang, who was originally a farmer. She succeeded in building a very large migrant boarding house in her urban village and had since become a millionaire. This tale of entrepreneurship shows how urban villagers maximize their land rights while resisting government demolition of such illegal structures. The lack of resettlement provisions and compensation often results in highly resilient nail households or *dingzihu*. Xiao Liu, also known as XL, was a rural-to-urban migrant turned millionaire. He instigated a chain migration of thirty men, who now form the basis of his highly lucrative construction-contracting team that builds art installations for some of the leading Chinese contemporary artists. The third story recounts a day in the life of an "Ant Triber" who lives in an urban village in the northeast of the city. Members of these "Ant Tribes" or *yizu* tend to be recent college graduates of universities in Beijing. They prefer not to return to their hometowns even though jobs are scarce and low-paying in Beijing due to the overabundance of educated youth. As sociologist Lian Si writes, "They share every similarity with ants. They live in colonies in cramped areas. They're intelligent and hardworking, yet anonymous and underpaid."[1] These subterranean dwellers comprise five percent of the city's population.

Story #1: Everyone Goes Out and Buys a Buick, and Chaiqian in Styrofoam Village
Styrofoam Village and Dawangjing Village, Beijing   39°59'54.26"N 116°29'7.77"E

Just north of the fifth ring road near the airport expressway, land surveyors from the municipal *Chaiqian* (demolish and resettle) Bureau arrived at an urban village to measure the built-up areas of all the migrant boarding house structures built by a former farmer and landholder. This farmer is in fact an entrepreneurial leaseholder of farmland largely owned by the state. The surveyors measured the footprint of the buildings and counted the number of stories. As a part of the relocation and compensation package, landholders of urban villages to be demolished are compensated according to the size of their buildings, including improvements and added structures.

Once the compensation and resettlement arrangements were made, a government-appointed contractor moved in to demolish the buildings. The demolition crew was surprised to find that the upper stories of the structures came down quite easily as they were constructed not with the standard concrete frame and brick infill, but of Styrofoam. It seems that after being notified of the forthcoming demolition of their village, the villagers rushed to add square meters of space not to serve as rentable housing for migrants, but to prepare for the government surveying crew. Fast and economical, Styrofoam would do. The village appeared to be experiencing a surreal state of snowfall for months following the demolition, as the foam particles became airborne in the heat of the Beijing summer. This story was recounted to us by the late Frank Uytterhaegen, a Belgian art patron who was the first to hire Ai Weiwei as an architect. Uytterhaegen was also a developer and producer of nuclear medical equipment and systems, and he lived in Caochangdi, an urban village in Beijing. In addition to being passionate about art and health technology, he had a great curiosity in the environs of urban villages.

Another village near Styrofoam Village and adjacent to Caochangdi, Dawangjing Village was chosen by the government as the site for "Beijing CBD Number Two." SOM won the international design competition, and in 2009, the villagers with land leases were well compensated for their properties and given good resettlement housing. Because of this, there were no hold outs or nail households. In a matter of months, the village was completely gone. The joke around Caochangdi was that the day after the compensation money came, all the villagers of Dawangjing went out and bought new Buicks, which were considered especially desirable in China as luxury and a status symbol.

---

1   Lian Si, *Ant Tribe II: Whose Time* (Beijing: CITIC Publishing House, 2010). Lian was interviewed and quoted in "China's 'Ant Tribe' still struggling," *China Daily*, Dec 14, 2010. Accessed on Nov 10, 2016.

Story #2: Nail *Dingzihu* Household
Changdian Village, Beijing 40°00'02.38"N 116°32'54.16"E

Li Zhonglai lived with her husband and an extended family of eleven in an urban village, where they had what remained of their small supermarket. Most of the buildings and houses in this Changdian Village, northeast of Beijing, have been demolished. Li's household was what is referred to in China as a *dingzihu*, or nail household—akin to a rusty stubborn nail that is impossible to pull out of a hunk of wood. Li recounted the complexity of her situation. Every house had a certification that proves ownership, but Li did not. Without the certification, the government would not compensate her for any of her business investments when the buildings are demolished.

The Li family was there for nearly two years when the *Chaiqian* Bureau and the landlord demanded their removal. Li had signed a contract with the landlord for ten years, and the landlord had promised that this area would not be demolished within the next five years. The supermarket business Li invested in opened in May 1, 2009. The business application and registration, along with the renovation and furniture, cost her RMB 300,000. A month later in June, the government declared that the village would be demolished. The landlord began to evict the family, refused to return their security deposit, and hired thugs of the "black road" to hasten their removal. In supporting Li, her friend's husband was severely injured by broken glass and hospitalized for quite a long time. The police came with a video camera to conduct an investigative interview, but it never led to anything even though there was video evidence of the crime. Evidence was also drawn from the hospital, but the police did nothing. Li and her husband had prepared weapons to defend themselves against the gangs. With almost nobody left in the village, the supermarket shop had no business, and public safety became poor. Gangs dominated the area, and harassments were commonplace. Living conditions deteriorated, with no water or only foul water from a contaminated well. Municipal gas and electricity had been cut off. Families must travel far to buy vegetables and food, and wood had to be used for cooking, and heating water for bathing.

According to the demolition policy, a house may be torn down once it is empty. Hence, the Li household must have someone at home at all times. This had a bad effect on the work patterns of the family, and the children's studies. Li claimed that after going through much hardship, they had little hope for the future. Their savings had been spent. Without government compensation, they were not able to go back to their hometown. A return to their hometown was usually the "Plan B" for rural-to-urban migrants. Yet, they cannot, and would not, move anywhere else. They rather stay right there until the day they die. By 2010, half of the village had been demolished, and with each year, more houses were razed. But the empty land has remained in an undeveloped stated for six years now. The view from Google Earth shows that their building in Changdian Village still stands proudly along with a handful of other nail households.

Story #3: Young Obata Spent Two Nights as a Member of the Rat Tribe
Building #1, Room #21, Beihua Apartments Beijing 39°54'23.96N 116°33'13.19E

Max Obata was a member of the BASEbeijing research team, and as a part of his research, he spent two nights as an undercover in the Rat Tribe or *shuzu*. The Rat Tribe is a slang term for underground dwellers. Obata's story tells an exceptional tale of human resilience and adaptability, and how little it takes to establish a "home" in China. There were over 1,374 civil air defense shelters that exist in the underbellies of Beijing's mid-rise housing towers. These windowless and illegal rental housing served approximately a million people, or five percent of Beijing residents in 2015. Approximately 727 people lived in each air raid shelter. Most of the members of the Rat Tribe were migrants who performed essential services for the city. One out of three Beijing residents were migrants.

During a visit to the Beihua apartment complex, Obata came upon several large walls filled with multi-colored apartment rental advertisements.[2] While most of the listings were for the huge above-ground apartment buildings, there were a few that stood out as much cheaper than the rest at only RMB 200 per month, or about USD 30. These ads turned out to be for the hundreds of Rat Tribe apartments, several stories underground in the required-by-law bomb shelters that each building in Beijing must have since Chairman Mao laid down this ruling. BASEbeijing coordinator Echo Xiang,

Basement apartment of Rat Tribes. Image courtesy of Sim Chi Yin

a native Mandarin speaker, called the four numbers on the listings to see if a room could be rented for a few days. Each of the four landlords were renting for RMB 30 a night, or about USD 5, and were all very eager to rent the many rooms available in the elaborate tunnel system as soon as possible. It seemed like a very simple procedure for each landlord: arrive at the building, call them, and pay for as many nights as one needs. The landlords were more than happy to accept any type of temporary tenants, but foreigners were strictly forbidden. This rental policy was strictly upheld, even though the rental of these underground spaces for habitation was *laissez-faire* and illegal in the first place. Xiang arranged for a rental, and Obata had to be snuck in past the landlord's office to get to Room 21. There was a small padlock on the door to the rather spacious room that was about 3.5 by 2.5 meters with a double bed. There was a desk with a television, a little bedside table, and a clothes dresser.

Obata spent the night with dinner outside, then wandering around the local subway stop. He was amazed by how vibrant the area was on the street level. There was a dizzying array of life, with thousands of people eating and cooking adjacent to a huge vegetable and fruit market. Coming back to the underground room felt normal, except that instead

---

2   The following passages were excerpted directly from Max Obata's account of his undercover experience as a member of the Rat Tribe.

of walking up some flights of stairs, Obata was walking downstairs. It would be wrong to call these spaces inhumane. Obviously, some are very low in quality and tiny. Obata's room was pretty comfortable, until he tried to get to sleep. It started to get pretty rough at about eleven in the evening, because he could not get over a paranoia about getting padlocked from the outside. He kept waking with a little shock of panic, and at about two in the morning, he sheepishly went over to the door, cracked it open just to make sure his fears of getting locked in were unfounded. Multiple televisions were playing well after 1am, with some of the worst programming in China. There was a woman watching some horror movie and constantly letting out bloodcurdling screams, while another film had plenty of yelling, crying, and screaming. The bed was pretty terrible, as it felt like a thin blanket laid over planks of wood. Mosquitoes were the norm, as the blankets were damp. The whole room felt generally humid.

Once the initial annoyances were overcome, the sleep was routine. The strangeness came in the morning, when there was no indication of sunrise or a change in the quality of light. Once awake, Obata had a hard time dodging the morning crowd as he had to sneak out of his room and out of the underground without being seen. He could not use the bathroom like everyone else, fearing he would be thrown out by his landlord because he was a foreigner. He spent the daytime wandering and merging with the neighborhood above ground. To his surprise, Obata felt comfortable returning "home" for the second night. He quickly settled down in his room, connected his iPad to the WiFi, then proceeded to have his "routine" sleep.[3]

The Production of Space

As these short narratives reached their conclusions, a homeless encampment across the street from our studio in Los Angeles is being dismantled. They have to move on after being served an eviction notice by the police. Nearly fifty thousand people in the City of Los Angeles are homeless. Many of them live in the multi-block area known as Skid Row. Meanwhile, in the village of Caochangdi in Beijing, where our other studio is located, migrants are living in illegal but dry and warm boarding houses. In the United States, there are a multitude of causes for homelessness: the failure of public housing, mental health policies and practices, insufficient veterans care, and domestic violence, to name a few. In China, the primary cause of homelessness is related to natural disasters such as the enormous earthquake that hit Sichuan in 2013. Taking in these basic facts, there ought to be a reversal of the stereotypes of what constitutes a First and a Third World country.

---

3   Many news documentaries and films have covered similar occurrences of the Rat Tribes in Beijing. Katie Hunt, "Meet the 'rat tribe' living in Beijing's underground city," CNN, Feb 18, 2015. http://edition.cnn.com/2015/02/17/asia/china-beijing-rat-tribe/. Accessed on Nov 16, 2016. Ian Johnson, "The Rat Tribe of Beijing: Under the Streets, a Hidden Warren of Rooms for the Thrifty," Al Jazeera America, Jan 24, 2015. http://projects.aljazeera.com/2015/01/underground-beijing/, Accessed on Nov 16, 2016. See also Chinese director Li Shaohong's film entitled *Stolen Life* released in Apr 23, 2005.

In the urban villages throughout China, former farmers had the entrepreneurial smarts to transform the land for which they held the land lease from a single-family home to multi-story boarding houses. While technically not legal, government authorities from village leaders to mayors, and "higher-ups" in the Communist Party act as "Winking Owls," keeping an eye open and the other closed.[4] While the usual interpretation of this proverb is that those in power pretend not to see what is an undesirable situation, in this case they pretend not to see in order to allow the non-legal activity to go forward, since the construction of this substantial amount of housing "of the people, for the people and by the people"[5] provides the necessary housing for migrants that the government does not account nor build for. By placing a winking glance toward this activity, the government actually empowers individuals and collectives to participate in and claim rights to the "production of space."[6] Observing this right to the production of the city, and in sharp contrast to the evicted homeless encampment on the public sidewalk, one might reflect differently upon the understanding of what constitutes freedom and democracy.

---

4   "The saying describes a sneering aloofness or a resigned stance pretending not to see what is essentially an undesirable situation. Once the visual form is reduced to a discursive proposition, it is easy to attach an interpretation to it." Eugene Wang: "The Winking Owl: Visual Effect and Its Art Historical Thick Description," *Critical Inquiry*, No. 26, Spring, 2000, p.454.

5   "Gettysburg Address," Speech delivered at Gettysburg Pennsylvania by President Abraham Lincoln, Nov 19, 1863.

6   Harvey outlines eleven basic human rights, with number nine being "the right to the production of space." David Harvey, *Spaces of Hope* (Berkeley: University of California Press, 2000), p.251.

FOUR REVOLUTIONS IN BIG DATA

LONG YING

Quantitative urban research is a scientific understanding of cities by applying different forms of data and methodologies based on clear theoretical foundations. It aims to better understand cities scientifically, identify patterns in the city, diagnose its condition, create models of the city, evaluate the impact of various policies on urban development, and thereby find solutions for the society it serves. Under the condition of rapid urbanization, the Beijing City Lab is analyzing current rural-urban planning conditions by documenting and evaluating existing urban plans. Current urban planning practices are not widely employing quantitative methods, but it is quickly becoming relevant, because the discovery of objective patterns in the city would lead to a better distribution of resources in China. The city, as a repository of social activities and the like, would be expanded in a more equitable way. Chinese urbanism has entered into a new era, where a scientific form of urban planning can enhance the quality of life of the ordinary public. Big data can be superimposed over the social and cultural forms of public health, education, crime, housing, public services, and others. Principles based on social theories can be brought into any data set for a more complete analysis.

One of the long-standing research questions in urban studies is whether the administrative boundaries of cities accurately reflect its actual social limits. For example, should the suburbs of Yanjiao be considered as acting within the urban limits of Beijing when as many as 300,000 workers commute daily to Beijing, even though it is under the administration of Sanhe, Hebei? For the larger metropolises, Chinese scholars would have no problem delineating the urban limits, based on decades of research; but for the countless smaller urban and suburban contexts, there is no data. If we define the operational limit of a city as bounding an area in which at least 10% to 15% of its population commute to, it is imperative to obtain "live" data from public transportation services and other urban amenities to map where these limits are in various Chinese cities, instead of relying on the formal measures of urban administration. Big data modelling helps administrators identify patterns within Chinese cities, and lends additional support to the smaller cities by narrowing the gaps in terms of infrastructure, policy, and talent. In the context of this rapidly changing epoch, the use of big data is quickly altering state policies. Quantitative urban research is undergoing four dominant revolutions in China today.

Spatial Scale: Reducing the Statistical Gaps, and Building a More Just Society

Urban research used to focus on the singularity of a city. But with the support of big data, it is now possible to develop a trans-regional analysis of a number of cities, or even all cities in China. Existing urban research can be divided into two types. Firstly, it can be an in-depth analysis of a single city, such as a close examination of poverty in Guangzhou, or the quality and service reach of public amenities in Beijing. Secondly, it can take the form of a regional analysis, such as an analysis of macroeconomics across the entire China. The unit of study would tend to be coarse, especially in the provinces and counties. There is always a compromise between the geographical breadth and the fineness of the research. Large data models would be a viable option for research covering a great expanse of geography without losing the minute details of individual parcels of land. Infinite amount of data can be stored for the imaging of such big data models. They are able to cope with the scale of research as well as the fine units of study. Such a tool for urban and regional analysis represents a tectonic shift in research methodology. Through the data model, it is possible to consider multiple cities at the scale of an urban building, a lot, a city block, a city, the entire country, or even a continent, traversing all scales at once. It is even possible to conduct both intra-city and inter-city research.

The Mega Vector Parcels Cellular Automata model has the capacity to capture a fine-grain land-lot scale urban model across the 654 cities in China. With the use of this model, it is possible to address how various social and economic policies may impact the urbanization processes in the next five years. At the scale of each land lot, researchers could begin to access its history, current conditions, and the trends of its future development. In the meantime, land use mapping by means of urban street networks and points of interest have been developed in Computer Aided Design or Geographic Information System formats in China, especially for companies invested by foreign capital. Through the development of a public information domain, land use maps for three hundred Chinese cities are readily downloadable for everyone in a common format, including information of land use, urban boundaries, development density, and level of land use mixture.

By virtue of practical necessity in China, most research and consultation work are currently focused on metropolises, and it is still difficult to conduct in-depth research on second-tier or smaller cities. However, these cities also need to be objectively investigated. The lives of its citizens need to be improved as urgently as the more prominent cities. The vision for the big data model is to reduce the technical and statistical gaps between large, medium, and small cities. Every piece of land in China ought to be considered precious, and every city and region needs the best possible attention. Big data can aid China in building a more just society. Furthermore, through big data modelling, we hope to find overall patterns in the development of Chinese cities. Once the planning logic

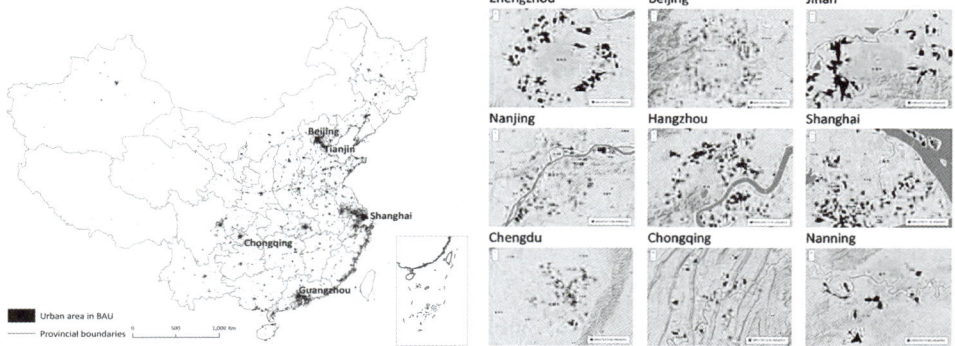

Urban area growth in business-as-usual (BAU) scenario. Images courtesy of Long Ying / Beijing City Lab

and rules of resource distribution in each city is discovered and analyzed, the problems of urbanization in China can be better handled. It is insufficient, if not negligent, to research only one city at a time. Yet because of a lack of knowledge and tools, researchers are rarely capable of research on multiple cities at the same time.

Time Scale: Retrieving Commuting Patterns, and Rectifying Inherent Inequalities

In the era of big data, transformations in a city can now be understood and analyzed across various time scales, no longer limited to the standardized timespan of a year or a week. Current urban planning regimes tend to define its annual statistics to reflect the accomplishments of their bureaucrats within the year, or report on the state of the city at the end of each year. Research of a smaller scale, such as the study of urban renewal and rebranding in a district, would make use of data that reflects a daily cycle of movement, an interview of a protagonist, or a record of activities that occurred in the past twenty-four hours. It is now possible for big data to retrieve a pattern of each commuter's travel habit, down to the second from each swipe of the metro card, in the creation of an accurate snapshot of a city. Imagine if the spending activities of a credit card user are made available over the course of a decade or two, the corresponding data would reveal clear behavioral patterns that an individual or a merchant is totally unaware of. Big data promises to make possible the mining and accurate interpretation of such detailed information, so that strong solutions for the city can be responsibly deployed. For example, credit card activities from the past twenty years could show a shrinkage in traditional businesses. Traditional bookstores may have been superseded by online booksellers, while small owner-run restaurants may be giving way to bigger fast food chains. It reflects the change of time and the spread of wealth in the city.

The cumulative data collected over the years can show how technological advancement changes our lifestyles and our city. What can researchers do with a week's data of metro card swiping activities in Beijing? Within a sample of 100,000 Beijing citizens, it is

	Beijing	Nanjing	Changsha	Weifang	Gongzhuling
City Level	1 MD	2 SPC	3 OPCC	4 PLC	5 CLC

Density

Low
High

Function

COM
EDU
FR
GOV
GRE
RES
TRA
Not classified

Land use mix

Low
High

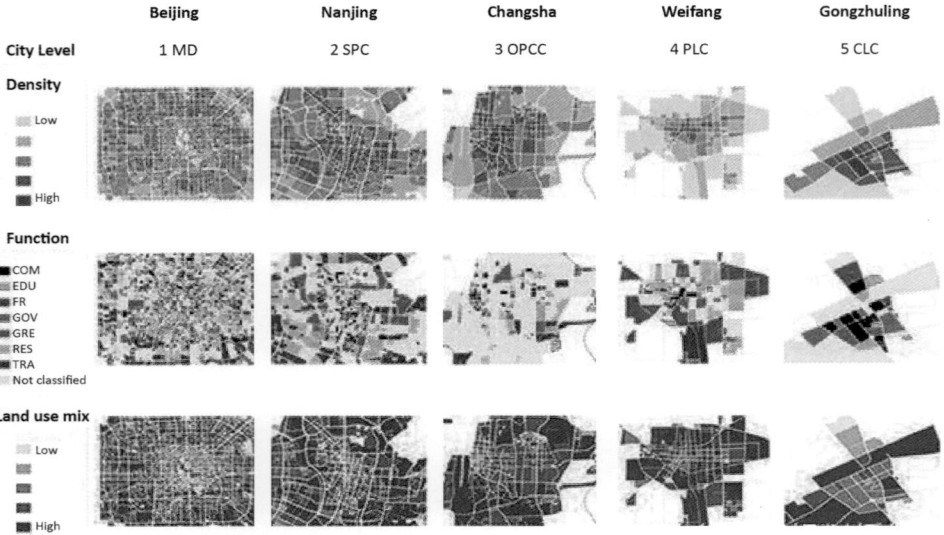

Comparison of densities, functions, and land use mix of cities. Image courtesy of Long Ying / Beijing City Lab

shown that 95% of them have full-time jobs of over six hours. Using this as a standard, it is possible to identify where they live and where they get on the transfer buses. In fact, 99.5% of them would leave from their homes in the morning, the remainder from hotels or other locations. Rules and patterns can also be discovered through the study of traditional data and redeployed for big data mining. There are about 10 million metro cardholders in Beijing, with billions of travel records. The weekly commuting pattern can be visualized. Deducing from the radiating patterns, the workers in the Central Business District arrive from a greater diversity of places than workers in the Shangdi and Financial Street areas. Workers who live in Tongzhou district would need to commute for at least an hour every day. The data collected in the past six years also showed that there are more than 10 million people making over 100 million travels both in 2008 and in 2014. Fewer commuters were taking the bus, choosing to take the subway instead. It also showed that most of the card holders would keep reusing their card over long periods because of the cost of replacements. Therefore, one card is an accurate representation of one person, and by extension, it is possible to deduce whether a commuter has moved, changed jobs, became unemployed, and so on.

Socioeconomic data can also be mined to rectify the inherent inequalities associated with commuting. For instance, commuters with decent jobs or of a higher economic class in Beijing would not spend more than three hours a day for commuting. One research hypothesis reveals that commuters who spend long hours on long-distance commuting are of the lower social classes, and with the help of this data, the Beijing authorities can consider recalibrating this inequality by shifting more of the cost of travel from the long-distance commuters to the short-distance commuters. From the study with a sample size of 100,000 people, it was shown that the low-income group of commuters tend to take more bus transfers, and spend more time on commuting. Their occupations tend to be subject to exploitation, or they are outright illegal. There are at least 112,000 of such long-distance commuters in Beijing, who would toil like this every day. During the past six years, 80% changed homes, and only 13% were retained in the same job. What kind of attention and assistance should society provide to stabilize the social well-being of this group of commuters? Did the processes of urban planning, urban village renewal, and affordable housing design consider their commuting patterns carefully enough? Were their identities within the city under consideration by mainstream planning policies? Urban research of this nature must consider their implications towards corrective policy making and urban design. With this fine-grain data, it is possible to deduce the lack of functionality of bus service system designed in 2008, 2013, and 2014, and thus hasten the evolution of the mass transit system and its impact on urban processes and change. With the many years of data, it is possible to study the evolution of cities through the success and failure of its public policies and urban services and their impact on society.

It is important to realize that there is a transformation of a social scale through the rise of social media and new forms of decentralized data.

Human Scale: Unaccounted Social Support for Floating Population

New urbanization strategies ought to be centered on people. With an increased need to return to the human scale in Chinese cities, the base unit of research has to be finessed. In the past, most policy designs are object-oriented and rely on coarse research data. Given that greenfield land development has become practically non-existent for first-tier cities in China, future projects would likely to be geared towards smaller scale urban renewal, rebranding, or redevelopment. Current urban research methodologies are not suitable for such projects. Crucial steps must be taken to refine the scale at which the research is conducted. Up until now, academics and consultancies are still unable to get obtain a map that shows the change in population density at the scale of villages, towns, and sub-districts in China. In the past decade, one-third of China's suburban or non-urban conditions are not thriving, with decreases in population density; but researchers and governments know very little about the prevailing conditions of these shrunken areas, and there is an urgency to continue to provide proper social functions for such areas.

With a recent set of exploratory data, researchers have found that this shrunken phenomenon exists not only at the scale of the village, but towns and sub-districts are also suffering from the same condition. Known popularly as a *kongxincun* or a hollow village, these extended problems at the sub-district level are in fact occurring within the municipal boundaries of the cities. Out of the 654 cities in China, 180 of these are low in population. What does this mean for urban planning? Urban planning in China tends to favor expansions in territories and increases in population. Urban development

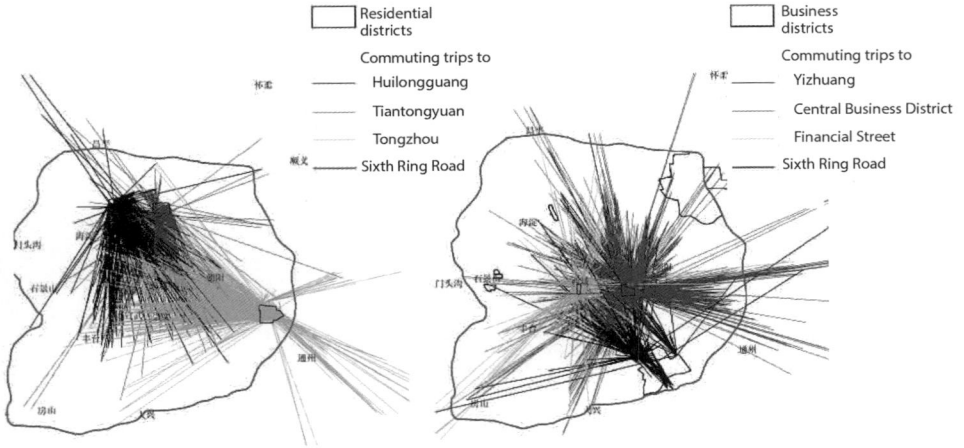

Commuting pattern analysis for typical residential (left) and business (right) districts.
Image courtesy of Long Ying / Beijing City Lab

is designed as economic engines, where the government is fundamentally looking for new land to sell. The planning for the 180 shrinking cities would have to break out of this economic dogma. The initial forecast shows that the Chinese population is moving towards the metropolises, no matter how hard China pushes for the development of small and medium sized cities, or develops the central, western, and northeastern parts of China. The reality is most cities around the world are typically not very big: for example, the United Kingdom has only one metropolis, London, and her second largest city may only be half or one-third in scale. Given the anomaly of Chinese cities, it may be possible to predict, with the help of big data, that the rate of migration into cities would still consistently high even after a decade of urban development. For these 180 shrinking cities, how should theirs planning methods be different? Should they reevaluate the need to develop more greenfields, and instead aim to improve the quality of life and increase job opportunities for their residents? Within the planning research community, there is a growing concern about ghost cities and the vacancy rates of residential neighborhoods or *xiaoqu* in these shrinking cities. Through the use of Baidu Maps and Weibo, there is an ongoing research assessing the occupancy rate within five hundred meters and one kilometer of any given neighborhood. The rate of urban growth that culminated in the current 654 cities and 1,000 towns in the past decade has exceeded growth rate in the past century, yet vacancy remains a serious issue. With the use of big data, a general pattern can be discerned by tracking as many as 800,000 building developments suffering from high vacancy rates. This can be supplemented with economics data to reliably inform the design of policy.

In another example, researchers discover that as much as 50% of Beijing's construction activity is informal, falling outside the reportedly planned construction activities.

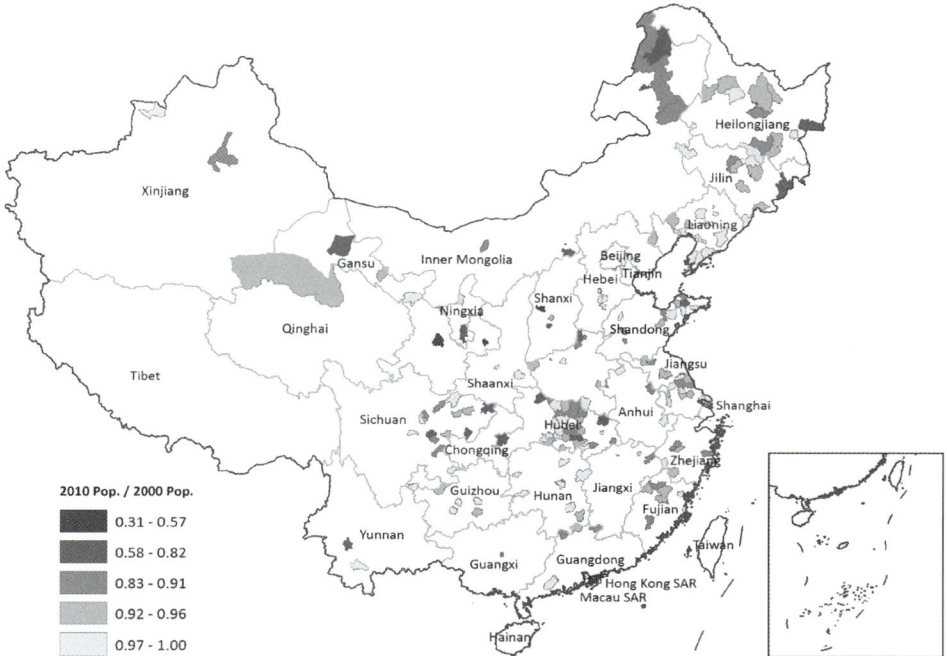

Shrinking cities in China, 2000-2010. Image courtesy of Long Ying / Beijing City Lab. Data by Wu Kang, Wang Jianghao and Long Ying

The importance of this is magnified by the fact that 95% of all human activities and movements take place within the physical planned boundaries of Beijing, which implies that the unaccounted and informal construction laborers and their families would be finding support from within the actual social sphere of Beijing, not its planned sphere. Analyzing data pertaining to human activity and mobility, researchers also realized that there are distinctly different urban functions between Shunyi and Tongzhou in Beijing—two outlying residential districts with substantial migrant populations, even though both share the same commuting distance to the city center. Shunyi turns out to have the capacity of being a more successful secondary core outside Beijing than Tongzhou, because Shunyi can serve other northeast subdistricts of Huairou, Miyun, and Pinggu, and act as a mid-point between these sub-districts and Beijing.

Social Scale: Decentralized Participation and Open-Source Models

In the research of cities, it is difficult to determine what kind of time frame is required for a fuller analysis. For example, pouring massive amount of research resources into the 180 shrinking cities may not be wise because the situation can be really dynamic. Some of these cities may no longer shrink after a decade or two. Hence, with the use of

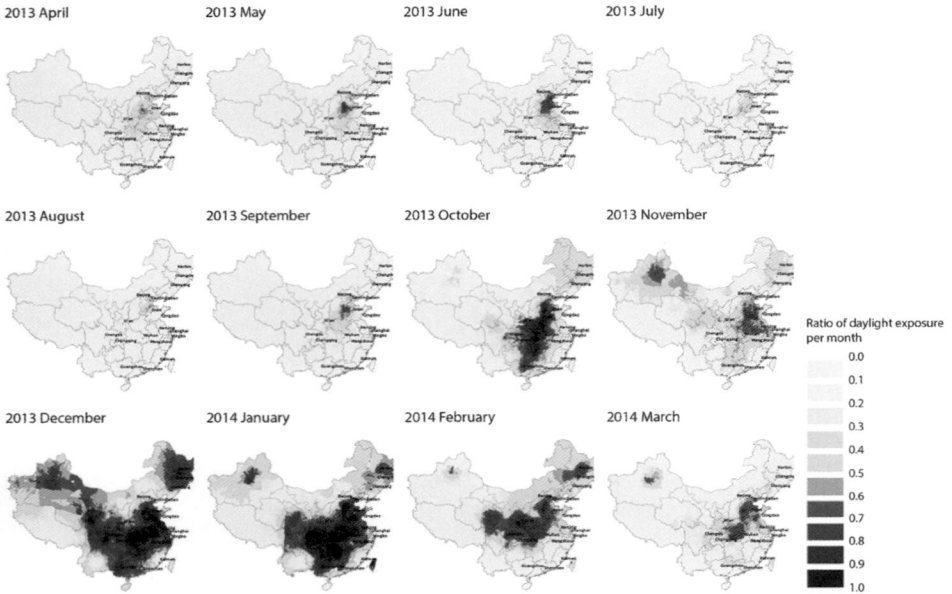

2013 April   2013 May   2013 June   2013 July

2013 August   2013 September   2013 October   2013 November

2013 December   2014 January   2014 February   2014 March

Ratio of daylight exposure per month

0.0
0.1
0.2
0.3
0.4
0.5
0.6
0.7
0.8
0.9
1.0

Rate of daylight exposure per month. Image courtesy of Long Ying / Beijing City Lab

big data, the results can be published in social media, and a method of crowdsourcing can be employed to determine the reliability of the data. For example, results of the five-year forecast of urban development under research can be published on the Internet, so that the methodologies are made transparent, and the residents can offer opinions and corroborate results. Weibo and other social media users of participating cities can be invited to assess the data from an ordinary perspective, in a truly open-source, decentralized, and collaborative model. Urban researchers have long been constructing large data models, but because there are too many cities in China, it is crucial to develop modelling methods that draw upon the participation of ordinary citizens. The general public often possess knowledge of a highly local situation unfamiliar to the researchers, and the capacity for such social-level data to be plugged into a big-data model can help ascertain the validity of the research and aid in the design and improvements of the research.

Evaluations of urban solutions tend to be done by urban planning departments, and their focus and analysis are mainly on the spatial scale. The concept of crowdsourcing would add a social dimension previously not available to the planning process. Everyday citizens can volunteer their information in an equally digitized platform, which is quickly overlaid over the formal land use and planning data of their home cities. At the moment, there are as many as two hundred Chinese cities gearing up to participate in the collecting and digitizing of a new range of social vectors for such combinatory urban maps. Like Baidu and Google Maps, such an online map is scalable and openly available to all online users. This way, there can be a new understanding of the extent of the social space that defines a city. Overlaid with the existing urban street grid, discrepancies between the urban plan and the existing conditions could be visualized and rectified quickly. Developers, for example, would be able to understand the current status and planning of a specific location and better evaluate the planning strategies in time to come.

With a big data model, it would be possible to grasp the extent of actual urbanization in each of the Chinese cities in the past decade and compare it with the extent of the formal urban plan to estimate the level of control or deviation over what had been planned. Through such the model, researchers come to realize that any control of urban development typically attains a fifty percent rate of success, and this is one of the unique patterns of Chinese planning practice. This translates to a reality in China where fifty percent its urban development is legal, while the other fifty percent is informal, but not illegal. The notion of an illicit urbanism in China is perhaps too sensitive a word for the government, as it means that the planning bureau would have a lot of rectification work to do. Through a big data model, it is possible to come to terms with the overall pattern of the Chinese urban planning system. It has been shown that conducting research for just one or a few elite metropolises have proven insufficient in anticipating the larger urban problems of China. It is important to realize that there is a transformation of a social scale through the rise of social media and new forms of decentralized data, where the enlarged sample size and the range of complex variables would enable every citizen to evaluate and participate in the urban processes of the city.

TOWARDS A SUSTAINABLE CITY

ZHAO LIANG

Architecture ought to refer to the whole built environment. For a long time, it was only referring to a specific set of buildings within the discourse of architecture, or unique buildings designed by a select group of architects. Therefore, research in architecture ought to also consider the broader built environment that society had constructed for itself. In academia, the buildings that are considered interesting are very limited. In terms of the numbers and types, perhaps they represent less than a millionth of the whole built environment. Research that ignores ninety-nine percent of society's architectural production due to such a view is neither conclusive nor objective. Such research remains unscientific and irresponsible even if it is genuinely ignorant. Traditional historical research had been concerned predominantly with the narratives of the powerful, and transitions between dynasties and kings. However, contemporary historical research is showing a greater concern with the general public and the nuances in society. This reflects a shift in society on both micro and macro scales. In other words, there is a shift from the histories of iconicity to the more impactful histories of mass society. Such research would have a greater use of big data.

Research of the Ninety-Nine Percent

The creative and unique buildings designed by starchitects or cutting-edge architects are exemplary, and therefore extremely seductive. But the plethora of normative architecture in the everyday surroundings should not be underestimated, because they accommodate the realities of life and reflect the real demands of society. Some may think that these buildings are unimaginative, banal, and reveal the backwardness and inertia of society. Such notions are complete false. The impact of such everyday architecture—from homes to neighborhoods, from offices to shopping malls—is far greater, because the common and frequent contact with such architecture is far greater. If one avoids the study of these buildings simply because they are common and mundane, it only shows that such academic research is not yet relevant.

In common neighborhoods, especially low-density ones, there is always the chaos of self-made architecture. Each addition from each household is uncoordinated in relation to its neighbors, embodying the different depths of design and levels of need of the families that constructed them. For every hundred households, one would find as many unique ways of construction and interior furnishing. The real interest behind such design interventions is the way they capture the variety of lifestyles and the ingenuity of design in order to attain them. It would be particularly meaningful, should research begin to examine such conditions in China. Current research rarely delves into China's real estate development. There is a lack of rigor in identifying the effects of mass construction towards society. The ubiquity of such topics are in fact good research areas for one to truly understand the society, lifestyle, culture, philosophy, and economy of China. The upheavals in the past three decades can be witnessed through the study of building construction, not only in the ubiquitous residential type, but also across typologies of offices, shopping malls, museums, entertainment districts, and public parks.

Research has the specific duty to excavate and reveal the unique qualities of such social architecture. For example, the design of the standard apartment units in China has probably attained one of the most refined and efficient iterations, because of the developmental progress made in high density cities such as Hong Kong, and adaptations of other typologies such as townhouses and multi-story dwellings from around the world. Over the years, China has adapted well to the complexity of being a large nation, capable of reconciling geographical differences between the north and the south, while working through the labor-intensive nature of its society. Thus in an analysis of a common neighborhood, one must hold off preconceptions of the mundane, unintellectual, or ugly. Instead, one must carefully examine its historical context and economic patterns, and arrive at a stronger understanding of why the general population would be drawn to such environments.

Such findings would be invaluable to society if researchers can fully register the real mechanisms at work and share the knowledge, because the depth of work required is in fact enormous. It is a pity that most architects, particularly those who are featured in design and professional magazines, are not concerned with such issues, in part because they may not have the design solutions for these issues. However, an architect's true contribution to society lies precisely in the solving of these complex but mundane issues. If an architect can design an apartment that meets the demands of a newlywed couple

Baishizhou Urban Village. Image courtesy of Arjun Rosha, 2013

and beyond, it may turn out to be the most significant contribution an architect can make towards society. This may be the truest meaning of architecture.

Housing as Commodity

There is nothing intrinsically wrong with treating housing as a commodity. In fact, the main value of housing is its function as a dwelling. It is a commodity whether it is built by a single owner or by a developer, comparable to a crop farmer who grows crops as a means of subsistence, or a farm owner who grows crops to sustain the rest of the community by taking up thousands of acres of land to do so. All these forms of housing provisions satisfy the universal demand for shelter. Even alternative types of housing or temporary shelters constructed by the homeless are derived from the same universal need. Thus the difference is only in terms of its supply. A house that is built by a developer is akin to a product that is manufactured by a factory. Both represent intensive means of production that guarantee efficiency and quality. Unfortunately, due to standardization, products manufactured in this way tend to be less diverse and less geared towards personalized requirements. However, it is really not such a strange phenomenon. For example, consumers would not make their own mobile phones simply to personalize it. Instead, they purchase them from reliable manufacturers such as Apple, Samsung, Huawei, and so on.

The industrial civilization has historically tended towards mass production in order to augment labor and transfer the competitive savings to the consumers. A greater emphasis was put on personalization in recent history because of the newer technologies in customization and computation in manufacturing. Essentially, the world is still in an industrial paradigm and still moving towards greater specialization, where professional institutions continue to provide highly specialized products and services. As the most capital-, energy-, and labor-consuming industry, architecture cannot escape from this basic industrial mechanism in society. It is impractical, even nostalgic, to resist the modern and industrial nature of architectural production.

Working within a civilization based on the market economy, architects should realize that the production and use of architecture exist in the same universal paradigm. Architects cannot afford to be ignorant or resistant about the values of the current civilization, and persist only in a limited sphere of influence. The basic theory of economics stipulates that for each commodity to exist, there must be an effective means of production to meet some form of demand by society. If no one buys the product, it means that either there is no demand, or the price is too high because efficiency is not high enough. For something to become a commodity, it should be able to strike a balance between its cost and quality, so much so that an effective demand can arise around it.

Architecture is a commodity and a physical container, most commonly made of reinforced concrete. Its production requires cost, in form of land, labor, capital, and physical building materials. It aims to satisfy the needs and wants of habitation, work, entertainment, and so on. To meet demands there is an exchange value that can be met, or a price to pay. These are the basic attributes of architecture. Since the rise of modernity and the fall of monarchies, no one builds just for pleasure alone. Architecture is such a huge labor and capital investment that everyone ought to treat it with seriousness. Yet there are many architects and allied professionals who would willfully undermine the fact that architecture is an important capital asset, or the fact that an owner would have to spend an exorbitant amount of money to build. These architects treat the design process as a very personal act, akin to writing a novel, a poem, or a song. Such absurdity detracts architecture from its innate character and its role in society.

Architecture is first and foremost "a machine for living," or "a machine for work," as Le Corbusier put it. Only after it has served such roles can it be a vessel for romance and culture. This does not mean that architecture cannot be a carrier of culture, but such a purpose must always secondary. It would be putting the cart before the horse if one were to mix up this hierarchy. Naturally, the best architecture would satisfy both requirements. This remains the greatest challenge for architects. The balance between the two aspects is what makes quintessentially good architecture. Architects who neglect the function and purposefulness of architecture in pursuit of personal aspirations or cultural representation cannot be considered successful.

Experimentation and the Developer

Developers in China are a special group of people. In the United States, real estate development companies may be comprised of only twenty or thirty people, most of them in finance. They would subcontract much of their work to architects and contractors. Architects thus act as the main consultant, bearing responsibility for the entire physical construction. In China, for a variety of reasons—perhaps due to low design fees, fewer architects, or higher standards set up by the developers—designers are unlikely to act as the sole supervisor for the entire project. The project team in a Chinese developer's setup is likely to be better-rounded and more professional, from the liaison with the local government for the filing submissions to building material sourcing, construction pricing, value engineering, and so on. Therefore, architects housed in Chinese developers' offices tend to have a huge role in the realization of the built environment.

It is often the developer's architectural design team who is the true master or decision maker of the building process, whether it is described as a "commodity" or as "architecture." Architects tend to be credited as the authors of the finished buildings; but this is not an entirely accurate recognition, due to the complex roles played by the developer's in-house professional teams. Consequently, developers have a great responsibility to bear. Unfortunately, this is also why architects have sometimes tragically degenerated into draftsmen, following orders during the production of design drawings. Critiques or research on architectural phenomenon in China must begin to account for the consequences of such a unique set of professional relationships.

In a market economy, there are always alternative models for architecture, especially housing for the low-income groups. In order to afford the rents needed to cover the costs of construction, someone must be able to fill in the gap between cost and price. However,

Tulou Commune,
Urbanus Image courtesy of
Xavier Tan, 2013

if there is no sustainable and systematic solution to the problem, then any subsidies, trials, and experiments will ultimately remain unsustainable. In Singapore, housing is completely built by the government, and the cost is covered by taxation. In the States, there are also various methods of achieving low-income housing. Architecture that reflects social ideals, such as social housing, must have direct support from the larger context.

The creation of new contents or new architectural forms is a process that originates from a confluence of passionate and aspiring architects, developers, and patrons who are willing to test their viability and receptivity by society and the market. If it is proven to be feasible, such new architecture will be replicated to become the new architectural form of society. There are countless experiments, from the social housing of Germany in the 1930s to that of the former Soviet Union in the 1950-60s. In China, the Tulou Commune led by the developer Vanke and designed by Urbanus in Guangdong Province is one such high-profile experiment. It is an alternative residential, commercial and office complex that was generally considered a successful architectural experiment, it was not economically sustainable. The fact that the Tulou Commune has not been replicated since is a clear signal that it was flawed in its operational logic. Vanke was searching for a new typology with smaller flat sizes, in the hope that low-income groups, such as security guards, street janitors, and housemaids, may be able to rent them. Regrettably, such rental returns proved unsustainable. As a profit-making enterprise, Vanke had no choice but to discontinue this experiment.

There are constantly new types of architectural solutions emerging around the world. For example, co-working spaces created by WeWork or flat sharing by Airbnb are starting to show some degree of success, aided in a big part by social media and affordable technology. With the mismatch in demand and supply between first-tier cities such as Beijing and Shanghai and other lesser cities, new industries have emerged from older ones. Industries that are less scientific and crude are being taken over and redefined by a bottom-up form of social and economic power. Taikang Community is another example of how the provisions of social needs can be combined with an economically sustainable model. It started out when its founder Chen Dongsheng combined a traditional welfare sector with the affordable chain hotel model. Taikang Community has been developing housing community prototypes for the aged by seeking new forms of medical and healthcare collaborations with more traditional medical institutions. Such experiments combine the needs of society with the market and position the aspirations of an enterprise with good architecture, leading to radically new forms of industry and architecture.

Urban Sustainability

Living patterns in China have undergone massive transformations in the past two decades since the 1990s. Through the process of urbanization, millions of families have moved into new apartments: commodified housing with higher standards of ventilation, daylight, building finishes, landscapes, and quality of life, compared to the traditional *danwei* low-rise housing, courtyard housing, and village forms. The new apartments are usually built and sold by developers on land purchased from the government. As a result of market forces and design research, there have been new formulations of housing typologies and urban innovations unique to China. Yet China's urban and housing communities are not sufficiently sustainable by contemporary standards. A more holistic framework is therefore required for the following reasons:

Destruction of the Natural Environment. Continuous and intense urbanization and crude planning are rapidly altering natural landscapes—mountains are being flattened, tributary systems filled, and green coverings deforested. Hasty construction and an uncontrolled rate of urban development have led to the degeneration and destruction of the natural ecosystem formed by the hydrosphere, lithosphere, and biosphere.

Unsustainable Use of Resources. The market economy has instigated an over-consumption of resources across the world, leading to a massive emission of pollutants. There is crass planning in terms of how resources are used, be it energy, water, land, or labor. Air and water pollution generated by factories, automobiles, and construction sites threaten the health and survival of man and other life forms. The massive waste that is produced has been all too simply treated before being buried. Even though China has been promoting low-carbon and energy-saving measures, it has yet to attain the critical mass of infrastructure, political support, and social awareness to mobilize a conscientious movement within society. The code of practice for environmental building construction, which emphasizes four aspects of saving measures and environment protection, has yet to be broadly applied. Cutting edge concepts such as the industrialization of housing construction have only been practiced in very few projects.

Ineffective Networks. In many cities, open spaces, transport, education, healthcare, entertainment, and other forms of public facilities are often difficult to access and unfairly distributed. Ineffective planning and uncoordinated construction of such auxiliary programs lead to their unequal distribution and disruption in service networks. Hospitals, schools, and shopping malls overflow in the old districts, but are scarce in new cities, such as Shenzhen, or emerging ones. Deteriorating traffic conditions have made it time-consuming and costly to reach the public facilities. The disjunction in land use and traffic planning has caused an over-reliance on privately owned automobiles, thus increasing carbon emissions and inhibiting slower forms of movement such as walking

> Such experiments combine the needs of society with the market and position the aspirations of an enterprise with good architecture, leading to radically new forms of industry and architecture.

and cycling. First-tier cities are facing intolerable traffic jams, and extreme restrictions such as purchase quotas are required.

Challenges in Demographic Changes. The initial stages of urbanization have come to a completion as economic development stabilizes. With the advent of a new consumption pattern in an aging society, a revolution in living patterns is inevitable. Society has not yet adapted to these changes, and piecemeal studies on elderly housing and mixed communities have not matured. Although there is an increased construction of security housing, its mechanisms of planning, construction, distribution, termination, and management are not refined. The separation of the wealthy from the poor is leading to possible social unrest. While the price of housing remains high, the separation of neighborhoods of commodified housing from that of security housing would exacerbate social disharmony. Even though newly built housing communities have self-organized ownership committees, the participation of the residents remains limited.

Disconnection between Urban Planning and Design, Real Estate Development and Management, and Unsound Social Sciences Research. Contemporary planning theory in China is based on the theory and practice of Germany in 1920s and the former Soviet Union in the 1930s. Although such urban theories are constantly being refined, they are still incompatible with emerging developments in rapid urbanization and the market economy. Land use planning and management have overly simplistic and imprecise regulatory guidelines. The management and monitoring of plot ratios, green coverage, and public facility ratios stipulated by law are still being exploited and maximized for profit. Within the discourse of sustainable living, there is no consensus on the definition of high-quality living. Is a good living experience merely found in environmental friendliness, convenience, or efficiency? Or is it also becoming luxurious, superficial, and a willful contributor to the widening social gap?

Steven Holl's Vanke Headquarters, Shenzhen. Image courtesy of Elaine Thian, 2013

Over the course of the six years of teaching and research, the Department of Urban Studies and Planning at the Massachusetts Institute of Technology, Vanke, Professor Tunney Lee, my students and I developed a theoretical model termed sNice—Sustainable Neighborhoods through Inclusiveness, Connection, and Environment. sNice arises out of an overall interpretation of the principles of sustainable development and its specification towards neighborhood planning. Under this theoretical model, there are four sub-models: nature, community, mobility, and housing. Each sub-model has its own standards, methods of analysis, and case studies.

Research workshops were conducted, and the standout one was in 2007 in the urban village of Bantian, ten kilometers from downtown Shenzhen. These early communities preceded formal planning, and such villages-in-the-city are juxtaposed with industrial areas as a result. Rent and purchase prices are considerably lower than that of downtown Shenzhen. The Sijihuacheng housing neighborhood developed by Vanke is an example of a beautifully maintained compound that starkly contrasts the chaos of Shenzhen. While major highway and metro networks have extended to the outlying districts, the principles of sNice would explore how the two distinct urban conditions can cross-pollinate and be revitalized, with opportunities to create new secondary centers alongside unplanned yet highly urbanized districts.

Fundamentals

In many cities, housing construction at the scale of the neighborhood has no relation to the overall planning of the city. There is also a disconnection between the actual construction of a city to its planning vision, and a similar lack of coherence in its resource planning to its operations as a social economy. There is a lack of reliable data and an ineffective means of research. Important research findings widely discussed abroad are often withheld in Chinese agencies, such as the coordination between land use and traffic planning, factors that impact housing value, and the effectiveness of public infrastructure. The highly visible architectural form would become the most important consideration to decision makers. They would liberally scale up the iconicity of architecture to the size of the city. In terms of academic research, the division of traditional architectural studies with urban planning has led to a vacuum in the research of medium-sized and neighborhood-scale issues: its planning, construction, maintenance, and management, as well as its relationship to the city. Such a scale has yet to be recognized as an independent design or planning discipline.

In the discourse of urban sustainability, the three widely-agreed principles are the environment, economy, and equity. Even though this concept has been discussed for many years, research on the subject matter has stagnated on a theoretical basis. There is no credible research specifically on the scale of the neighborhood. There is not yet a theoretical framework to discuss what a sustainable neighborhood really is. Urban research must aim to develop a set of theories and methodologies to discuss sustainability in the ubiquitous neighborhoods throughout China. Extensive case studies and theoretical research must be adopted with the use of fieldwork, questionnaires, interviews, and planning simulations. Architecture and a healthy city must reflect the diverse communities of different ages, incomes, and social backgrounds. This is the most fundamental. One can relate to culture, space, and aesthetics on top of this; but good architecture, neighborhoods, and cities must first satisfy the fundamentals.

03
LABORING

Architects are often intellectually oriented, conducting their work from the drafting board, visualizing a future that would more likely be utopian, communicating and transmitting ideals through highly provocative imagery and lucid arguments. Critics suggest that there tends to be an inherent alienation from the actual production of architecture in its construction. The *shangceng jianzhu* or superstructure of society conceives and manages the realm of the professional bodies, cultural institutions, and political organs in an ideological capacity. They do so without directly shaping the built environment in the role of the base formed by actual laborers, contractors, and builders of architecture and cities. However, in a more contemporary or late-modern distortion of this relationship between the superstructure and base, architects and other urban professionals have lost their ideological command over the field of architecture, and instead they become merely a service provider who produces forms to suit the prevailing capitalist market of real estate. This is a fiercely contested argument, as other critics believe that the only way to achieve social equity today is to work within the mechanism of real estate production, rather than to seek an autonomous or separate ideological space for architecture.

A worker rests in the construction site of Urbanus' Dafen Art Museum. Image courtesy of Xavier Tan, 2013

LAND WILL DO WELL.
LAND CAN DO WELL.

MA QINGYUN

The root of the problems of Chinese society lies not in the cities but in the villages. Urbanization is not the cure-all to the issues China is facing. Based on the current rate of urbanization, another five hundred million of the rural population will be migrating to the cities. Urban infrastructure in China would collapse under such immense pressure. Instead of high-density cities, China ought to develop high-density villages. The emphasis of such density would lead to an expansion of China's agricultural economy. Without an understanding of the make-up of villages, it would not be possible to truly grasp the city. Without a strategy for the rural, there cannot be a viable strategy for the urban. It is theoretically possible to fit the density of an entire County of Lantian into a 120,000-square-meter skyscraper, following the utopian vision of Frank Lloyd Wright. Such density can be encapsulated in a concept called Agri-Urbanism.

Building for Production

The greatest intensity in the architectural discipline ought to be the activity of building, not the process or iconicity of design. Mankind builds for living. Mankind builds for production. And mankind builds for the land. Hence, one can create two new modes of work, namely, Landwill and CAN. Landwill refers to an awareness of the will of land. It is a developer without land, but a developer focused on the production of the land. CAN stands for Culture, Agriculture, and Nature. It speaks to the potential of the project. It is also part of the Chinese word *canlan*, which describes the splendor and magnificence of a place. A working framework of Landwill and CAN situates a body of work as a reminder that one should be most creative and respectful to the provisions of the land.

There is a depth and wealth of life to the land aggregated in the form of planet Earth, nothing like the superficial surfaces of other planets that cannot support life form. Land is the only source of origin of mankind; one can either flourish with it, or waste it. Land is that which exists between the mountains and the seas, between heaven and earth, between mankind and creatures of the earth, between the city and the village. Land has given mankind an abundance of life. Does mankind learn to organize its resource, or flee from such grave responsibility? Land gave mankind a civilization founded upon agriculture. Land gave mankind a civilization founded upon cities. These resulted from the choices made by humanity. Humanity grew tired of urban life not because the rural was more attractive. It grew appreciative of the rural not because the cities had fallen into decline. Humanity does not need a false choice between the city and the countryside, but an alternative that transcends the physicality of location or place. This third reality is a state of mind, a context and a new spirit. Land is the dominant expression of nature's destiny, offering agriculture as part of mankind's instinct to expand, as well as offering time for mankind to nurture a culture.

Land is Splendid

Land can. Land CAN. Land is confident. Land is reliable. Land is splendid. Its splendor grants mankind the opportunity to recover dignity, confidence and trust. *CANscape* is a region defined by natural parameters, and it flourishes through a symbiotic and dynamic network of culture, productive economy and natural environment. A *CANapolis* is a zone that accommodates the most vital system of production and habitable density. A *CANacropolis* is the nucleus which ignites the growth of a *CANapolis*. It is important to reclaim what land has once given mankind—creativity, originality, and productivity. Creativity is the inspired use of intellectual and technological prowess to exceed the limits of geography, space, and time, as well as to satiate mankind's hunger for the faraway and the unknown. Originality is borne out of mankind's deep sense of belief and a sense of grandeur. Productivity is the resilient capacity of all mankind, of all

Productivity includes men, land, and living. Image courtesy of Ma Qingyun

land mass, and of the state of living itself. The best way to show gratitude is to share the architecture, the produce, and the passion harvested so brilliantly from nourishment that the land provides.

Since the dawn of time, the wisdom behind the art of agriculture was in an efficient use of land and the methods responsible for an increased harvest of crops, such as corn, rice, and wheat. In the West, viticulture and winemaking are some of the oldest agricultural activities, and the Chinese is only recently getting acquainted with these activities. Wine is the most profitable product that one can get out of grapes. It would be most interesting to combine the ancient art of viticulture with an ancient place in China. This slow and methodical process of production has begun to show signs of stimulating the place and mobilizing its society. This stimulation bears a certain similarity to the impact architecture has on a locale. Irrespective of its physical form or conceptual position, architecture is a social actor, necessitating a social responsibility. Architecture is a spatial construct, undertaken by mankind using the limited resources one could conjure. Architecture would not able to break free from the contradictory and interdependent attributes of "what it is" and "what it wants to be." However, architecture has the capacity to revolutionize society precisely because it partakes in these two attributes. Architecture is the manifestation of the society it serves—architecture is a function of the constraints of its economy, and it is shaped by the kinds of architects emerging out of the very society.

Agent of Social Change

If architecture were to be the agent of social change, then architects must be able to translate social forces into a meaningful architectural language. An architect must also be able to make legible the meaning of such a language in society. This is a formidable task because an architect must be able to decipher the subtexts of different social forces in order to truly grasp the essence of the social issues, and assert a purposeful role for architecture in society. For architecture to have a social voice, it must have the courage to explore a multitude of issues, so that it can be involved in solving problems and shaping the future. Only by intervening on this broader environmental level can architecture fulfil its potent potential and redefine an obsolete mode of construction.

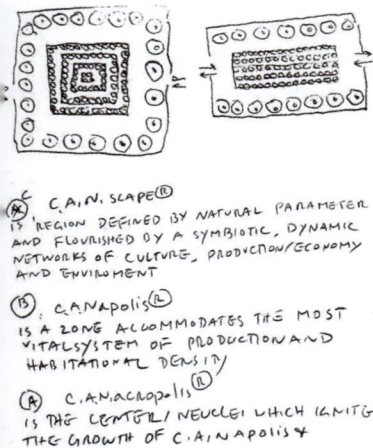

C.A.N. SCAPE®
IS 'REGION DEFINED BY NATURAL PARAMETER AND FLOURISHED BY A SYMBIOTIC, DYNAMIC NETWORKS OF CULTURE, PRODUCTION/ECONOMY AND ENVIROMENT

C.A.Napolis®
IS A ZONE ACCOMMODATES THE MOST VITALSYSTEM OF PRODUCTION AND HABITATIONAL DENSITY

C.A.Nacropolis®
IS THE CENTER/ NEUCLEI WHICH IGNITG THE GROWTH OF C.A.NAPOLIS+

Curatorial sketches of C.A.N.:
The Projects of Agri-Urbanism
Image courtesy of Ma Qingyun

Architecture in China has to be reassessed from the point of view of society, economy, and functionality, in order for new values, new insights, and a new public image of architecture to emerge. While contemporary architecture in China has not been as badly diminished in its social standing compared to its counterpart in the West, it does not change the fact that architecture has lost much of its critical voice in society. Architectural design has become either non-existent or it has reached a pointless fuss. Architectural theory and experimentation have either been too ponderous or so badly criticized for its social failings. If architects continue to fail to understand the basis of the discipline, architecture in China would soon meet the same fate as its counterpart in the West.

The generation of architects born in the 1960s would be the leading proponents of a new cultural revolution in China, because they had witnessed a China in social transition when they were coming of age between their middle school and their early university education. This generation had crossed the divide between two kinds of social form—from the planned economy of the socialist system to the market economy of great social mobility. Such a period of social transformation had led to new modes of operation. Architects from this period had the benefit of gaining an education in both the East and the West and developed an exceptional position in response to China's unique developmental problems.

They would likely display a particularly strong courage in their work and not rigidly adhere to the mere aesthetics of the built environment. This reflects the thrust of a new architectural culture.

Cultural Renaissance

A civilization must be progressive and forward-thinking in order to demonstrate the highest ideals of the present society. If one does not understand the purpose of such high social ideals, there is little meaning in advocating China to become the focal point of architectural excellence in the process of so much construction and urbanization, as well as such intensive internationalization. The sheer amount of resources poured into building and infrastructure construction should not benefit just the architectural or urban development community alone; instead, such formations should be indicative of a comprehensive kind of social growth and attainment. While the general public are routinely critical of architects and their work, not many have contemplated the relationship between the cultural activity of building, the role of architects, and the progress made as a civilization. The social and economic boom experienced by China today has conditions very similar to Japan in full flourish in the 1970s. It was precisely in that period when Japan rapidly formed its unique social and architectural character, combined modern materials and innovative forms with traditional ones, and forged a leading position in the culture of making and in the construction industry. The Japanese architects were able to lead the process of this cultural formation through the activity of building itself. Now, China has to establish its own cultural renaissance.

It is important to reclaim what land has once given mankind— creativity, originality, and productivity.

The mere materialization or realization of architecture alone is not adequate in suggesting the fuller significance of architecture. Any form of materialization today would be exceeded by a superior form tomorrow. For an architect to only endeavor to give material form to design concepts is to seek too low a standard for architecture. Such ambitions would not lead to any new architectural paradigms. All architecture would be superseded by newer and more innovative ones, and the speed of supersession would only increase in the future. Since antiquity, and even more so in modernism, the architect was flawed in the pursuit of authenticity and a form of professed authority, because of an originality seen in one's work. The notion of permanence and the creating of an immortal legacy are fallacies of self-centered modernist ideals. Instead, architects should learn to think and adapt, and to effect changes in society through activities of building.

C.A.N.: The Projects of Agri-Urbanism at 2015 Shanghai Urban Space Art Season
Images courtesy of Ma Qingyun

The City is Not the Only Reasonable Outcome for China

The biggest curse was brought about by modernism, as it deified new innovative forms as the only permissible form of architecture. Modern architects failed to comprehend the purpose of tradition found in the cultural heritage of past civilizations when they sought to establish their form as the only true "heritage" in architecture. Yet tradition should not be received blindly, because it is also shrouded in problems of inertia, politics and human error. Tradition is not always the most intelligent, and it is always possible to make changes to old methods of construction. The sense of stability and permanence is the least important criteria in architecture, but rather, architecture ought to bring a sense of warmth, comfort, joy, and harmony. In the final analysis, there are many reasons to believe why the city is not the only reasonable outcome for China. It is always more impactful for one to find non-traditional possibilities within the trajectory of tradition itself. Architects in China have to grasp the true instrumentality of influencing society through the incredible activity of building and the multiple forms of tradition.

BIG FOOT REVOLUTION

YU KONGJIAN

A *Baihuawen* Revolution for Design

For centuries, rural women in China were regarded as backward and ugly. Only those who had their feet bound are considered beautiful. Comparing women of a different class status or character, the woman with a pale complexion and small three-inch feet would be regarded as classical beauty. A woman with tanned complexion, big feet, and robust body would be of a lowly class, because she needed the robustness to labor. A woman should not be able to stand upright as well, otherwise she would appear indecent. The ancient Chinese had an extremely strict set of rules for feet sizes. Feet that were three-inch long were adored as a "golden lotus," four-inch feet were called a "silver lotus," and five-inch feet were called an "iron lotus." Those with bigger feet beyond these sizes would not be able to find a suitor, because they were destined to be a village laborer for life.

As one of the Four Beauties of Ancient China, Xi Shi was renowned to be the prettiest. She walked bent, probably due to poor health. Later, historians deduced that she may have suffered from heart disease. Why we would perceive a sick person as beautiful, but a healthy and robust body as ugly? It is because beauty was defined by the minority who have been living in cities for centuries. To elevate themselves above the village folks, or *xiangbalao*, the urban elites defined beauty and taste by treating healthy people as abnormal—the healthy as sick, and the productive as lazy. This was how the ancient Chinese dealt with the aesthetics of the body. We may be glad that we no longer have to adhere to the foolish practice of foot-binding up to a century ago. But a century since, we may still be binding our feet so to speak, as our aesthetic sense and values in the treatment of our environment are still driven by the same technological elitism that value small feet over the big and robust feet. The May Fourth "New Culture" Movement promoted the language of soy milk and *youtiao* (the Chinese cruller) to prose and poetry, becoming what is now *baihuawen* (modern vernacular Chinese), and replacing the classical Chinese language of high culture. This essay is about a revolution of our land and our living environment—a *baihuawen* revolution of design.

Current Landscapes

Compare the landscapes of our cities and our villages. The rich paddy fields appear fertile and aesthetically pleasing. Yet we replace them with cities and turn them into glossy lawns. We have to fertilize and irrigate these landscapes with a ton of water for every square meter each year so they can survive, and we consider this beautiful. We uproot trees full of peaches, plums, and pears in our villages, and replace them in the parks of our cities into plants of the same species that only flower but bear no fruit. The reproductive organs of these trees have become defunct. We treat our fish in the same way. Fish reared by our fishermen or fish in their natural river habitats both have dull appearances. At home, we would prefer a pet goldfish, a specialty of China. In reality, it is the ugliest, most unfit fish, with a distorted head, bloated waist, and a weak tail. If it is released to Huangpu River today, it will die tomorrow.

We treat our land and rivers with the same small-foot aesthetics and distorted values. Our rivers and streams, like the Huangpu River, are all "bound" by concrete levees, to protect against floods that would occur once every half or one millennium. They are excessive hydraulic engineering works for flood prevention. But flooding is becoming ever more serious and occurring every year, because nature's feet have been bound. Our rivers can no longer self-regulate against water logging and flooding. In the great number of rivers in China, there is not a single complete river today. We are investing hundreds of billions of renminbi into the "managing" of river channels, with water conservancy projects, flood prevention schemes, and beautification projects. These rivers have become lifeless and incapable of self-regulation. China has less than seven percent of the world's water resources, but we drain it away completely every time it rains, to the detriment of the groundwater supply. The groundwater level in the entire North China Plain is dropping by a meter each year.

> We must advocate the return of our land such that the wild grasses and paddy fields would be alluring again— our Big Feet can be beautiful.

Our cities are terrified of flooding after heavy rain. How they wish to drain all the water away the very night the storm is over. Therefore, the pipes we construct are ever bigger and wider, with massive investments to widen the pipes and even install mechanical pumps, so that the water can be drawn out and drained away immediately. In this engineering process, we are ruining the big feet of nature, whose self-regulating system is lost. Liken to a gravely ill person who has been hospitalized, our drainage system is dependent on transfusions and artificial machines to sustain its life. Flooding has become more serious than before. In 2012, flooding-related deaths in Beijing stood at seventy-seven. In Changsha, a female university student was pulled into the underground pipes during a rainstorm. Countless number of accidents are happening every year.

We have invented highly sophisticated machines and membranes to purify our water, passing through more than ten levels of filtration and purification, some with the aid of nanotechnology. Yet, water has become dirtier. Seventy-five percent of surface water in China is contaminated. Water from the Huangpu River is not even of the lowest acceptable grade by government standards. Twenty to thirty years ago, water from the rivers had substantial amounts of nutrients and was precious to farmers. Today we drain it away as dirty water, or construct expensive sewage treatment plants to purify it. Paradoxically, it results in a greater pollution of water. New constructions in the rural regions have turned robust and meandering streams into ornamental canals with white marble railings, mimicking the ancient Golden Water Bridges. The fields of paddy, maize, and sorghum on both banks of these rivers have all been razed and replanted with ornamental plants for the enjoyment by inhabitants of the new cities. Canola flowers and beans were replaced by unproductive horticultural species such as purple barberry and golden boxwood in the short span of a month. We perceive them as beautiful and pour out money and labor to sustain such manicured beauty.

Our entire city is in pursuit of a distorted beauty, not unlike ancient foot-binding. In the process, we have consumed fifty percent of the world's cement, thirty percent of the world's steel, and thirty percent of the world's coal to destroy our healthy feet. We continue to deplete our underground water every year, affecting the water supply of four hundred cities out of the six hundred in China. Fifty percent of China's wetlands—the kidneys of nature—have been destroyed. Our altered watercourses have become uncooked noodles. They were transformed into long and straight canals of cement and flood walls, with no more wetlands on either side. As a result, our land has lost its ability of self-adjustment. A little rainfall would lead to serious flooding, in the same way that our legs are no longer fit for walking. We need a revolution—a Big Foot Revolution! Beginning with the environmental professionals, we must alter our sense of aesthetics and recalibrate our values!

Water and Floodplains

We need to change our attitude towards water. We should befriend floods. My recent research demonstrated that only 0.8% to 6.2% of land would be affected by floods, should we not have the flood walls and dams across China. In other words, the flood prevention measures we have been investing in for centuries are effective for protecting as little as 0.8% of our land. Why do we fight a battle that we are destined to lose? With this in mind, we need to tear down these reinforced concrete, flood prevention structures.

My first engineering project was for a river in Taizhou, Zhejiang, over ten years ago after my return to China. It was a very beautiful river, meandering with lush wetlands on both banks. As the flood enriches the alluvial soil, indigenous wildlife and fishes were flourishing. Unfortunately, the water conservancy department would later commission a RMB 200 million construction of new flood prevention walls. Midway through the project, the mayor received petitions from farmers because their buffalos did not have a place to drink water. Herds of buffalos used to drink at the floodplain daily at dusk. A child was also discovered to have drowned because he could not climb back up the newly constructed high walls. The natural ecosystem was being destroyed. Frogs had disappeared along with the wetlands, as the tadpoles could no longer reach the shore after spawning. The mayor sought solutions from me, and I suggested the flood walls construction must be stopped. It was a political risk to discontinue a RMB 200 million infrastructure project. The mayor was nonplussed, "How can you ensure that my city would not be washed away?"

Upon a deeper analysis, the extent of flooding caused by massive floods would occur once every ten, twenty, and fifty years. We discovered that the city would not be threatened even without the flood walls. If the floodplain can be turned into parks, green spaces, and wetlands, including paddy fields and lotus ponds, what would necessitate the RMB 200 million flood walls? How many years do farmers need to work in order to overcome such debt? It is lamentable that the public can no longer get close to the fearsome river because of the perceived risks of flooding. After the flood walls were taken down, we carefully designed shallow and deep shores along the floodplain to bring back the natural habitat of fishes and frogs. The old buffalos can drink water from the river again, and the public can stroll along its shores. In the event of a flood,

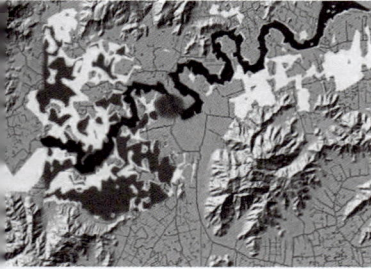

Flood analysis of Taizhou, Zhejiang. Image courtesy of Turenscape

the shores would be flooded for a couple of days, up to a week, but the public can still access the wetlands park along elevated walkways. The lush vegetation can serve to reduce the severity of flooding, as long as we can minimize our interventionist attitude towards the natural water systems. We must allow the natural elegance and functions of these watercourses and wetlands to return.

Production and Paddy Fields

The Big Foot Revolution is also very much about going back to the basic productivity of our landscape. Our land was originally fertile, but today, they are mostly earmarked for urban construction. Crops are forbidden; even the vegetables grown by urban residents are uprooted. Labor production is looked upon with disdain. Yet the harvest from our land is a healthy way to express the beauty of our landscapes. Because food is such a basic need for mankind, we should be vigilant towards the use of our land. In other words, where possible, crops should be grown on them. Instead of appreciating the ornament of flowers, we can anticipate the beauty of a harvest.

In 2002, the principal of a school in Shenyang sought to create a field for his school campus. It was barren but he wanted a landscaped field in six months. Given the short notice, a lack of funds, and the absence of irrigation facilities in the city, we proposed a rice field for the project. We collected free rainwater—a gift from the heavens—and we showed that growing rice is even easier than growing a lawn. We would even be able to get food at the end of a season without having to maintain a manicured and ornamental lawn. Farmland is a precious resource in China as only one-tenth of our land is arable.

In the past three decades, we have assimilated ten percent of this arable land into an infrastructure of concrete and steel. Only thirty to fifty percent of the arable land are greens. Most legislated urban green are conceived with the mentality of "small feet." But the rice field project had transformed the school campus into one with a healthy "Big Foot," where there are festivals for planting and harvesting. Food is being produced organically for the school's canteen and offered to visitors as souvenirs of rice packets.

Students have the freedom to keep goats and investigate new methods of husbandry. Teachers would stroll along the fields and the students would read and farm. This pedagogy is a forgotten tradition of China.

Shenyang Architectural University Campus.
Image courtesy of Turenscape

Memory and Industrial Forms

The past three decades of urbanization functioned under the slogan "*tui'erjinsan*", which means a suppression of the secondary industry and development of the tertiary. Shanghai was a part of this urban renewal process. The site of the Shanghai Expo used to be a great expanse of steel mills, factories, and fertilizer plants, and home to the Jiangnan Shipyard. I systematically surveyed these chimney industrial buildings just before they were demolished. While these buildings were clearly the source of pollution, they belonged to a unique part of China's industrial history. Their demolition was a form of an erasure of our memories. Xi Jinping reminded us that "our mountains must remain visible, the depths of our water discernible, and our memories held close." Unfortunately, China has been systematically removing these key aspects of our physical environment in the last three decades, and we have lost our ability to remember them.

In a project in Zhongshan, Guangdong, we advised the mayor again his intention to tear down a dilapidated shipbuilding factory to make way for a brand new cutting-edge building. To demolish the old building would be regressive as it erases the history and memory of the place. Therefore, we decided to conserve, reuse, and, with a few alterations, turn it into a habitable place. The river banks along the factory were ecologically restored. With a terraced form, visitors are able to walk all the way down to the stream and be close to nature. The rusty factory became a popular site for wedding photos in the Pearl River Delta, receiving more than five thousand engaged couples every year for their photography. This is a piece of history even if it was merely utilitarian three decades ago. We spend so much time figuring out how things were like in the ancient dynasties of Zhou, Han, Tang, and Ming, yet we forget what things were like just yesterday.

Over a dozen years ago, we were the first to plant weeds and wild grasses in a park along a rusticated railway track of a preserved factory. The walk along the robust railway tracks, surrounded by a tallgrass prairie landscape, would possess the beauty of the Big Foot Revolution. It is indisputable that gardens of Suzhou and the Yu Garden of

Zhongshan Shipyard Park, Guangdong. Image courtesy of Turenscape

Shanghai are beautiful as well, but these gardens are suitable for non-productive folks who could only walk with their waists bent.

Sponge City

When most of our Chinese cities have turned to the aesthetics of "small feet," they suffer from flooding every time there is rain. Our monsoon climate has a characteristically heavy rainfall in the summer. Unfortunately, the centralized drainage systems have not been able to adapt to it because these newly installed pipes are paralyzed with two hundred millimeters of rainwater per day. No matter how wide the pipes are, the heavy rainfall could not be accommodated. Only natural systems can adapt to nature. Therefore, cities ought to return to an absorption system that is elastic. We should build a "sponge city." Rainwater is a scarce resource, but we unwittingly drain it away, fearing floods. On the other hand, there is a shortage of water in most cities in China. If the sponge system is implemented across the whole country, rainwater will be stored, and we would no longer need to divert large amount of water from the south to the north. Beijing drains away one billion cubic meter of rainwater, which is almost equivalent to the amount of water that we divert to Beijing. The sponge system could change our city by eradicating the extremities of flooding and drought, while creating a landscape system that does not require excessive management or irrigation. Residents can wander along bridges under which the artificial sponge system would be located. We must liberate nature's big feet and let them self-regulate.

As I visit the Shanghai Houtan Park each year, I would see the public engaged in the harvesting of beans, corns, and sunflowers. It conveys an elegant relationship between people and food, between people and land. The water that flows naturally through the water system in the park is starting to be clean and crystal clear, despite the industrial brownfield history of the site as the former No.3 Steel Factory. Water takes approximately a week to percolate downstream from the upper reaches of the park, and 2,400 tons of water is cleaned and stored here every day. In fact, part of the water used during the Shanghai Expo was extracted from here. There is a sophistication in the way Shanghaiers relate to the park. An elderly visitor described the Houtan Park as a water purifier. If we implement this purification method to all our watercourses, and recover the ecology of our wetlands, then our water system can become cleaner. Currently, the streams in park are lively, but they remain behind fences and inaccessible by the general public. We should advocate greater accessibility for everyone and let the skyline of Shanghai be visible from down close to the waters. The old factories should be updated with means of water purification, turning the industrial heritage into a factory of life.

To build an ecology of the Big Foot Revolution, an ecological corridor can be attained with the transformation of the watercourses within the city. The branches of these water systems can be activated as lively and vibrant public spaces, and the nodes within the system can be turned into a series of sponges to absorb rainwater. Rainwater would enter into the watercourse indirectly only after sedimentation and filtration. If pollution can be intercepted through the rainwater as it enters the ground, our rivers and lakes

Houtan Park, Shanghai.
Image courtesy of Turenscape

can become very clean with all the necessary nutrients for a richer ecology. In fact, all six hundred cities in China are facing the same problem. As this method of is being adopted across China, two hundred cities are starting to implement various technologies of rainwater storage, leading to a purification of the wetlands, the land, and the water system.

Contemporary wisdom in water conservancy projects in China tends to rely on increasing the speed of flow, such that floodwater can be drained away rapidly. The designs of these river channels usually employ a straight or stepped section that is polished on three sides, a technique described as *sanmianguang*. Planting of trees and shrubs are strictly forbidden. Instead, water conservancy techniques require the exact opposite. The flow of water must be slowed down. Like a slow lifestyle, it takes time to nourish and digest. If the natural system can retain water longer, the wildflowers and plants would be able to absorb the nutrients in it. At the same time, it would become a scenic resource for the public. In Liupanshui, the local authorities elected to straighten out the rivers when its wetlands were destroyed by polluted water, sewage, and garbage. We used three years to change the entire watercourse, utilizing the earliest farming technology in China called the Pond Irrigation System. The system allowed the flow to slow down instead of

accelerate, so that the pollutants could be intercepted and contained. Fishes and wildlife were restored, and the vegetation on the river banks were reinstated to its original lushness.

Productive Architecture

In China, only one percent of nearly fifty billion square meters of architecture is energy-saving. The majority of buildings are neither energy-saving nor environmentally friendly. They consume one-third of China's electrical energy for air-conditioning. In light of this, I suggested what a generic energy-consuming high-rise might look like—one where vegetables could be grown on the top floors, pigs reared in the middle section, and mushrooms and fish grown and reared at the bottom floors. This would be a new form of a high-rise pig farm! The notion that every building can become environmentally friendly can be attained quite simply, even from one's home. I have been collecting rainwater and solar energy on the balcony of my Beijing home, located at the top of a five-story apartment building. In this relatively small footprint, I have collected fifty-two tons of rainwater for growing thirty-two kilograms of vegetables in a year. In another smaller enclosed balcony, as is customary in Beijing, I have developed a greenhouse for growing jasmine with the help of passively collected rainwater. This balcony has become an educational venue—a place for popular science frequented by neighbors, environmental organizations, and even real estate companies who wished to learn.

Greenhouse at Brown Stone Apartment, Beijing.
Image courtesy of Turenscape

Such greenhouses can be made indoors as long as there is enough sunlight. Rainwater may be collected and brought indoors, aiding in the irrigation of a biological wall of ferns and mosses. Such walls would act as ecological air-conditioners. This reduced the amount of electricity used for air-conditioning during summer or winter and led to annual savings of two thousand kilowatt-hours of electricity for each household. Apart from that, the wall would release an earthy aroma, akin to a sense of being part of a natural cliff-side environment. This earthy aroma can potentially cure symptoms of fatigue and depression. Through small and passive interventions in our buildings, there is the potential to mitigate bigger problems in urban living.

The Chinese literary revolution was manifested through a daily and affordable form of food. The words of grocers selling soy milk and *youtiao* were transformed into poetry, and the folk songs of fishermen became music. We must advocate the return of our land such that the wild grasses and paddy fields would be alluring again—our Big Feet can be beautiful. Our land needs an intensive revolution. This revolution follows in the footsteps of the May Fourth Movement in a real and profound manner, advocating a new form of culture, a vernacular language, and poetry that heralds the return of nature.

AGAINST ELITISM

ZHANG KE

China is massive. Many of the elites are concerned with the findings of the social sciences and humanities, and many have made theoretical advancements on these topics. The actual application of such academic knowledge falls on the practices of architects and other professionals. Unfortunately, instead of collaborating with the academics and adopting the new knowledge, architects are either cozying up with the government officials and contractors, or deceiving the media with stories of self-promotion. The architects are failing to act on the opinions and research findings of the social scientists and scholars. Many would blame the new generation of architects for lacking in a sense of social responsibility, but this situation would soon change. Many issues in our built environment are urgent and worthy of greater attention, and architects need to deal with them from the perspective of society, and from the perspectives of ordinary people. It is much more meaningful and real if solutions from the architects can represent the majority. Of course, architects are always seduced by cutting-edge technologies or stylish designs, but ultimately, we need to reflect on who the architecture is serving, and what can architects do about it.

Social Life and Architecture of the Superstructure

Architects ought to ask what the ordinary folks would do if they are allowed to plan their own vacant spaces. More ordinary people should have a stake in the city. The city can provide more work-live spaces, more shophouses, with residents living above and their shopfronts on the street level. The most fascinating example seen in China must be the "toilet-residence," where a home is located above a street-level public toilet. As long as the family living above is willing to take on the public responsibility of maintaining the hygiene of the toilet, they should be able to enjoy the right to live there, and to even run some small business from it. Architects and designers must consider how their spaces and designs can be utilized by the ordinary public. For example, architects can take on urgent housing problems by providing young graduates with an affordable, temporary, fashionable, and portable home—one that has access to water and electricity. This way, the fresh graduate would have great mobility with only a few essentials. In Beijing, for example, one may choose to stay at Houhai one day, and head off to Xidan the next. Growing out of a limitation of resources, a new approach may bring about an interesting sense of freedom. By thinking through different and experimental ideas, architects can choose not to be hampered by the pragmatism constraining the real world. Again, a city like Beijing is sometimes too unforgiving and takes itself too seriously. The distinctions in hierarchy between different districts are becoming increasingly pretentious. Everyone wants to demarcate their own territory, calling one a "financial street," or another a CBD, while human relationships continue to deteriorate and become segregated. It is not interesting to boast of how big Beijing is, or how many Bird's Nests, CCTVs, or World Trade Centers there are. Every city has landmarks, but they are meaningless if the ordinary people remain alienated in the city.

Chinese culture is comparatively cosmopolitan. The younger Chinese generation is less cognizant of the specificity of their culture or nationality. They thrive on the present, and the contemporary condition is all there is. They may not differentiate between Chinese and Western architecture. Architecture *is* architecture. The terms used by the nation-building generation such as "Chinese architecture," "modern architecture," or "Western architecture" are concepts that are irrelevant to the younger generation of architects. Only the decisive act of making architecture really matters. Architects no longer need to discuss what is ours and what is theirs. The most critical position of the contemporary is to be creative. Since architecture and the making of our cities are important aspects of our culture, architects, especially the younger generation, must develop a clear set of values. We belong to a new generation of architects, but not all young architects belong to this new generation. Just by producing something that looks trendy does not mean it is good architecture. Moreover, there may be two types of young architects. There are those who are still drawing inspiration from the West, or selling Western ideas in China without critical discernment and real innovation. Alternatively, there are architects who would excavate profound concepts from China and parade them in the West. These architects would choose to stubbornly hang on to the Chinese tradition, proclaiming to create a modern Chinese architecture. There is nothing new in either of these polarizing views that caricaturizes culture and identity. They are mere acts of smuggling or vending.

It is equally interesting for architects to reflect on the concept of adaptation in the everyday practice of architecture, because it helps to determine the degree to which one may change or struggle within the cultural, societal, or architectural frameworks.

The making of a great city, from a layperson's point of view, would be one in which every corner I turn to, I would be able to find a spot to sit down and find someone to chat with, or a place where I can choose to keep walking and exploring. In Beijing, this is obviously impossible. In New York, I can find an enjoyable walk between Central Park and the World Trade Center supplemented with segments on the subway, if I choose to. I am concerned about how fragmented Beijing is as a city, and whether it is really acceptable by the ordinary people. Is it still a city that is full of imagination? The quality of life of the Chinese people is not one that finds conflict with city life. Traditional urban life in Beijing was found on the streets. Before 2002, large populations were still found in the Old City along the streets of the residential *hutong*s, where they sunbathed, played mahjong and chess, dined, or sold their merchandise. The streets were extensions of the ordinary people's living rooms. Now there are no longer intimate and bustling streets of such nature. The bigger problem is the lack of continuity. This is a problem at the disciplinary level of urban planning. An enormous amount of urban space is being wasted during the planning stages, because the roads of Beijing are generally too wide. Roads are not the only solution to resolving the traffic problem. Moreover, the distance between one road and the next is too far. Comparatively, every urban block may be five to ten times the width of those in Manhattan. There was no critical inquiry when China was blindly following the urban planning approach of the Soviet Union. Chinese society need not modernize in the same way as the Soviets, even if there was agree-

Micro-*hutong*, Beijing. Image courtesy of Budi Lim, 2015

ment in adopting socialism. The *hutong* blocks used to be tiny with a walking distance of thirty to fifty meters, determined by the dimensions of back-to-back courtyard dwellings. Instead, the length of a single Beijing city block is about four to eight hundred meters. Many lots have stayed empty and not been fully utilized; hence it is ever more important to leave them for the public for informal recreational activities.

The shortage of affording housing in China has confounded everyone. Architects have the capacity to act. I want to propose the existence of three types of dwellings—the three-*bao* dwelling, three-*xiao* dwelling, and three-*liu* dwelling. The three *bao*s stand for condition of protecting, especially the service or servant class, who are in fact the ones in greater need of social protection—*bao'an* (security guards), *baomu* (nannies), and *baojie* (cleaners). These people live in the same communities as the majority of the middle class, but often live their lives hidden from the sight of the rest. The nannies live in their employers' homes, while the security guards and the cleaners live in subpar underground apartments. During the planning of the residential districts, more consideration should go into providing adequate spaces for these people who serve. The three *xiao*s refer to yet another belittled and marginal group in our society—*xiaojie* (prostitutes), *xiaoshangfan* (hawkers), and *xiaotou* (thieves). Many rural migrants have to survive in these marginal, or even illegal occupations, but the fact is they do serve society in their own ways. Then the three *lius* stand for a banished segment of society with no economic capacity and an equally disenfranchised disposition—*liuxuesheng* (students), *liulang* (wanderers), and *liumang* (hooligans). Marginal as it may sound, the resolving of the housing question for the underclasses such as these would not only lead to an improvement in the security of our society but also teach us the importance of compassion in our society.

Adaptation and Praxis

The recognition of social ideals and the purpose of architecture is only the beginning of the process. It ought to lead to an active formulation of practicable and highly adaptable architectural methods for China. The process of adaptation in China can take on two layers of meaning: one physical, and the other conceptual. At the conceptual level, the approach in thought and idea must adapt to the local so that it works, and this is realized by a precise coordination between climate, landscape, local materials, and traditional construction techniques. Architecture must grow naturally from the ground, adapting to the properties of the place. This may in fact be an amalgamation of both conceptual and physical realms. This methodology of adaptation helps to situate my studio's work, which differs depending on where the site is located, from Yangshuo, Suzhou, Hangzhou, and Shanghai to Beijing, Tibet, and Chengdu. The projects would adapt to the place

Niyang River Visitor Center, Tibet.
Image courtesy of standardarchitecture

and its local building traditions, but always imbued with critical contemporary perspectives as points of departure. The physical aspect tends to be more visible and formal, and it mutates and adapts as a building takes shape. There is an urgent need to adapt to new spatial programs or the aftermath of unexpected events and natural disasters.

The Niyang River Visitor Center in Tibet is a relevant example that speaks to the process of adaptation. The construction method of this building adopted and developed the techniques of the Tibetan vernacular architecture through the use of local resources. Standardarchitecture and Zhaoyang Architects came together in 2009 to develop a solution that would resonate with the site. The result was a small 430-square-meter space so geometric and abstract that it has a sense of being carved into, with an interplay of voids and solids. There were experimentations in the construction process. Over the course of an inspection visit, we brought along some local mineralized color pigment that could be applied on the stonework of the transitional spaces. Evaluations were made with the client and builders on site, and quick and decisive measures were taken. The architectural stonework and structures were handmade, and this site-specific ruggedness and directness was accentuated by adding color to it. Perhaps for a different project, this site-based decision-making process would not have been possible. When the sunlight strikes the colored stonework, the effect is indeed quite magical. The inboard surfaces of the transitional spaces and courtyard benefited from the use of the Tibetan colors, but at the same time, the abstract geometry evokes a sense of contemporaneity. There was difficulty in the use of colors, because in the Tibetan tradition, only religious buildings would be painted with strong colors. Ordinary architecture would at most have white paint on the stonework. Eventually, the colors were reverted to white. There was still a sense of modesty about the visitor center because the colors only appeared on the inboard surfaces, and white was equally alluring. But the impact of color was nevertheless complex, drawing in the curious locals in their exploration of the meaning of the colors in the building.

During the design process of the Niyang River Visitor Center, we had argued with the locals, suggesting a desire not to directly imitate their culture, nor impose anything foreign on them. When confronted with our position, the locals are mostly divided into three types. The first were the ordinary folks who found our ideas easy to accept, because our construction methods were familiar. The second were unable to accept the absence of Tibetan symbols usually found in doors, windows, and colorful ornaments, because of their partially Sinicized expectation. Lastly, the Tibetan intellectuals favored our design very much, agreeing that any imitation would be vulgar and dishonest. One would be easily be misled to believe that modernity and regionalism are in conflict with one another. On the contrary, such an adapted approach would provide enormous room for interpretation and sociocultural development. Learning from Ou Yangxu, the Chairman of Tibet Tourism Corporation, we were reminded to show an equal degree of respect to foreign cultures in Tibet. When one is overly superstitious of the culture of a place, one would uncritically "look upwards" to their high culture, which tends to lead to imitation. Yet when confronted with globalization, one would "look downwards" with arrogance, which is in fact an act of ignorance to assume that the economically or technologically advanced urban solutions would rescue those in less developed places. Metropolitan architects in China have often appeared foolish when they lack a true respect for the local, natural, and human environment.

As a humanistic way of life for twenty-five centuries in China, the ethics behind Confucianism was essentially about adaptation. It is about how one manages the balance between the self and the universe. Adaptation is not something that can be easily found in the scientific realm, especially when it comes to the maintaining of harmony in everyday Chinese society. Hence, the Confucian teaching of a cultivation of the self was impactful in creating a positive influence in society. It is equally interesting for architects to reflect on the concept of adaptation in the everyday practice of architecture, because it helps to determine the degree to which one may change or struggle within the cultural, societal, or architectural frameworks. By developing such an ability, an architect becomes agile and proactive in developing buildings that can adapt to the local conditions in a more humble manner, even when it comes to the handling of complex cultural questions that speak to the prevailing interests of a global audience. Should architecture be wrapped up in the world of symbols that represent a culture? Or should architecture be more subtle and delicate? These are productive problems that ought to define the search for contemporary architecture in China.

PROGRESSING FROM TRADITION

LIU JIAKUN

My generation has been deeply involved with the politics and social issues of China, and we tend to care more about our world. Compared to architects, artists tend to express this concern in their work more conspicuously. However, even amongst the artists, one can discern a clear difference between artists born in the 1950s and artists born in the 1970s or 1980s. The former tends to think about contributing to the betterment of society, or arousing public awareness in social issues. The latter tends to focus more on themselves. This is most probably due to the education they had received. The generation born in the 1950s had experienced life under collectivist ideology, and they grew up under Maoist slogans such as "Fight Selfishness, Repudiate Revisionism," "Fight against even a Moment of Selfishness in One's Mind," and "Serve the People."

On the other hand, an older generation of architects that I have met would also have a focus on the practical and economical aspects of architecture, especially the ones from previously state-owned architectural design institutes. Their attention was centered on the construction and function of a building, and they tend not to focus on issues of aesthetics. This older generation of architects had a way of fully expressing themselves in their work. For instance, some of the surviving industrial buildings designed from that period would embody a kind of functional aesthetics that is not superficial like buildings built in the contemporary era. The functional buildings might seem dull, but they express some of architecture's most powerful and innate qualities.

Unfortunately, well-intended social agendas in architecture are often hijacked by the formal aspects of design. This is exacerbated under the curious gaze of the global media. In the case of the Tulou Collective Housing by Urbanus, while principal architect and co-founder Liu Xiaodu repeatedly stressed that the essence of the project was to contribute to the low-income community, the media instead chose to hype up the formal resemblance of the project to the vernacular earthen structures known as *tulou*. Let us rethink this— the traditional *tulou* from Fujian also takes the rectilinear form as well as the circular form, but had Urbanus decided to implement the rectilinear form, it would probably not have gained the same level of attention from the media. Furthermore, it was not the architect, but the client, who had suggested the use of such a typology. The authority of the regional and the local has weakened in the age of global forms of practices and media. Critical Regionalism was an attempt to strike a balance between international and regional aspects of architecture, and has been adopted by many contemporary Chinese architects. In fact, cosmopolitan urbanites imagine the rural conditions in a similar way the West imagines the East. Both imaginations favor pictorial and symbolic ways of seeing and depicting, and quite often, they are also self-projected realities.

Outside of China, there are fewer opportunities to build, and architects would grow old trying to secure a project after years of experimentation. In China, we have the luxury of making countless mistakes in the same process of experimentation year after year. Experimentation is an important process of learning from mistakes and attaining perfection. There has to be a motivation for progress. Yet many architects in China try time and time again without realizing the mistakes they had made, so they fail to reach the next step. There is rapid improvement in China, but the social and environmental costs are relatively high. I want to make use of my work in this prevailing context. Each generation of architects has a statement to make, but it is important to be humble and treat one's own work candidly. The dissemination of a message may require the effort and time of an entire generation. For example, our contemporary innovation of *zaisheng* materials might seem irreverent to tradition. These "rebirth" materials are very much unlike the vernacular gray clay tiles, which have a simpler and more direct link to the history of China. A foreigner would immediately recognize the gray clay tiles as a traditional Chinese feature, but in the pursuit of a more authentic and contemporary design approach, I want to present a realistic China, rather than an impressionistic one.

A foreigner would immediately recognize the gray clay tiles as a traditional Chinese feature, but in the pursuit of a more authentic and contemporary design approach, I want to present a realistic China, rather than an impressionistic one.

Integrity of Materials

There would be considerable differences in attitudes towards design even amongst Chinese architects from the same generation. Zhang Lei, for instance, prefers making architecture to a high level of completeness, regardless of its scale. He is more concerned with architecture as an entity, while I am more concerned about relationships among the constituencies of architecture. Wang Shu and I differ in the ways we handle materials. He is more interested in the direct reference to traditional use and the intentional misappropriation of materials. Taking his China Academy of Art in Hangzhou as an example, the clay tiles were added on top of a complete steel roofing system, which means the clay roof tiles have no role to play in terms of the waterproofing function. It was merely a reference to cultural forms of a particular era.

An observant critic may suggest that there is no inappropriate way to use traditional roof clay tiles, as there were instances where such tiles were also used in places other than the roof, even in traditional usages such as ground paving. Even in traditional craftsmanship, there was a possibility of misuse. Perhaps even the placement of clay tiles on a wall as a vertical cladding material may be construed as an innovative form that follows the logic of tradition? In reality, tiles are tiles, in the sense that the intention behind the arched form of each tile came from the necessity of waterproofing roofs. In short, in response to the use and reuse of this traditional material, I would prefer to maintain a stronger connection to the original form of overlapped tiles that served the purpose of waterproofing. Traditional materials are like idioms and old sayings, and I choose not to use them. I am also skeptical about the clever misuse and referential use of traditional materials. I prefer to speak in the plain language of architecture. I would prefer to take a widely-used contemporary material, and find ways to elevate it. Many years ago, brick kilns proliferated in China, but they have been replaced by small cement factories today. Bricks and cement blocks are the most basic construction materials emerging from the specificities of their own times.

The elemental quality of the construction materials we choose to build with is by far the most important consideration in architectural design, and each architect should attend to the specific invention and transformation of materials that have emerged from their own era. Building materials form the vocabulary of architecture. They not only reflect the practical functionality of architecture but also the characteristics of their time. I wish to extract the most naturally-produced form of material from the most ubiquitous of contemporary resources, and to use them appropriately. Even if the ambition is to attain a spiritual connection to "tradition," my hope is to yet express it through contemporary materials. If there was no adequate transformation, or a mere inheritance of a traditional form of materials, then it is perhaps best just to follow the traditional use of such materials faithfully. The selection and treatment of building materials sometimes arise only at the end of a design process after a fully idealized architectural form had emerged, yet at other times it can be a deliberate intention to consider the building materials right at the beginning of the process. Because the materiality of architecture has such a spiritual connection to our artistic conception of architecture, and because it has such immediacy in affecting our senses, an architect should always attempt to engage with the consideration of building materials at the beginning of the process.

One should not underestimate the way contemporary building materials can carry deeper stories that have yet to be discovered. Each material has its own unique characteristics on a deep cultural level. Iron is comparatively rough, reminding us of the more durable tools and weapons from the Iron Age, while the bronze reminds us of the earlier Bronze Age with the first discoveries of metallurgy. Brass would conjure a sense of grandeur and magnificence, and sometimes the fineness associated with the decorative arts and commercial forms. One ought to study a contemporary building material with the same reverence as a traditional one in order to gain an understanding of its essential characteristics.

Rebirth bricks. Images courtesy of Jiakun Architects

The use of local materials is the most basic common sense in the process of creation. Examine how buildings from different regions of China utilize them. Consider how architect Mu Jun turned to rammed earth construction for his work in Sichuan after the earthquake. For the commoners who built their own houses in rural China, they would always choose the path of least resistance. Between the multitude of villages, ancient towns, and mountain settlements, the distinctiveness of each vernacular form is distinguishable because each region would construct their dwellings with the most readily accessible materials. It is most natural to appropriate building materials and resources that are within immediate reach. From this vantage view and especially in practice today, the generic availability of building materials and the distances these resources have to travel between the source of production and the site of construction are no longer relatable to the conditions of the past. Architecture in the contemporary era tends to rely on pretentious and ultimately unsustainable ways of using the building materials available to us.

Rebirth Bricks and Low-Tech Strategy

I prefer to use cement blocks or rebirth bricks because it is a contemporary material. The idea of rebirth bricks first dawned on me when I was on my way to the earthquake-stricken area in Sichuan, where I witnessed extensive rubble and straw materials in the aftermath of destroyed buildings. Then learning about the readily available technologies of small brick factories, I decided to turn my brick idea into a real building material. I do not see it as an invention, but rather as a way of recycling. It is more accurate to describe it as a process of discovery and utilization. Rebirth Bricks can be made by everyone. It is affordable and easy to make, and the raw material can be found everywhere. They do not need to be fired, and the size of the bricks can easily be adjusted according to the different needs.

The idea of a low-tech strategy came from my experience of rural construction, and it is a responsive and realistic strategy we applied in the face of construction constraints at the time. Regardless of an urban or rural context, the approach remains the same. We have to stare reality in its face, use the constraints, and even turn it around into an advantage. We can transcend this reality by making the most of both the positive and negative conditions, and transforming them into the basis of our resource and design. Despite the increasing multiplicity and availability of construction materials, technologies, design ideas, and methodologies, the conditions for construction may not have improved. At the fundamental level, it may have even deteriorated. This is the existential purpose of such low-tech strategies. Buildings in China are often poorly finished, which may be caused by a combination of factors relating to the availability of skilled labor and building resources. While each situation should be analyzed independently, the use of a low-tech strategy can be an effective approach in China.

Rubble of the Wenchuan earthquake.
Image courtesy of Jiakun Architects

I would like to avoid being attached to a singular framework, where I have to adhere to certain building principles without evolving. Hence I would approach each project differently depending on its situation. One can develop a dynamic attitude towards change, avoiding a constant insecurity about progress, or a stubborn resistance towards change. It would be sufficient as long as one has a well-considered direction, and can be prepared for eventual change. In my case, I prefer to adapt to the circumstances of each project, following the Chinese saying *yindizhiyi*, which means to suit one's measures to a local condition. The word *di* literally means the ground, but it can also extend towards a territory, as in *dikuai*, as well as broadly encompassing its customs and practices, as in *fengturenqing*.

It is important to contemplate further about the understanding of gray and red bricks as building materials. They are very similar in terms of their material nature—red bricks would become gray bricks when they get wet. Red bricks were hardly used during the Republican era, but they became representative of the planned economy era, corresponding to the proletariat, the working class, and the revolution. Even though these two materials are similar in physical nature, they embody different meanings and essences. In a recent renovation project that seeks to transform a historic film studio into a cinema park, I had selected red bricks over gray bricks in order to evoke the historical period associated with the year 1958 as the commencement of the film studio. On the other hand, gray bricks were preferred when I was operating on more classic and vernacular renovations, such as residential projects in the Kuanzhai Alley in Chengdu. I am not against the many means of applications in each building material. However, when a building material is turned into a specific product through a specific usage, it acquires an innate or cultural function. For example, the stacking of arched gray roof tiles against a wall does not adequately expressing the full functionality of these tiles. It would be for a decorative purpose rather than an authentic purpose. I would only occasionally apply these aesthetic techniques, but always in a more controlled fashion and as a secondary intention. I am more inclined towards authenticity.

The Invisibility of Materials and the Aesthetic Condition

The choice of materials in our design of the Sichuan Fine Arts Institute Design Department came from an understanding of Chongqing's history and regional character. The ancient Ba Empire was populated by mountain-dwellers and hunters, but as the imperial city of Ba, Chongqing was definitely not rural. Chongqing had an enviable status as the subsidiary capital of China during the Republican era. The city has always been a weighty base for heavy industry in the modern era and a leader in progressive industrial culture. People from Chongqing tend to be more tempestuous, their cuisine tends to be strong, and the harshness of their dialect contrasts sharply with the softer Chengdu dialect. The rawness of these traits led me unambiguously to the evocative quality of red bricks. Any attempt to rationalize this choice of material would prove rhetorical, but when one is standing in the presence of the unpolished red shale bricks, one could feel a decisive resonance.

The seven buildings for the Fine Art Institute were designed as seven variations of the same system, which includes the industrial-form roofs, the external staircases, and so on. The gable ends of each of the seven buildings and their angles of rotation are all controlled by red bricks. Variations only occurred in the middle sections. Building materials form the language of an architect, and they can often be the driving force behind a design. Small design decisions can lead to bigger ones, and an intricate detail can bring architecture into being. There were subtle changes made at the Fine Art Institute that were not immediately perceptible—the ten-by-twenty-centimeter bricks used were smaller than the normal bricks. This reduction in brick size and a corresponding increase in the visual density of the walls made the walls appear well-finished. Larger bricks may expose the crudeness of the workmanship, while bricks that are too small may lead to a loss of tactility in the wall.

There are aspects in the crafting of materials that may not be noticeable when one only reads the construction drawings. There is an important lesson in the use of plaster and corrosion-resistant aluminum boards for the Department of Sculpture at the Sichuan Fine Arts Institute. Located in the extreme heat of Chongqing at the old campus, hollow cavity walls were built to allow for ventilation and heat insulation. The environmental performance was fine, yet it was the plaster that demanded a lot of attention in construction. Plaster walls in Chongqing tend to crack easily, appearing like turtle shells, even if a coating layer is applied. It turns out this was caused by the silt sand in the plaster. By the time sand from the Yangtze River is deposited in Chongqing it has become too fine to be sufficiently adhesive. In the old days, the sand used for plastering was collected from the mountain, instead of the river, and we returned to the old wise way of obtaining our sand from the mountains. No coating layer was required, and the plaster finishes at the Fine Arts Institute did not crack. Iron oxide was added to the plaster to bring this experimentation to another level. A crack-free plastering exploration does not have the flamboyance of a formal expression, but this subtle reworking of a material can very much become the basis of an aesthetic condition of architecture.

An Artist's Humility

If a painter flaunts his or her techniques, or if a writer only cares about embellishments in the writing, it could lead to a lack of precision in the content, or a lack of content altogether. Ostentatiousness, even with the right techniques, is never considered to be of high virtue in Chinese artistic judgment. While good techniques are required to solve problems or to complete an expression, it is not about displaying everything you know at once. Architects are often too heavy-handed in the pursuit of a design sensibility, making obvious every single detail and fearing that their intentions would not be noticed.

There are many ways to capture fine details in a piece of work, and it is especially important to be observant. A good use of detail can be achieved without jeopardizing the whole work. In the same way, a lengthy piece of narrative can be punctuated by a particularly excellent piece of detail, aiding in the development of the whole story. Being ostentatious can be dangerous, as it destroys our soul and harms our inner virtue. A good craftsman exercises restraint in service of the art form, and in service of the society that needs a good piece of work. There is no place for arrogance, and a craftsman would only engrave a small detail or an understated initial on their work. As a question of culture and class, artists and craftsmen can be categorized into different levels by this measure. Architects are craftsmen. Should we become too self-indulgent too early, we would fail to express the deeper aspects of our work. In the highest order of our craft, there has to be a deliberate obscuring of the techniques behind the work, in order to stay focused on the message.

This essay is translated and adapted from Liu Jiakun, *"Ziran yu chuantong"* ["Nature and Tradition"], *Interior Design and construction, Volume 3, 2016,p.102*

GRAVITY IN LOCAL CONSTRUCTION

HUA LI

Globalization is a form of colonization. Any regional practice of tradition would inevitably face external challenges, as traditional craftsmanship would be replaced in the advent of mechanical production. This form of atrophy points to the impossibility of remaining unaffected in a global system of construction, because there is no cultural system that can be kept in isolation. Instead of being heralded as a false binary opposition or a rigid dogma, tradition can be better defined as an organism that constantly absorbs, adapts, and evolves. Only the spiritual and intangible forms of tradition can be transformed and transmitted. Tangible things would eventually be destroyed and fade away with time. In order for a tradition to survive, it requires a conduit to connect with the present ways of life; otherwise it will quickly become obsolete. Of all the forms of Chinese traditions, the notion of "returning to nature" is the most valuable. Coming from China's agricultural civilization, this tradition manifested itself through various forms of Chinese gardens, shaped by the literati from ancient and modern days. Yet the uncouth act of spitting by farmers and the less educated rural community today can be said to have come from the same agrarian tradition. Since nature is not directly accessible or attainable in a city, the association or sentiments with physical aspects of a garden became a way to return to nature.

In the context of a village, the land has a way to recycle everything by absorption and re-nurturing. There is an all-encompassing effect of nature—everything returns to the earth as a way of returning to nature. In this holistic manifestation, the practice of tradition can indeed be described as a spiritual and intangible force. Architectural tradition can also be passed on through a careful and practical consideration of construction constraints within a contemporary context. To build a house in a rural village, local conditions and materials must be considered foremost, because of a great limitation of resources. This is a way to return to nature in itself. In the current process of urbanization in China, farmers would build their homes without any professional help. In keeping up with modernization, they would invariably use large quantities of industrial materials such as steel and ceramic tiles. This may look aesthetically crude at first glance, but it is in fact authentic to their everyday life, in the manner of gaining quick access to these affordable materials.

When a local government decides to demolish and redevelop a piece of land, the outcome for architecture is predictably dull and repetitive. The mechanics of urbanization does not encourage positive architectural change. Ideally, urbanization should be a bottom-up and self-initiated process. Even with a top-down approach, architecture must avoid crude methods that negate critical relationships between the new construction and its context. Urbanization of the rural would inadvertently transform the lives of people. Given the demand for a responsible architectural proposition, there must be continuity between architecture and the urban fabric in terms of their scales, and between architecture and its methods of construction. All continuity would be lost if the urbanization process begins only with the bulldozing of the old; then, architects would have no choice but to adopt new and foreign planning concepts and construction methods.

Architecture for the People

In every project, there should be an utmost concern with the "essence" of architecture. Should such an essence exist, it would be especially meaningful to identify this rudimentary and internalized order. One has to look through the busy mirage in a world that is surrounded by countless excessive and imaginary forms. My design philosophy can be described in terms of the "initiation" and "gravity" of architecture. Architecture must have a sense of commencement. It must make a return to the fundamental questions of place, space, and construction. Gravity is the material presence of architecture in its precise place and time. An initiation in architecture is simple and formless, while gravity is complex and formal. Gravity enables architecture to become entwined in the livelihood of a people and artifacts of a location, akin the relationship between plants and the earthly ground. For example, if the initiation process is an exploration of the fundamental significance of architecture, then gravity points to relatively social and practical considerations. An initiation in architecture is an overall concept that is universal by nature, while its gravity would be the specific strategies that are needed to face the particularities of place, climate, resources, tradition, construction technology, and costs. This philosophy is a holistic consideration of architecture with its context rooted in place.

Architectural tradition can also be passed on through a careful and practical consideration of construction constraints within a contemporary context.

The Paper Museum in Gaoligong in Yunan Province can be considered a piece of architecture that is grounded. The main idea was for it to be rooted in the local. This further determines how the architectural form responded to the village—the consideration of form, scale, landscape, and climate. The total use of local material for its construction are as relevant as the hiring of local village craftsmen for its construction. At the same time, it is also something new—a marriage of inventive concepts with local tradition. It marked the formation of a new composite that might become part of a local tradition in the future. Many of the initial ideas were realized only through the construction process of eventual building. Even though the handcrafted details seemed raw, they matched the character of the building. Craft brought in a unique sentiment, while the locally available materials reaffirmed a sense of time, as well as a heightened sense of vitality and fullness of expression, to architecture.

The localization of construction meant a consideration of design only in terms of locally available resources and constraints in construction knowhow. This project was designed to become part of the local socioeconomic regeneration, not just being a beneficiary of an external funding source or externally-aided expert construction. The method of construction played a big role in the Chinese debate of regionalism in architecture. There must be an avoidance of simplistic localization as a predetermined style, especially architectural designs that only strive for an external visual effect without a deeper consideration of the role of the construction process. It is important to adhere to the fundamentals of construction, avoid mimicking wood construction with newer forms of construction in concrete, or tiling over a surface to give the appearance of masonry construction. Merely addressing the visual appearance or architectural style would only lead to a highly limited and rigid understanding of the role of architecture in China's rapidly transforming society.

Tree Clubhouse, Beijing, designed by Hua Li. Image courtesy of Budi Lim, 2015

Architecture is for the people. It cannot afford to be an abstract and autonomous order. Therefore, in the process of the spatial and construction aspects of design, the priority has to be given to the people. To give a specific example, the main contribution of the Xiaoquan Elementary School was its provision of a collective space that allowed students to be active in order to enjoy their school life. Happiness is really important for a student, and it was important to reflect this pedagogical principle in its architecture. Architecture has the subtle capacity to change the lives of people, and in so doing, architecture can lead to a value change in our society. The Paper Museum became a place for communication between the villagers and the visitors. This gradually helped to enhance the lives of the villagers, in terms of improvements in their income and exposure to cultural exchange. Visitors have come to learn about the paper-making process with their own hands, and it gave a genuine sense of self-worth and empowerment to the local craftsmen. The experimentation of local construction during the process of the project also gave the craftsmen and architect the opportunity to rediscover and reinvent new methods of adopting the traditional mortise-and-tenon joinery. New alternatives and experimentations are being further developed from the lessons established in this project.

Potential of a Construction Site

To develop realistic design concepts and maintain control over the construction, the peculiarities and constraints of local construction must be considered during the design stage. There must be close communication with the local builders during the frequent site visits, in order to ensure that problems are solved immediately. There will always be new challenges during the execution process. For example, despite having the best plans in place for maximum communication and site visits during the construction of the Bamboo Raft Factory at Wuyishan, Fujian, the quality of the fair-faced concrete blockwork was still not up to par. This was a result of basic competency issues with the builder's management and workers, which means the choice of concrete blockwork would need to be reevaluated as well. In another example, the earth dug out for the foundations was reconstituted for a rammed earth wall for a new building. The stones dug out from the site was reused for new masonry walls, and the earth can be adapted as formwork for concrete casting. These methods fall outside of modern industrial methods, but they can survive with the right application at

Hua Li at an exhibition in Beijing. Image courtesy of Budi Lim, 2015

the right place. There has to be genuine creativity in every effort to solve problems during the construction stage of a project, addressing the problems with limited resources, while relying on experience and knowledge in the design stage.

It is imperative to keep a team small, with a tight control over the number of ongoing projects a team has to engage. Because the making of architecture is still a deeply local, personal, and vested process, there is a need to see the whole process through. By being close to the ground, each architect has the duty to evoke a distinct regional character through every project. A strong sense of place and region need not be limited to rural or remote areas. Investigations in urban centers and peripheries are equally valid. There should be a fundamental relationship between architecture and its site or the broader environs, and different sites ought to possess different problems, with the seeds of various unique solutions. Architecture must not be limited to any typological constraints. Architecture's supreme concern should instead be about the use of local materials and construction methods, and their correspondence with locally available craftsmen and their community of users.

An exploration of the general features of disciplinary power would naturally lead to critical explorations of governmentality in a society in a Foucauldian sense. In China, this is asserted through institutions and technologies of the state for the purported good of society. Theorists describe the planning and building of cities as one of the institutionalized forms of economic development and social control, and all levels of local government from provincial, prefectural, county or township levels, are beating to the drums of urbanization. No local government leadership would want to fall short of the demands of city building and infrastructure building, even if they are thinning out China to such an extent that the new cities are too big and too empty. Apart from the more obvious class-based stratification of society, there is a real lack of discourse of race in a geographically and culturally diverse China. This proves that the regime is continuing to evade the need to find an equitable way for a more genuine kind of multiculturalism to exist.

A surveillance camera at the Guangzhou Opera House by Zaha Hadid. Image courtesy of Takeo Muraji, 2013

04 CONTROLLING

THE RAPIDLY THINNING CITY

WU GANG AND CHEN LING

Seventeen years have passed since the dawn of the new century, and the social and urban development of China is still facing a serious crisis. This is reflected by an insufficient population and an extreme lack of population density in the city core. This seems to contradict common sense. People tend to detect more tangible problems in a city like air pollution, traffic congestion, short supply of resources, and the like. Many are misled to believe that such urban malaise is mainly due to an overpopulation and high densities in the city. As such, even the experts have started to actively discuss how to relieve cities of its metropolitan population, how to develop small and medium cities or towns, and even idyllic village proposals are receiving undue attention. Chinese cities are expanding at an unprecedented speed, but under such a misguided logic. From 1990 to 2015, the rate of urbanization doubled from twenty-six to fifty percent, and the urban population grew one and a half times from 2.8 to 6.9 billion. However, the amount of land being developed as cities more than tripled from 12,200 to 50,000 million square kilometers over the same period. This is based on the official statistics, but the actual amount of developed land may be well over 100,000 million square kilometers. Officially, the urban population density over the same period has decreased by forty percent, implying that the real population density may have decreased even more. This implies that during the twenty-five years of rapid urbanization in China, the urban population density is rapidly decreasing. China is experiencing a rapid suburbanization of cities.

Illusion of Urbanity

Chinese cities are being thinned. They can be seen as the making of a thin-crust pizza—to use a food analogy—but what is worrying is that the pan does not have a boundary. The rate of adding flour and water to the crust is lagging behind the stretching of the dough, thus the pizza succeeds in becoming thinner and thinner, and holes are forming in many places. American cities had expanded along its highways, while Chinese ones are expanding along its high-speed railways. The railway stations that are being constructed often add a direct and exponential boost to the growth of the urban built-up area. Islands of high-rise residential neighborhoods in large-scale urban blocks are being scattered along the railway lines, isolated by kilometers of low-density and poorly urbanized areas. Even basic urban amenities along these stretched areas are not secured. There is an illusion of urbanity, as their access to social functions and the capacity to serve as communities are more rural than rural. New land leases are rare in the original city center, and urban development can be slow in the urban core. By comparison, newly urbanized areas are encouraged to develop rapidly. Advancements in engineering and infrastructure building, including the construction of tunnels, bridges, sanitation and other municipal services, and communication networks, and the reclamation of lakes and seas, have lowered the cost of land development as China expands horizontally on a plan. Together with other transportation expertise, such as high-speed railways, metro systems, and highway systems, low-density urban expansion is being propelled at an enormous capacity. China has entered into an era of thinned cities.

Insufficient Population Density

The most serious problem is China's population growth is dropping fiercely. There is no longer sufficient population to fill these rapidly thinning suburban cities. Within a decade, the Chinese population would peak at 1.5 billion, just 0.1 billion or a hundred million more than that what China has now. Based on the sixty percent urbanization rate predicted for this time, cities currently totaling 100,000 square kilometers in area would accommodate an urban population of 900 million. This means that the population density would not be able to meet the government target of 10,000 persons per square kilometer. The relaxation of the one-child policy to allow for two children per family is failing to deliver the required population growth rate at the moment. China may even need to relax its immigration policy to attract immigrants from around the world to boost its population. Chinese cities are being rapidly thinned under all types of divergent, if not contradictory, policies. As a rapidly aging society, would China be prepared to abandon the old and retired to the desolate thinned cities? A high concentration of a diverse population in a city is still the best environment to generate a socially sustainable and harmonious urban development. But a thinned city would not only have a sparse population, it would have the characteristics of a homogenous enclave with limited social capacity for outsiders to integrate.

Land prices have surged in city centers because new land is non-existent or limited in supply. Hence, they tend to be planned only to yield the highest economic returns. When these pieces of land are being redeveloped, they would likely become high-quality Grade A offices, commercial centers, luxury gated residences, or other mono-functional programs. By new means of mass transportation, urban inhabitants would be able to transit between different locations and urban functions in the city. Unfortunately, because of extremely high land cost, the city center would eventually be monopolized by industry giants, making it difficult for small holdings and start-ups to find affordable work spaces. Many would resort to commuting long distances to find affordable homes or work spaces, and this phenomenon has become a painful experience in many cities in China. A great deal of resources, disposable income, and time are being spent on commuting. In major Chinese cities, the average commuting time per day is over sixty minutes. Productivity is eroded, and the quality and stability of family and community lives are being challenged. Moreover, both the clearing out of the city center and the expansion of yet more outer metropolitan ring roads would further lengthen the commuting time.

Isolated Islands

The type of urbanization undertaken by China in a short span of three decades has turned cities into isolated islands connected only by commuting. The Chinese city is trapped eternally in the opening stages of the *Go* board game, where the urban inhabitants are hemmed in by the playing stones. Dispersed on the game board, they are alienated and unable to enjoy the boundless space around them. Yet the board keeps expanding outwards because of an uncontrollable economic development. What is then a good attitude towards urban design? Should Chinese cities support or oppose the idea of urban expansion? Enrique Peñalosa, the Mayor of Bogotá in Colombia, once argued that "a city can be friendly to either pedestrians or automobiles, but not both simultaneously." Chinese cities must regain its compactness and density, and they must become more walkable. By attaining a higher density of 40,000 persons per square kilometer, or 25 square meters per person, Chinese cities can create more social intensity as the foundation for a more socially and economically sustainable development. A 62.5-by-62.5-meter pedestrian block is the ultimate dimension for solving the issue of traffic, but traffic should not be the final goal. There must be a more idealistic return to a vibrant street life in the city. There must be a pleasant experience for the future of Chinese cities. There ought to be a central park within walking distance for recreation. It can take up to one-sixteenth of the urban land in a city. The city can be a twenty-four-hour space for everyone, where its citizens can spend an equal three parts of eight hours each on living, working, and resting. It is important to have nature both inside and outside of the city, making it easy for the society to reach it, whether it is the countryside or the city. It is important to understand that these values should be relative, not absolute. China does not lack people. It is suffering from cities that are too big in relation to its population. China does not need to fill empty cities with ghosts.

THE OPEN CITY

LI HU AND HUANG WENJING

As design practitioners of the built environment in China today, we are often faced with two types of cities—the old, inherited from history and poorly preserved, and the new, built in haste often without thoughtful planning or careful execution. In both cases, public spaces for the people are severely lacking. This is largely because public space never existed with great importance throughout the history of Chinese urbanism. In the master plans today, which are driven by capital and market profit, public spaces are still not receiving the attention they deserve. By and large, the urban history of China was a history of closeness, totalitarian control, and forced compliance.

The old city plan of Beijing was absolutely beautiful as a graphic, to the extent that Le Corbusier, in his book *The City of Tomorrow and its Planning*, would use the plan of Beijing of the Ming dynasty to describe the importance of order. Yet he had never been to China and would not understand that all its order and beauty would happen only within the high city walls. There was no concept of public social life—not in the Forbidden City and the imperial gardens, nor in the courtyard dwellings, which had an inward focus on individual families. This Beijing was a city that embodied absolute control by an autocratic and privileged class.

Open Office's school campus at Fangshan. Image courtesy of Budi Lim, 2015

Drive towards Modernity and City of Generosity

In the process of China's overdrive towards modernity, historical urban structures are no longer practical or functional, yet new structures are still being constructed. In the age of globalization, our cities have been greatly transformed on the superficial level; yet internally, the cities still have a long way to catch up. The scale of our cities is so much grander, extending both horizontally and vertically. But on a social level, openness, generosity, and freedom are largely ignored. The root of the problem lies in our culture today. We lack real respect and care towards every individual. We are in urgent need of cities that are open and adaptable to the processes of modernization. Confining Chinese society within the courtyard walls can no longer be sufficient. We must see the great needs of public spaces in all forms and scales, all open and free, serving society at large.

We have an immediate need for a city of generosity based on common respect. There would be no loneliness or nobleness in a city where people are more honest with one another, in a city where everyone has a job. Public spaces ought to be far more generous, especially when they are established in different forms and scales. Green urban squares and community centers would certainly be open to everyone, encouraging a coexistence of the noble and the common, of individuality and collectivity. In this city, architects must value every chance to build as an honor to serve society. We ought to spend more time thinking and achieving details that are more socially provocative. In this city, natural systems would be highly respected. We must seize every chance to protect and restore our natural systems. We must not cut off rivers irrationally in the name of protecting our urban environment, not deprive native habitats in favor of urban sprawl, and not damage our rural areas. Eventually, we must realize that the more the natural environment and the rural areas are improved, the easier our cities will become more habitable. The awkward situation we are in must come to an end.

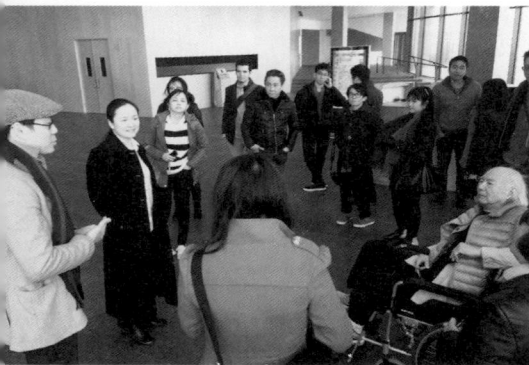

Study trip to Beijing No.4 High School Fangshan Campus. Image courtesy of Jeremy Chia, 2015

The planning of entirely new cities and the complete redevelopment of existing cities are both daunting tasks. They are incredibly difficult and time consuming. On the other hand, buildings can have a faster and more direct impact as catalysts in the re-energizing of our urban lives. Buildings are charged with the responsibility of connecting people, linking new interventions with history, and opening up cities that were previously closed. Buildings must stitch together broken communities, bring together new narratives of events and spaces, and regenerate cities with pleasant surprises and dynamic energies. When the number of such buildings increase, they will form networks of urban energizers, enhancing their impact on urban repair and regeneration. We hope that open and pleasant buildings will remedy our self-centered and short-sighted urban condition, and eventually redefine our future cities. The open cities we hope for might not be very clean or orderly on the surface, but they must be lively and energetic. Open cities must allow the harmonic coexistence of the rich and the poor, and of the individual and the collective. They are cities of high density and efficiency, but with ample and diverse public spaces; they are cities in which the artificial and the natural are balanced.

Lost the Power of Thinking about the Future

In the past decade or so, changes taking place in our cities were too drastic. We have lost old relationships between the city and nature, as we rush to build new ones. Our planet is being transformed not only by old cities like Beijing, but also new ones such as Shenzhen. Having lived in Beijing and New York for a decade respectively, we have made some observations about the two cities. We have contemplated the interactions between their spaces, and critically examined the aspects that were lost in Chinese urban spaces and the alienated relationship between architecture and society. In the transition from New York to my home country, we had changed our focus from materiality, space, and light to broader issues of society and the natural environment. There was always a strong fixation on the tectonics and construction of a building, yet we gradually realized that these were not the most urgent issues. We ought to think about the issues pertaining

Discussion session at the Linked Hybrid, Beijing.
Image courtesy of Budi Lim, 2015

to our city instead. Thus, in some of our larger undertakings, we have been trying to create public spaces even within privatized projects. We still believe that architecture can change the world, hence we are looking for a new type of practice that can directly confront the challenges of our times. Our attention to the city is an attempt to implement changes that can influence the social lives of the public.

In China, the process of social and architectural modernization is taking place without a deep consciousness. Architecture is supposed to generate a widespread social and urban revolution, but architects and professionals of the built environment have not started to think. The focus has been given over to superficial aspects, such as the thin surfaces of facades, artistic expressions, and other forms of design refinements. Or architects would simply follow market trends, or practice in rural areas so as to avoid the challenges of the city. Compared to China, the development of architectural theory in the West and Japan are considered more far-reaching and universal. Western and Japanese societies had experienced modernization at the same stage, but people still did not fully understand the spirit of modernism. Modernism is not an architectural style, as is generally misunderstood. Instead, it is a revolution of spirit. We simplified it as an architectural style when we did not know what it actually stood for. I believe that this misunderstanding has misled us for too long. While architecture in advanced societies such as Japan remained popular, architects in Japan have come to realize that they have lost the power of thinking about the future since the Metabolist movement.

Restore the Revolutionary Power of Architecture

Nowadays, the city is always saturated and has a healthy foundation, and its inhabitants can live a relatively comfortable life. Architecture in the West and Japan have shrunken in scale, as they continue to strive for perfection and small pleasurable moments. Certainly, there is a need to pay more attention on the noumenon of the building, but the definition of noumenon in architecture is still up in the air and differs from person to person. Before a big revolution, we do not have to focus on the small moments of pleasure, but initiate moments of small revolutions. In a building or a neighborhood, we can create a culture of generous and open spaces. We can challenge the thinking of the old and create a new type of architecture. We can stop simply relying on existing modes and types of architecture that are imported from other regions. No matter where they are and when they are occurring, China needs something different now!

For a long time, Chinese scholars have not been brave enough to reform. They chose instead to revel in the peaceful landscapes of yesteryears, without realizing the aspect of the Chinese scroll painting had changed from the vertical, with a focus on the grandeur of landscape, to the horizontal, with an emphasis on the expression of narration. Step by step, Chinese culture has begun to lose its power, not to mention its capacity to uphold independent thinking. Today, the situation is very different because of consumerism and a misplaced social hierarchy, but we seem to be still looking for the same general benefits. As a discipline, architecture has been misguided as the maker of an image or an object, without realizing it has no impact at all if it does not participate in an urban space. The emphasis on aestheticism is seen as the only recourse when our overloaded visual identities and instant media environment have become increasingly acceptable. Architecture no longer strikes any nerve in society or challenges our conservative customs. There is no cause for revolution. This kind of thinking has existed in China for a long time. We must restore the revolutionary power of architecture! Architecture is a force that can change the future with creativity!

RECASTING SHOUGANG

JEREMY CHIA AND ANDREW LEE

Beijing barely has time to catch its breath in the nation's pursuit of economic development and prosperity. Rapid industrialization was a prominent factor in spurring growth, and the Shougang Steel Mill has long loomed large as a visual depiction of the engine at work since 1919. As a one-time largest steel mill in China's, Shougang produced a whopping ten million tons at its peak output. The steel it produced fed the Chinese economy for nearly a century, as well as several thousands of workers and their families. We had the benefit of visiting the blast furnace of the Shougang Steel Mill No.3 Plant, and as we clambered up the steep slope towards it, we got truly acquainted with the magnitude of its physical size. An entire society flourished from this industry, and like the size of a small city, the district that surrounded the mills benefitted as a whole. By the turn of the century, Shougang started to become an embarrassing liability—manufacturing processes were constantly permeating the environment with sooty pollution, and the wasteful consumption of resources during production meant it could no longer be tolerated.

Field visit to the Shougang Steel Factory. Image courtesy of H. Koon Wee, 2015

Against the showpiece of the 2008 Beijing Olympics, decisive measures were taken to construct and preserve the image of an ascendant China. Even Shougang's reputation as a center of industry was inadequate. Plans were made to gradually relocate the factory to a neighboring province some two hundred kilometers away, and steel production was halted before and during the Games.

Soft Power in the Form of Culture, Politics, and Diplomacy

The end of 2010 marked the closure of Shougang's activities in Beijing, coinciding with problems dogging the steel industry nationwide. Overcapacity and low prices had forced many steel makers to go bust. The authorities were instituting reforms to modernize the steel industry, but more crucially they determined that the country would re-orientate itself away from manufacturing, and towards knowledge and services sectors instead. This was the advent of a new Chinese economy it claimed—and what would be more apt than to rehabilitate the abandoned Shougang site into an industrial theme park attraction? Taking cues from the art zones located in and around other parts of Beijing, such as the famed 798 Art District, the proposal would appeal to artists to set up workshops and studios in the disused facilities, and subsequently draw in the visitors and tourists. How successful would such a project be?

In China's advancement to become a global superpower, the government has not only built on its "hard power" in the elements of the military and economy, it has also taken steps to broaden its "soft power" in the form of culture, politics, and diplomacy. The most noticeable campaigns include the setting up of multiple Confucius Institutes worldwide to teach and disseminate the Chinese language and culture. Arts and culture fostered within the country can likewise be used to generate further interest both domestically and overseas. Such cultural production would easily reach a critical mass, should the government continue to support the growth of art districts, where creatives can live, work, and exchange ideas conveniently. But can government-sanctioned art zones be truly successful in providing a new space and institutionalized support for artists? Or are they just another attempt to reap commercial advantage and accumulate profits from artistic activities, as evidenced by the uncontrolled property speculation that has occurred in some art districts? Is it possible to strike a balance to achieve both aspirations?

A man walks past the dilapidated Shougang Metal Factory. Image courtesy of Budi Lim, 2015

A man walks past the dilapidated Shougang Metal Factory. Image courtesy of Budi Lim, 2015

Post-Industrial Commons and Nostalgia

In understanding the new economy that Chinese urban planning strategies must operate within, a few principles and key requirements stand out. First, there is increased awareness of the need for urban designers to appreciate the local society and context and to work from the ground up. This is the only way to attain maximum value for the lives of the inhabitants, rather than to unwittingly serve big businesses and corporations that capitalize and extract value from the art districts. By engaging the locals, planners can determine accurately what components are necessary and beneficial to the district. This will entail establishing new cooperative models for engaging the grassroots and civil societies, and abandoning top down or overly prescriptive planning guidelines. Second, a provision of the commons is crucial. The commons include resources that are made accessible to all members of society, such as public spaces and other forms of urban amenities. They represent inclusivity and diversity, and celebrate sharing. Such commons will encourage and meet unintended and spontaneous uses and needs, promoting a genuine culture of creativity. Third, the modernist approach of functional division must be rejected, because the success of any urban precinct ought to be based on ensuring that it remains lively and occupied with constant social activities. The monolithic condition of single-use districts bears great risk with the rapid change of economic cycles and technological advancements. Heterogeneity across the activities within such a district would boost the exchange and confluence of ideas.

As our visit to the blast furnace concluded, we had a glimpse into the life of a steel worker, as he would have experienced the city of industry in its heyday. We were led to ascend further up a nearby hill, where an ancient temple complex was located. From this vantage point, a mix of deities cast a watchful eye over the factory grounds. Here lay what had been the spiritual center of Shougang. Gazing at the rusting husks of the mills, a number of questions inevitably came to mind: What was the significance of retaining the factory buildings? Were there tangible benefits, or was it mere nostalgia? How would such monumental architecture fit in forthcoming conservation plans for Shougang? In our speculative opinion, careful appropriation of the existing buildings and their historical forms would be an important factor. There also ought to be a strategic melding of the planning and vision of the state, together with the district's future inhabitants and their needs, to collectively determine just how bright the future of such industrial heritage would be. With intermittent streaks of the midday sun piercing a sky tinged in grey, the cathedral-like spire of the No.3 blast furnace cast a long shadow on the rest of the industrial surroundings in Shougang. For now, they stand as markers for a period past. It remains to be seen if these well-grounded structures can be polished to reflect and shine as future representations of a strident Beijing.

Heterogeneity across the activities within such a district would boost the exchange and confluence of ideas.

DAILY LIFE AS WORLDVIEW

WANG SHU

Architecture in contemporary China has been mired in a kind of inner poverty as it does not have an interiority to speak of. If the connection between the interiority and exteriority of space is most important, as affirmed in traditional architectural theory, then architecture, without its interior, would not have an exterior. All that is left would be a hollow appearance. From this point of view, if the city is the exterior of contemporary China, then the rural is its interior. In the massive tide of urban construction in China, no one with a sense of history can afford to be complacent. Within three decades, the urban civilization of this country has fallen into ruins. Villages, which formed the basis of such a civilization, have all either been turned into ruins or are in the process of destruction. It is poignant to recall the eight years of rural reconstruction between 1931 and 1937 in Shandong by Liang Shuming. As the leader of the Rural Reconstruction Movement, Liang's visionary and intellectual efforts are undertaken by few today.

The urban village of Tengtou served as a powerful topic for the contemplation of China's state of architecture today. As the basis for the design of a city pavilion at the 2010 Shanghai Expo, the Ningbo Tengtou Pavilion remains an interesting commentary for rural reconstruction in China. In the outskirts of Ningbo, Tengtou is an orderly and clean village. There is almost no trace of the countryside in this urbanized fabric, composed of five distinct districts. The first district has orderly row houses constructed for migrant workers in the 1980s, the second has eclectic Neoclassical European villas built by the locals for themselves in the 1990s, the third for a country club for tourists, the fourth for an agricultural laboratory with greenhouses and aeroponic farms, and the fifth consists of a forest of trees planted by government officials, adjacent to a monumental wind turbine.

Deep Civilization but Depleted Interiors

Streets are complete with pedestrian walkways, traffic signals, and road signs, and aligned with a row of trees on each side, just like those in cities. Industries are developed beside the adjacent village, with up to RMB three billion worth of annual production. There are only eight hundred locals. But several thousand migrant workers, employed for the village-run enterprises, have caused great upheavals over the decades. Social stability was achieved by successive generations of strong and combative party committee, a democracy based upon open elections, and up-to-date and strict laws. In this village, one only plants trees but does not cultivate. The village is renowned for its ecological advocacy, specifically for its upkeep of water quality. Tengtou was honored with the United Nations Global 500 Award for Best Villages in 1993. In recent years, Tengtou started to put greater emphasis on cultural constructions. As the traditional buildings in the village were long gone, an ancestral shrine was moved from a nearby village, where tea is served and rural plays are performed. A large site model of a new masterplan developed by a university in Shanghai is placed in the office of the village committee. There are proposals suggesting new clusters of villas, typical of an American suburb, for tourist rental.

Tengtou has achieved remarkable and exemplary success. It is immensely difficult for a civilization, the result of millennia of accumulation, to systematically reconstruct itself once it has collapsed. Everything the villagers of Tengtou have achieved was accomplished by themselves in order to survive. The sheer fact that they were able to maintain at least the ecosystem, despite the collapse of its civilization, is an important lesson for our cities to learn. Unfortunately, Tengtou has no more than an efficient, high-density, and well-organized communal living, with an absence of anti-social behavior such as gambling. The problem is that Tengtou is not a primitive society, but one with a civilizational history of several millennia. It is apparent that the civilization of Chinese villages is almost fully depleted.

If Tengtou can be understood as a microcosm, then this microcosm has only a rough exterior. Its interior is almost devoid of the intricate structures associated with the realities of life. Claude Levi-Strauss made a remarkable suggestion that the greatness of all civilizations lies in the richness and variety of details. Such depth arises from the details of its social and aesthetic structures—to read the details is to understand its whole. In architecture, the interior of its microcosm can be revealed by its section, and the current state of Tengtou would reveal that it is as banal and dry as its exterior. Tengtou has no volumetric quality; in other words, it is deprived of a sectional quality. It is unproductive to only grapple with Tengtou in its present state. Instead, it may be worthwhile to explore the distinctiveness between its past and present architecture through its section, and it would be possible to conjecture its future.

Perceivable Visions and Structure

If one is authentic in the social and material experiences of daily life, its consequences should be directly perceivable. Its nature would not be concealed in something that is not observable. To perceive reality, one would need to have a real and particular vision. In architecture, there was an extraordinary technique of visual projection found in representations of reality, such as the Ming-dynasty woodblock prints of *The Plum in the Golden Vase*. A low viewing angle with a field of vision of about two to three stories defined the typical height of buildings in a projection of the "worldview" of its time.

Panorama of Tengtou. Image courtesy of Wang Shu

This drawing was an oblique projection where the horizon was held constant, and the vertical skewed to one side to maintain the continuity of the horizontal. This drawing analysis led to a new way of depicting the village life of Tengtou. In the panorama of Tengtou, the courtyard houses were divided at six to seven locations by walls, and the drawing was directly cropped at the edges of the paper to imply the continuity of the world it was depicting. Six or seven events of daily life were occurring simultaneously, each corresponding with household artifacts and clothing items, plants and animals, and constructions and scales, allowing a world of rich intricacies and details to be observed. In traditional Western architectural thought, an interior courtyard elevation of daily life would not be considered a façade worthy of depiction at all. In fact, the absence of formal façades in an everyday population of high density would require a drawing of multiplicity to be effective. This type of drawing would not be a bird's eye view, but a sectional view from a gently raised angle. It would not merely be a drawing, but a catalog of daily constructions capable of accommodating different social and material expressions as a new worldview.

Another exploration of social spaces began with a drawing that was horizontal in nature. There was really only one type of architecture in Tengtou, namely, the courtyard houses. The other types were merely variations with similar appearances of a high wall, and a small opening for access. One of the most comparable exemplars is the Hui Chun Tang Traditional Chinese Medicine Hall along the Hefang Street in Hangzhou.

Its form came out of a similar residential typology. It had a generic street front, but peering through the door opening, one would be struck by the confluence of complex timber construction and spaces, and dynamic movements of people living and working in it. Architecture must be an obsession of meticulous detail. There were more people conversing, socializing, and daydreaming than those getting medicine and seeing the doctors. The scene was highly theatrical. But if one examines more closely, the people were harmoniously spaced around the two main halls on the first and second stories, and between the front and rear courtyards. In terms of its tactility, the outer wall was heavy, yet the interior was light and delicate. In terms of its illumination, the exterior was bright as day, while the interior was clear even in the shadows. In terms of its quality as an architectural drawing, it was akin to having an ability to enter the organs of the human body, and circulating with a freshness of space. The opening was a hole, within which one could only observe the surroundings section by section. The two sectional methods of observation constructed a world that would be particularly compassionate and tolerant of the highly differentiated social lives in this world. This anticipates a humanism that is visible, a spatial realm that can be drawn and built, and a structural possibility for the future.

It is immensely difficult for a civilization, the result of millennia of accumulation, to systematically reconstruct itself once it has collapsed.

Land and Density

There is a relationship between the unique tectonics of architecture and the population and density of a place. Zhejiang was heavily populated and land was scarce. As a result, its buildings and their use of land was always efficient. Traditionally a whole clan would live together in a domestic dwelling with a clearly demarcated exterior, whereas each unit of its interiors would be a microcosm of intricate details. Each branch of the family tree has its independent area in the interior. Each clan has a dignified front along the street façade—something Italian architects had a great talent for. The frontages of various clans along a street would establish a dialogue with one another due to their important but subtle differences. Inside the exterior walls, architectural order was established in essence by a syntax of sections and elevations that has been carefully laid out since antiquity. These were ethos well adapted to the region.

The fact that the site model in the village committee office resembled an American suburb represented an inevitability of urbanization that took place in Tengtou. This laid the groundwork for an alternative Tengtou architecture. It was not merely to articulate the logic and understanding of traditional and regional dwelling form, but to structure the tactility of its essence. Novel artifacts could then be constructed through fragments of memory, without the burden of history. Because the past is always fragmented and blur, its appearance would always be expected. Land would be highly collective, where each building would be three stories tall, the lowest level for a home factory, shops, and warehouses, while the two upper floors would be a series of courtyards for three generations of around four households or ten inhabitants. Greening would be implemented to the maximum, covering more than fifty percent of the area under roof cover. Variations could be developed for every possible type of village building, from schools, offices, and hospitals to hostels, hotels, and museums. In terms of the relationship between landscape and its architecture, one must not forget that the tradition of the region had already attained a highly poetic form, not mere agricultural production. This required the new vision to match the greater depth of the region.

With a particular vision in mind, one would begin to notice that Chinese paintings have always carried the crucial languages of the visual realm. The condition of shelter in *The Mountain of Five Cataracts* by the painter Chen Hongshou from the Ming dynasty revealed a new possibility for rural architecture. A series of layered openings were created by enormous trees, which seemed to reach the skies. Even a geometric language could be found in the hills in the background far above the trees. This represented a typical but immensely architectural worldview prevalent in China. This two-dimensional scroll painting revealed a section that cut between human society and nature, transcending any specific historical time or event. As one of a few painters skilled in painting human figures in the Ming dynasty, Chen only drew a single scholar in the clearing who never looks outside the painting. In Lu Xun's collection of essays *Literature in the Age of Revolution* written in the 1930s and 1940s, he rearticulated the distinct relationship between nature and Chinese society as "branches so dense it shadows the sun."

Chen Hongshou, *The Mountain of Five Cataracts*. Image courtesy of Cleveland Museum of Art

Materiality and Labor

In traditional Chinese architecture, the choice of *wuliao* (materiality) remains the top priority, whereas *cailiao* (material) is an imprecise term. *Wuliao* entails *wuxing* (a sense of qualitative form), which is humanist by implication. Drawn to the earlier Ningbo Museum of History, the government of Ningbo explicitly requested the use of old ceramic tiles and bricks, as well as bamboo formwork concrete for the Tengtou Pavilion. In an effort to question the distinctiveness between the exterior and interior, the bamboo formwork concrete was applied to the internal finishes of the Tengtou Pavilion. It immediately changed the meaning of the architecture, where the exterior was supposed to possess a heaviness in its materiality, and the interior ought to feel light. It may seem there was a pathological obsession with materiality, but the other extreme would be an obsession with conceptual realm of architecture.

Concepts tend to be abstract, while materiality is always concrete. In this analysis, history would not be of people and events, but of the visual culture of materiality and its making. Architecture must not rely only on concepts. This understanding of materiality brings to mind a certain physicality of music, an equally abstract form, described by Roland Barthes. In his description of "The Grain of the Voice," in the remarkable anthology entitled *Image, Music, Text*, Barthes analyzed the voice of a performance, "which is directly the cantor's body, brought to your ears […] from deep down in the cavities."

There is always an anxiety with modern-day construction, where the large and formal construction companies would not comprehend a more artisanal and informal approach in the making of architecture, especially the vernacular clay tiles, the bamboo formwork concrete, and the bamboo cladding panels of Tengtou. The Tengtou Pavilion was finalized in May 2009. It was the last pavilion to start construction in the Best Practice Exhibition Area, and the first to be completed. Everything progressed well. The team responsible for the Tengtou Pavilion had been practicing with me since 2003 as apprentices, developing a combination of traditional techniques in contemporary experiments. They have built five free-standing pavilions and the Museum of History. Their awareness of the labor-intensive techniques was mature. This was the first time I did not have to work on the construction site. My apprentice would assure me, "Master, I know what to do." A Bukina Faso architect and friend thought it was a dream to be able to have such a well-developed team and construction methodology. For all of such brick-and-mortar projects, he thought he would need to be on site all the time to ensure instructions are being adhered to, otherwise everything would go wrong.

Memory without History

Closer to the completion of the pavilion, I had given my graduate students a drawing exercise to use eleven sectional axonometric drawings to reconstruct a field of vision of one kilometer. The context of this exercise was first two paintings of a long scroll painting of eight panels called *Mountain Villa* by Li Gonglin, a painter of the Northern Song dynasty. Li was renowned for his detailed line work, but in this context, the notion of detail not only referred to the physical density of the line drawing, but more so to a vision that combined the mind and the body. The first two paintings in question portrayed a view at a distance of one kilometer away in the first instance, but the second instance, a close-up view of one-to-one scale was portrayed. In other words, the former possessed an extroverted view, while the latter had an introverted view. However, upon closer analysis, the human figures in both paintings were completely identical. Both were at one-to-one scale, implying that both manners of observation can coexist conceptually.

Through their sectional qualities, the eleven reconstructed sectional axonometric drawings were implicitly able to assert control on the entirety of the architectural form. It

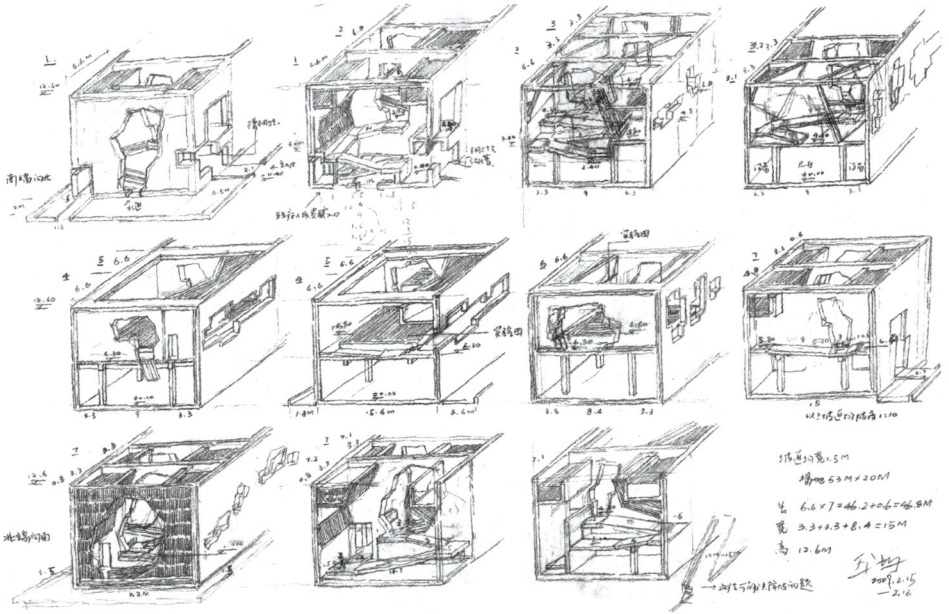

Eleven section sketches of Tengtou. Image courtesy of Wang Shu

became possible to holistically describe a new village through Tengtou, capturing all the highly differentiated intricacies of the world we live in. It raises the question of whether the resurrection of memory would still be possible if there was no viable history to cling on to. The anecdote in *A New Account of the Tales of the World* depicted Wang Rong as an esteemed government official, wearing ceremonial robes and riding in a wood pavilion-like carriage, passing by a wineshop and apprehensive about the past. This was a humble place where he used to drink and make merry with his friends Ruan Ji and Ji Kang, who had since passed away. Wang could only lament, "Even though it is so near, it seems as far away as the hills and rivers."

This essay is translated and adapted from Wang Shu, "poumian de shiye" [A Sectional Worldview], *Time+Architecture*, Issue 112, 2010/2, pp.81-87.

MULTIPLE IDENTITIES AND TEXTURAL DIVERSITY

MICHAEL KOKORA

Since the market-based economic reforms of 1978 and the resultant economic and physical transformations, China has been working to understand the tension between the dramatic scale of its urban growth and the richness of its cultural identities. To cope with the massive shift in population, new cities were built and villages were reformatted. This reformatting is physical as well as social, and it is used to support the sociopolitical state agenda. While not the only factor, these new urban plans have a powerful impact in shaping the current cultural identity of China, and in an effort to promote stability, they lead to increasing homogeneity and disaffection with the urban environment. This essay is a plea for architecture in the city to accommodate and innovate not only at the level of the built environment. It must also develop a range of highly tactile urban textures of diverse scales and types in its unbuilt and open spaces. Architects and landscape architects must create a framework for the open spaces and voids in the cities of China, in order to better relate to the past, and influence the emergent social and cultural forms.

One-size-fits-all Planning Module

The economic programs that led to China's shift from rural to urban were one of the main catalysts for large-scale urban planning. Documented by the World Bank in 2012, China crossed a threshold with more than fifty percent of the population living in cities, compared with eighty percent living in the countryside in 1978. This means close to five hundred million people moved from the countryside to cities between 1979 and 2012. In the 1950s, some ten thousand Soviet advisors were invited to assist in the postwar reconstruction. Like formatting a hard disk with a new operating system, two primary urban models were superimposed on the country to cope with this transformation: the superblock and the commune, according to Lu Duanfang's historical analysis. A third type, known as the urban village, evolved almost by accident to house the massive migrant labor force used to build the superblocks and communes. These urban villages are continuously upgraded and retrofitted, and their form persists today despite efforts at demolition. This shift from the rural to urban has come with a loss of cultural identity. In an informal survey that was discussed at length at the 2014 Mercator Salon XII hosted by the Ullens Center for Contemporary Art in Beijing, Stiftung Mercator found that many urban citizens still have strong feelings toward their *guxiang* or hometown, but few believe they will ever return. The provocation of "How to Construct Heimat?" formed the basis of a discussion between Michael Kahn-Ackermann, Shi Jian, and myself in Beijing.

The Soviet-style superblocks were problematic from the start. Their configuration as six-story slab blocks with symmetrical axes combined with a long perimeter meant street-facing units suffering from noise pollution, poor cross-ventilation, and broad façades facing west. Besides afternoon heat gain, west-facing windows are undesirable in China. In Chinese tradition, the west points toward the direction of death and afterlife, and therefore has poor real estate value. Chinese developers would often ask to minimize west-facing area or cut away floor area in west-facing floor plates to reduce the leasable area on west-facing facades. Communes often followed a similar layout as the superblock, with factories in place of some of the slab blocks for housing. The Soviet-style slab block is increasingly an endangered typology, but the 250-square-meter superblock unit remains the dominant urban planning module.

Architects and landscape architects must create a framework for the open spaces and voids in the cities of China, in order to better relate to the past, and influence the emergent social and cultural forms.

Superblocks are still used today, however, the internal organization has been distorted by new planning codes, and Euro-American influences. Planning codes address issues of orientation in residential development by enforcing a specific number of hours of direct sunshine in every apartment, resulting in more centralized building footprints. In the Shenzhen superblocks, one can find large, organically shaped swimming pools with tropical gardens surrounded by residential towers averaging forty stories—super-high-rise versions of gated communities in Florida draped with old European-style décor. Apart from high-rise housing or offices, these superblocks are also well suited for vast shopping malls. Given the size, almost any use would fit these superblocks—apartments, offices, convention centers, malls, or museums can occur in any block without any specific rationale or zoning. Even though Chinese cities have a well-developed metro and public transportation system, the scale of the superblocks force a reliance on automobiles and taxis, even to travel just a few blocks. For the uninitiated, imagine how walkable Manhattan would feel if there were only long blocks. Despite the superblock's flexibility and the mixed use grid, the overall result of the superblock is homogeneity. Audiences at the 2014 Mercator Salon XII echoed this concern, specifically the fact that every city feels almost identical in terms of its structure and planning, despite the radical cultural, climatic, and topographic differences across China. The superblock has become a one-size-fits-all planning module.

Often found adjacent to superblock developments, urban villages evolved out of the sheer necessity for workers housing. Yet, they represent one of the most vibrant pedestrianized urban forms in the modern Chinese city, particularly those in Guangdong. Once a source of urban crime, unseemly businesses, and a target of redevelopment, urban villages have persisted due to the continuous demand for an affordable workforce. Urban villages now provide affordable housing and offices adjacent to their high-priced superblock neighbors. Their dense urban form consists of a tight grid of square plan extrusions ranging from eight to fifteen stories in height, often not more than 1.5 meters apart, and less if the exposed duct work, gas lines, and plumbing are included. Their

Baishizhou, an urban village in Shenzhen, Guangdong. Images courtesy of Angelene Chan, 2013

small ten-square-meter footprint enforces a pedestrian environment, and their small retail spaces would spill out onto the narrow streets—wood panels are cut in a workshop next to hair salons, and clothing is washed next to massage parlors. Their population density can be as high as thirty seven thousand persons per square kilometer, according to David Wang in his 2016 book on Shenzhen urban villages. As a result, bustling informal markets and food stalls appear in the breaks where one grid meets another. In an urban village, migrant workers from vastly different regions and cultures in China would come together to form new communities.

Cultural Governance: Destruction as Protection

From a planning perspective, the superblock is extraordinarily efficient, and now that its dimensions are so engrained in Chinese planning it has become ubiquitous in reformatting large tracts of land. Whole cities can be built or destroyed, and rebuilt in a relatively short period of time. These state-mandated urban forms are not by accident, they are based as much on the urban economics of redevelopment as they are for social integration. Not unlike imposing a unified language requirement and national education testing standards, urban plans are also active tools for social formatting. There could be no more vivid examples than Kashgar, a city located in the Xinjiang Uyghur Autonomous Region. Xinjiang means "New Frontier," and Kashgar has been on the front line of cultural assimilation through urban reformatting. As a strategically important city along the Silk Road, Kashgar has a rich history of over two millennia. George Michell traces the history of Kashgar, showing it to be one of the most well-preserved Islamic cities in Central Asia. The Medina-like mat structures of stepped internal courtyards create privacy for the Islamic family unit, forming cloistered outdoor spaces for women to spend time with their families while unveiled. The clustered organization of thick masonry walls provide shade from the sun and thermal mass to negotiate the climate. In addition to housing, the old city is dotted with mosques, madrasas, stalls, and markets.

In the 1990s, a number of policies began encouraging more Han Chinese to move to Kashgar. The teaching of the Koran in mosques was banned, and all Uyghurs were required to learn Mandarin. The moat surrounding the city was filled and paved, and a central road was cut through the old city, opening a plaza directly fronting the main mosque, and henceforth allowing direct vehicular access by the police or military to subdue any social unrest. Eventually, tensions boiled over resulting in a number of Uyghur attacks, and a particularly violent one occurred in 2008. The next year, after the devastating Sichuan earthquake, a plan was announced to "save" Kashgar from a similar earthquake by demolishing and rebuilding as much as eighty-five percent of the old city while "respecting" local culture, and this was widely questioned by preservationists and the media. In 2009, Michael Wines wrote a *New York Times* piece entitled "To

Demolition works in Kashgar, Xinjiang. Image courtesy of Estelle Chan, 2010

Protect an Ancient City, China moves to raze it." In 2010, Kashgar was turned into a special economic zone for the greater Han Chinese population to live and invest, with the side benefit of diluting the existing Uyghurs population. By 2014, most of the Old City was leveled and Uyghurs were relocated into superblocks comprised of Soviet-style slab housing. Beatrice Kaldun, UNESCO's cultural specialist in Beijing, described the aftermath as a "desert in the city." The remains of the Old City have been turned into an ethnic theme park with a thirty-five RMB admission charge. In the same article featuring Kaldun's opinion, Dan Levin reports the distress and violence in the city, even though the Beijing Zhongkun Investment Group has leased the area from the neighborhood

Demolition and protection of the old city of Kashgar, Xinjiang. Images courtesy of Estelle Chan, 2010

Communist Party Committee for a "living Uyghur folk museum." Now, with teaching of the Koran banned and the urban fabric completely reformatted, the struggling Uyghur ethnic minority will be gradually swallowed into the growing state-sponsored Han Chinese population. Only a small theme park will remain after two thousand years of urbanized history.

High Tactility and New Identities

Beyond the much-needed conservation efforts in the historic cities of ethnic minorities or the lower economic classes, the mat-like developments of urban villages in Shenzhen, the *hutong*s in Beijing, or the medinas in Kashgar are forming within their remaining public and communal spaces an atomized collection of interconnected, loosely organized and alternative societies. In his 1967 lecture "Of Other Spaces," Michel Foucault described such conditions as a heterotopia, outlining a wide array of spaces from hospitals, libraries, museums, and cemeteries to gardens, brothels, colonies, and ships. These spaces, from the hierarchical to the chaotic, are all premised on the potential for multiple meanings, interpretations, and uses, despite their designated functions or intended meanings. The markets, streets, and plazas would certainly fit within Foucault's "heterotopology." Public space in China is rarely so reductive or scripted prior to the Cultural Revolution. Now, every space seemingly needs to be given a prescribed meaning. Public spaces are more often vast symbolic plazas fronting government headquarters, such as the Citizen's Square in Shenzhen, or commercially co-opted environments in shopping centers. While these spaces are heterotopias in their own right, they do not contribute as much to the layering of public space or a sense of intimacy that could be found in the cities and villages from China's past. Conservation efforts tend to thematize them or transform them into shopping districts like Lijiang or Kashgar, providing yet another sanitized or prescribed meaning.

To relieve the relentless homogeneity of the superblock, and its sharp and sudden scalar differences, China has to allow the creation of new and highly tactile urban forms, with a more gradual gradient and layering of public spaces and voids. Recently, much attention has been placed on the aesthetic of Chinese architecture and design. From copies of European buildings or whole European cities built as theme parks to the proliferation of *qiguai*, or weird, buildings. Instead of focusing on the design of architectural objects, planners, and architects should focus more on the fabric—the negative space as an object itself. In other words, they should engage in developing textural diversity in the open spaces. These spaces do not need to be so heavily planned and imbibed with meaning. If scaled well with their surroundings, these new textural spaces can derive their own meanings over time through their use and adaptation. During the discussion at the Ullens Center for Contemporary Art, Shi Jian described an example of creative public space development in Shenzhen. The government wanted a basketball court so people could have more communal space. Since there is virtually no free space available, and no high-rise was going to be demolished to make way for a basketball court, it was built on the top of a five-story building complete with a slide to reach the bottom. Imagine a highly tactile, continuous, and stepped roofscape of public sports venues and park spaces—such transformations in urban identity need not only be two-dimensional. Since its inception in the 1850s, a few active adaptable void-plans have been developed like the Ildefons Cerdà block plan for the Eixample District in Barcelona.

Although the puzzle-like void structure could not be fully realized, and it may too easily be co-opted by commercial developers, the idea of a sequence of recombinable voids could have resulted in a dynamic series of open public spaces. These spaces would require no particular programming other than community use and appropriation. In this context, aging superblocks in China must be rethought, and their current forms cut and subdivided. Large plazas and selected sections of open park spaces would allow more buildings at differing scales to coexist. New visions of textural diversity and high tactility in the open spaces of China should be allowed to evolve from the specific cultural and contextual conditions in China. New prototypes could be referenced and further innovated based on successful examples. Space planning is not the only response to an increasing cultural diversity in China. If the spaces themselves were less polarized and less rigidly defined, urban development would be open to multiple meanings and cultures. New forms of identity would come together to transform a country that is anything but homogenous.

URBAN RENEWAL AND THE ARCHITECTURE OF POWER

ZHAN YUAN AND RUAN HAO

The Chinese city is no longer the blank slate that it used to be during the period of mass construction. While urbanization is slowing down as a process, cities are turning from mass construction to urban regeneration. Old elements are being washed away every day from existing structures, while new contradictions are bedding in. Chinese society must start to confront the aftermath of the explosive period of construction. This essay presents the new campus of Tiantai No.2 Elementary School as a meditation on the problem of land shortage and urban renewal in China, while cognizant of the power of architecture in this process. Situated in the old city of Taizhou in the province of Zhejiang, this project explored the possibility of resisting mass demolition in urban renewal that is widespread in China. Since its conception, the design of the school struggled with the dilemma brought about by urban renewal. The site is a surprisingly near-perfect rectangle situated as the remainder of an old urban block, but it occupies an interiorized urban condition, facing mostly the rear-windows of other street-lined housing blocks as an urban infill condition.

With the introduction of a two-hundred-meter roof-top running track, mandatory for schools of this scale, the school gained over three thousand square meters of usable floor area on the ground. This freed ground would facilitate a stronger continuity with the existing fabric on the ground level, with three distinct vistas connecting to the main entry of the school, the side entry, and a south-facing garden. In order to break the monotony of a parallel setback from the neighboring buildings, and to create more green courtyards to be shared with the neighbors, the building was set at a fifteen-degree angle against its rectilinear site. With the smaller pockets of spaces between the new envelope, its site boundary, and the neighboring buildings, there can be a more animated interaction with the older urban fabric. The lifting of the running track created the possibility of a lower four-story building, instead of a five-story form planned as part of the original competition brief. This lowered height allows the new school to remain very close to the prevailing

01 SITE AREA AND BOUNDARY   02 AREAS OF SPORTS FACILITIES   03 EXTRUSION OF MASSING

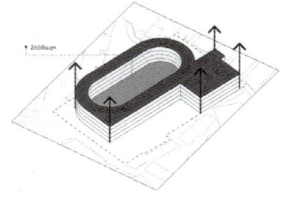

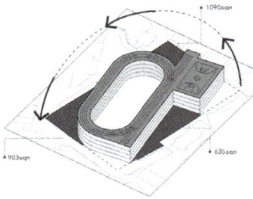

04 ROTATION OF MASSING   05 GROUND SPACE CONTINUITY   06 VERTICAL CIRCULATIONS

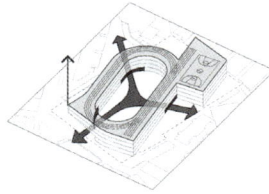

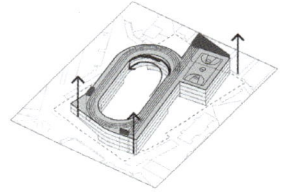

Connectivity and reversed Panopticon. Image courtesy of LYCS Architecture

heights of the neighboring residential buildings, taking on a more sympathetic approach towards its surrounding urban context. Given the conundrums and contradictions brought about by urban renewal in China and the multitude of limitations that had to be confronted, architecture has an important role to play in helping to resolve the problems of land shortage through a win-win solution. New typologies have to be invented, so that architecture can defend the freedom and rights of its users while satisfying its regulatory functions. Even when confronted with urban renewal issues, architecture must remain central as a courageous and powerful intervention while blending harmoniously with its surroundings at the same time. It is precisely the uniqueness of the land use criteria in the face of urban renewal, and the complex and high-regulated requirements of the program, that had forced a more imaginative architectural response.

Fragmentation in the Metropolitan Condition

The placement of the race track on the rooftop of Tiantai No.2 was a strategy that is foremost a response to the emotional needs of the children. Most urban buildings would ignore or even suppress the emotions of the users. Due to the tight site boundary and the safety requirements that confine the school inwardly, the children's desire to break out to express themselves is exceptionally strong, and this necessitates a moment of breakthrough in design. The design of the school opens key spaces up to the sky, and it reflects this emotional need as well as defends the rights of the children to feel the freedom and happiness of an unrestrained sprint. The outline of the building's massing traces precisely the shape of the standard race track, unencumbered by unnecessary

Aerial view of the elementary school and vicinity. Image courtesy of Su Shengliang / LYCS Architecture

formal language or excessive ornaments. The utility of the race track is apparent, hence its authenticity. This seemingly romantic response is backed up by strict rational thought. The massing of the teaching block is extruded upwards from the outline of the rooftop track, creating an extensive amount of activity space on the ground floor for students to run around and interact freely. At the same time, the oval teaching block gives students a sense of security through its introverted character. By placing the race track on the roof and opening up the ground level, natural lighting and ventilation between the front and back of the building are optimized.

The raised race track was a method of dealing with the restricted conditions of the land. This unexpected vertical redistribution of functions brings to mind a kind of functional stratification discussed by Rem Koolhaas in his analysis of the Downtown Athletic Club in his 1978 book *Delirious New York*. Koolhaas describes this as a classic capitalist representation of the "culture of congestion," where the sports club experiences a disjunction between its exterior and interior, and between its form and its function. While its exterior appears to blend in as a typical Manhattan skyscraper, its interior houses an exercise and sports program that is distinct from, but complementary to, the financial and office programs that dominate Manhattan. Each story of the building is unrelated to the next in the horizontally divided skyscraper, relying on the elevators to shuttle the users and visitors vertically to their spaces. Every floor plan of the Downtown Athletic Club is an abstract composition of social activity, with no prescribed order or hierarchy. While the raised race track subscribes to the vertical separation of functions in a similarly congested old urban district, Tiantai No.2 did not share the intention to keep the kind of social fragmentation that Koolhaas observes in Manhattan. His argument was that such autonomy and alienation were allegorical to the fantastical and fragmented realities of the metropolitan condition. While Taizhou is not nearly as congested or as deliriously capitalist as Manhattan, the autonomy that Koolhaas observed would not serve a school particularly well. Instead, Tiantai No.2 introduces a highly visible staircase that allows students and the weekend public to connect directly between the ground and the roof track.

Bottom-Up Power and Open Architecture

There is another project that bears a resemblance to the unique sense of being lifted up from the ground. Instead of students running freely and more closely to the sky, it was a track on the roof for the testing automobiles, in operation in Turin since 1923. In a social sense, this was an experiment and expression of the process of industrial production, and the capacity of the workers serving in it. It was so remarkable that Le Corbusier would suggest it as a suitable model for town planning in the Avant-garde era. By placing the test track on the roof, the Fiat Lingotto Factory achieved a wholly integrated system of production, assembly, testing, and product design. The ring-shaped roof of the factory was an enclosed production system, where the building form was itself an attributing factor in the great efficiency of the production line. The intensification of production was to improve efficiency and land utilization. There is, however, a poignant relationship of these Avant-garde industrial forms to the society of Italy in the 1920s, especially when armed workers had taken over and occupied factories in a demand for social change. It was unfortunate

> Old elements are being washed away every day from existing structures, while new contradictions are bedding in. Chinese society must start to confront the aftermath of the explosive period of construction.

that this forgotten and failed revolution of 1919 in Turin would pave the way for the emergence of a Fascist regime. By the 1970s, Fiat would recuperate some of the missed opportunities of its architectural innovations by reintroducing new social functions to the Lingotto Factory, in what Jeff Diamanti describes in his 2014 essay "The Cultural Work of Architecture: Fixed and Social Capital at Fiat" as new socially-minded investments in recreational, educational, cultural, and entrepreneurial start-up facilities.

As the Lingotto Factory was set apart from the city environment, the existence of the ring-shaped test track on the roof was a rendition of top-down authority. On the other hand, the roof race track of Tiantai No.2 should be seen as the ground pushing upwards to the sky, with clear and visible connectivity and porosity. The factory can be seen as a highly efficient yet narcissistic machine for production, and its authoritative power was hugely strengthened and centralized in the ring-shaped architecture. Yet, Tiantai No.2 ought to be seen as an excavation of the power embedded in the classic concentrated ring-shaped spatial form, albeit in a different scale. The rooftop sports ground serves the children and neighbors of the school. Due to the media attention gained and social impact delivered, Tiantai No.2's strong urban intervention turned the school into a center of the neighborhood. This kind of centrality is one not of the authority but of its citizens. The ring-shaped race track is open to the public during the weekends, so there is not only social interaction and recreation but also a way to get closer to the sky. The race track has become a public space and a space of respite in the midst of the bustling urban living environment. This ring-shaped architecture is definitely a concentration of power, however, this power belongs to the children and the public, as an expression that is bottom-up and open.

Introversion and Security: Weakened and Reversed Panopticon

The ring-shaped inner courtyard of Tiantai No.2 provides a sense of introversion and security to students. As students move through the transitional entry plaza from the city to the central courtyard, they would experience a spatial sequence of openness of the city to a compression under the ring of classrooms, and open again in the courtyard. These are clear psychological clues that guide students and the public as they enter into the school. They are able to see one another across the courtyard void, and as a result it augments the playfulness of the space. There is room for wandering and upward movements. Teachers can see students better as there are no hidden angles. This ring-shaped typology can be traced back to Jeremy Bentham's Panopticon and its spatial model of surveillance. In his conception of a prison, a conspicuous observation tower is located at its very center, yet it is also the darkest and most secured space. Prison cells are arranged and lit in such a way that the prisoners are under surveillance in such a way that they have no knowledge of who is watching and when they are being watched. Tiantai No.2 is a weakened and reversed version of Bentham's behavioral control model. Here, the authority is not at in the center of the ring. The center is hollow, and flooded with natural light that makes everything open and visible. The visual control is not outspread from the center, but mutually observable from the periphery to the center. Along the corridors of the ring, students and teachers are illuminated by healthy sunshine, with a sense of community brought about by the visual interaction. Against the school's white walls, the clothing and movements of the students and the general public add color to a gray city like paint on canvas. The students and weekend public have become the real subjects of the architecture. Just as the sightlines and spaces intersect, so do the students and functions of play and learning. The inner courtyard and roof race track have transformed this new school into an openly interactive learning space and a public space in the middle of an urgent and intense urban renewal process.

This essay is translated and expanded from Zhan Yuan, "Chengshi gengxin zhong de 'wuding paodao' Zhejiang Tiantai di'erxiaoxue" [Rooftop Track in Urban Renewal: Tian Tai No.2 Primary School, Zhejiang], *Time+Architecture*, Issue 129, 2015/1.

05
RESISTING

The notion of resistance can be taken quite literally as the opposite sides of the same coin within the regiment of control. On a technological level, unsuspecting developments of infrastructure and other seemingly positive urban improvements for the purpose of efficient commuting can end up distorting and producing massive inequality. There is an unpredictable but dynamic acceptance of the spaces of contradiction, where boundaries between the private and public are blurred, and the limits of the legal and illicit are vague. Everything is under negotiation. The appropriation or borrowing of resources, especially from the public and the state, was prevalent in a China with scarce resources. Many would exploit the provisions by the Communist Government, calling it *chi guojia* or feeding off the country's resources. This can apply to a segment in the Chinese population who are disenfranchized by the upward mobility promised by the ethos of new consumerism. This brings to mind Michel de Certeau's idea of tactics in everyday spatial practices, in order to subvert the power of control over these spaces. Such tactics of resistance are themselves not freed from the necessity of an economic form of survival.

Banners are hung by a *xiaoqu* in Shanghai in protest of adjacent public construction works.
Image courtesy of Lam Lai Shun, 2014

POWER OF THE GROUND

ZHU TAO

What are the core values of Hong Kong? Without hesitation, everyone will declare they are freedom, democracy, human rights, rule of law, and so on. These are important values we should strive for. As an architect, I would like to point out that there is another core value of Hong Kong that is equally precious—the ground of our city. It is less abstract than freedom and democracy, but it is often ignored. The ground is the foundation of freedom and democracy. The ground on which we walk about comfortably and freely is also the place we rest, gather, organize public activities, and act collectively.

End of the Pedestrian

Hong Kong is a city governed by technocracy. Many government officials and planners hold onto outdated ideas that the ground is supposed to serve primarily vehicular traffic—the faster they go, the better. They are used to letting highways and parking lots occupy the ground, and they deal with pedestrians in three ways:

By putting them underground, as in Tsim Sha Tsui and East Tsim Sha Tsui. For the convenience of traffic, more and more pedestrian crossings are blocked by balustrades, forcing them to burrow into the underground network to get to the other side of the road.

By lifting them up, as in the Central Government Complex in Admiralty. During the Yellow Umbrella Movement, having walked and chanted all the way from Victoria Park, demonstrators would have lost their energy by the time they arrive at Admiralty. The rally is forced to divide into three, and one by one they have to line up to take the escalator, the elevator, or the stairs. Then they have to walk past the elevated podium and over the expressway to reach the government headquarters that is ironically known as "the door that is always open." How mean is this suppressive and ridiculous bottleneck effect in front of the government complex towards public space and civil actions?

By connecting the underground with the overpass, for example, from the Central subway station to Exchange Square, IFC, and the Star Ferry pier; or from the Wanchai subway station to Wanchai Exhibition Center and Wanchai Ferry Pier. Notably, the connection from the Admiralty subway station to the promenade, following the typical local strategy, was supposed to be a double connection with both an underground tunnel and an overpass. Especially for a civic space frequented by the public like the Government Complex, it is important to provide easy and convenient transportation for the citizens. But according to a Legislative Council report from 2003, the government was worried about terrorist attacks and decided not to construct any subway stations or tunnels underneath the Complex. The result was negative—the government's "door is always open," but "open" mostly to the cameras of the tourists in Tsim Sha Tsui on the north side of the harbor. On the south side, there is only an overpass connecting it to the busy streets in Admiralty, making it very inaccessible for the citizens of Hong Kong.

> **The ground is the foundation of freedom and democracy. The ground on which we walk about comfortably and freely is also the place we rest, gather, organize public activities, and act collectively.**

The Central and Western District Promenade is built on reclaimed land, and it provides an amazing view of the harbor. Despite having invested heavily on land reclamation, these views are not easily reached. The development of Hong Kong Island has relied on sequential reclamation over the decades, and highways are always constructed along the water edge, blocking pedestrians in the city from accessing the promenade. This 1.5-kilometer-long promenade from Star Ferry Terminal to Wanchai Exhibition Center has only three major connections with the city—the Star Ferry Pier from Central, the Government Complex from Admiralty, and the Exhibition Center and the Ferry Pier from Wanchai. None of these connections offer the public a decent and comfortable access on the ground. The Hong Kong technocracy has nearly destroyed the Victoria Harbor, one of the most beautiful urban shorelines in the world. A study in 2007 showed that 60% of the shoreline of Hong Kong is occupied by highways and roads, 9.5% of the shoreline is still under development, and only 30.5% of the shoreline is accessible to its citizens. Yet this so-called accessibility is a deeply uncomfortable and undignified one, where pedestrians, like rats, are forced to burrow through tunnels and climb over bridges.

Megastructures and the Destruction of Pathways

Hong Kong is a city dominated by real estate development. For many developers, the commercial value of land, not its value as public space, is its core value in Hong Kong. Since the eighties, there has been no restriction on the size of the urban grid and the amount of commercial development on reclaimed land. This has encouraged developers to acquire bigger plots of land, build in a massive footprint, and aggressively misappropriate the ground. In the past three decades, megastructures have started to emerge. Most of them adopted the podium-and-tower typology—where their site coverage is maximized by means of a single large-scale shopping center as a podium. Outdoor public spaces that should have belonged to the city were assimilated into the indoor space of the mall, with a token compensation of public space on the remaining roof of the podium. Out-of-scale and super-tall towers would sit on top of these legally required but relatively inaccessible roof top public spaces. Pedestrians who want to get to the other side of these megastructures have no choice but to be absorbed into the shopping mall. After the developer assimilated the ground, the roof level "public space" becomes a privileged space for the people who live or work in the towers. The lack of control by urban planning authorities and the over-development of megastructures have led directly to the loss of large expanses of land in Hong Kong. Hong Kong has become interiorized and privatized.

The Union Square in the West Kowloon District is a notorious example. Arriving in Hong Kong from New York, a friend of mine took the Airport Express train to the Kowloon Station, and ascended the Union Plaza to his room at the W Hotel. The entire trip took around twenty hours, and he never left an interiorized condition. The floor he had walked on had been either artificially elevated or was mechanically moving, covered with granite, carpet, or metal. He never for a second walked on ground that is exterior. He could tolerate it anymore, exclaiming, "Gosh, I really want to see Hong Kong, with my feet on the ground!" The next day, he asked the concierge at W Hotel, "Where can I get to the ground?" The response was, "Ground? You wanna take a taxi? You can do it here—in the sky lobby." After ten minutes of exploring the place, he finally reached the ground of Union Square, and it turned out to be a very monotonous environment for walking! The thirteen acres of land at the Union Square was completely occupied by the podium, as permitted by the planning code. Not a single storefront was facing the street, nor was there a public street that one could pass through. There were only exits of parking lots, massive exhaust vents, fire escape exits, and the entrances to the Elements Mall and the Kowloon Station. My friend gave up finally, went back into the mall, and proceeded to get lost in the labyrinth of thematic spaces and shopping. Every time I visit the Union Square, I get utterly confused. How could its developer and architect be so perverse and disconnected from the idea of walking on the ground of the streets?

In Hong Kong, such megastructures are proliferating, their quality deteriorating with each project. The reconstruction project in the old town center of Kwun Tong is another prime example. At 5.3 acres, it is said to be the biggest urban renewal project in Hong Kong. This project is being co-developed by the Urban Renewal Authority and some developers. Unlike the Union Square, this is not part of a reclamation project to create a new district, but a renewal project of an old district. Unfortunately, the Authority gave up the existing layout of the streets completely and adapted the abominable podium-tower megastructure. The shopping mall podium will take up nearly the entire site coverage, swallowing up as many as ten public streets. One of the most famous streets was the Yue Man Square, once a historically rich community park consisting of a theater and many small shops. This precious public square will be completely assimilated into the new shopping mall, and the park will be turned into a decorative green atrium. There was much resistance against renewal some years ago, but they were related to the inadequacy of compensation to the private property owners. There was little consideration of the loss of public spaces—how should we calculate the loss of public streets, parks and plazas? What are the ways that a citizen of Hong Kong can resist against such barbaric misappropriation of public resources?

Will Hong Kong become an extra-large and completely interiorized private shopping mall? A friend of mine at the Hong Kong University of Science and Technology had bought an apartment a few years ago. I was shocked when I visited him the first time—the lobby of the building was directly connected to the subway station. In the dark station, it was impossible to tell if one was on ground level or underground. Perhaps it was not important, as the escalator in the lobby would take you directly to the podium, from which you can access the elevator to your apartment without any experience of the outdoors. If my friend had taught at the City University of Hong Kong instead, he may never need to come into contact with the outdoors or the actual ground the whole year round. One could descend to the basement and into the subway, alight at Kowloon Tong station, pass through the Festival Walk mall, and walk directly into the main floor of City University. What are the real effects of being trapped all day in an interior space?

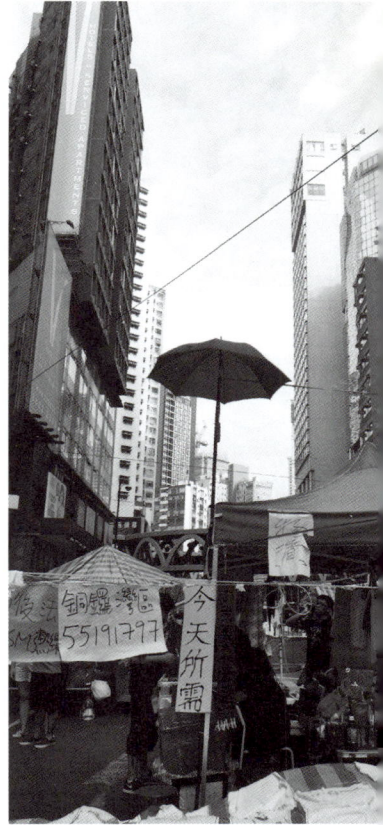

The Umbrella Movement protestors in Causeway Bay.
Image courtesy of
Cherry Cheung, 2014

Effects of Being Ungrounded

First of all, in both physiological and psychological terms, we are going to deform. We will become "ungrounded," a species that is only used to polished granite floors, air-conditioned spaces, and walking within shopping malls. After the first highway to Tibet was built, a group of Tibetan antelopes tried to pass it. They froze the second they stepped onto the tarmac or concrete ground, and for a long time they were afraid to move. They were used to stepping on surfaces with a rich tactility—rocks, dirt, and grass—and had never stepped onto such smooth surfaces. Their migratory route was disrupted by the artificiality of the ground, and they may not survive it! Our situation is as tragic, even if completely opposite—we are so used to the granite and cement floors that we have lost the opportunity and capacity to step on natural ground.

My daughter was born in Hong Kong, and she spends most of her time on the Hong Kong Island. When she was two or three, she was afraid of coming into contact with the natural ground and other natural surfaces. I brought her to the grass and asked her to walk on it. She refused and instinctively retracted her feet. The same thing happened when I asked her to walk on the beach. Are all Hong Kong children going to suffer like

An exterior wall of the Government Complex was nicknamed the Lennon Wall Hong Kong and acted as a billboard for protesters to express their opinions and aspirations. Image courtesy of Cherry Cheung, 2014

this? Psychologists study how human interaction in one's childhood can play a significant role in forming one's personality. They should extend their study to the psychological and physiological consequences of the loss of real ground on our children.

Secondly, from a sociological perspective, we will completely lose the ground that supports our public and political life. We have become apolitical. The first problem could perhaps be solved by taking the whole family away from the city center for a recuperative time in the natural outdoors. But the decline of public political life by the loss of outdoor spaces in the city center will be more difficult recover from. Politics not only links together the intangibility of power, values, and rules but pertains to tangible urban spaces as well. Politics is an ancient Greek word referring to that which is associated with the city and its citizens. Where do these public events occur—in a city, or in the center of the city? The etymological root of politics is *polis*, which means city, citizens and the city-state. In ancient Greece, the center of a *polis* is the *agora*, meaning the marketplace, where people can gather and hold social events. Such a place is called a *forum* in ancient Rome, and it is also a base for the public politics of the Republic. There is perhaps not such a clear definition of republican politics and public space in the Chinese tradition, but the Chinese word for the city is *chengshi*, composed of two characters *cheng* and *shi*. The latter *shi* means the market or forum, and by extension, the temple fairs, tea houses, and opera houses. The former *cheng* is the basic form of public space. Both the republican tradition of Europe and the civilizational power of China showed a relatively high awareness of the sense of the public. Politics is based in the city and public political life is dependent on the public spaces of the city center.

Fast forward to the twenty-first century, advancements in technology have made long-distance communication a lot easier. But it has not weakened the close relationship between public politics and the tangible public space. Citizens are most aware that public spaces in the city is the foundation for forming public politics and collective action—from Martin Luther King's speech on the steps of the Lincoln Memorial in Washington DC in 1963 to the insurgency in the Parisian streets in 1968, and from the crowds who gathered to fast at Tian'anmen Square in 1989 to the citizens who occupied Tahrir Square in Cairo in 2011. Citizens in Hong Kong have similar experiences. Hong Kongers gathered on the streets to support the democratic movements happening in Beijing in 1989. They marched to oppose the legislation of Article 23 of Basic Law in 2003, and they occupied the Government Complex to protest against national education in 2012. Through each act of resistance, not only did Hong Kongers express their democratic aspirations through collective action, they also exercised their rights to urban public space. Hong Kong needs to walk, gather, and occupy in order to take back the public space that belonged to Hong Kongers in the first place.

Acts of Resistance

In Hong Kong, the developers and the government are working together to destroy the public spaces of the city. They are occupying the ground of our city center with either vehicular traffic or private shopping malls. The so-called "public spaces" that they provide in shopping malls, tunnels, and overpasses are totally detached from the ground, merely acting as pathways that passively create passages of movement. Once drawn in, the pedestrian can only stop to shop or pass through the tunnel hurriedly like a rat. The pedestrian can no longer proactively

Protesters built steps to climb over the concrete road dividers at Connaught Road Central, Admiralty. Image courtesy of Cherry Cheung, 2014

experience the space or gather to communicate and interact with one another. There is no possibility of constructing a viable public life. The government has set up a plethora of regulations and restrictions to limit how citizens can use the little public space that is left. For example, the open space in front of the Government Complex—a piece of reclaimed land that cost the city a fortune—was supposed to be the best place for citizens to express their opinions. Through strict regulations, however, protesters are only allowed to stay on several isolated, palm-sized areas, preempting any possibility of gathering on a larger scale. The "openness" of the "door always open" has become merely visual and symbolic. The collusion between developers and the government not only embezzled

Connaught Road Central, Admiralty, before and after the Umbrella Movement.
Images courtesy of Cherry Cheung, 2014

the commercial benefits of the ground in the city center but also destroyed the spatial foundation of public politics in Hong Kong. This cannot be controlled and stopped through existing channels of public opinion; thus I argue that citizens have the right to protect and reconstruct this space through more forceful acts of resistance.

The "Occupy Central" movement most vividly triggered our imagination of space in the history of protest in Hong Kong. The mode of resistance directly and strongly connected two core values of Hong Kong: that which is intangible —freedom, democracy, human rights, and the rule of law—and that which is tangible—the value of public space on the ground of our city center. This movement can have a long-term effect. Will it be able to catalyze a long-term and comprehensive process of "enlightenment?" Will it encourage the public to participate through active discussions and actions? Is it going to help people understand the true value of freedom, democracy, human rights, and the rule of law, while at the same time draw attention to the political health of its citizenry in these public spaces? Would more people share the tasks of rebuilding the society and its urban spaces?

SHANZHAI AND THE PHENOMENOLOGY OF RESISTANCE AND ASSIMILATION

WANG YAN AND WANG FEI

There was a profusion of a specific type of architecture on the Internet and mass media starting around 2005. Most prominently numerous law courts and government buildings in Chinese cities built at that time bore great resemblance to the Capitol in Washington DC. There was also an imitation of Ronchamp in Zhengzhou, Henan. The Wujiao Commercial Complex in Shanghai was modelled after the Pentagon, and Thames Town in Songjiang was a replica of an English town. Noting their similarities with the knockoff phones and copy products that came about during the same period, the Chinese media called them *shanzhai* architecture. The sarcasm seemed to manifest an exuberance of mass consumption, as well as the conflict between an inflated desire and a lagging mode of production. To date, such architecture has accompanied the broader *shanzhai* phenomenon that pervades all Chinese society, implicitly motivated by events that carried symbolic meaning to the state, such as the Olympics and the World Expo. The question is no longer, "What is the difference between *shanzhai* and copying?" or, "What are the negative implications of *shanzhai* architecture to the architectural profession?" but more provocatively, "Has *shanzhai* architecture created a new productive force for the architectural profession?" Studying the etymology of the term *shanzhai* and its sociocultural context, this essay analyzes two cases of *shanzhai* architecture to reveal how *shanzhai* architecture can offer new directions for the profession under extreme conditions.

Social Context of Assimilation

Shanzhai originated from a Cantonese term that means a mountain stronghold. Opposite of the formal or the official, the term conveys a sense of informality, outlawed with no regard for authority, or a smallness in scale. The term was popularized from the *shanzhai* mobile phone phenomenon. In Guangdong, *shanzhai* factories specifically refer to family-based workshops or small- to middle-scale factories that specialize in the fabrication of foreign-branded goods and do not have in-house design teams. In order to assimilate rapidly into the world of outsourcing and manufacturing, these factories have to remain nimble in order to minimize their cost in design, and research and development (R&D). By avoiding the costs associated with American-styled intellectual property (IP) laws, they disrupt the monopoly held by the large corporations and attempt to create a more genuinely open, innovative, and competitive market in China. A large number of products are being copied in appearance but augmented in functionality to suit Chinese needs. The term *shanzhai* has evolved from a noun into a verb to specifically refer to the acts of imitation and low-cost R&D that aim to meet the demand for rapid production.

In fact, *shanzhai* has always existed in China, from Soviet firearms to domestic appliances such as cameras and bicycles. Early *shanzhai* came from a desire for high productivity instigated by rapid development, and reproductions were more faithful to the original. Not driven by market demand, the issue intellectual property rights were considered less relevant. The manufacturers had a deeper understanding of the principle, appearance, and structure of the original artifact. This is why products such as the double-lens reflex camera by Hai'ou or the bicycle made by Feige were considered excellent industrial products and is still much appreciated by a contemporary society that yearns for stylish vintage products. The current generation of crude and consumerism-oriented *shanzhai* manufacturers have the potential to develop into innovative practices. *Shanzhai* phones, for example, can integrate the two competitive mobile operating systems, Windows Mobile and Google Android, and rapidly add new functionalities required of specific needs arising out of China, such as dual-SIM capability required for the masses migrating between provinces, as well as between the rural and urban. In an interview with the Swiss newspaper *Sonntags Zeitung*, Jörg Selden, a professional at a German trend research center, argues that Western enterprises should learn from the experiences of Chinese *shanzhai* manufacturers, who were innovating openly and producing *shanzhai* phones that can overcome inefficiencies in corporate brand protectionism.

From the vantage point of the design profession, acts of *shanzhai* continue to be seen as low-brow and illegal—acts of copying that erodes IP rights and financial gains. They are opposed, even warred against, by many designers. Such acts of resistance were disseminated in mass media to educate the public about the concept of IP rights, as China is required to demonstrate its compliance as a member of the World Trade Organization. It reveals the architectural profession's uneasiness of towards their own means of production, because an architect values creativity and the creation of highly original work. This value system is markedly different, if not alienating, to the expectation of the broad users of architecture, who values the functionality of architecture considerably more than its aesthetics. The architectural form merely acts as the medium that communicates the aspiration of the product to the users, but until the needs of the users are satisfied, the medium and the form do not matter.

A group of students visit the *shanzhai* Champs Élysées at Tiandu City, Hangzhou, with the *shanzhai* Eiffel Tower in the background. Image courtesy of Lam Lai Shun, 2016

The bulk of architectural production in China is undertaken by the photorealistic renderers and visualization profession that support architectural practices. In the rapid pace of visual production, external forms are easily replicated by referencing photographs of acclaimed works of architecture—some of these exemplary forms or façade treatments already preexist in the three-dimensional digital libraries of the renderers. In the process, the craft and technique of making architecture, as well as other factors that determine the true quality of the architecture, are often neglected. Thus, architectural production in China is itself replete with *shanzhai* architecture, with a repeated use of not only consummate forms from the West, such as the Eiffel Tower or Erechtheion, but also state-approved forms such as the Beijing "Bird's Nest" National Stadium or the Beijing "Water Cube" National Aquatics Center. But is the treatment of *shanzhai* architecture as utter disgrace by the architectural profession overly pessimistic, even disingenuous? Are architects neglecting new possibilities that have arisen out of changes in social conditions in China? Or are they underestimating the social dependency that *shanzhai* architecture offers? Is the production of *shanzhai* architecture itself the ordinary society's tactic against the tyranny of high professionalism and creativity own by the elites? Or is *shanzhai* architecture an uncoordinated protest against the unbearable speed of architectural production and greed in China's urbanization? The following are two conflicting cases that exceed the general understanding of *shanzhai* architecture today, no longer a simple term that denotes cheap taste and quick money. They could act as the new foundations for contemporary architectural thought in the sociopolitical and economic contexts of China.

Poetry and Longing

In 2010, Warren Buffett's trip to China made headlines. His attendance at a charity dinner in Beijing was covered in great detail by the *South China Morning Post* and other mass media. The dinner was held at the *shanzhai* Château Laffitte at Changping, a suburb of Beijing. In his blog post "The 'Buffet-Bill' Charity Dinner in the Potemkin City," Zhu Tao cited a 2004 *New York Times* article that described a certain Beijing official's quest to replicate the seventeenth century Château Maison-Laffitte beside the Seine after a highly impressionable visit. Besides adapting the drawings of the Château accurately, his team took more than a million photos over multiple visits, basically performing a "full-body scan" of the original château. Thereafter, a garden was designed, based on other French examples, but different from the original

The *shanzhai* Champs Élysées at Tiandu City, Hangzhou. Image courtesy of Lam Lai Shun, 2016

Versailles. Exotic yet functional landscape elements, including fountain sculptures of Greek mythology and a semi-circular colonnade, were repurposed to achieve a Chinese gated residential *xiaoqu* compound. Security guards wearing traditional French army uniform were included for added authenticity. Beyond the aesthetic question, or the vulgarity due to the boundless power and capital shown in China, there is a deeper question surrounding the social discourse in architecture.

In his book titled *Built upon Love: Architectural Longing after Ethics and Aesthetics*, Alberto Perez-Gomez, professor at McGill University, discusses the bipolar extremes in architecture of form and function. Does architecture exist to satisfy social interests beyond an art form? Is it a form of rational expression, or a poetic one? To answer such questions within the most ancient of Greek contexts in his book, he raises a fundamental and pedagogical question of architecture—can architecture be motivated by love? Since the Renaissance, architectural theory has been driven by the pursuit of reason, and it ultimately failed to serve humanity in a more holistic way. Perez-Gomez argues that architecture must continually "be built in the name of love," where the focal point of architecture is not limited to merely the fashion of form, the economy of housing, or the sustainability of development. Perez-Gomez's phenomenological analysis is an attempt bring back the poetics of architecture at a time when architecture has become obsessed with other rational determinants, such as society, humanity, structural logic, symbolism, linguistics, and historical criticism. Architects have lost the ability to recognize the poetry that is fundamental within architecture.

The *shanzhai* Laffitte is an important lesson for Chinese architecture. China is in a period when capital has hijacked society's imagination and aspirations in architecture. The cynicism architects have expressed can be seen through the compromises made in their desire to satiate the whims of their clients. The client of the *shanzhai* Laffitte may have been interested in the symbolism of luxurious living, and was likely not knowledgeable about the Baroque period in architectural history. But from an architect's perspective, the client is an individual obsessed with Baroque architecture, because it represents the extravagant lifestyle of the Western elite. The *shanzhai* Laffitte critically reveals the dilemma that contemporary Chinese architecture faces. On the one hand, architects are looking towards other fields to remedy the profession's disempowerment by capital and power. On the other hand, capital and power are making use of their love for extravagant architecture to establish their amateur "architectural discourse." Through this painstakingly created replica rooted in capitalist desire, the *shanzhai* Laffitte has become an interrogation of architecture. Architecture is standing trial for having lost its aspirations and values.

Rapid Evolution of New Modes of Practice

A young graduate architect would quickly realize that the work of an architect is not as "pure" as one expects in school. In practice, architectural design and construction is usually repetitive and commodified. An example of this is the European-styled commodified housing, which has long been regarded as crass and out of context in China. In the 1990s, when commodified housing was still rare, the first-generation developers with capital demanded architectural design that symbolized an identity of wealth. But for the masses who lack architectural knowledge, it was impossible to fully decode, let alone understand, the replication of such architectural signs. Over time, this uncoordinated thrust in the escalation of China's real estate bubble turned European-style buildings into the first *shanzhai* architecture.

The initial impetus of the faux European styles came from several American design firms who have had years of experience in commercial architecture, such as Joseph Wong Design Associates in San Diego. Having been long exposed to rigorous corporate operations and commodification, they developed a reputation for designs in the Californian and Spanish styles and were able to rapidly respond to market demands. The application of the Californian style to high-rises in China was difficult: facing extreme requirements to achieve high saleable floor area ratio, they initially found it difficult to adapt to the Chinese market. This was compounded by extremely short design-and-construction cycles, imprecise construction methods, and minimal technological support. These teething problems were easily resolved when they had the opportunity to collaborate with more mature developers, who were able to put more emphasis on the quality of their products and improve the aspects of management and brand creation. Early commodified housing estates such as Junlintianxia Gardens and Shengdehengya were able to retain the authentic detailing and quality of architecture from California. This process of maturing helped to consolidate a solid reputation for many American design companies in the Chinese real estate market. To achieve greater adaptability of this style to more typologies of varying heights and densities in China, many of the American firms started to streamline their design processes. Different teams were in charge of master planning, unit typology design, elevation design, and landscape design. Responsive communication and effective collaboration became critical in the design process. It not only increased the efficiency of design production but also yielded a new housing product in China that was completely different from the original Californian style across the Pacific.

This is an example of *shanzhai* architecture that is forced to mature under the pressure of market forces. Like the creative struggles of *shanzhai* designers, commodified architecture that can stand the test of the market has to go through a process of competitive selection and survival, where the majority are eliminated. This kind of *shanzhai* architecture has the power to change the field of global practice and the mode of architectural production. Nowadays, most *shanzhai* architecture would still be ridiculed upon, but there are successful cases that meet capitalist desires and instigate new architectural development. Traditionally slow and thoughtful practices must find a new driving force to compete with the rapid evolution propagated by *shanzhai* architecture under extreme socioeconomic conditions. Whether it is an authentic, poetic pursuit of architecture or a commodity fetish by capital, China will take time to grow confident about its own architecture. In the meantime, architects must learn to live with the juggernaut of *shanzhai* architecture.

This essay is translated and adapted from Wang Yan and Wang Fei, "Jixian tiaojian de 'shanzhai jianzhu' ji liangge anli" [The Extreme Conditions of 'Copy Architecture' with Two Case Studies], *Time+Architecture*, Issue 119, 2011/3, pp.40-43.

BOURGEOISIFIED PROLETARIAT

H. KOON WEE, DARREN ZHOU, AND EUNICE SENG

Urban development and modernization in China is butting up very awkwardly against the social needs of the people. There is a real need to broaden the discussion of the many agencies that participate in the daily use and making of architecture. This essay is a reflection of an inaugural exhibition event that took place in an experimental mixed use building located in the Dongjing Industrial District of Songjiang, Shanghai. The complex of Jia Little Exhibition Center and Ateliers, comprising an exhibition hall and three work-live atelier buildings, integrates the display and production spaces into a multifunctional sequence. It reimagines the traditional relationship between production and consumption, thereby deriving a unique design solution that is encourages new social and production networks.

Developer, Curator, Artist, and Architect

This essay brings together the ambitions of a number of key protagonists surrounding a building. Firstly, there was the developer who selected the site and invested in the building; secondly, the self-made curatorial coordinators who envisioned the role of art in the city and were hunting for affordable spaces for the artists; thirdly, the artists who produced the site-specific art that were exhibited in the building and were invited to live in the building; and finally, the architects who created the interconnected spaces of production and exhibition of the art works. There is a critique of global market and production relations, where manufacturers seek the highest profit by locating production in places with the lowest labor and production costs, with little regard for what the production brings to these places in terms of real social and environmental costs and benefits. The primary strategy in the design of Jia Little is to create a potentially seamless relationship between the once alienated spaces of production and consumption, so that visitors have the opportunity to be reconnected with the functions and knowledge of back-of-house processes.

The global manufacturing and industrial complex in China is arguably the greatest culprit in the increased alienation between the producers, their products, and the consumers. Prior to the full completion of the building in 2009, the inaugural exhibition *Bourgeoisified Proletariat* was a lightly veiled criticism and observation of this alienation. Curators and artists were aware that the naming of the project recalls an awkward and not unproblematic position against the ideals of communism in a supremely capitalist China today. Forty-four individual artists and groups were involved in the exhibition, including household names, such as Yang Fudong, Yu Ji, Hu Jieming, Zhang Peili, Yang Zhenzhong, Wang Jianwei, and Liu Wei, and art collaboratives, such as MadeIn and Yangjiang Group. There were multiple voices and visions in the project, including those of the developer and curator; and when evaluated together, they capture the complexities and contradictions surrounding artistic practices, urban development, capitalism, and socialism.

Yang Zhenzhong, *Fatality*, installation.
Image courtesy of Art-Ba-Ba, 2009

Conflicted Proletariat

In an age where consumers are no longer acquainted with the origins and production of the goods they fetishize and consume, they expose themselves to materials that may be hazardous to their health or goods that are produced under unfair production practices and so on. In pursuing this project, there was a clear responsibility to bring visitors to these industrial and production spaces. And conversely, the gritty and unadorned spaces of production must be made visible and accessible. The saturated state of industrial production in China is dominated by an uninspiring industrial landscape, often with nothing more than large sheds built at minimal cost and with little consideration for the workers. The design agenda for this project aimed to generate a more responsible approach towards this very system of exploitative production, whether it is art or other forms of design and fabrication industries.

When the lead coordinator from the self-organized curatorial team Vigy Jin surveyed Jia Little during the selection of sites for *Bourgeoisified Proletariat*, she felt there was a conceptual gap between the form of the exhibition center and the old courtyard house across the stream. It had an odd bourgeois feel about the place, given how the large courtyard house may have been home to a wealthy merchant a couple of centuries or more ago, or how the exhibition spaces had a museum-like quality. Instinctively, there was an interest to set the blue-collar workers in the industrial complex against such a contradictory sentiment. Most of the works for the exhibition were made as site-specific installations or performance pieces, the concepts of which were based on the spatial qualities of the building.

There were four factories built in the first phase on this site, a few years prior to the Jia Little Exhibition Center and Ateliers complex. For a stronger connection to this earlier phase, the developer Li Gang decided that the new buildings should retain aspects of the production and industrial functions. However, adding purely industrial buildings would be rather unchallenging. In addition, the economic logic of industrial production and its highly standardized architectural forms would rapidly normalize and arrive at a very foreseeable limit, hemming in the possibility for greater profit. There would be no room to grow spatially, programmatically, or economically. The fascination with an innovative form of architecture was in fact spurred by a deeper interest in financial gains and the added potential that may come from a differentiated and augmented form of architecture. This also formed part of the land banking strategy of the developer.

Bao'an (security guards) at the exhibition. Image courtesy of Art-Ba-Ba, 2009

The exhibition intended to explore the themes of the bourgeoisie versus the proletariat in contemporary China. The curators began the experiment by immediately seeking out the family backgrounds of the artists, asking them to outline their genealogy and social strata three generations back. Artists were even asked to recall the most expensive art work they have sold. This awareness was something that was more visible in the 1950s and '60s, where one was much more conscious about one's identity as a landowner, worker, farmer, capitalist, or proletariat. All the participating artists had their bio-data drawn up for the exhibition.

"The theme of this exhibition comes from a debate about so-called class struggle. Discovering this strange sentence from Engels about the 'bourgeoisified proletariat' is absurd in that it could be used to describe the political and economic life and thinking of nearly everyone in contemporary China."

Yang Zhenzhong, artist, *Bourgeoisified Proletariat Exhibition Catalog*, p.33

"Looking at the past in retrospect, the so-called *Bourgeoisified Proletariat*, the title of this exhibition, has only given people a direct feeling: 'materialization,' the actual process of 'modernization.' This modernization process is bitter, accompanied as it is by an evasion of modernity. If we say that 'transformation' is the main theme in China today, then the realization of modernization has already been felt by the people. In a country in which the 'worker class' is the main actor, the workers are all concerned with maintaining their legal rights. Even if we've reached an era of a 'bourgeoisified proletariat,' what can we do?"

Jin Feng the Elder, artist, *Bourgeoisified Proletariat Exhibition Catalog*, p.38

Industrial and Cultural Relations

The project was originally filed with the building authority as industrial land use, even though it had cultural functions. It was not considered a problem, as there were inroads made into new forms of urban development where land use patterns were always more dynamic and mixed. In Songjiang, many developers were further ahead in the real estate game, anticipating changes in urban and economic policies, and bidding for land as a land banking strategy. Industrial sites used to have a maximum gross floor area of 1.0, and green landscape coverage cannot be under forty percent. In recent policies, local governments are allowed to adjust land use policies to encourage greater densification, even in the urban outskirts. According to Li, he took a leap of faith in this project because he was fairly certain that the government would eventually become more enlightened. The benefits of such flexible and expansive plans would yield greater profits, which explains why there is so much speculation in real estate in China, including industrial land. Li further suggests that his decisions followed three crucial principles of mutuality, where his project must benefit the society, government, and businesses. Once these aspirations are met, there would be no compelling reasons for any government official not to support a development such as Jia Little.

This building integrated the display and production spaces of creative industries into a single mixed-use building complex. The primary spatial strategy was to create a continuous relationship between spaces of production and consumption, so that visitors and consumers could be reconnected with the knowledge and appreciation of the processes of making and production. Exhibition programs have sometimes gone hand in hand with manufacturing and industrial programs in China, hence the proliferation of highly commercial exhibition centers in every major development. In the Chinese housing market, this exhibition function takes the form of temporary sales gallery and show flats, where sophisticated visual techniques found in the design of art galleries and museums are employed. Perhaps in the same dystopic but realistic way, the curators of this exhibition tended to see artists as the cannon fodder of the creative industry. In 2002, a number of the exhibiting artists moved to Moganshan Road as a non-profit arts group when rental was considerably low. There were numerous forms of industries, such as print shops, metal workshops, wood studios, and many others. But once the artists arrived, the industries gradually moved away, because the artists were somehow considered cleaner and more desirable tenants. Soon after, the design and creative firms would come in and begin to force the artists out because they would pay even higher rent. The original artists were priced out and had to move to industrial area of Taopu; but the same story of gentrification can be told there. The developer said that he would not reveal the real economic motivations behind developing the cultural dimensions of the site to the local authorities. As long as the government did not hinder the progress of the project, Li felt he would be able to enhance both the capacities of his development and the ambitions of the artists, forging a win-win relationship. In response to one of the curator's class-based question to the artists, "Where do you think China's advantage lies? What are your expectations? Are they related to your work?" the following response from Liao Guohe suggests that artists are acutely aware of their roles in the production of art in the current Chinese society.

> "Differences in who owns the means of production determine differences in historical evolution. In a socialist society, the masses hold power, where in a capitalist society the monopolist class holds the means of production. A communist society, however, is the conscious choice of a people who already enjoy material prosperity. Slave-holding society depends on heredity, feudal society on class relations, capitalist society on concealment and exploitation, and socialist society on ability and moderation."

> Liao Guohe, artist, *Bourgeoisified Proletariat Exhibition Catalog*, p.61

In searching for a language of connectivity between the living and production spaces, and between the public consumers and resident producers, one returns to the potential of the production core itself. The architecture of Jia Little Exhibition Center borrowed a formal language from the well-honed linear industrial core that facilitated mass production, but it updated its linear logic into a complex knot. This was made visible through a formally expressive wood and steel curtain wall. This continuous core circulates visitors through the buildings on multiple elevated levels, enveloping the otherwise separate spaces. Weaving through the complex across the bridges, visitors are reoriented at different levels of communicating lobbies and stairs, and are allowed to reach other spaces without getting off the circuit of exhibition. The core is stretched through a retail strategy of linear persuasion, weaving visitors through different spatial experiences—from interiors to exteriors, from sleek exhibitions to untidy fabrication studios. The experience of the exhibition was rethought through this project with the hope that one's experience can be authenticated by the connectivity between production and consumption.

Center versus Periphery

Even though the site is located at the periphery of Shanghai, there was a recognition that this new kind of space had to be designed to build community. Set on the premises of Jia Little, the 2016 Chinese television series *Love O2O* is the best possible vindication of a new form of community growing from such an industrial site. A romantic story revolves around a second-year university student and her senior fourth-year computer science student, who is also the CEO of a technology start-up that designs online games. This TV series boasts of nineteen billion views on the Youku online video channel. The form and orientation of the exhibition hall were determined by a need to create smaller zones for social interaction and circulation between the atelier buildings. This forms the pretext for the micro-urbanism of the site. The resultant pockets of landscape and courtyards become social spaces of engagement that could be used by workers, and the bridges allows for unexpected encounters and shortcuts through the spaces. Li considered a number of industrial areas outside the central city, including Nanhui and Jiading. Songjiang was

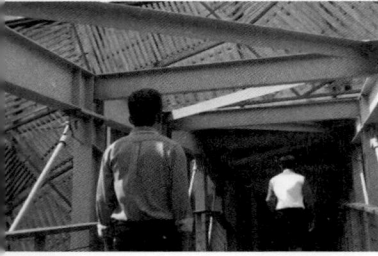

Film still of *Love O2O* TV series.
Image courtesy of JSTV

favorable because it was the most developed district out of the One City Nine Town masterplan. It is also sandwiched between Shanghai and Zhejiang. From a geographical standpoint, it is extremely convenient. At its inception in the early 2000s, the infrastructure and urban development of Songjiang was not mature, and not many university graduates from the Songjiang University Town remained behind in Songjiang to seek employment after graduation. Part of the reason was factories and industrial areas did not require many graduates. In fact, the positive effects of the University Town on our project can only be felt more recently. This indicates that over a decade is required before one can see the long-term effects of education in an area.

Li wanted the artists to stay to set up their production studios after the inaugural exhibition, but according to Vigy Jin, the Jia Little location was too far. Back in 2009, all the ateliers of the artists were within the inner ring road of Shanghai. A year after the exhibition, it turned out these artists still had to look for a new space outside of the city center. They found a new collective space next to the Middle Ring Road in Taopu, which is half the distance to the city center compared to Songjiang. By 2013 and 2014, the artists had to move again when the space at Taopu became too small. They could no longer find a space in the city area and resorted to approaching Li to take up his offer from 2009. Unfortunately, he had no more room at Jia Little or in the Dongjing area. By coincidence, the Sheshan Hui in the Sijing area right next to Dongjing approached the artists, and they eventually resettled there.

The initial goal of Li was to develop a creative cluster because he was inherently interested in the arts, and he had developed deep friendship with a few friends within the artistic circle. Moreover, the adoption of industrial spaces for art is not new in the city. However, in the early decades, real estate developers had to distance themselves from artists, because much of the early art works in China were considered quite political, and many artists were under the scrutiny and direct surveillance of the police. During the planning stages of *Bourgeoisified Proletariat*, there were always concerns that it would be overly politicized, even for the peripheral location of Jia Little. There were risks in allowing the theme to be autonomously developed and self-curated by the artists. Every few years since 1999, this group of artists have self-organized exhibitions together. There were fewer restrictions and self-censorship imposed on them by other art organizations, and self-expression was greatly promoted. This 2009 exhibition corresponded to the larger socioeconomic patterns and gradual permissiveness in China, where urban and economic development in China was moving along a neoliberal capitalist system, even though China remains ostensibly a socialist state.

Growing up, artists and cultural workers in China were told that they were proletariats, but increasingly they have become more bourgeoisie. Hence, the exhibition name *Bourgeoisified Proletariat* echoed the deeply contradictory mental state of every Chinese.

During the promotion of this exhibition, it was marketed under a much more innocuous name, *Contemporary Art in Songjiang: The Great Songjiang Art Exhibition*. Even up to this day, the title *Bourgeoisified Proletariat* remains sensitive. Jia Little was a natural choice for the exhibition because the artists found the space to be large and beautiful—and of course, the space was available for free.

Exhibition Center and the Art Effect

Many developers in Songjiang are doing what Jia Little and *Bourgeoisified Proletariat* had accomplished in 2009. Large groups of artists have been attracted to Sheshan Hui, as well as the Sheshan Art Valley. However, these real estate developments are more speculative and risk-adverse in nature, and they lack the kind of courage and commitment the original *Bourgeoisified Proletariat* artists had. This is a problem in China where developers would merely use a gimmick "art" strategy to generate interest, and quickly sell them off for a profit. Sheshan Hui eventually committed to promoting the arts, because they had run into a legal problem with the zoning characteristics of the land, which prevented them from land subdivision and resale. In fact, the success of Sheshan Hui was in a large part due to the original *Bourgeoisified Proletariat* art collective. Even so, the artists soon left it to seek larger spaces. Today, a number of the original artists are located in a building with a ten-meter high space next to Jia Little. These spaces are five thousand square meters large, or about twice as large as the ateliers at Jia Little, and they remain the only art-base collective in the area. There is not enough cultural capital to influence the local government to make specific policies to encourage cultural industries. Instead, the artists are in compliance with the market forces of real estate, and seeking out affordable rentals. Jia Little generates RMB 50 million in revenue each year, but it remains negligible compared to the entire revenue Songjiang.

Artists do not like governmental interventions. Unlike other cultural or creative industries, artists do not like to be pigeonholed or directed by the authorities. Hence, government-led cultural districts or science and technological development zones, meant to induce economic and urban development, would not work on the artists. According to the curatorial coordinator Vigy Jin, even if the local government were to set up something really conducive, the artists may shun it. However, the reason for the burgeoning of the artist community in Shanghai in 2013 and 2014 was due to the cultural development of the city itself. There are not many artists born and bred in Shanghai. Artists across

当代艺术展在松江
Bourgeoisified Proletariat

Bourgeoisified Proletariat exhibition catalog and poster, indicating a different Chinese name used for marketing. Image courtesy of Hipic Culture & Art Ltd., 2009

China were drawn to the rise of the private museums. Their works are being collected and exhibited in the Yuz Museum founded by Chinese-Indonesian entrepreneur and art collector Budi Tek, the Long Museum founded by art collectors Liu Yiqian and his wife Wang Wei, and countless others. There is also the new West Bund Biennale, on top of the foremost Shanghai Biennale. With these come an influx of a large number of artists, as well as their attendant art economy and auction houses. Many of these artists come from outside of Shanghai, while others are fresh graduates from reputable art schools. Traditionally they would follow the *beipiao*, or "north drift", to Beijing, but now many come to Shanghai with the Shanghai drift, *haipiao*. As the artist community grows, there is a larger demand for production spaces for art, and pockets of art communes, such as the one in Dongjing and Sheshan, Songjiang, would benefit. Art communes have grown from ten artists to a hundred to two hundred today. These artists may not be household names just yet, but there is a growing sense of community.

Art and Urban Development

The focus on art and cultural industries, as well as other innovative industries, came about because these industries mirror the rapid growth patterns in the development of cities in China. Because of Jia Little's position at the fringe, the outward spread from the city center would inevitably reach it. According to Li, the benchmarking of Jia Little was done in such a way that its development would be intrinsically tied to the development of the city. As the city becomes more expensive, there would be more opportunities for the pioneering developers in the outlying district. Following urban development, Jia Little also has the ambition to address its socioeconomic sustainability. While projecting itself as an architecture of industry and exhibition, the architecture was designed as a critique of both the exhibition of commodity and the various interrelated modes of consumption and production. It reinvents new relationships between the key constituencies or users through newly configured architectural forms and programmatic adjacencies. At the same time, the project also demonstrates the as yet untapped design innovation of industrial spaces in China. The industrial landscape is still dominated by prosaic factory complexes today.

The effects of art and cultural industries on the urban development of a district are much slower, and they cannot bring about instantaneous solutions such as increased employment, greater tax revenue, or intensified daily consumerism. The immediate effects of art and cultural industries are weaker. But in the long run, the results are stronger and more sustained. Therefore, the developer saw an economic need to couple the creative industries with other design professionals and hi-tech innovation industries, such that Jia Little can yield immediate socioeconomic benefits. From the perspective of the organizers, *Bourgeoisified Proletariat* represented a year of consolidation. The art collective that was originally based at the M50 Art District on Moganshan Road was quite fragmented by that time because of the escalating rental costs. It was extremely difficult to identify a space that was large enough to host a collective exhibition. In the formative years prior to 2002 or 2003, the artists were readily able find spaces to exhibit in the city center. By

2009, the collective had to hold it at Jia Little, which was considered to be very far away. The only way to attract the audience was to specially charter shuttle buses for them. Ironically, Songjiang has grown to become a major site for the contemporary art scene in Shanghai, and it all began at Jia Little.

Politics, Censorship, and Artist as Bourgeoisie

According to Vigy Jin, politics is still completely taboo in China. With respect to censorship, the government's stance on the display of sexual content in art has somewhat softened. In the past, nudity of the sort displayed at *Bourgeoisified Proletariat* would have been immediately censored. Improvements are slow, but as the artists continue to work with public media companies and cultural enterprises, they are better able to convey their ideas to the government. By the same token, the censors were much more authoritarian in the past. If artists failed to obtain a permit for the display of their art works, the paranoid censors would have thought there was something unseemly. The civil servants today are not only younger and more attuned to the sentiments of the grassroots but also have a stronger empathy and understanding of the different aesthetic values in society.

> "Confronting a new social landscape raises questions of focus, of how to select and interrogate the appropriate phenomena, how to anticipate the future. The important question is what art can build in its confrontation with life today. How much of our work shakes at the fundamental question of art?"
>
> Zhou Xiaohu, artist, *Bourgeoisified Proletariat Exhibition Catalog*, p.29

On the other hand, artists have become less extreme over the years. The sharp bristles of paint brushes, once wielded by the most provocative of artists, have been toned down by the society they were critiquing and the reality of a consumerist public. This is inevitable with the rise of commercialism in art. Back when there was little or no commercial art, many artists felt they had to resort to a kind of violence or sacrificial struggle to sublimate

Polit-Sheer-Form-Office, *TOFU Wall*, site-specific performance art. Images courtesy of Art-Ba-Ba, 2009

their art. Over the years, the artistic community has diversified and grown inclusive, and many do not really care about political or critical issues on behalf of the society they serve. In fact, most artists are no longer willing to do engage contentious or political contents in their art. Reflecting back on the 2000s, up until the period of *Bourgeoisified Proletariat*, the artists were perhaps struggling proletariats. But today, Vigy Jin describes them as having embraced a completely bourgeois lifestyle, as they own houses and cars, smoke cigars, and drink whiskey as they perform their roles as artists.

> "When I was younger, I had a very negative approach to money, I saw it as the root to most problems and inequalities in society. I rejected it and believed experiences were what mattered. I still hold these views, however, as life continues I have realized that money can also be a tool. It is not just one thing, it can help you do and change things in a positive way."
>
> Seth Joseph Augustine, artist, *Bourgeoisified Proletariat Exhibition Catalog*, p.77

> "Human history is driven by interest. Capitalism is an ideology of the rich minority, where socialism is an ideology that can allow everyone to be rich, but this still depends to an extent on competition and does not ensure total equality. Capitalist society prevents monopolies. Socialist society aims, in addition to this goal, to allow people without ability to enjoy wealth."
>
> Liao Guohe, artist, *Bourgeoisified Proletariat Exhibition Catalog*, p.80

With the rising purchasing power of the public, artists invariably change their works to cater to the tastes of the buyers. In many sense, art is becoming much more superficial. However, in the case of *Bourgeoisified Proletariat*, the economy in 2009 was terrible, as Asia was only starting to recover from the financial crisis in 2008. Art galleries were barely making any sales that year. The artists were not enamored of the market then. A closer examination of the site-specific art works of the exhibition shows that many were art installations or performances that cannot be purchased. A good number of the works were directly responding to the alienating processes of urbanization and the blind

Yang Zhenzhong, *Fatality*, installation. Images courtesy of Art-Ba-Ba, 2009

consumerism in China. This was because they were focused on self-expression rather than the commercial aspects. For the audience, most of the works were considered too angry, too crude, or too difficult to understand. It was precisely during this period, when art was still extremely pure and unencumbered, that the artists did not have to think about the marketability of their works. For the raw and free space of Jia Little, there were no intentions to sell any of the art works. In commercial art galleries today, artists are sometimes told to think about these commercial aspects.

"There has been a change, before when I would enter a restaurant I would first feel my pockets, but then I started daring to enter any restaurant at all, sometimes forgetting to check if I had even brought enough cash."

Yang Zhenzhong, artist, *Bourgeoisified Proletariat Exhibition Catalog*, p.79

In the lowly years, perhaps the artists had no families. It may have been easy for artists to move around and live a relatively less comfortable and stable lifestyle. But with age and a declining health, they can no longer really do that. With a family in toll, artists may have different material responsibilities and needs. Vigy Jin argues that it all comes down to a process of maturing as a nation, and as a profession. Especially in Shanghai, everything is about money. Back in the 2000s, apprentices in art would work as assistants for the sake of art and for the sake of learning. It was purer. These days, even volunteers need to be paid. Reflecting on *Bourgeoisified Proletariat*, Jin's last words in the interview closes this chapter in Shanghai—"when everything around you is about money, there is no way you can talk about being a proletariat."

PROTECTION AS RESISTANCE

SHI JIAN

At the beginning of the early Modern era in 1914, Zhu Qiqian, Beiyang Government's Chief Minister of Interiors and Supervisor of the Municipal Office, targeted Qianmen, an area in front of the old city main gate dominated by historic *hutong* courtyard housing, as the first choice for modernization and renewal of the old city of Beijing. The significance of Beijing Old City's urban renewal was pointed out in the *Construction Proposal for the Alteration of the Capital's Qiansanmen City Wall*, describing that "the Capital, as the finest place of the country, which evokes the admiration of its quintessence in both foreigners and locals alike, should be well equipped with all sorts of facilities and display orderliness and solemnness, so that she may be an exemplar for the rest of the nation."

Originally numbering in the thousands, the courtyards were reduced to approximately six hundred by 2014. The remaining courtyard housing that are severely under threat are currently located in an area south of Chongwenmen River West, east of Qianmen East Road, north of Dongchashi *hutong*, and west of Caochang Third Alley. With elevations along the streets—of courtyard gates and walls—restored and unified to resemble other parts of Old Beijing in 2008, the eastern part of Qianmen area seems to have been artificially frozen in time since. Fortunately, the majority of the traditional alleyways and courtyard fabric of the *hutong*s has not been altered much, despite falling into disrepair due to the decline of the area. It is one of the few areas that managed to preserve the style and features of the Old Capital.

In anticipation of the changes taking place to this Qianmen East Area, an international exhibition entitled *Cheng Nan Project: Qianmen East Area 2014* was held at the Beijing Center for the Arts from October to November in 2014. Artistic Director Weng Ling, under the auspices of Tianjie Group and the Center, invited nine architectural and research teams to participate. They included the Beijing Institute of Architectural Design and MAD from Beijing, Jiakun Architects from Chengdu, Kengo Kuma and Associates from Tokyo, Keenen/Riley from New York, MVRDV from Rotterdam, Neri & Hu from Shanghai, Urbanus from Shenzhen and Beijing, and Position from Shenzhen. The proposals of the participating design and research teams were based on comprehensive

1750/2014: Qianmen East Area Study in 'Qianlong Capital City Map' Context (illustrated book, 6188×5951mm) at *Reverse Spatial Combing: From Qianmen East Area to Zhengdongfang*, 2014
Images courtesy of Position / Shi Jian

investigations of the site, including the meticulous research and complete documentation of spatial information. Over the course of the exhibition and academic forum, the teams reached a consensus for the enhancement and development of the site.

Enhancement and Development of Qianmen

Restriction of Mass Demolition and Mass Development. The damaging results of demolishing and reconstructing on a large scale is evident, as proven by many previous cases. This method of redevelopment must be changed. Although some courtyards have already been demolished and opinions as to how to utilize these spaces differ, the consensus is that existing buildings should be maintained, refurbished, and protected.

Comprehensive Cultural Protection. Comprehensive cultural protection is a widely agreed principle. Zhu Xiaodi suggested combining the city, the buildings, and the people together as one protected cultural entity. Liu Jiakun suggested no further demolition or relocation of residents in the areas under protection to ensure that the cultural identity and memories of the place remain unique and flexible and practical functions can flourish. Should residents be allowed to return to the original splendor of the place, such a scheme of cultural protection would be duly justified. Kengo Kuma raised an alternative concept of an exterior emptiness and interior protection, in an effort to minimize the changes made to the old city. Ma Yansong and Terence Riley shared a similar view on developing the outer region and protecting the inner. The remaining buildings and its residents are kept, while a new population of youngsters and the middle class are brought in to balance traditional and modern ways of living. Urbanus suggested the protection and renewal of old courtyards, with an emphasis on cultural heritage, and a reintegration of existing and new residents. The concept of comprehensive cultural protection remains key to this site, where the physical fabric and people residing within are held with equal value.

Courtyard as Unit in a Progressive Renewal. The protection of the old town must include the streets, *hutong*s, courtyards, and roofs, as such renewal can only be done progressively, by incremental units of individual courtyards, according to Zhu. Urbanus' proposal suggested courtyard renovations based on land lots, encouraging residents to be more creative with their living spaces. Winy Maas stressed the importance of development in phases, to create a platform on which different owners can work with the architects to achieve their goals, and have a diverse array of utilities in different courtyards. The method of progressive development and refurbishment was also raised by Ma.

Financial Offset from New Developments Towards Protected Areas. The question of funding and financial balance is an important issue in the protection of the old town. Zhu, Liu, and Ma suggested using financial gains made from already demolished spaces to cover the funds needed for protection and renewal of the inner areas. Liu further suggested commercial developments in the perimeter areas, forming a wall of protection for the inner region. The revenue from the commercial activities would cover refurbishment and protection expenses. Ma suggested a similar method of outer region development. He proposed high density residential buildings in selected spaces to act as a catalyst to increase vibrancy and attract new residents into the area with relatively low investment from the city.

Xi Da Mo Chang Jie 105-242 (video, 15mins) (left). a *hutong* in Qianmen (right)
Images courtesy of Position / Shi Jian

Development of Underground Spaces. The usage of underground spaces to increase the volume and capacity of the area, as well as solve utility issues such as car parking were proposed by Zhu, Maas, and Rossana Hu. Zhu suggested two levels of underground development in cleared lots, with the first basement as an extension of the courtyard and personal space, and second basement as public space for parking. MVRDV's "Dig Project" presented various ways in which the underground spaces can be integrated with the conventional courtyards, such as the underground cellar courtyard, the underground gallery and the transparent floor courtyard. Neri & Hu emphasized the concept of excavation, as the underground spaces can have practical uses such as civil defense shelters and an underground city with plazas, courtyards and public connections.

Various doorways of Qianmen *hutongs*. Images courtesy of Position / Shi Jian

Social and Historical Research as Basis

Drawing from social and historical research, Position provided the basis for this collective exhibition by contributing an in-depth study of the Qianmen East Area, carried out over half a year. As an independent research and advocacy group, Position is led by Zhu Tao, Zhao Lei, and myself. The exhibition was entitled *Reverse Spatial Combing: From Qianmen East Area to Zhengdongfang*, and it was composed of three parts, namely the installation *Qianmen East Area Spatial Research*, measuring 4,650 by 5,400 millimeters; the video installation *Damochang West Street No.105-242*, lasting fifteen minutes, and the set of illustrated historical maps *1750/2014: Qianmen East Area Study in 'Qianlong Capital City Map' Context*, measuring 6,188 by 5,951 millimeters. *Qianmen East Area Spatial Research* was conducted on the existing *hutong*s and courtyards in the specified area, and it concluded with photographic documentation of every entrance of each courtyard residence, as well as measured drawings of all the illegal structures, also known as *jiajian gouzhu* or annexed construction. For a deeper understanding of the sociopolitical undercurrent of this site, this spatial research was complemented by oral records and interviews of the residents, and a compilation of the historical maps and documents. The purpose of these documentations is to comprehensively comb through the spaces of the region and construct an authentic condition of the area, in order to establish the core effects of the courtyard fabric on the evolution of urban space.

Residents and illegal construction at Qianmen *hutongs*. Images courtesy of Position / Shi Jian

Due to the limitation of the exhibition format, the exhibited works were unable to reveal the context of courtyard fabric protection at greater depth. While the reality that the large-scale bulldozing of the Old City is now confined to history, the irony remains that present-day historical preservation of historic urban districts still often revert to large-scale constructions in the name of the protection of the *hutong* fabric. Based on the consensus established in the 2014 exhibition and forum, Position and Urbanus went on to co-curate a follow-up exhibition entitled *Projective Preservation: Conditions and Strategies for the Future of Beijing Qianmen Hutongs* in Beijing, from September 25 to November 19, 2015. Through further research and design, the 2015 exhibition revealed a

在这一特殊语境里，现状的强化保护，至新基础设施，置入活力因素，既是对新的唯我独尊的旧城无序扩张的抑制，也是一种有序的新陈代谢。

Tower installation, 2015. Images courtesy of Position / Shi Jian

clearer spatial essence of the Qianmen East Area *hutongs* and courtyards. Strategic advice was further provided to the government for sustaining and regenerating the existing fabric, as well as the "vanished" areas under protection. The installation *Tower*, measuring 2,300 millimeters square and 3,600 millimeters tall, was reassembled as a tower form from the *Qianmen East Area Spatial Research*. This allusion of a tower was created by juxtaposing and stacking, and it symbolizes the dilemmas, plights, and challenges faced by the inhabitations of the Qianmen East *hutong*s.

In the context of this conservation and educational efforts, the strengthening of the courtyard fabric is in fact a form of suppression or resistance against the disorderly expansion of the new capitalist construction projects within the Old City of Beijing. The research behind the exhibition and proposals, and the advocacy for the protection of the courtyard fabric, is no longer limited to mere academic investigations. As a whole, they represent a substantive study on, as well as a call for, strategies for the protection of the urban fabric of the Old City of Beijing. The protection of the courtyard fabric speaks to the cultural sustainability of a people, and the last line of resistance of a place.

EIGHT URBAN MEMOIRS

HU YAN AND LI HAN

Dashilar *Hutong* District: Public-Private Alliance

Dashilar is an old *hutong* district of Beijing. *Hutong* districts have long been considered having density that is too low for a contemporary city. The *hutong*s of Beijing are traditionally single-story courtyard residences, which have a very different density from the historical districts of European cities. This problem of a lack of density is exacerbated by the fact that Beijing today has become one of the most expensive cities in the world. In the downtown districts of Beijing, where the *hutong*s are located, the land prices are exorbitant. Thus, it is difficult to expect any good financial returns if one were to invest in such a low-density form. It is not surprising that the revitalization of the *hutong*s of Dashilar has become a state-funded program. The state would first provide the investment capital to repurchase the homes of the residents, then attract young creative professionals to establish creative start-ups in these spaces. The quasi-governmental developer would offer rental incentives to attract the more promising creative enterprises, especially those with high cultural value and staying power. Through these enterprises, they hope to reinvigorate the *hutong* district and raise the quality of the district as a whole.

The public-private alliance model achieved great results in the beginning. During the process of redevelopment, numerous exemplars emerged in Dashilar. As the number of *hutong*s available for repurchase dwindled, however, the spaces available for redevelopment became increasingly scarce. It became even more problematic when the creative enterprises were unable to form good communal relations with the local residents. The new enterprises tend to complain that the local inhabitants were arrogant and unreasonable in their ways of the old, while the local inhabitants could not relate to the newcomers. In fact, both parties were equally alienated, and social interaction was practically impossible. This greatly hindered the spread of the redevelopment, and the positive effects remained elegant but highly isolated. The district as a whole could not enjoy the broader benefits of the interventions brought about by the creative enterprises. The original idea was to induce change through short-term improvements, with the hope of a sustained economic effect and profitability in the long term. But Dashilar had to face great social challenges despite the well-intended urban acupuncture strategy.

Qilou Old Street of Haikou: Production of Space and the Expansion of Capital

Located in the city of Haikou, Zhongshan Road is famous for its old colonial district of row houses, known as the Qilou Old Street. The traditional architectural form was hybridized with colonial western influences. The street façades have a Western appearance, but the spatial configurations of deep courtyards have a distinctively Chinese history. The Qilou Old Street is in sharp contrast with the Beijing *hutong*. Downtown Beijing is one of the most important, expensive, and populous districts in China, yet the density of its vernacular *hutong*s are incredibly low. Haikou is a third-tier city with affordable land and a relatively small population, but its historic district has a relatively high-density form of three- to four-story buildings.

The *hutong* of Beijing is in decline because there is a severe lack of productive uses for the unique spatial form. On the contrary, the Qilou typology is in decline because it suffers from having too much space and a high level of vacancy.

The drawing *Qilou Old Street of Haikou* imagines a situation where the capital investment of Beijing is transferred to Zhongshan Road in Haikou. All the multistory spaces are used efficiently. They are transformed into restaurants, art galleries, educational spaces, and offices, creating an invigorated atmosphere in the city. However, this is merely conjectural. This speculative vision relies on a proper redevelopment of Haikou for the future, and it is not something that can be taken for granted in the short run. The production of space is an important vehicle in the expansion of capital. Yet as the economy continue to flourish around the connectivity brought about by the internet, the significance of a physical space becomes challenged. Does capital still require a production of space in order to grow? If the growth of capital is disengaged from the physicality of space, the future of the *hutong* of Beijing can be massive, but that of the Qilou Old Street can only grow more desolate.

Nanluoguxiang: Gentrification and Disillusionment

A classic prose in *The Peach Blossom Fan* serves as a stark reminder of the splendor of the alley of Nanluogu. This tragicomedy narrates a remarkable rise and spectacular fall of this downtown district of Beijing. "Look at him constructing the luxurious building, look at him dining with his guests, look at the building fall!" A decade ago, the alley of Nanluogu was renowned as the most beautiful *hutong* in Beijing. Young entrepreneurs would rent the old houses as reclusive cafes. Patrons would stay here for an entire afternoon in solitude, basking in the sun, watching the cat, or drinking a cup of coffee or tea. In time, more and more cafés, restaurants, and shops would gather along this fascinating alley. It would become the most famous shopping street in Beijing.

Dashilar (excerpt) Image courtesy of Drawing Architecture Studio

Countless visitors would arrive because of its charm, and the place would become the top destination for relaxation and a local haunt for Beijingers. However, skyrocketing rental prices would gradually force the highly original and small bohemian shops to leave. Only low-brow souvenir shops, barbeque restaurants, and bars are left today. The locals of Beijing had fled Nanluoguxiang, displaced by the regular tourists from low-budget tours. Even though the hustle and bustle continued, the unique character of the place was long gone. In a remedial effort to prevent more budget tours from congesting the district, the alley decided to opt out of its heritage status and its accreditation as a national AAA tourist site in 2016. Subsequently, the government joined in the remedy efforts. All it took was a decade for the elegant street, the most sought-after urban oasis, to fall into the savages of cheap tourism. The case of Nanluoguxiang caused an unfortunate disillusionment amongst advocacy efforts towards a bottom-up urban redevelopment.

Sanlitun: Illegal Conversions and Landmark of Everyday Culture

Sanlitun is filled with the trendy and the creative, as well as expatriates; hence there is a prevalent bar culture and nightlife in the area. The first generation of street bar culture in Sanlitun was long gone because of urban renewal, and the remaining street bars tend to be found along the back alleys. The buildings along these alleys are residential in nature. In particular, the residential buildings in the drawing are being occupied by bars, cafés, restaurants, and salons, with a direct relationship to the street. These buildings demonstrate a sense of great cultural diversity, with a mix of whites, blacks, Arabs, and Indians. There are high-end restaurants as well as spicy hot-pot shops of an affordable nature. There are pedicures and tattooists. With the popularity of online video streaming websites, DVD shops are all but disappeared, but here in this neighborhood there are still two. They are probably well-patronized by foreigners who are looking for a fine selection of global arthouse films that may be censured by their home state.

In China, it is illegal to convert a residential building into a commercial one. Since this year, the government has enforced state-level regulations on this problem, and many non-compliant buildings were demolished and walled off. Surprisingly, this building was not affected. Not only was the conversion not curtailed, the situation became even more out of hand. The illegal conversions reached even greater heights, from the first to the second, third, and even the roof levels. In the context of heavy enforcement by the local government, this abnormal proliferation and chaotic development of commerce is a miracle. It still faces a highly volatile future. Since it is severely illegal, it would not be at all surprising if the local government chooses to demolish it. On the other hand, it would be even less surprising if this building was left to its own devices. As a landmark of everyday culture, this Beijing locale has the extremes of a dual personality.

Tuanjiehu: Tactics of Extreme Privatization

Tuanjiehu is a residential neighborhood in Beijing built in the 1980s. Even though the buildings in the neighborhood are relatively old, it is still very vibrant because of its lo-

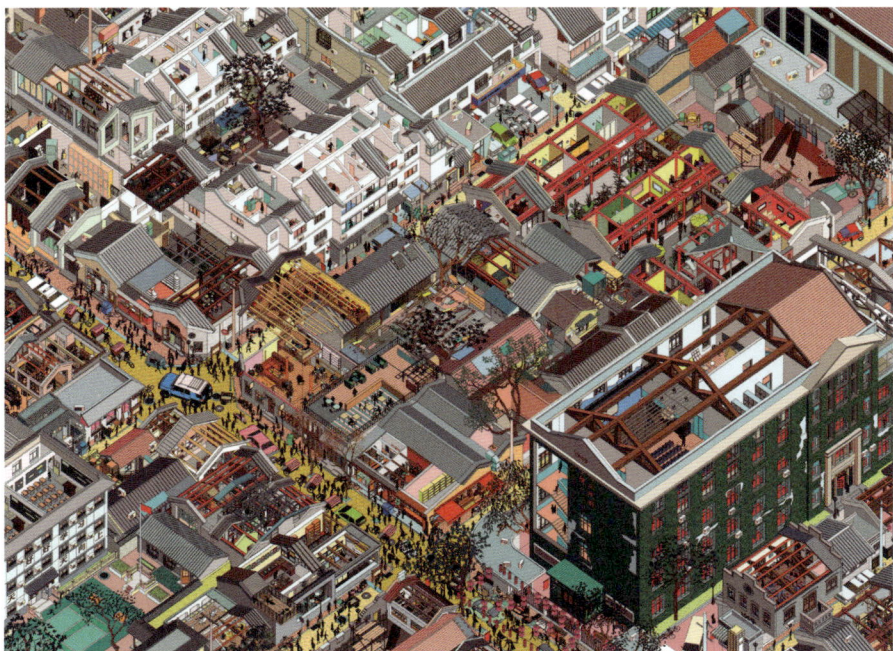

Qi Lou Old Street (above) and *Nan Luo Gu Xiang* (below) Images courtesy of Drawing Architecture Studio

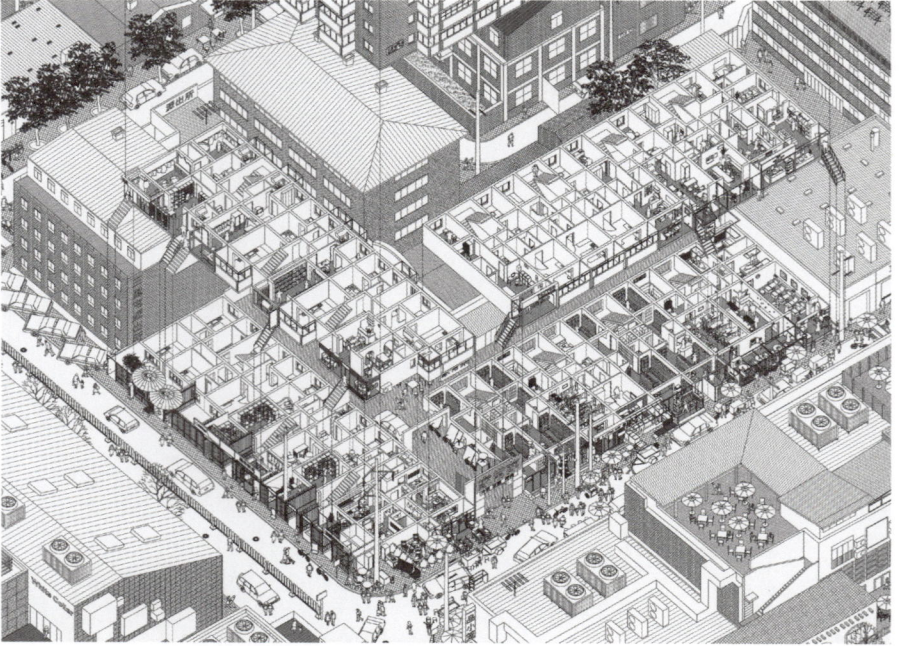

Sanlitun (above) and *Xibahe* (below) Images courtesy of Drawing Architecture Studio

cation next to the Central Business District. In this neighborhood, cars are not required. Every necessity required in life is within walking distance, including shopping, leisure, food, medical care, school, and work. In terms of its scale, Tuanjiehu is very livable. It is an excellent neighborhood made up of poorly designed buildings. In such a neighborhood, one can observe an unexpected privatization of the public realm. One can find shabby furniture strewn across certain portions of the public spaces. They look like garbage, but they are actually strategically placed by specific owners. They exist to occupy specific public spaces and privatize them. The logic behind is that furniture is private, no matter how badly they have fallen into disrepair; hence no one else can contest it.

This privatization of public space is very common in the old neighborhoods of Beijing. Due to relatively lax management, all sorts of tactics are used to gain a bit of private benefits in the public realm. Similar tactics include the use of rubbish bins or broken bicycles to reserve parking lots along the street. Locked cages are used to transform public green spaces into private nurseries and vegetable farms. In the most curious cases, Beijingers would exploit the use of exterior security grilles. Installed on the exterior of windows, this security contraption would project outwards of a building to accommodate the outward swing of the casement windows. Such three-dimensional security grilles are popular with practically every household, because they serve a more significant purpose of allowing each window to gain air rights over the projected window space. The addition of this small enclosed volume allows each owner to pile up their private belongings inside it. These projected security grilles are becoming infinitely larger and protruding further to claim even more space.

Xibahe: Pets and Urbanity

Xibahe has a lot in common with Tuanjiehu. They are both relatively old residential districts in Beijing, but they are geographically well-located. This depiction attends to the spaces of the animals, as much as they are interested in spaces for the human inhabitants. Pet keeping in China is an extremely interesting business. Elsewhere, most pets may have the opportunity to live outdoors in a kennel or a semi-outdoor environment, allowing them to retain much of their natural character. However, in a dense living environment as Beijing, pets would live in high-rise conditions as their owners. These pets would dress up when they head outdoors. Some may even wear shoes to keep clean. They would take the elevators and even learn to look both ways when crossing the road. The life of a pet has become exceedingly urbane.

Apart from pets, there is an equal fascination with the large number of stray animals in Beijing. On the one hand, there are media reports of black market butchers selling stray animal meat for barbeques. On the other hand, compassionate residents and animal welfare activists would organize care groups to feed stray animals at regular intervals and locations. Beijingers have always had the tradition of keeping pigeons, for example. This tradition was brought into new conditions of high-rise living by the elderly residents. The cages that they build in their balconies would bring about a severe nuisance to neighbors

Tuanjiehu Image courtesy of Drawing Architecture Studio

Xizhimen Image courtesy of Drawing Architecture Studio

and be a source of conflict. There are frequent social media reports of fights between residents over whether pets can be allowed in lifts. Xibahe can be imagined as a high-density zoo—a new form of composite habitation. The green spaces of the neighborhood would be transformed into mini pastures with tiny ponies. Animals would be managed with the help of microchip implants for identification tracking. The city would belong not only to man but also to the incredible animals of Beijing.

Xizhimen: Chaos and Ugliness as Everyday Textures of Life

The portrayal of Xizhimen was made in 2008. The Xizhimen metro station today is very different from the one depicted in the drawing. Rapid urbanization made it possible for the metro station to be understood as a moment confined to the memory of the old. Today, Xizhimen is an interchange of three metro lines, with relatively short walking distances between them. In 2008, there were only two metro lines, and they were located very far apart. Passengers had to walk from three stories above ground to a location deep underground, through countless steps and long distances, and even through a passageway on the street level. The highlight of this 2008 interchange was precisely the oddity of this passageway. From this passageway to the narrow steps leading to the concourse of Line No.2, there was a maze-like barricade to slow down the crowd. This lengthy spiraling sequence remained a very primitive method, not too different from the American farmers, who would use the same technique to guide galloping wild horses into their stables.

This remarkable transfer sequence left an indelible impression on all commuters in Beijing, even though Xizhimen station was much criticized and cursed at the time. This collective memory lies in the temporal nature of China's urban transformation, utterly crude and poorly planned, yet hugely vibrant. In fact, there were small electric fans above the spiraling passage in order to generate the slightest of breeze in the extreme forty-degree Celsius summers. With the completion of this interchange, passengers can transit from one line to another in the comfort of an air-conditioned environment. The transit experience has become more convenient and comfortable by far, but it no longer triggers any strong feelings about the place. The irrationality, mundaneness, crudeness, chaos, or the sheer ugliness of the built environment can sometimes yield a space with the greater textures of life.

Old Town of Xinchang: Dynamism and Unfixed Perspectives of a City

Xinchang was built in the Song dynasty more than eight hundred years ago. Its original townscape boasts of a rich heritage of traditional architecture. The urban development over the recent century turned Xinchang into an exemplar, where there can be a coexistence of traditional and contemporary architecture in the historical towns of China. All the buildings in the *Old Town of Xinchang* are aligned along the streets or rivers, as one row of buildings would appear upside-down, mirroring buildings from either side. The documentation of the historical buildings was made as a journey down the streets and through the town, observing and recording all the activities around the architecture. As the streets and rivers slope, turn, and bend, the buildings would adapt to their angles accordingly. Taking a macro-perspective view, if the viewer can approach the upside-down buildings as an ant crawling along the streets, the viewer would experience exactly the same urban scenes as observed in the city.

While the drawing itself is static, it has the capacity to mobilize the viewer because of the unfixed perspectives, bringing dynamism to the experience of the city. Different from an emphasis on objective documentation of earlier urban panoramas, *Old Town of Xinchang* tries to represent this particular area of the city with an illusionary structure. Both figurative and abstract, concise and abundant at the same time, the panorama is a flattened picturesque projection of the real world. The true nature of architectural drawing is in its ability to conjure a new view of the world. Heavily inspired by Persian miniature painting, each building in *Old Town of Xinchang* is drawn with a relatively condensed approach, collaged with a large amount of pre-rendered components, such as ridges, gables, *matouqiang* gable walls, doors, and windows. The abundance of architectural details is not represented in individual forms, but it is shown in the diverse combination of the components and perspectival changes, as well as the multiplicity of textures, fills, and shapes. This drawing is based on the redevelopment plans and a vast 3D model by AMJ Architecture and Planning Design Company for Xinchang Town in Shanghai.

Old Town of Xinchang Image courtesy of Drawing Architecture Studio

SEVEN YEARS AGO?
THIS WAS ALL COUNTRYSIDE!

DAAN ROGGEVEEN

Airport: Connected

It was sweaty and warm when I walked down the airstairs in the direction of the airside transfer buses. The first thing I saw when I walked over the tarmac was a blue KLM Boeing parked at its gate—the proof of an Amsterdam-Chengdu connection.

The airport that served as its backdrop was the second testimony of Chengdu's progress in global connectivity. When we visited this city for the first time seven years ago, the construction of Terminal Two had just started. Now, the glitzy airport connects this western Chinese city directly to fifty cities globally, including London, Paris, Moscow, and Los Angeles.

Flashback One: Truly Different Development Model

Between 2009 and 2011, journalist Michiel Hulshof and I traveled extensively to cities in central and western China to understand the development model of what we considered to be "potential" world cities. We visited upcoming metropolises like Chongqing, Xi'an, Kunming, and Guiyang, and investigated their urban growth model. We published a book, *How the City Moved to Mr. Sun*, in which we described a new type of urban progress driven by the combination of a strong state, and an entrepreneurial spirit of its inhabitants.

Our conclusion was clear. Chinese cities have a truly different development model from cities in the West. They focus first on the expansion of their tangible infrastructure—roads, railroads, airports, and skyscrapers. But their ambition would eventually shift to the intangible, soft side of the urban—education, cultural life, and the environment.

Compound: Focus on Software

Our reason to revisit Chengdu was a design pitch for a real estate company, of which Zhan Xianglong was the Vice Director. Mr. Zhan was a fashionable man, dressed in a slim white shirt, fashionable gray pants with inside-out seams, and bone glasses. He drove us around the area to show us the context of their real estate projects. We drove along Tianfu Dadao, the main axis of Chengdu that connects the heart of the city with its southern developments, including the new business district and the new exhibition center. It appeared that the explosion of real estate development we observed nearly a decade ago has never stopped.

Through a gate we arrived at a gigantic building made of red stone. The structure turns out to be a large sales center for the residential compound that sat behind it, in a sort of archipelago of villas and high-rises. Mr. Zhan took us to the deck outside the clubhouse, overlooking a small harbor. Dressed in a yellow polo shirt emblazoned with the "Luxelakes Yachtclub" logo, a young man steered a motor boat with potential buyers into the dock. We boarded a similar catamaran boat with gray leather sofas, and started our journey through the gated community.

Mr. Zhan exclaimed, "You can swim here!" After a ride through the remarkably clean water, we visited the equestrian stables, the company of which, we were told, followed the French equestrian system. After picking up an ice cappuccino, we visited the show apartments. They come in different designs, catering to either an eclectic Baroque preference, or a minimal neo-historical Chinese style.

Bigger Picture: Industrial Economy to Export Economy

The story about China's urbanization is frequently told. During the process of economic liberalization initiated by Deng Xiaoping, China made the move from a rural to an urban society and economy. Where only one-fifth of its population lived in cities by the end of the seventies, China reached a fifty percent level of urbanization by 2011. Along the way, the country transformed its economy into an industrial one, focused on an export economy.

Since 2011, urban development in China has gone through a rocky period. Urbanization continued, but the real estate market resulted in a number of economic bubbles. This influenced the economy of many Chinese cities, with real estate markets cooling and urban development slowing down. At the same time, both labor cost and the level of education increased immensely. China then made an opportunistic shift from industrial production to service oriented industries. China refocused its economy from export to its internal market.

Tai Koo Li: Consumerism and Leisure

After visiting Mr. Zhan, we decided to head downtown. When we left the car at a busy crossing, we passed by a couple of expensive stores and a *Joghurtwerk* shop, a frozen yogurt franchise from Berlin. Next to the shop, a street musician is playing rock songs. I felt lost. Seven years ago this was a rather backward and provincial city with a slow pace and an extremely laid-back attitude. Somehow, it has changed into a swanky version of its former self.

Tai Koo Li is a shopping concept in a Kengo Kuma-style by a Hong Kong developer. Kuma is the panda bear amongst architects because he is impossible to dislike. His work is recognizable as both modern and nostalgic. We passed by a couple of high-end stores, including a Gucci flagship store with a six-meter-high glass façade. Then we entered a Nicolas Andreas Taralis boutique. The place was completely white, with a white translucent ceiling and a terrazzo floor. Its Raf Simons style jackets cost RMB 6,000.

Flashback Two: Gijs and Gentrification

The second time we were in Chengdu, we went to visit the Machu Picchu bar, started by former squatter Gijs. His bar had a domestic atmosphere, with posters and paintings on the wall and a low sofa with cushions lining the walls. Local hip youngsters were having a drink here and there. Gijs made a clear description of the background of his customers, "You have to realize, they just come from the countryside. Their parents are still wearing uniforms from the Cultural Revolution era."

The bar was located in a small apartment building in a quiet street in a 1990s apartment block. Gijs acknowledged that his bar was part of this gigantic urban transformation. "The place we are now was still rural only fifteen years ago. Outside the second ring road, only just five years ago it was countryside."

Walnut: the Service Economy

The next morning, we decided to pay a visit to an old friend Mike. He is a Guizhou-born entrepreneur in his mid-twenties with an American accent and a couple of serious tattoos. With one eye on his iWatch and another on his smartphone, Mike ran Walnut, a co-shared workspace concept similar to WeWork in an office park in the northwest of the city.

We met him in the lobby of the office, at a bar with fake Chesterfield sofas decorated with cushions printed with slogans "Fuck Average" and "I Can. I Do. End of Story." Mike talked about revenue, management fees, and how the shared workspace company was becoming a tech firm. He was about to enter the Shanghai market. Inside Walnut, there were three floors of young people, programmers and designers typing away on laptops. Mike reiterated, "Our average age is below thirty." They even developed their own app. To unlock the door to these premises, you only needed to swipe your Walnut App. We ordered an Uber, and Mike saw us out. "See you in Shanghai, when we set up shop there!"

Flashback Three: Real Value

"I think we have lost direction and do not know the real value of things anymore." Liu Jiakun was very skeptical of the urban development in Chengdu when we visited him in his office in 2009. "We are lost in the woods. They built new living quarters in a

Western style. And Kuanzai Alley has turned into an area like Shanghai Xintiandi."A local architect in his late forties, Liu has been locally engaged for decades.

"I let myself be influenced by local building materials and by the historic processes of building." By 2009, Liu was able to develop his ideas into a small sculpture museum in the western part of the city. But he is very concerned about the future of the city center. "It's usually very difficult to persuade the client. And what we do is only a small piece of everything that is being built, of course."

The Great West Village Beisen Yard

The Uber dropped us in front of a massive building in raw concrete and wood. We entered the minimally designed concrete showroom of a real estate company. A pregnant woman in her twenties welcomed us and showed us around.

Liu's most recent project was an inner-city development that consisted of a concrete structure with five floors. It covered a full urban block. On one side, the building entailed a running track that spiraled up the floors. At the heart of the building, there were three soccer fields. Throughout the whole building, tenants changed, altered, and added to the structure, creating a very lively environment. Next to the elevators, the floors were open. We walked on the streets in the sky, hovering over the trees. Fully accessible, with public facilities and a structure that can change over time, this urban project represented all of Liu's ambitions.

Final Drive: Lost in Chengdu Again

We left the building impressed by so many changes in Chengdu, and headed for our final meeting over hotpot. Halfway through the dinner, I had to leave to catch my plane. At the crossing, looking for a taxi, I felt a bit lost again. I told the taxi driver that I had visited Chengdu seven years ago, but I did not recognize the city anymore. His response was as straightforward as it was dismissive. "Seven years ago? This was all countryside!"

06 NETWORKING

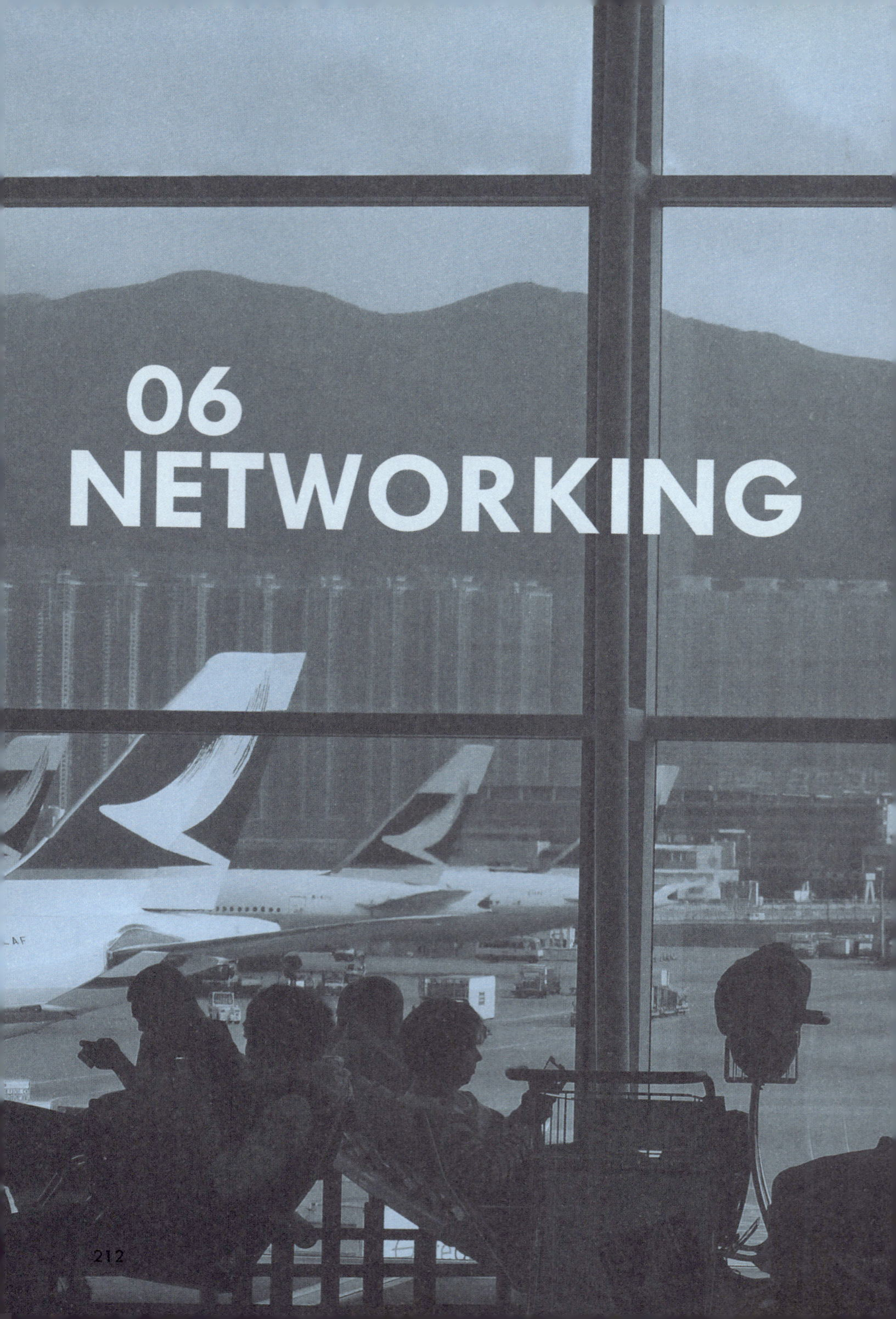

China's bullish economic growth has a lot to do with its investments in mass communication and digital networks. Yet it is also the same networks that serve as the "grounds of services" for the rise of social media and mobility that threatens China's ability to control its society. This McLuhanite notion of a concealed environment of services, and the fetish for innovation can be very true of China's approach to media. Manuel Castells made numerous observations about China under the same influence of the global informational network in the context of the state and the economy. He questions how class struggles are being transformed by the availability of mass communication and new types of networks. How do the structural changes in the "spaces of flows" radically improve lives? While sociologists, economists, and political scientists examine these complex organizational relationships, they are always looking for evidence of how it affects the lived reality of people. It is important to examine how such abstract forces "hit the ground" in a city and get subsumed into architecture. As a methodological necessity in this volume, the real site can be found in the spatial dimensions of art, culture, and production networks.

Passengers connected to the social network in the Hong Kong International Airport. Image courtesy of Budi Lim, 2015

INSIDE-OUT PARTICIPATION

ZHOU YI

The architecture of the Inside-out Art Museum and its interior were done separately, typical of projects in China. An architect's work is considered complete when the building is constructed. In the case of a highly specialized art museum, another architectural design office had to be brought in to design its interiors. Hence the building and its interior, or the outside and inside of the museum, were results of a collaboration of two architecture offices. The architectural shell was designed by Cui Kai's office in Beijing, and the inner casing was designed by Obra Architects from the New York. In the years of running the full program at the Inside-out Art Museum as its Curatorial Director, I was actively involved in the process of Obra's design of the interiors, especially the functional aspects of the museum.

There was an effort to try to think much further ahead of its current use. Obra Architects began by "softening" the white box. With very limited choices, a hierarchy and a series of transitions around the main exhibition space were created. Variations in lighting and in types of furniture, transitions in material, height control, and spatial orientation gave legible character to each area. When the museum is in use, such qualities not only offered opportunities for visitors to find their own space in the museum but also challenged the curators and content-makers to fill the layers with more content and to create a tempo with diverse activities for the visitors. As the exhibition program matured, the spatial potential of the museum was thoroughly explored in collaboration with artists from the International Residency Program. Every single pocket of space, every corner, and every hallway was utilized for temporary exhibitions at different times. These spatial experiments gave the museum an unpredictable edge, and a vital connection to the communities around. Spaces were used for multiple purposes. The meeting room, for example, was a popular classroom for the fast growing educational program. It was used for running classes in art history, painting, printmaking, and handcrafts several times a week.

Once the museum opened, the operational territory expanded and exceeded the initial expectations. This is not a reference to a need for more space, but simply that the activities grew beyond the confines of the walls. The museum took on a greater experimental mission to sustain its fundraising efforts and its public program for the surrounding local communities. The museum found itself in situations that demanded that each space becomes less formal and more flexible for different purposes. It was almost akin to asking the institution to take on an ability to mutate. There was experimentation with exhibitions to add or contain an extra layer of functional space. In one instance, a classroom was built inside an exhibition, and another occasion, an exhibition was curated on the inside of an existing exhibition. Special opportunities reveal themselves in such a way that the process of exhibition was afforded the same creative process as the art projects, catching the right moment to develop a new portal to another dimension in the world of art.

Inside-out Museum, exterior and interior. Image courtesy of Budi Lim, 2015

Energy not Quality

The German artist Thomas Hirschhorn adopted the slogan "Energy not Quality." In the everyday reality of China, there are great applications for such a slogan. From a practitioner's point of view, quality is always exclusive in China. Given the fast-changing and unpredictable circumstances, there is an urgency to meet multiple demands in the daily operation of the museum. The main conflict is between rapidly changing needs and the rigid walls of museum. Designing it from the inside out, the giving up of quality should not be understood literally. Instead, there can be a renewed focus on the exchange of quality for greater participation. In the end, it is for no a lack of quality but a totally different kind of quality—a richer definition of quality that favors openness and participation. The spaces of the museum can become less and less defined, less categorical, and more open to diverse social groups and multiple functions. It seems that there is a growing need for an ever broader sense of architecture.

Experimentation and Openness

In the reality of realizing a building from its conception to construction, there are complex factors at play. In 2013, the main proponent behind the Museum requested the hiring of a sculptor to create a relief for a stretch of wall along the staircase ascending towards the entrance of the Inside-out Theater. With a preference for a more holistic and conceptual approach, an architect was selected in place of a sculptor. Long-time collaborator and architect Thomas Tsang took the opportunity to further experiment within the premise of an exhibition space. Tsang eventually proposed a Miniature Museum—the creation of an exhibition space by hollowing out the two-meter-thick wall. It was a discovery of something out of nothingness. Tsang intends it as a space to exhibit and collect events

and memories. In other words, it is to be a space to inspire art, not to contain it—a vision for the future of art institutions. Architecture becomes quite literally a site where things would happen in a more open manner. The Miniature Museum does not exist until one discovers it. Waiting to be defined, one could begin by asking what it can be. It is a site of imagination. It appears useless, an enigma. One may call it architecture, just to provoke a reaction. It is like a brick, calling for an external force to give it form.

Visitors outside the Miniature Museum.
Image courtesy of Budi Lim, 2015

Taking an unconventional approach, a two-channel sound installation and performance piece called *Jericho's Mouth* was installed and performed at the Miniature Museum in 2014 by artist Ken Ueno. Using his voice and body together as a performative instrument, Ueno gave the best answer to this challenge. During Ueno's two-week residency at the Inside-out Art Museum, he experimented with his voice inside the space, and incorporated his vocal style into the narrow space—a four-meter-tall, 1.6-meter-wide and nine-meter-long chamber that featured four holes, a door, a window, a skylight, and a sound portal. Ueno recalled the experiment, "Working within the Miniature Museum, I sang and recorded myself singing sub-tones that I calibrated in a way to shake the building, make it roar."

The finished installation was too loud for the visitors to be inside, so one has to experience the piece from the outside. Ueno sings, listens, and improvises in this special chamber of resonance. Was he was performing inside an instrument, or was he operating a massive and heavy body from within? Drawing on the destructive volume of heavy metal, sub-tonal singing, and the resonance of the concrete walls, Ueno used his sounds to possess the structure. The walls became a carrier of his voice and will, to the extent that a distracted observer may be under the illusion that the thick concrete walls were breathing. This performative exhibition took place in the world's smallest museum, or it created the world's largest musical instrument. It really depends on how one looks at it.

THE INDIVIDUALIZED COLLECTIVE

HAN TAO

"The Gemeinschaft is the lasting and genuine form of living together."

Ferdinand Tönnies, *Gemeinschaft and Gesellschaft*, 1887

This essay proposes a new form of community for China, as an update of the dichotomous concept of *Gemeinschaft* (community) and *Gesellschaft* (society) proposed by the nineteenth-century socialist Ferdinand Tönnies, and the three types of collective form in Karl Marx's theory. At the core of both concepts is the rethinking of the relationship between the individual and the collective. In *The German Ideology* (1845-1846), Marx differentiated three types of collective form, namely, nature and politics, alienation, and free association. In this instance, Tönnies' work is comparable to that of Marx. Tönnies' *Gemeinschaft* echoed Marx's natural and political collective form—a cultural form rooted in pre-industrial society, where social relations were founded on natural kinship, as well as leadership and obedience. There was a controlled political hierarchy established on relationship by blood. His *Gesellschaft* would echo Marx's concept of alienation—an uprooted cultural form that existed in capitalist society. Such social relations were established on material dependence and human independence. The natural relationship by blood was replaced by materialist social relations.

With respect to China, the social transformation from 1949 to 1992 as a whole can be understood as the displacement of traditional village communities by political communities. In other words, the kinship community of village societies, composed of autonomous settlements within a traditional patriarchal society, was replaced by the political community of *danwei* societies. The *danwei* forms were designed as compounds in the city, or the people's commune in villages. On the other hand, the social transformation from 1992 onwards could be understood as the displacement of the fabric of a community by that of a society. *Danwei* compounds were displaced by middle-class real estate compounds and gated communities. The neighborhoods along the public streets were displaced by the homogenized masses, shaped by shopping malls in a global consumer culture. Traditional settlements in the rural area would become tourist destinations and theme parks.

How can we transcend the aforementioned dual social formations? Marx proposed a third category of collective form, the free association of producers. He suggested that there was a prerequisite that every individual had free possibilities for development. Corresponding to the current social reality, with modern communication technologies and the Internet, various social media have prematurely infused "free association of producers" into the spectrum between Tönnies' *Gemeinschaft* and *Gesellschaft*. Thus, the traditional community is making a return in a new form under the new guise of digital technology. Society can no longer be simply described as individualized or dispersed. According to philosopher and socialist art theorist, Boris Groys, contemporary society can be understood as the combination of communist software and capitalist hardware. This is precisely the context generated by a new Chinese community, where the simple dichotomy of community and society would change to reveal a third path—which can be termed the New Community. The society of the twenty-first century would return to a state of community from its dispersed state. In short, the New Community is the combination of traditional community and modern society. It appropriates the current social logic that respects the values of the individual, in order to correct the community form of the pre-industrial era. It also uses the community form of a pre-industrial society that emphasized the value of the collective, in order to correct the state of an individualized modern society. The New Community is a kind of individualized collective, which is a form of collectivism that takes individual value as its premise. An individualized collective does not reject the collective. On the contrary, it is a contemporary form of the collective, and a contemporary alteration of traditional forms of community.

Condition and Context

Where did the first individualized collective of the New Community first appear in twenty-first-century China? Was it in the urban or the rural? In a city entirely ruled by politics and capital, it is almost impossible for a New Community to exist. However, there is potential for it to emerge in the rural areas. The reason is two-fold. Firstly, land is collectivized in the rural, which means land is collectively owned by all villagers. Rural land is not nationalized, unlike how urban land belongs to the state, and the right of use is separated from that of possession, since the constitution of 1982. Secondly, for a long time, the rural was isolated from basic infrastructure, due to the urbanization processes. These conditions created an autonomy that provided relative political freedom on the one hand, and prevented early contamination of capitalism on the other. These factors made the New Community possible.

At the terminus of the Beijing Ancient Canal at Gaobeidian sits the Chinese Academy of Oil Painting. This was once a node of the extremely well-developed shipping network and agricultural landscape. However, due to industrialization after the People's Republic of

China was established in 1949, Gaobeidian turned into a semi-industrial rural landscape, isolated from the outside by railways, sewage treatment plants and elevated roads. Before 2012, Gaobeidian would be disconnected from the world for five hours every day, because of the high-speed train departing from the city center. Under such circumstances, it was almost impossible to make use of existing urban resources. Everything had to be self-sufficient. As a village, Gaobeidian is less than thirteen kilometers away from Tiananmen, yet it existed primarily in isolation. This was the foundation on which a community was formed—a community in a pre-industrial society was founded within a relatively isolated condition. Gaobeidian gradually transformed within such a state of isolation. The Academy was also responsible for initiating the transformation of the village of Gaobeidian from an agricultural and semi-industrial rural landscape to a post-industrial rural landscape. At the same time, the condition of isolation drew groups of artists to the place. They formed a community with a similar artistic language, but lacked a relatively close personal working environment, or they lacked an aspect of production and a real social space. It was a conscious desire for a closed environment that drove the artists and students to this relatively isolated area.

The Chinese Academy of Oil Painting is situated amidst an intersection of various collective fields. The land is rented from the village community of Gaobeidian. It receives political support from the Chinese National Academy of Art, a national institution of education. Its organization is based on a community of freelance artists, with Yang Feiyun, dean of the Academy, as its core member. These three fields correspond to the collective forms of the rural, the institutional and the individual respectively. From this aspect, the artist group is neither fully official nor individual, but a folk group with official support. The Academy is neither a top-down national investment nor a real estate development. It was not founded by individual artists renting studio spaces in an organized manner. Since 2000, the Chinese art market had gradually integrated with economic capital, as the group of artists led by Yang gained cultural capital and symbolic capital with their artworks. They garnered economic capital for the construction of the Academy in a collaboration with various real estate developers, instigating a primitive form of bartering in an eight-year construction process and producing a total of 22,000 square meters. This is also why the construction of the Academy in Gaobeidian was not formally registered. The Academy was a temporary and illegal structure that would be "legalized" only in the future. Such an informal construction did not necessarily violate the building code. It existed as a stratagem that resulted from special conditions of social production, where practice preceded official documentation and registration. Unregistered construction usually occurs at urban peripheries or areas undergoing urbanization, where ambiguous areas of a social space gets filled under uncertain social conditions. In China, new communities are constantly emerging in gray areas of relative isolation. Isolation is the starting point that nurtures difference. In twenty-first-century China, the New Community can be described as an "individualized collective," and physical and social conditions of isolation are its context.

Social Transformations in Architecture

While the transformation of Chinese societies did become more prominent in recent conditions of rapid urbanization, it was never truly a new phenomenon. In fact, the fundamental demand for social change can be attributed to rapid development during the late-nineteenth-century capitalist period of industrialization. Based on this principle of social change, architectural historian Kenneth Frampton narrates architectural evolution in the twentieth century through Tönnies' concepts of community and society as early as 1980. From Frampton's point of view, architects in the early twentieth century responded to two forms of collectivity. On the one hand, there were numerous forms of habitation and work environments produced by such new societies, such as Le Corbusier's three planning visions for Paris and their relationships with Fordist production methods, or the spread and homogenization of the suburbs for the middle class in the United States during the 1950s and 1960s. On the other hand, social transformations arose after the disintegration of traditional communities, such as Le Corbusier's La Tourette Monastery and Unite d'Habitation at Marseilles, or Louis Kahn's Jewish Community Center and Bath House. These new forms and materiality evoked discussions on new forms of monumentality. The work of numerous architects from Team X also reinterpreted the role of mass-produced architecture, and initiated new discourses on the relationship between the individual and the collective.

New architectural variants emerged after the 1970s and 1980s, brought about by the arrival of the post-industrial society, and the expansion of liberalism under globalization. The "culture of congestion" was an extreme case that responded to the growth of a capitalist society, as articulated by Rem Koolhaas in his writings about New York during his time at the Institute of Architecture and Urban Studies. In another alternative concept, Critical Regionalism was suggested by Alexander Tzonis and Kenneth Frampton in the early 1980s as a strategy addressing the cultural crisis of the community. Since 2000, the digital revolution, economic globalization, and rapid urbanization have been pushing these problems to the next level, that is, the internal conflict and integration of a place or community within the logic of the city, and a global consumerist society under the logic of urbanization. The extreme case of the former took the form of commodified housing and iconic architecture under massive real estate growth in China. The thinking behind the logic of an urban form was captured by Italian architectural scholar Pier Vittorio Aureli in his 2011 seminal book The Possibility of an Absolute Architecture. The interactions between the two theoretical paradigms of "community" and "society" would form the foundation of social transformation in architecture in the twentieth century, and in the twenty-first century, the sites of extreme transformations would be found in the cities of China.

In the future processes of urbanization, new social spaces are being restructured with various phenotypic means, and new subjects are emerging.

Multiple Scales, Multiple Light Conditions, and Independent Control

During the design stage of the new studio and the building for teaching purposes, the artists requested that the space should enable traditional still life drawing, sketching, serial and large painting, exhibition, and a comfortable space for habitation. How can these differentiated and specialized functional demands be deployed in the design process, with an enhanced architectural form? Starting from the criteria of light requirements and scale, the different functions were first organized by their scales, and spaces of similar scalar requirements were organized around their distinctive lighting needs. By doing so, all spaces were instilled with a unique meaning—as one walks along different rooms, one wanders through a variety of spaces with different lighting conditions. In this way, the lighting condition of each space in itself is unique and stable, while the scale between spaces are different and variable. These differences are also expressed as a sequence of spaces with direct or indirect light, and with dominant or supplementary light sources at various sectional intervals. The angles of the light source would also be carefully determined based on the demand of exhibition, art production, and habitation, as the lighting conditions aid in the dispersion or dissolution of the spaces from one scene to another.

The lighting condition and scalar qualities of the new studio were defined by typological studies based on multiple criteria of historic archetypes, collective memory, and the character of the region. However, the new building for teaching purposes would emphasize the experience of alternating lighting conditions across the different spaces. The specific scalar requirements imposed by the functions of exhibition, art production and habitation induced the development of a unique architectural type in the design of the Academy. In other words, the section of the building was designed by juxtaposing the three scales of different proportions. In the creation of this new typology, the lighting conditions of various historical studios were analyzed and integrated with the memory of the everyday life of the artists growing up in China. Light sources would be controllable by the users, especially the south-facing direct sunlight suited for habitation, and its integration with north-facing diffused skylights suited for work. These light sources could be used independently or combined in various ways, depending on the mood of the artists, which may change during the course of their stay. Ventilation windows are provided on the side to facilitate the dissipation of odor produced by the art production, which is often ignored. The conditions for the production of art would differ drastically from those of the exhibition spaces.

The greatest expectation from the artists would be the provision of a professional studio that has a skylight, spaces for working and dwelling, and spaces large enough for the moving and producing of large-scale paintings. Light conditions and scale could be entry points to the core of the architectural condition, and solving these two problems is equivalent to solving the most critical demand of an individual's space. And this is the only power that can bring highly individualistic and influential artists together. The demand for a collective space would be a natural occurrence, such as the lecture hall in the third phase of the Academy, but it was not a prerequisite. This is a unique phenomenon in contemporary art practices, and also a common practice for the "free association of free men." It is no longer the collective spaces of traditional society that is truly attractive, it is the fulfilment of the intrinsic desire for individual space. The establishment of a collective space would occur naturally after the congregation of proactive and motivated individuals. The way the Chinese Academy of Oil Painting privileges individual space echoes Hannah Arendt's response to "privately owned spaces where one could hide." These independent studios represent a private shelter where artists could express their potentials, dreams and memories, heal themselves, and attain profound perceptiveness. An individual without a deep perception of the world is but a shadow on the street. An individual space of recluse allows each artist to better prepare themselves as their works emerge in the public realm.

Service Space after Modernism

What supports the individual and collective spaces, as well as the private and public spaces of the communities today? There remains a great reliance on service spaces even after modernism. The urban peripheral condition of the Academy alludes to the reality and specificity of the issue. The dependency of service spaces in modern life and a reliance on modern equipment not only became the prerequisite for design, but they are also the foundation of a community. Although Le Corbusier was the first to understand the relationship between the individual and the collective in the Chartreuse d'Ema, he did not investigate how important the service space would be to the collective form. It was Louis Kahn who deepened the contemporary understanding of such a service space, which is an issue more fundamental to the distinction of public and private spaces. The service space is relatively fixed, compared with the flexibility of spatial attributes, no matter public or private. It is restricted by multiple constraints in its realization, and Kahn resolved the differentiated collective and individual spaces, by distinguishing and structuring such a service space, and even the ability to perceive such a space.

There was a sustained investigation of the coexistence between different individuals in the design of the Academy. This was the first problem that arose concerning the layout of the service spaces. Should service spaces be centralized, dispersed, or networked? How can the layout of the service spaces support the multitude of individuals and the requirement of flexibility? The solution was to set up a networked organization of service spaces, and to structuralize them. This allows spatial units to disintegrate from the whole, supporting the multiple demands of differentiated functions. Each fragmented spatial unit would have the flexibility to accommodate the various users intervening in the space. It could then be collectivized or individualized. It could also respond to changes in time. Artists would come and go over the decade, but because of the networked structure of service spaces, the artists living in the Academy would find their needs fulfilled. The Academy would become a society of rooms, or a new collective life under contemporary conditions. The service spaces would also be experiential. The third floor of the second phase of the building for teaching purposes was an uplifted courtyard. Between each individual studio, there are *hutong*s or alleys which are the negative spaces of the structuralized service spaces. Whenever an individual artist walks along these alleys between the rooms, the Fifth Ring Road and the Jingtong Highway would be visible at a distance, and a nearby train would be speeding by.

Le Corbusier's discovery in Chartreuse d'Ema was recognized as a spatial prototype for the contemporary community. It motivated a number of his late works. This prototype was furthered by Louis Kahn, who investigated the physical composition of a community form from the lens of a service space. Pier Vittorio Aureli expands the debate by using the concept of separation to create a form of new community for the new working class, firmly establishing a new architectural form in the contemporary city, and fully confronting the capitalist form of urbanization. These ideological sources inspired the formation of a contemporary space of community in China. The decade-long project of the Academy did not shape architecture into a container of society for different individuals, but it shaped a spatial structure based on the existing collective relationship of differentiated individuals, that is the "individualized collective." On this basis, the future form of community space can be projected. Mobile networking and digital technologies would continue to create even newer and more diverse relationships in this "New Community." In the future processes of urbanization, new social spaces are being restructured with various phenotypic means, and new subjects are emerging. The spaces of the New Community in the Chinese Academy of Oil Painting were part of a response to rapid social transformation, and they also represent a projection into the future.

EXPERIMENTATION, EXCHANGE, LIFE, AND ART

XU TIANTIAN

Architecture has the capacity to transform lives, and to have an impact on the society it serves. At the same time, architecture has to follow the mandate of its times. As a number of architects addressed the urgent topics of the countryside in China in the past decade, the relevance of the countryside grew in importance in the discourse and practice of architecture. Unfortunately, this discourse also became a predicament, as ideas around the countryside developed into a singularly oppositional stance against the architecture of the city. In reality, the countryside and the city ought to be part of a harmonized whole. With a rural population at around one billion, the sheer size and territory of the countryside alone represent a massive social problem for China. Improvements made in the countryside can only lead to a corresponding and magnified improvement in the city. On an architectural level, there is no differentiation between the city and countryside when it comes to the strategies for coping with essential issues of the site and the wider environment, and end-users and their utilitarian needs. The sensitivity shown towards the natural environment and local culture in the practice of architecture in the countryside would serve to stimulate a similar reflection when one builds in the city.

Between the Countryside and the City

Songzhuang Artist Village is the largest and one of the most renowned art districts in China, and it is the ideal context for the discussion of this intersection between the city and the countryside. Prior to its expansion, Songzhuang was primarily an area for agriculture. Located on the edge of East Sixth Ring Road of Beijing, its artist population has reached over four thousand artists by 2008, and this growth has invigorated the expansion of studios, art galleries, museums, and art centers in and around Songzhuang. The transformation of Songzhuang began in 1994, when the Yuanmingyuan Artists Village located by the old summer palace on the west side of Beijing was demolished. To escape the watchful eye of the authorities, the relocation of this artist community to a relatively remote area was led by the famous art critic Li Xianting. He was joined by many artists, who became successful commercially in the recent two decades, such as Fang Lijun, Yue Minjun, and Wang Guangyi.

From the mid-1990s to early-2000s, Songzhuang was known as the base for artistic experimentation. Photographed in Songzhuang in 1994, artist Zhang Huan's famous performance *To Add One Meter to an Anonymous Mountain* was achieved by stacking naked bodies upon one another to form a mountain. In its early days, this artist community

Songzhuang Art Village. Image courtesy of Budi Lim, 2015

was akin to a commune, where artists rented houses from the local villagers. As they pursued their artistic dreams, their meager living circumstances soon began to change when the art market experienced its first boom in early 2000. Artists from all over China seemed to have a preference for Songzhuang when they first arrive in Beijing. The sheer number and diversity in both the creative genre and economic status of the artists were unique characteristics of this community. As it grew, it became necessary to build an art museum for the community, where local artists could exhibit their artworks, hold academic conferences about art, and conduct artistic exchange programs.

As the first public art facility in the artist village, the structure of the Songzhuang Art Museum was inspired by local forms and materials. The red bricks used for the exterior of the museum and the gray paving tile in front of the museum that extend into the interior were references from the brick buildings and courtyards in the village.

Reflecting traditional courtyards in the village, the individual art blocks of the museum were extruded from a rectangular envelope from a simple layout. The box-like forms were scattered on the public ground, carrying services and functional demands of this facility. The glass enclosures used on the perimeter of the ground floor offer a sense of transparency that draws the community and visitors in. Vertical spaces within the museum connect visitors to a white-box exhibition space for the display of artworks. The handrails of the staircase leading up to this classic space are made of a crisscross mesh of steel, evoking the fences in the existing village. The exhibition spaces on the second floor are rather cut off from external views in favor of an uninterrupted experience and appreciation of the artworks, yet viewers are exposed to plenty of indirect light from the courtyards and skylights. Designed in the spring of 2005, and completed in the summer of 2006, the Songzhuang Art Museum has continued to meet the flexible demands of showcasing creative projects and hosting community events. It is also successful as a platform that brings ideas from both within Songzhuang and the international community.

Architecture must serve to experiment, exchange ideas, and present life and art.

Art and Social Economy

With the boom in the Chinese art economy, prices of contemporary Chinese artwork soared in auction markets. Songzhuang soon became a hotspot, not only for artists but also for investors interested in its real estate and art program. In another related project, the Songzhuang Artist Residence was the result of one such developments—a rental property that serves the purpose of living, working, and exhibition for twenty artists. Built on an outdoor industrial storage lot, and facing a pond decorated by faux Scholar's Rocks, twenty container-like boxes are stacked into an enclave. Each box-unit consists of a six-meter-deep artist studio space and a three-meter-deep living space. The studio spaces are composed of a simple rectangular form, while the living room, kitchen, and restroom have a more complex geometry. The living area is plugged into the same volume, either on the same level or in an upper duplex level. Each unit has its own entrance, and is lit by either a slit of ceiling light or windows that draw natural light into the space.

Walking through this complex, the interplay of solid and void, as well as light and shadow, allows artists and visitors to constantly explore and experiment with the outdoor community space. Such "unexpected encounters" serve as an experiential extension of the production and presentation of art. For the exterior of the complex, the dark gray concrete of the vertical surfaces match the color coding of district zones, while the horizontal surfaces are coated in brick red that act as an extension of accessible surfaces from the local village. This red hue not only contrasts with the gray but also brings a sense of warmth to the interior, as one traverses through the spaces. Like Zhang's artwork, the Songzhuang Artist Residence drew from the idea of stacking, random at first glance, yet carefully composed structurally and functionally. The units of the composition maintain its character of individuality within an artist community, while allowing a place of intensive exchange of ideas to emerge.

The conceptual drive of these two projects were rooted in an understanding of the functional requirements of the users of architecture. It drew from the artistic, cultural, and historical references of the place and its people. The overall architecture emphasizes the presence of community and creativity, as well as a minimalism that does not compete with the artists who live and exhibit in these spaces. Through the particularities of these first projects, the work of DnA has evolved to design spaces to inspire and draw communities together. Architecture must serve to experiment, exchange ideas, and present life and art. If Zhang's performance contributed to the development of contemporary art through the collective, then the two projects, Songzhuang Art Center and Songzhuang Artists Residence, can serve to broaden the social discourse of architecture in China.

POSTMODERN SUBLIME

LI SHIQIAO

The store-lined interior corridors of Yiwu are more provocative than they first appear. At the first glance, they are almost embarrassingly modest next to the aspiring grandeur of those of the Venetian in Macau and the determined luxury of those of Central in Hong Kong. They have none of the contrived totalities of meaning embedded in the signifiers decorating the Mall of America and the Dubai Mall. In Yiwu, the corridors offer a physical setting for a normative encounter with commodities. They suggest affordability and choice, not semi-packaged lifestyle choices but economic value at its barest essentials. Yiwu's modesty radiates the attraction of bargains, which can be intoxicating. However, very quickly, the excitement of this first encounter turns into something that is difficult to define. Perhaps it is the inability to grasp the sheer number and range of commodities, or perhaps it is a lingering fear of striking the worst deal out of all possible deals. Perhaps it is the total exhaustion resulting from the primal motivation for an overview of value, or perhaps it is the frustration with sameness in endless variety.

Hedonistic Utopia of Value and Dystopia of Entrapment
It is something akin to flipping through hundreds of television channels, surfing over thousands of websites, prompted by the thought that perhaps the next channel or page is better, but eventually finding nothing worthwhile to watch or buy. There seems to be an extreme monotony in the corridors that provides the key to this experience; clearly no one teaches Kevin Lynch in Yiwu. As one shifts from animate excitement to abject inaction as a consumer, Yiwu's corridors take on a menacing character. Like in a science fiction or a horror movie, one is overwhelmed by the sensation of being trapped in never-ending tunnels of commodities. Their welcoming smiles now turn into malicious grins, threatening to engulf you, extracting all energy out of your biological frailties, and all financial resources out of your limited bank accounts. All of a sudden, the hedonistic utopia of value and choice turns into a Gibsonian dystopia of entrapment.

Arranging stalls along a walkway is as universal an instinct as making wheels. One does not have to go to architectural or planning schools to learn how to do this. Street markets, as they are found in almost all human settlements throughout the world, are perhaps the most enduring features of communities and cities. The arcades gave Paris its character in the nineteenth century, the Christmas market defines Vienna at times of festivity, the five-foot way makes Singapore and Kuala Lumpur the tropical city, and the Golden Computer Arcade puts Hong Kong on the map of affordable tech that inspired enduring classics such as *Blade Runner* and *Ghost in the Shell*. Shopping malls are ideals. They mimic the street but romanticize it at the cost of the city. Draining its central energy into a container, shopping malls leave the city to die a slow death, replacing it with rows and rows of homogenous spaces for contented consumers living in relative and abject isolation. Walkways can be spiritually and socially elevated. The stoas of the agora, the passages of the forum, the colonnades of the Vatican, and the corridors of imperial Beijing make use of the potentials of linear walkways to advance political, social, and religious goals.

A corridor at Yiwu. Image courtesy of Li Shiqiao

But the corridors in Yiwu are something else. Lining the corridors of the International Trade City and other market places are over 72,000 stalls with a total building area of 5.5 million square meters. These stalls sell 1.8 million distinctly different kinds of commodities in twenty-six broad categories. They employ 228,000 sales persons, and attract 210,000 visitors per day. In 2015, Yiwu's total transaction reached RMB 12.5 billion, an almost sixteen percent increase from previous year. Among them, sixty percent was domestic and forty percent international. These commodities reach all corners of the world through direct export clearances from Yiwu, fanning out from Yiwu to the major land, sea, and air transportation hubs in China then to other parts of the world. One recent development was the dedicated "Yiwu-Xinjiang-Europe" rail line—"a caravan with no need to feed on grass" as China's CCTV dubbed it. This was a clear reference to the much-cherished history of the Silk Road. The rail line stretches thirteen thousand kilometers from Yiwu to Madrid over twenty-one days, passing through important locations of Kazakhstan, Russia, Belarus, Poland, Germany, and France. In 2015, 1,988 containers were transported from Yiwu to Europe, while 204 containers were transported from Europe to Yiwu. Yiwu, a *stallopolis*, has been designed and constructed at the very outset with this enormous network of exchange in mind—which is in itself a mind-bending reality as it is almost impossible to "imagine" this network of exchange as physical entities.

Consequence and Creator of Throwaway Culture

When Jean-François Lyotard wrote his *The Postmodern Condition: A Report on Knowledge* in 1979, he anticipated an ever shortening of contract cycles which allows outsourcing to take place—outsourcing of not only knowhow but also emotions. This is a most recent material manifestation of the logic of capital, as David Harvey argues, through a "spatial displacement"—an ability to spread contractual arrangements across geography in search of larger and larger profit margins by shedding more and more moral responsibilities—that results in globalization. Perhaps they did not quite anticipate the scale and speed with this has taken place today. Yiwu, among countless other cities in China and throughout the world, have taken this spatial displacement in the world system to heart and for granted. Instead of undercutting the pricing of commodities through specialization and efficiency, Yiwu chose to build the ultimate market place to gather all commodities under the heaven. It plays a central role in the distribution of commodities that are produced in the surrounding Yangtze River Delta. This makes perfect sense for Yiwu. When Lyotard was musing over the shortening of contract cycles in the 1979, Yiwu did not have enough food to feed its population, let alone ponder over neoliberalist strategies of making a profit. In 2015, Yiwu's GDP is USD 16.2 billion.

Yiwu did not have sufficient farm land for its population. In the past, during inter-crop seasons, small farm peasants began to trade brown sugar for chicken feature to enrich the soil and increase the productivity of the soil. Initially seen to be "capitalist" enterprises, this practice finally received government approval in the early 1980s; an explosion of trade took place and it expanded to all kinds of small commodities. China's Open Door Policy, and its eventual joining of World Trade Organization, gave Yiwu an extraordinary opportunity to play a role in the new world economy. If the Opium War was China's first entry into the fledgling world system in the nineteenth century, the Open Door Policy was China's second entry. This time, technologies, transportation, multinational finance, and the development of consumer society are dramatically new features, resulting in Yiwu's determination to maintain its mono-function as a *nonplus ultra* of commodities market—an urban condition that descended from the lineage of Liverpool and Detroit. Yiwu is both a consequence and a creator of today's throwaway culture—a manifestation of Lyotard's shortening of contract cycles in the lives of commodities—that is so fundamentally different from Liverpool and Detroit.

Spatial Displacement: The Corridors of Yiwu

Fredric Jameson speculated on a notion of "postmodern sublime" in his classic essay "Postmodernism, the Cultural Logic of Late Capitalism." First published in 1984, he noted a reduction of depth in the arts. From Van Gogh's peasant shoes to Warhol's diamond dust shoes, from Munch's scream figure to Warhol's Monroe, there has been a profound shift from depth of meaning and alienation of subjectivity to surfaces effects, and physical and emotional burnout. This movement captures Lyotard's observation of shortening of contract cycles, Harvey's argument of spatial displacement, and Richard Sennett's narrative of the decline of "careers" in curriculum vita and the rise of "job experiences." If the sublime of the machine age gave us Futurism and Le Corbusier, what would be a postmodern sublime of intensities? Is it William Gibson's *Neuromancer*,

Ridley Scott's *Blade Runner*, or Wachowski brothers' *Matrix*? Is it the feedback loop of data and matter in the form of parametric design and three-dimensional printing? Is it the tectonic abandonment of warped planes and twisted volumes? All of them are too fictitious or symbolic to give us a sense of the twenty-first-century sublime that can rival the great imageries of modernity—the smoke chimneys, the steam locomotives, the automobiles, and the airplanes.

The physical presence of our machines that enable spatial displacement is a flat screen, deliberately mute in its tectonic manifestations through a series of "reduction" of visible features in the design of computers and mobile devices. The symbolic feedback loops, the warping planes and twisting volumes in architecture fail, by a large margin, to capture the immense, powerful, and menacing nature of the world system in its enormous and ever moving systems of goods, people, money, and commodities. Instead of the analogue approximations of feedback loops in parametric design masquerading as sublime, the sheer presence of throwaway commodities is perhaps a much more effective measure of the immensity of the system in its complexity, its impulses in material forms, and its pathologies in commodities abuse. Yiwu's corridors are not comparable to a Hadid opera house, a Gehry composition, or a SOM slickness. The corridors are very much unlike a themed development, a *xiaoqu* community, and a *danwei* commune. Yiwu's corridors have no pretension and no ideology. Yiwu's corridors do not simulate meaningful and pleasurable human experiences: subjectivity, creativity, aesthetic pleasure, love, care, community, and society are faint conceptions receiving little mention in Yiwu.

World System and Banality

In their ability to simultaneously excite emotions and thwart the urge to make sense, Yiwu's corridors stand a chance to be an object of postmodern sublime in the world system. Designed by the throwaway culture of today and enabled by the impatient multinational capital, Yiwu's corridors redefine human life within them. Children would be doing their homework in commodity-filled glass boxes, while playing hide and seek underneath escalators. Yiwu would also alter societies in distant places, locations of consumption with excess and abandonment, in their own image of ungraspable immensity and banality. In its honesty, Yiwu's corridors create the bonds between data centers, manufacturing bases, transportation systems, and shopping malls as the great intermediate and expansive gray zone, where spatial characteristics of tenuous and absurd usefulness are exchanged and tedious logistics of movement are actualized. No meaningful ornamentation and dramatization can be found. At Yiwu, the relentless drive for efficiency and profit of the world system at the expense of the environment is the most manifest. When globalization finishes its energetic and reckless expansion, the corridors of Yiwu can be preserved as the tantalizing future "postmodern heritage" in architecture.

When globalization finishes its energetic and reckless expansion, the corridors of Yiwu can be preserved as the tantalizing future "postmodern heritage" in architecture.

CITY AS TACTICS: CURATION AND REACTION

JIANG JUN

As one of over a hundred biennales in the world, the Bi-City Biennale of Urbanism\ Architecture (UABB) owes its uniqueness not only to double-city or urbanism and architecture attributes but to its dynamism behind the organic urbanization of Shenzhen. The UABB is more than a documentation or a hermetic inner-circle activity. It is an integrated urbanization model that systematically combines geography, economy, society, politics, culture, history, and space. The geography of the city can be understood in terms of its land resource and urban layout, and its economy in terms of economic structure and industrial distribution. The society is most evident in terms of the capacity of the city to encourage public participation and enhance social security, and politics describes the relationship between government and enterprises, as well as tactical planning by the municipal government. Culture is most visible in terms of the cultural expressions a city and forms of identity, and history can be understood in terms of agriculture and industrial and post-industrial moments. Lastly, space is always expressed through the city, its architecture, and its objects.

As an organizational model with a focus on duality and urbanism, the UABB sufficiently distinguishes itself from the myriad of other biennales around the globe. This model of integrating organization and content into a coherent form sustained the UABB for a decade, leading it to become one of the core competitive forces of Shenzhen. To understand its history would require an examination of this model in terms of its outer organization and inner content. It would reveal how the Biennale has been a keen observer and participant in the past decade of the urban transformation of Shenzhen and China's national strategy of urban growth. The curation of a city is no longer confined to the organization activity of a city exhibition. Instead, it is a platform to introduce a new form of socially conscious action—a capacity to cu-react (curate + react) *vis-à-vis* exhibition-making and reacting to the deep-rooted changes of the city and the nation.

The political model in China, *dashou xiaofang*, can be described as follows—through revolution, the state would *voraciously absorb* power and resources (*dashou*), and through reform, it would *slowly release* them (*xiaofang*). The former points to centralization of power, where core resources are to be publicly owned. The latter points to the selective distribution of decision-making power to the lower ranks, and to the privatization of rights to use and operate publicly-owned assets, such as land and state-owned corporations. China's economic model is to *grow first* then *amass*. To grow first means to adhere to a three-step core tactics. First, to *anchor* the economy through investing in heavy defense industries, then progress to *activate* development through building basic infrastructure, and lastly to *invigorate* the economy through a fostering of privatized businesses. To amass is to turn the attention to public services and cultural accumulation. The turning point is when the macro-strategy—in terms of geopolitics, industry patterns, and urban-rural structure—gradually comes into shape, and the government shifts toward a more intensive and fine-grained financial policy aimed at developing the economy through public service. If the nation is not self-sufficient in the providence of public service, it may lead to the tragedy of the commons. The launch of Shenzhen coincided with the moment when China moves from *dashou* to *xiaofang*, while the commencement of the UABB coincides with Shenzhen's shift from growth to amassing and subsequently to a *rebirth*. These processes were set against the background of the nation's shifting attention from rapid industrialization to rapid urbanization, in a city that has begun its self-renewing process in under thirty years. As a creative endeavor, the UABB is a product of the changing times, but as an organization, it is also the catalyst of this very change. This transformation can be summarized in five tectonic shifts in the realms of the geographic, economic, social, political, and the cultural.

Shifts in Geography: All-Rounded Connectivity

The opening up of Shenzhen began with Deng Xiaoping's response to "Thirty Years of Strategic Opportunities." He suggested a connection with the Three Worlds—the First World of the Western developed nations, the Second World of the former-Soviet and Eastern Bloc, and the Third World of developing nations—by means of an Open Reform. This national policy involved both a reform from the inside, and the opening-up of the country to the outside. The second opening-up of Shenzhen now faces a shift in a new geo-strategic situation in terms of a re-balancing of power over land and sea rights. China's economy took-off peacefully after a primitive accumulation of capital. It must now evolve to achieve an "all-rounded connectivity" through the design of institutional systems, technical support, and financial structures. Institutional systems would include free-trade zones, and renminbi offshore and onshore markets. Technical support points to the necessity of basic infrastructure such as the Express Rail Link, highways, canals, and energy pipelines, as well as business amenities such as ports and industrial parks. Financial structures are to be set in place by institutions such as the Asian Infrastructure

Investment Bank; the Brazil, Russia, India, China, and South Africa Contingency Reserve Arrangement; the Silk Road Fund; the South-South Cooperation Fund; or the Cross-Border Inter-Bank Payments System.

The distinctive relationship between Shenzhen and Hong Kong that led to the organizational character of UABB stems from the fact that it is geographically situated at an intersection between a country of land rights and a world of sea rights. The bi-city trait is witness to a regional institutional form in transition. The UABB is set against the larger context of the free-trade Closer Economic Partnership Arrangement (CEPA). There are a series of "All-Rounded Connectivity" strategies, which are disparate yet closely related regional tactics and nomenclature, such as the Shenzhen-Hong Kong integration, the Greater Pearl River Delta (PRD), and the Pan River Delta. The underlying goal is not simply to develop the economy or to domesticize Hong Kong, but rather to push for domestic reform through capitalizing on the effective elements of Hong Kong's market economy. Hong Kong is thus used as a springboard to compete with the rest of the globe, as well as a firewall to defend against the periodical risks that inevitably would arise during competition.

The UABB-decade accompanied the gradual development of CEPA. Shenzhen, on the Biennale's tenth anniversary, entered into the Free Trade Zone (FTZ) Era, leading China in her national strategy of One Belt, One Road—a policy with the ultimate goal of establishing a China-led, renminbi-centric economic circulation system. Such FTZ strategies would consolidate Hong Kong with Shenzhen, bring the Canton-Hong Kong-Macau bay region together under the Greater PRD, further consolidate the South Asian Sea, and exert control over Central Europe, Asia, and Africa by the One Belt, One Road policy. These policies obey the global strategic policies of China, aimed at globalizing the renminbi. While connecting the seaport, the airport and the vital nodal cities along the Sea Silk Route, an intensified renminbi offshore market system, constituting the stock market, futures market, bond market, and currency market, is formulated. This enables China to participate in worldwide competition and cooperation in all domains. The organization and context of the UABB must be able to *cu-react* to this shift in geospatial strategy.

Shifts in Economy: From Industrialization to Urbanization

The UABB-decade corresponds to ten years of regeneration, one which can be best described as *tenglong huanniao* (emptying the cage for new birds) for the coastal industries along the PRD. In essence, it means to complementarily integrate the more developed coastal region with the less developed hinterland in terms of resources, industries and markets. This is an area carrying one-third of China's total population. As the CEPA framework strengthened the transportation networks between the coast and hinterland, low-end industries have the choice of moving inland, while the coast undergoes a strategic industrial upgrading. During this hierarchical process of redistribution, the coast and hinterland formed two sets of industrial systems which complement and safeguard each other. The economy along the coastal system would compete with Japan and Korea, as it is densely populated with mid to high-end skilled labor and high value-added industries. The inland system would compete with nations from the Association of Southeast Asian Nations, consisting low-end labor-intensive, and low value-added industries. These two systems form the two international trade passages of the coastal sea and inner land route. This corresponds to Deng Xiaoping's "Two General Pictures," advocated thirty years ago to pioneer economic development in the east, and the opening-up of the mid-west.

Under such economic shifts, the UABB provides a catalytic thrust, channels for communication, and an exhibition platform for cultural and creative industries in terms of its creative content. As an organization, it also reactivates degenerated areas of the city by giving the organizers the freedom to develop a new exhibition venue for each installment, based on their curatorial direction. Furthermore, the UABB adds value to land through creativity in cultural production and procurement of high-end services. This relieves the bottleneck situation of the Special Economic Zone, and pushes the city's transition from industrialization to urbanization.

Shifts in Society: Rising Civil Society

A decade of the UABB saw Shenzhen move from rapid industrialization to rapid urbanization. As a municipality with an independent planning status, Shenzhen's gross domestic product per capita has reached the level of a developed economy. This economic base gave rise to a rising urban middle class, and as a result, a civil society in Shenzhen. The establishment of the FTZ will create further divergence in different social roles and social stratification. But this society is being mobilized by dynamic economies, new forms of social settlements, new social interests and a willingness to participate in the forces of production. As such, the socioeconomic growth model is making a shift from an emphasis on an efficient means of production to an emphasis on the quality of life. It would also indirectly lead to renewed appreciation for public service and a real civic sphere.

The curation of a city is no longer confined to the organization activity of a city exhibition. Instead, it is a platform to introduce a new form of socially conscious action—a capacity to cu-react (curate + react) vis-à-vis exhibition-making and reacting to the deep-rooted changes of the city and the nation.

Architecture in the city was once the ivory towers of professional planners and architects, yet such architecture is also inextricably connected to the interests of the public. Through its content and organization, the UABB is able to reveal the potential and colorations of the long monopolized discipline of sociology by the state. The UABB is also gradually evolving as a platform that fosters fair competition, as well as constructive collaboration between the different stakeholders of society. In the increasingly dynamic and tolerant city of Shenzhen, many of the research-oriented UABB exhibits were able present to the public the multivalent conflicts that inevitably arise during a complex urbanization process. The ultimate achievement of the Biennale is not the branding or the making of Shenzhen, but rather its ability to inspire and enlighten the public through the very friction produced by a socially-sensitive regenerative process. These are the foundations for the making of a sophisticated civil society.

Shifts in Politics: Experimental Ground for Personal Freedom

The geographical interface between land and sea enhances the role of Shenzhen as a dynamic theater of domestic and international politics. The UABB began with a bi-city vision of a new Shenzhen-Hong Kong Metropolis ten years ago. Unfortunately, Hong Kong entered into a state of crisis as the largest renminbi offshore market in the world, and as the transitional market for global capital to enter into China. These cross-boundary investment channels can take the formal forms of the Shanghai-Hong Kong Stock Connect or the China Power Holdings, but they can also take covert forms through underground and shadow banks. These functions are sometimes overshadowed by the geopolitical friction that inevitably occurs due to a constant alternation of a domineering Chinese authority over the land and sea territories, and a resolute search for political independence within Hong Kong itself.

The purpose of the FTZ is not merely to attract the advanced management and service industries from Hong Kong, but it also acts as a substitute in a contingency plan against future political or financial crises in Hong Kong. The Chinese regime would be keen to avoid a Hong Kong-led "cultural" revolution in the form of the 2014 Umbrella Movement, as well as shelter China from major financial crashes, such as the 1997 Asian financial crisis

The 2015 UABB at Shekou, Shenzhen.
Image courtesy of Lam Lai Shun, 2015

triggered by the collapse of the Thai baht. Shenzhen's role as a backup is pertinent to the networking platform of One Belt, One Road, as it takes on the role of being China's gateway for inbound global capital, and a launch pad for a New Silk Road. Shenzhen continues to thrive as the springboard for Chinese enterprises to venture overseas, and in the process, globalizing the renminbi. Chinese enterprises tend to cooperate more with one another when they venture overseas, in the form of a *baotuan chuhai* conglomeration tactic, to safeguard against potential financial tsunamis.

To position Shenzhen as an "enclave economy" or a "cross-border financial zone" is to suggest that it would take the opportunity to absorb Hong Kong's tradition of greater sociopolitical freedom and the rule of law. These values would end up exerting a great deal of influence on Shenzhen's model of governance. As a quasi-official and quasi-autonomous public event under the auspices of the municipal government, the UABB would also become an experimental ground for civil liberties or personal freedom, in terms of the participation by the public, and the rule of law, in matters of administration.

Shifts in Culture: Selective Decentralization of Power

There are three interrelated processes that imply that the structure of cultural practices in Shenzhen would become further diversified in the years ahead, namely, the systematic liberation process of the FTZ, the selective decentralization of power held by the regime, and the organized participation of the citizens in matters concerning the society. The cultural role of public events such as the UABB have transformed from an official thematic rhetoric that narrates national solidarity, economic prosperity and social stability, into a sociopolitical instrument that stimulates creativity, and a social platform that fosters collaboration. In his 2011 book *On the Hong Kong City-State*, Hong Kong localist scholar Dr. Chin Wan suggests that such a transformation is "a turn from the residue of great policy to the origin of great policy." Such a shift would enable cultural workers and groups with different interests to find their own niche amidst the irrepressible trend of social diversification, and allow distinctive yet creative communities to form in harmony.

There is sufficient evidence to suggest that the co-stimulation amongst geographical, economic, societal, political and cultural factors, as they come together to generate a new vitality and motivate positive changes in the city. The UABB has more or less, wittingly or unwittingly, become the platform that reveals these changes through a spatial narration of the urbanism and architecture of Shenzhen, and to a certain extent, Hong Kong. The Biennale fixes five invisible dimensions on highly visible and highly targeted space-time coordinates, thereby reifying the meaning of *gewu zhizhi* (attaining knowledge through investigation) with the spatial attributes of architecture and the city as the primary vehicle. In summary, the UABB has attained *dadao,* or the great truth, of divine and universal values through *xiaodao,* or the small reasoning, of earthly everyday practices. The conviction of a different form of the same structure may have be distilled from *yiguo liangzhi,* or the One Country, Two Systems policy, but it is this same duality that is being represented in UABB's content structure as "great truth," alongside its organization model as "small reasoning."

07
MEDIATING

Cities in China are very much part of a system of infrastructure and people, technically and socially coordinated in such a way that it does not implode. Working towards a philosophy for cities today, one would have to understand the implicit role of architecture within the wider field of aesthetics and politics in the global arena. Virtual spaces and other forms of mass media are the true civic spaces of contemporary society, more powerful than the agoras and piazzas of yesteryears. This is described as a new institutional aspect of space, and the governance of such spaces must be open and accountable. While China still has a poor reputation in overcontrolling and censoring information, with less-than-transparent surveillance bureaus such as the Golden Shield Project, critics are optimistic that the leveling effect of technology will inevitably put power back in the hands of the people. Contributors in this chapter examine the civic potential and committment emerging in various unique conditions in China.

Grassfields and the Vanke Headquarters, Shenzhen, by Steven Holl. Image courtesy of Arjun Rosha, 2013

MASS MEDIA AND CIVIL SOCIETY

OU NING

The definition of "civic" in architecture is born out of a political concept. A civil society is a demonstration of how people can participate in public issues in the process of creating an orderly and optimal society. Architects are first citizens before they are design professionals. Regardless of profession, everyone must have some form of civic awareness. This is a basic duty of every citizen. In a sense, the formulation of a "civic architecture" is wishful thinking. The slogan adopted by the *Southern Metropolis Daily* in its biannual Chinese Architecture Media Award, "Towards a Civic Architecture," was based on the hypothesis that there is insufficiency in civic awareness in the practice of architecture in China. If every architect possesses such civic awareness, there would be a natural initiative to create more public space in every design project. As civil society in China matures, such public spaces would become all the more effective. In his book *Society Under Siege*, Zygmunt Bauman argued that civic architecture had too great a responsibility to bear in society. Yet, in China, it is precisely within this tumultuous and imperfect institutional system that such an award for civic architecture is most needed. The goal is to catalyze everyone's lives through civic architecture. With this inversion of causality, can the award still retain its capacity to stimulate society?

The Olympic Games of 2008 acted as an accelerator for urbanization in China, especially for the city of Beijing. There was a significant increase in the quantity of architecture built within a short period of time. The large stadium constructions also brought to the minds of the public the concept of civic architecture. Architecture today cannot simply be understood as individual buildings, but they form part of a larger context of the city and its people. As a broad and physical concept, the city is an aggregation of many buildings and the built fabric, but its vitality comes about only when these buildings are being used. The city is a space where people connect and interact, and many of these activities occur within architecture.

Governance and Institutional Aspect of Space

If architecture is a mere physical space, there would be limits to its influence on society. There is an additional institutional aspect of space, in which powers of governance can have a normative range of operation within the space, and the rights of the people using such spaces can also be effectively protected. When physical and social spaces have an effective connection with one another, there would be an elevated standard of a public nature in a building. Civic architecture arises out of such a calibration of relationships. The urban planning of downtown Shenzhen is remarkable in this context. The office building of the local government is not named as a "Municipal Government Building," but it is instead named as a "Civic Center." This name carries a strong notion that the government exists to serve the people, and the office of the government is where it strives the hardest for its citizens. In front of the government building, there is a "civic plaza," surrounded by a concert hall, a library, a youth center, and the Shenzhen Stock Exchange Building. Unfortunately, there is hardly anyone using this plaza.

The Shenzhen Stock Exchange by OMA offers a new horizon of pedestrian open space in the center of city! A platform raised from the ground! The sight line is elevated to view the surrounding city, which introduces a new vantage point for the people and the city! A peaceful and quiet plaza is framed by the skyline of the city, and closed in with the cantilevered podium above. This isolation of an open space creates a sense of territory, and yet, one still feels free to move over to the edge of the plaza to gaze at the city. What a self-contained public space! But where are the people? Caption and image courtesy of Victor Su, 2013

Architecture and the city must be designed and planned in such a way that it can communicate with its users, because they will form a collective space, where the physical space is closely related to an invisible institutional and regulatory space. At the early stages of a project, architects and planners ought to think about the possibility of a space for the public. But they will always need to collaborate with stakeholders from other fields, especially if it has to function within a bureaucratic system. This collaborative process relates to the educational needs and political structure of society, and even to a certain extent it builds in the possibility of social mobility. A space can only be enjoyed and appreciated by the public if there is an energetic government to support it. In other words, civic architecture is a built artifact or built environment that precedes civil society, awaiting its maturity. It is important to see an architect taking responsibility to create more public space for everyone to use and enjoy. However, this is very idealistic, because the usability of these spaces by the general public is highly dependent on the openness of the bureaucracy that governs it. The spatial layout only creates a physical possibility for public expression. In order for architecture to support a civil society, a sustained process of complex social planning with a set of social intentions would still be needed.

Mass Media and Intangible Public Space

Mass media shares a similar function as civic architecture in society. In fact, it may be possible to argue that mass media plays a more important role than architecture in the creation of a civil society. Mass media is such a crucial element in a civil society, because it holds the critical functions of public education and monitors and guards the well-being of society. If a newspaper can really represent and speak for the general public, then it can be an intangible public space in itself. Mass media can be an invisible form of civic architecture where the public can express themselves. Much of contemporary Chinese architecture speaks of this public agenda. For example, Chen Zhihua, professor at Tsinghua University, has dedicated most of his life's work to the study and protection of vernacular architecture, when the dominant discourses of the architectural industry were focused on the city and its growth. Since the founding of China's new economy, farmers and spaces of the rural have been neglected. They made great and precise contributions to the progress of China during a particular period, but they rarely reap the benefits. Chen's work is focused on the protection of vernacular architecture in the rural area, giving a prominent voice to the spaces of an agricultural society.

There are many other radical practitioners in this field, such as professor Wen Tiejun and architect Hsieh Ying-chun. In this collaboration, they approached a village in the province of Hebei to teach farmers how to build new houses with his professional know-how. They promoted the tradition of "labor exchange" in Chinese rural society. Instead of paying a builder for the work done for constructing a house, the favor is returned by labor by the beneficiary when there are needs elsewhere. This kind of building cooperative still exists in contemporary rural China, continuing what constituted a core value of anarchism in the past. This represented a form of utopia, where labor is used as mode of exchange currency, avoiding monetary currency and the exploitative character of capitalism. Hsieh advanced his informal practice to a great extent in the process of discovering the vitality of village societies and reinterpreting the utopian values embedded in contemporary society. Hsieh was introduced to discourses in mainland China for the first time when Chang Yung Ho invited him to participate in the inaugural Urbanism\Architecture Bi-city Biennale in Shenzhen. Chang's remarks in 2005 was poignant: "Don't worship Koolhaas blindly, the importance of Hsieh can fully match that of Koolhaas."

CIVIC POTENTIAL IN EVERYDAY ARCHITECTURE

DONG GONG

Building construction in Chinese cities practically ignores the way of life of the ordinary citizen. New construction does not seem to be concerned with establishing relationships between architecture, the public space around it, and the ordinary people. In reality, there are many public spaces in Chinese cities. But they fail to stimulate meaningful public life, because their designs and construction fundamentally disrespect the everyday needs of ordinary citizens. Rapid urban transformation has mercilessly destroyed the old fabric of the city. This problem is compounded by the fact that, during this rapid process of change, Chinese projects tends to be very short, sometimes taking as few as eight months from design to completion for a medium-scale project. As this is fast becoming a serious issue in China, it is paramount for architects to be concerned more with the place and experience of a building, its relationship with the way of life around it, and the kind of public space it has the duty to support. When an architect examines a site, there ought to be a positive consideration for a spatial experience that contrasts with the city's less-than-ideal conditions, so that users could enjoy a moment of calm, both physically and mentally. Architecture must be able to give a brief respite from the hustle and bustle of the city. It should always be about creating a sense of place in any specific part of the city, and any architectural intervention has the capacity to evoke an entirely new spirit of the place.

Place for Living

Architecture is first and foremost a place closely associated with the way of life of the city, because it shapes the way ordinary users would use it. There is a great responsibility on the part of the architect to embark on an optimistic and proactive search that can promote different ways of life appropriate to a place. The question of place and experience of its users would likely be a more salient point of inception for a design project than the routine demand for creativity, creation, or a stroke of genius. It is more apt to describe the role of architecture in a place as an act of discovery or transformation, because there is a unique quality in each place. Architecture should reveal this quality, emphasize its presence, and establish a positive and irreplaceable relationship between an ordinary citizen and a place. Each architectural project ought to be the result of the *genius loci* of the site, without which architecture would lose its sense of origin. Architecture must be generated from certain origins, such as the local climate, users' habits, and site conditions. It must be able to offer to a place an experience that is unprecedented but somehow relevant to the user. Through such a transformative sense of purpose, architecture would be inspirational.

Public and Social Space

In a socialist country like China, where all land belongs to the state or the public, it is a surprise to find that there are in fact very limited social spaces that are truly for the people. The quantity of public space is disproportionate to its quality. Hence, there is an urgent need for architects to effectively replenish this lack by ingeniously creating spaces for the public within the spaces of architecture, even if it begins with a purportedly private use. Architects should endeavor to fight for such spaces in each project and generate conditions that can induce a high quality public life. A good public space should be able to offer unanticipated opportunities for communication between the specified users of the architecture and the general public, thereby inducing positive modes of exchange and integration. Architects must continue to try to bring public functions into their designs, and persuade their clients not to be impatient with the direct economic losses they may bring in the short run but instead be confident about the greater social good that can accompany the socioeconomic benefits in the long run. For example, it is sometimes possible to persuade a private client to install a public observation deck on the rooftop of a building so that the general public can access it as a public amenity directly connected with an easily identifiable public network. This can be done without compromising the private areas of the building, and such a useful deck would become instrumental in generating a powerful reputation and a sense of place around the building in the long run. A responsible public aspect of architecture would bring it into an intimate relationship with the ordinary citizen, which would go a long way in enhancing a healthy urban life.

Living Relationships and Everyday Architecture

One of the critical roles of architecture is to aid in the establishment of relationships between the overlapping functions of the everyday and the different lives of ordinary people. The multiple components of architecture ought to be designed according to relationships between different functional living units. By understanding the ambiguities and uncertainties of everyday life, architecture can create more possibilities for encounters. As a vessel of everyday life, the form, space, and construction of architecture can embody and enhance social relationships. By exploring this potential, architecture can create rich experiences for the ordinary users above and beyond meeting their basic needs. It can contribute to everyday life in ways. In an exploration of different kinds of living relationships, for example, it can come down to details such as the kinds of users one might meet in a particular space or the lighting conditions that are designed to facilitate that moment of engagement. The expression of the exterior form and the structure of the architectural space would capture such a moment. Architects must arrive at a few strategies for how these relationships resonate with how the spaces are being connected, in anticipation of the possible human interactions in these spaces.

Tectonics

The tectonics of architecture is about establishing a system and order, and it is to a large extent influenced by an architectural position. This relationship can be likened to a huge tree, in which the fundamental conceptual position is the root while the structural details are the branches. There are mutually dependent relationships between them, all connected by the same vein. To this end, the design of the construction process is a major undertaking in a project. The tectonics of architecture is often directly linked to the early conception of an architectural thought, whether it is the site or the relationships to its users. This tends to be a vital turning point of any project. Under different lighting, weather conditions, and times of the day, the tectonics of any architecture can reveal different visual relationships to the city and the ordinary users. Architects must be aware of the vivid relationships between architecture, its surroundings, and the experiences of the users. Hence, for each

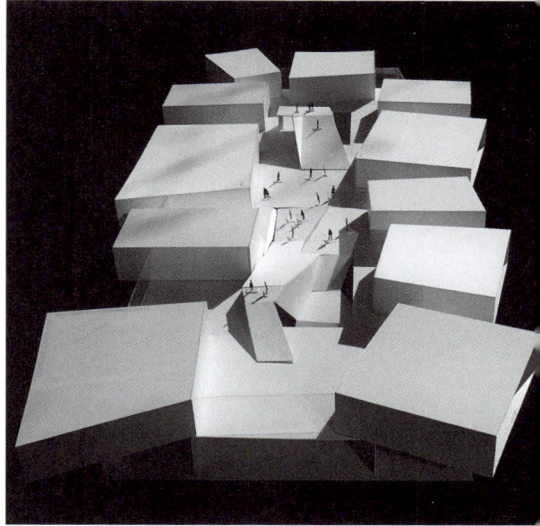

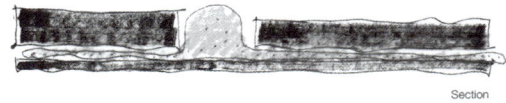

Section

Plan

Tectonic studies in sketches and model for Zhangjiawo Elementary School, Tianjin.
Images courtesy of Vector Architects

project, architects would have to undertake a whole range of comparative research to identify an accurate design direction and tectonic. This would include relatively large-scale working models, where various tests on lighting and materiality can be simulated, perceived, and refined.

Contradictory Problems of Civic Architecture

Given the inherent social and public potential for architecture, there is a notable civic form in China is that is faring particularly poorly. There are different types of civic architecture in China that is supposed to carry the aspirations of the public in the best possible way, yet they are more likely to overly monumental in scale and design, detracting from its most fundamental role as public buildings. Sometimes, they can be as large as eighty thousand square meters and include an entire complex of theaters, museums, exhibition centers, and libraries. To win competitions or design bids for such projects, architects would have to be cognizant of the disproportionate demands and grandiose ambitions underpinning the sites. Research on large-scale civic architecture in China reveals major structural and organizational problems pertaining to this type of architecture. The sites of such architecture tend to be located in areas in the city with deep political implications, such as plazas along a municipal axis in new towns, or sites of memory or with propagandistic value. In addition, in trying to derive or project a sense of grandeur or significant meaning, the briefs usually call for oversized and outlandish forms. Their relationships to the city, the public, and the market are often ignored.

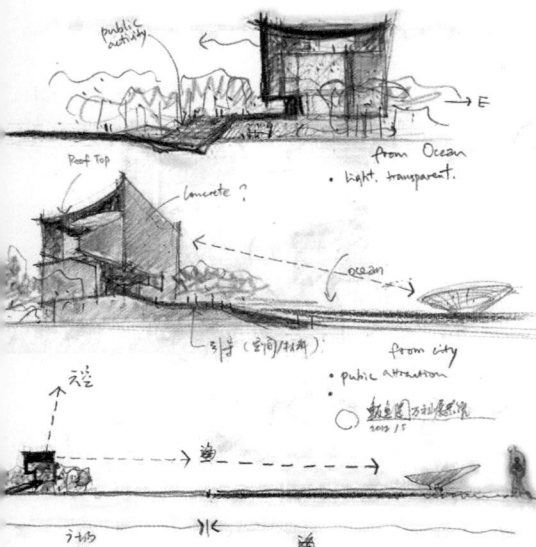

Public access of private space at of Bayuquan Vanke Exhibition Centre, Yingkou.
Image courtesy of Vector Architects

Large museums, art galleries, cultural institutions, and other civic venues are often unable to attract the expected visitors. They gradually become vacant due to a lack of good exhibitions, educational programs, and other public agendas; yet the city still spends millions, even billions, of renminbi on their maintenance annually. This is because these buildings were built not for the city's cultural needs but for political and propagandistic purposes.

Civic buildings are more accessible to the general public when they are dispersed within the city. The scale of the museums and galleries should also be in harmony with the city. The general public and pedestrian access should be favored in the location of this type of building. Even though there are good examples of national- or state-level museums or galleries that may be larger in scale, their realizations are based on long-standing collections with enormous artistic and educational value for the general public. Chinese cities have to evaluate the need for cultural buildings of a certain scale based on the contents being exhibited.

There are a number of approaches to this problem. Firstly, the Chinese government needs to change its view towards investment-driven construction widely accepted in China. It ought to begin to rationally analyze the specific needs of its public cultural investments. For example, perhaps only cities above a certain level would be permitted to construct large-scale public cultural buildings, and their scale should be planned with supporting data and extensive knowledge about the content of the space. Secondly, the planning and design of such buildings should be to gear heavily towards the public realm. In a well-planned situation, such cultural architecture could benefit the city as a whole. Despite its oft-criticized starchitect effect, the Guggenheim Museum Bilbao can still be considered successful in bringing in art and architecture lovers from all over the world. The success in reinvigorating the city is undeniable.

The relationship between architecture and the city, the openness of the architecture, and its organizational and events management support after the completion of the building must be considered from the beginning. If cultural buildings in China is aimed at benefiting a broader public, it makes sense to break down large-scale buildings into medium- or small-scale ones and distribute them throughout the city. By turning one 30,000-square-meter museum located in a vacant plaza of a new town into ten 3,000-square-meter museums that can be located within or adjacent to residential complexes, shopping malls, schools, and other everyday spaces, the dissemination of culture would be more deeply woven into the city. Such small-scale museums would be just around the corner when the general public are out taking a walk in the city. Once the benefits of this rich form of urban experience is better understood by the Chinese government and the general public, and once the scale is reduced, the management of such cultural functions could be simplified and made more accessible. Architecture would then be better integrated with public and private investments in this cultural function of the city. This remains a multifaceted issue that requires that multiple stakeholders pull together to succeed.

This essay is translated and adapted from Dong Gong, "Qinghua jianzhu xueren: Donggong" [Architectural Scholar of Tsinghua: Dong Gong], *World Architecture*, Issue 286, 2014/04, p.62, and "Shijian yu fanshi" [Practice and Self-Reflection], *The Architect*, Issue 164, 2013/04, pp.80-103.

CONTEXTUALITY AND CONTRADICTION

NARTANO LIM

The Cultural Revolution was meant to purge Chinese society of western capitalist ideologies and worldviews. It was successful in creating a vacuum in mass media and in intellectual activities, which extended beyond the obvious political dialogue into the humanities, the arts and, by extension, architecture. Whilst the Cultural Revolution was devastatingly effective, there was an earlier influx of internationally trained Chinese artists and architects that had left a legacy of modernism in China. The decades roughly between 1911 and 1942 saw a free flow of ideas and influences that was largely transmitted by a handful of influential Chinese students that returned back from stints at top universities in the US and Europe, funded ironically in part by the Boxer Indemnity Scholarship Program. Historians Ye Weili, Jeffrey Cody, Nancy Steinhardt, and the late Anthony Atkin edited and wrote a comprehensive account of these first waves of transmission in their 2010 publication *Chinese Architecture and the Beaux-Arts*. The École des Beaux-Arts was particularly influential, both as an institution and as a prototype pedagogy for architectural education. It was most notably adopted at the University of Pennsylvania, leading also to a proliferation of modernist thinking in various areas of the arts.

Unrepresented Canons

The influence and proliferation of the Beaux-Arts in China came through the first influx of western-educated Chinese students. Upon their return to a China that was actively open and absorptive of new ideas and thinking, the young architects were able to synthesize the influences from their native culture and upbringing with the lessons learned from abroad. This can be seen in the paintings of Beaux-Arts-educated Lin Fengmian, which had a blend of Chinese subject matter and western techniques. According to historian Ruan Xing, in his 2002 article "Accidental Affinities: American Beaux-Arts in Twentieth-Century Chinese Architectural Education and Practice," the modernist buildings by Pennsylvania-educated Yang Tingbao were held at high esteem and comparable to those of his classmate Louis Kahn. It would be disingenuous to say the modernist influence was rejected during the Cultural Revolution; rather, it was repurposed to become a political statement in support of the Communist ethos. Modernism, with its themes of rationality, functionality, and the rejection of ornament, seemed well suited for a range of interpretations, just as in the West where it had evolved from a jarring rejection of neoclassicism to the preferred ambiguous aesthetic of multinational corporations.

This recounting of modernism's roots in China lends weight to the transfer of sensibilities that is evidenced in the work of today's contemporary Chinese architects. This can be partially attributed to the lineage of western-educated Chinese artists and architects, who have had long periods of influence but were largely unrepresented in the canons of architectural history. Just as in the first generation of returning Chinese architects, the amalgamation of influences remains a highly personal interpretation rather than a simple "East Meets West" proposition. The role of the architect had also undergone a transformation during this early modern period, as the architect in China was previously more akin to a tradesman of a specific craft rather than the conductor and leader of all building works in the Vitruvian model.

The Hakka *tulou* form adapted by Urbanus. Image courtesy of Theodore Chan, 2013

Looking more closely to the cities of Shenzhen and Guangzhou, this modernist narrative meets the contemporary Urbanus with a degree of familiarity. Similar to their predecessors, all of the three principals were educated in both China and the United States, specifically at the Miami University in the State of Ohio. Partners Meng Yan and Wang Hui continued to beecome registered architects in the State of New York. Armed with a global view of architecture and urban planning, the three partners of Urbanus, including Liu Xiaodu, would deploy Western-influenced design methodologies to tackle issues that are results of intrinsic Chinese urban conditions. Overcrowding due to mass urban migrations, low-cost housing, and the enormous scale and speed of urbanization are prevailing realities in China, with few parallels in the developing world encountered by the Western world. The solutions proposed by Urbanus are often intrinsically Chinese as well—if not in form, then in their acceptance of the reality of the environment surrounding them. They avoid an idealized *tabula rasa*, which many Western notions of urban planning stem from. This was evidenced in the redeployment of the traditional Hakka *tulou* circular form as a modern low-cost housing development. The issues of safety, security, and community necessitated in the original form are still relevant concerns today. The acceptance of China's urban reality is probably best demonstrated in their Dafen Art Museum, which sits within an urban village in Shenzhen renowned for producing fake oil paintings of European masterworks. The siting of this museum in such an environment directly confronts notions of unauthenticity or worthlessness—notions many associate with reproductions. Yet there is a quiet recognition of the skills and indeed artistry in the reproduced works along the alleys surrounding the museum. In her 2013 book *Van Gogh on Demand: China and the Readymade*, art historian Winnie Wong argues that the social and labor context of Dafen allows for a reassessment of the definition of creativity within the larger scheme of authenticity in the global and perhaps Western sense. The architecture of the Dafen Art Museum succeeds in blurring the line between public and private, path and programmed space, ground and ramp, and even museum and village.

Intrinsic Pluralism and Complex Systems

There is an intrinsic plurality in the projects found in China because they deal with an urban context that is not a single condition. China is immersed in an ever-changing mélange of conditions and contradictions. The seminal 1966 publication *Complexity and Contradiction in Architecture* by Robert Venturi recognizes the pluralism and complexity of modern life as a key source of richness in architectural thought. He argues against a distilled or simplified understanding of complex systems and contexts. In the introduction of Venturi's publication, Vincent Scully describes it as "a very American book;" but the growing pains experienced in the United States in the late 1960s—such as overcrowding, cultural diversification, rapid urban migration due to post-war conditions, and structural shifts from an agricultural and manufacturing base to newer forms of economy—are similar to the present-day chaos in China.

A row of shopfronts along Dafen Art Village.
Image courtesy of Benjamin Chew, 2013

Much like China's modern history itself, contemporary architecture in China is a mix of bold statements, thoughts, beliefs, and responses. There is a sensitivity and acceptance of plurality and inherent contradictions seen throughout the work of many prominent contemporary practices in China. The idea that a contextual response is necessary today remains at the heart of global contemporary architectural practices, but the idea that such a contextual response can be itself contradictory seems uniquely Chinese. Whatever the influences may have been, the resulting adaptation and evolution have resulted in an architecture that can be site-specific and culturally specific in the most profound ways. Any preconception to find an "authentic" Chinese experience in Beijing, as compared to Shanghai, would quickly lead to one-dimensional truisms about the complex Chinese condition. Shanghai has always been referred to as the most western of Chinese cities with its history of autonomous foreign concession areas, hence it would be as easy to dismiss Shanghai as cosmopolitan as it is to project Beijing as bearing a more authentic Chinese identity. All simple categories about China would be woefully inadequate to understand the multiplicity and pluralism that is modern China. Contemporary practices in China are at a very exciting moment in time—having long accepted that the modern world is no longer only about rationality and authenticity, but about multiplicity as well. Architecture in China is not designed to conquer or control the irrational, but to find a space of coexistence.

Inside the Dafen Art Museum.
Image courtesy of Theodore Chan, 2013

DEFEATED ARCHITECTURE

KENGO KUMA AND SHIRLEY WOO

If one were to explain the *raison d'être* of cities and buildings today, it would be of utmost ignorance to address merely their primitive objectives of facilitating space and events. The impurity in functions can be explained by the fact that cities and buildings also became targets for financial capital investment under the impact of a global economy. China, without exception, authenticates the phenomenon ever since it became the world's fastest-growing major economy. Chinese cities today confront such frantic urban transformations that eradicate most of its out-of-date and valueless indigenous environments as they fail to catch up with the universal economic trend. Like any other monetary commodity, buildings in present-day China bear a more crucial identity—the proclamation of economic power and class of a city. Leading Chinese cities, especially Beijing and Shenzhen, continue to commission renowned international practices in designing major national buildings, resulting in a hyped proliferation of branded and collectible architecture. Even secondary cities hysterically reproduce knockoffs or adapt to distinctive architectural fashion in buildings of all sorts, regardless of scale, function, and context. The ability to achieve "placelessness" is now considered a plausible rationale in architectural design in China; buildings are no longer tied to their specific regional character, and they should bear a certain degree of alienation to be situated in contradictory contexts.

Ground for Experiments

Many have said that the booming economy in China makes it a resourceful ground for architectural experiments, yet the starchitects commissioned by Chinese clients are in fact tragically restricted by their own established design vocabularies. Their designs are also hindered by how the media portrays their work. It is considered willful to deny their vogue expressions for the sake of any design principles. Like other foreign practitioners, we encounter a similarly embarrassing dilemma when we receive requests or commissions to design buildings of distinct idiosyncrasy, despite the philosophy of weak and defeated architecture we argued for. It is definitely distasteful to erect in China today another M2 building, one of our earliest works infamous for its outrageous and discordant mix of historic styles and its satire of nostalgic architectural languages. Yet in the context of Tokyo in the early nineties, this represented a provocative attempt to break down the building elements to create architecture as an "anti-object." The theory of "anti-object" architecture seems to be perceived by Chinese audiences as merely a gesture of erasing the physicality of a building through a fragmented envelope. The use of louvers, perforated screens, translucent meshes, or otherwise became the architect's most recognizable strategy in dissolving built volumes, and the mesmerizing envelopes of our buildings are what is mostly commonly acknowledged.

Anti-Object and a Strong Visual Sense of Material Fragmentation

It is inarguable that the majority of our work establishes a strong visual sense of material fragmentation. However, the essence of this "anti-object" philosophy is not as simple as a visual illusion. Instead, it comes down to the distilled realm that a building creates in response to its surrounding contexts. We often use the exemplary case of Bruno Taut's Villa Hyuga in Japan as a pioneer that possesses the essence of an "anti-object." Instead of Taut's skillful manipulation of traditional Japanese artifacts, what struck us most is the intimate relationship between domestic space and nature. This observation led us to design the Water/Glass project, a guesthouse adjacent to Taut's villa, where he successfully dissolved the built space into the vast panorama of the sky and ocean. This belief in the "anti-object" capacity of architecture is further explored in our work in China.

To implement the philosophy of "anti-object" in contemporary China is particularly challenging because of its desire for visually distinctive icons. Rapid urbanization is also giving shape to a gentrified environment where vernacular characteristics are eradicated. Can "defeated" architecture validate itself, and respond to urban contexts lacking in character in present-day Chinese cities? How can such architecture mediate between universal and native expressions? Two of our recently completed Chinese projects continued with this experimentation of "anti-object" architecture, and they demonstrate how these edifices are "defeated" in the diverse urban and rural contexts of contemporary China.

Dematerializing the Shanghai Shipyard

As one of the major architectural relics in downtown Shanghai, the history of the Shanghai Shipyard in Lujiazui dates back to the 1860s. It is part of a major historical urban fabric that witnessed the city's transformation from an industrial port into a prestigious financial center. This project is not only an experiment in the revitalization of the old, but it also aims to reinstate the identity of an obsolete architecture in a renewed urban context. It is not a mere act of nostalgia; this would only lead to an outcome no more exciting than a replication of the past. Like M50 and the 1933 Slaughterhouse, creative clusters in Shanghai have shown the capacity to drive processes of urban regeneration in a city.

While preserving old industrial skeletons, interior spaces are renovated to accommodate various artistic productions, exhibitions, and new forms of transactions. These spaces are often collectively housed within an existing neighborhood with a well-established urban network, thus they mature relatively rapidly as new forms of cultural hubs.

The renovation of the Shanghai Shipyard has a similar objective, yet unlike the earlier cases, the shipyard is situated in the central business district where land value is highest. The context of this project is a synthetic outcome of global finance and real estate speculation—the glamorous Huangpu River, heightened by a series of formalist skyscrapers that constitute the relatively new financial center beginning from the 1990s. Built denser and taller than the last, each of these skyscrapers exerts a flamboyant visual rhetoric onto the dazzling skyline of the river. The challenge of this renovation project is to dematerialize or neutralize an obsolete warehouse into a man-made terrain of glittering glass curtain walls, when it already bore robust industrial features such as a red masonry façade and an arched roof. This surgical operation is carried out through two major approaches: program and materiality. While retaining the majority of the concrete structural skeleton, every piece of interior wall and slab was demolished in order to designate spaces for two new programs, namely, a four-story shopping mall and an eight-hundred-seat theater. A major longitudinal axis was reinstated to create an internal circulatory avenue, marrying these two programs while embracing a visual corridor of monumental concrete columns that was once the structural spine of the warehouse. While carrying on with their modern-day activities, visitors would have the opportunity to experience an elapsed industrial time, heightened by the presence of the historic "obelisks." The theater volume at the eastern end of the axis is further expanded beyond the original footprint to accommodate sizable performances and audiences.

Construction workers at work at the Shanghai Shipyard.
Image courtesy of Kengo Kuma and Associates, 2016

Materiality is another critical approach to this surgical operation. The entire red masonry wall on the north and east elevations are preserved. The colors and dimensions of bricks on these existing masonry walls were carefully surveyed in order to reconstruct a contemporary "masonry curtain wall" on the west and south facades. Pixels of bricks are suspended on stainless steel cables to form another layer of skin in front of a glass enclosure. This gradual fragmentation softens the colossal masonry wall facing Huangpu River into a porous curtain wall that fronts the south public plaza adjoining neighboring developments. Every construction detail of the curtain wall was carefully treated to achieve a screen of drifting masonry particles, visually uninterrupted by the more mundane structural components. A serene interior atmosphere was achieved through three adopted industrial textures: concrete, oxidized steel, and meshed stainless steel. Coupled with these interpretative materials are historic artifacts found discarded from the old warehouse. These remnants were dismantled from various parts of the original building, and recycled and revived with new functions in the renovated space. They include concrete beams converted into outdoor furniture, roof panels refurbished as interior wall finishes, old drainage pipes reshaped as signage and ventilation ducts, and so on. The juxtaposition of the old and new contents would dematerialize the building in such a way that the Shanghai Shipyard would blend back into the urban fabric.

Subsuming the Folk Art Museum of China Academy of Art into the Landscape

Situated within the hilly campus of the China Academy of Art in Hangzhou, the museum is located right on a slope where Hangzhou's most renowned Longjing tea plants used to grow. The slope was intentionally preserved such that the museum could seek ways to adapt its form to the topographic features of the site. The architecture is highly ambiguous between what is fabricated and natural. It was an integrated outcome of geography, climate, and vernacular elements. The planning of its space, circulation, and programs was guided by a network of rhomboid grids overlaid onto the sloping site. Embracing the mountain terrain, a chain of rhomboid modules spiraled uphill and served as both exhibition and circulatory spaces. A field of overhanging roofs folded over the crawling volumes by projections that abided by the strict rhomboidal grid. Together with the uneven level differences assigned between these volumes, the architecture was conceived as not a single edifice but a terrain of voids scattered over a field. The result resembled the spatial richness of a vernacular village. As visitors enter the museum from the lowest entry point, they are guided by an intuitive sense of direction as the exhibition space is both static and circulatory. There is no defined boundary between the display of exhibits and visitor's circulation, and visitors are progressively brought uphill through a series of oblique planes.

Materiality has always been a crucial approach in the work, in particular because of the regionalist character found in different parts of China. Not only does it offer the buildings a tactile envelope, it also crystallizes the intangible essence of nature, and encrypts them into the space of the building. Materiality represents a strong sense of regionalism, reflecting the resources and culture of the locale, as well as its climatic variances. The poetry of the museum is enhanced by a cascade of drifting tiles, like drapery over the glass curtain wall and roof surface. Unlike those that are customized or mass-produced in a factory, most of these tiles are in fact recycled from building materials from the neighborhoods bulldozed during Hangzhou's rapid urbanization. The weathered finishes of these wasted clay tiles offer a strong sense of ruggedness. This effect is equally

The roofscape of the Folk Museum at the China Academy of Art, Hangzhou.
Image courtesy of Kengo Kuma and Associates, 2016

compelling in the Xinjin Zhi Museum in Chengdu, where clay tiles were also adopted as a façade material. There is always a certain expected fallout in the process of China's rapid urban development. Upon completion, the completed building was left abandoned due to curatorial conflicts, and the museum was not maintained. Natural processes of rainwater stains, overgrown weed, and infiltration by all forms of birds and wildlife turned the porous façades into microhabitats with a vigorous sense of nature.

It is worth noting that the museum is paradoxically the most serene when it is uninterrupted by any exhibition. Immediately after the museum's completion when the interior spaces were still unoccupied, the design and photography team from Tokyo made a deliberate trip to Hangzhou just to witness the effect of sunlight on the façades at dawn. It was most breathtaking when the low-lying light filtered through the suspended clay tiles, throwing elongated shadows into the interior spaces. It felt like walking through a forest of tile foliage. The building is successfully "defeated" by its environment. It has a seasonal quality, when visitors can be refreshed every time they encounter nature made tangible. The ambiance of the architecture has arguably surpassed its functional purpose— the museum has become subsumed under the indigenous topography of Hangzhou.

DECENTERING BODIES

LEE AMBROZY

Thinking spatially is not a recent innovation in Chinese artistic practices but is established in traditions of art and architecture. There are sight lines integrated along the paths of Ming landscaped gardens, social hierarchies built into residential courtyards, and rituals designed in tandem with temple architecture. They demonstrate how space and movement are choreographed through the design of built environments. These are the three-dimensional arts, but a similar experiential dimension exists in the appreciation of ancient paintings and calligraphies on paper or silk. In traditional ink landscapes, viewers can "wander" through peaks and valleys using only their eyes, and even the physical act of unrolling a handscroll adds a participatory dimension by drawing the viewer's body into the pictorial narrative itself.[1] Opening this conversation on contemporary art with ancient paintings is not to force correlations where none exist but only to highlight that artists have taken an interest in spatial engineering for centuries.

There is a new wave of spatial experimentation unfolding at the intersection of contemporary art, architecture, and everyday experiences. I argue that artists living in megacities such as Beijing, Shanghai, and Guangzhou are translating the psychology and realities of life in urban enclaves into the context of art. While their spatial manipulations may seem expected within the medium of installation art, I believe the conditions in China's megacities have contributed to an interesting evolutionary trajectory. Also, in this exhibition culture, where freedom of expression is characteristically limited, and where political messages in art demand accountability, artworks that result in a decentering of the viewer can sometimes be read as ambiguous social critique. This essay will consider three contemporary artists and one collective, all of whom are working and exhibiting in Beijing. They all treat architecture, space, and preexisting materials or conditions as a commodity. Space here should be understood in the broadest Lefebvrian sense—from organic urban to

---

1   Wu Hung, *Double Screen: Medium and Representation in Chinese Painting* (University of Chicago Press and Reaction Books: Chicago and London, 1996).

infrastructure space[2] and the disparate social situations therein. Strategies include deploying architectural appropriations or interventions, translating architectural raw materials into an "art world" context, or inducing creativity that is contingent on the immediate built environment. What they share in common is the engendering of a phenomenological experience that decenters and disorients, despite the deployment of vastly familiar materials or scenarios.

The following case studies represent recent exhibition practices, all staged in Beijing, the silent central character in this essay. Owing to the experiential nature of installation art, it is important to note that I have personally seen and experienced each of these artworks, and have found the inspiration to write about them. Collectively, they represent larger trends which can serve as a theoretical foundation for future work. Readers will hopefully find that such an interdisciplinary approach is located on the spectrum of anthropological participant-observation, and materialist object-oriented art history. While an artistic preoccupation with space, architecture, or social contexts is not exclusive to China, unique socioeconomic and political conditions in Beijing have encouraged creative strategies that harness the flexibility of private exhibition spaces. Additionally, the relatively low cost of materials and labor affords the artists opportunities to create structurally ambitious encounters which sometimes encode a subtle form of embedded social critique. These artists responded simultaneously to local conditions and global demands without relying on iconographic "Chineseness." Dismissing cultural or ethnic tropes and iconographies, they instead choose conventional materials that respond to their architectural and social surroundings while the resulting art works similarly strive to resist consumption as either "image-event" or spectacle.[3]

Despite its importance to the discourse of art in China, a discussion of transnational flows of capital will be not attempted here.[4] But it must be acknowledged that international market forces as catalyst for art production is a foundational assumption of my work. There is good reason for such a focus, as contemporary art history in China has demonstrated[5] since the 1990s. Privately operated spaces have been consistently more experimental and trendsetting for art practices. Independent spaces are also capable of illuminating the boundaries of social and economic possibilities, and private galleries in China also tend to congregate in "art zones,"[6] a relatively new yet indispensable part of the urban cultural experience in China.

---

2   Keller Easterling, *Extrastatecraft: The Power of Infrastructure Space* (London: Verso Books, 2014).

3   Hal Foster, *The Art-Architecture Complex* (Verso, 2013).

4   For discussion of how the free market reforms influenced art production in China since the 1980s, see Jane Debevoise, *Between State and Market: Chinese contemporary art in the post-Mao era* (Brill: Leiden, Boston, 2014).

5   For the most recent and thorough treatment of the evolution of public and/or commercial exhibition spaces, please see Wu Hung writings on experimental art: "Experimental Exhibitions." In *Contemporary Chinese Art: A History, 1970s-2000s* (London: Thames & Hudson Ltd, 2014), pp.265-273.

6   This is a geographical status conferred usually at the municipal level, and most first tier cities in China now have at least one "cultural zone" or "creative zone." See Beijing, Shanghai, Xi'an, Guangzhou, Shenzhen, or

Tight Spaces: Linguistic and Non

When a body-space relationship is inherent to a work of art, whether quantified by its ability to be entered or defined by a constellation of objects in space, it is generally characterized as "installation art." Yet as theorist and art historian Claire Bishop notes, the term itself has become so vague as to be functionally ambiguous. Unlike *objects d'art*, whose purpose is activated by a viewer's gaze, these works act upon the viewer and provide heightened perceptual experiences for their audiences.[7] Bishop's definition takes the presence of the viewer's body as a primary characteristic of installation art[8], but the works discussed here move a step beyond, taking their specific architectural surroundings to be equally as primary in the creative formula.

Installation art, which is translated from English as *zhuangzhi yishu*, seems too simplistic in describing works of art which are contingent on their surroundings. In the interest of searching for a more emic terminology, the Chinese verb artists often use to discuss their own works in relation to the audience is not "to see" (*kan*, or *guankan*), but rather "to experience" (*tiyan*). A more robust expression of the body's spatiotemporal relationship to artworks is inherently expressed in the Chinese word *tiyan*, where the first character in the word *ti* refers to the "corporeal body" and the second *yan* "to confirm" or "verify." Using the body as a primary tool for deriving knowledge is an aspect of phenomenological experience that modern cultures have tended to ignore,[9] but inherently available through a *longue durée* art historical approach.

Of course the consideration of body in relation to artworks is a well-documented concern in modern sculpture,[10] minimalist and post-minimalist art, land art, earthworks, and museum studies. Examining ancient traditions, a similar consideration for bodily trajectories can be found in Buddhist art, beginning with the caves at Ajanta in India from the second century BCE through the sixth century CE, and continued in the Mogao Caves at Dunhuang in western China from the fifth to fourteenth century CE. The latter was a pilgrimage site for travelers on the Silk Road where hundreds of fresco-painted cave shrines aggregated over nearly a millennium. The body-space relationship here comes into play through the relational network of sutra tales painted around the walls and ceiling of the cave chapels, some of which were meant to be circumnavigated in prayer. Aspects of this art historical juggernaut have been recycled into modern Chinese art narratives since Zhang Daqian (1899–1983) in the 1940s, and formal connections with the Dunhuang caves can also be read in the work of the collective A Diao Dui.

Chongqing for examples.

7   Much of my thinking here is indebted to Bruno Latour's Actor Network Theory. See Albena Yaneva, "Actor-Network-Theory Approaches to the Archaeology of Contemporary Architecture," in *The Oxford Handbook of the Archaeology of the Contemporary World*, Paul Graves-Brown, Rodney Harrison, eds. Online Publication Date: Dec 2013 DOI: 10.1093/oxfordhb/9780199602001.013.00

8   By way of a general introduction to her work, see: Claire Bishop, *Installation Art* (London: Tate Publishing, 2005).

9   Tim Ingold, *Making: Anthropology, archaeology, art and architecture* (London: Routledge, 2012).

10   Michael Fried, "Art and Objecthood," *Artforum International Magazine*, June 1965, pp.12-23.

Their *Arrow Factory Grotto* (2011-12),[11] was a collaborative painting inspired by the cave chapels or "grottos" at Dunhuang, and by way of site-specificity, it also built upon the Arrow Factory's physical location and institutional purpose.[12]

The Arrow Factory is a non-profit, artist-run space situated in the *hutong*s near Beijing's Confucius Temple. Since 2008, it has hosted conceptual and experimental art projects which can be viewed around the clock through its sliding glass door. As a wrinkle in the urban fabric, Arrow Factory entangles itself within the capital's traditional residential neighborhoods, and reaches a hybrid audience of passersby who might constitute the widest socioeconomic art demographic in the capital—Beijingers and foreigners, tourists

Arrow Factory, Beijing. Image courtesy of Lee Ambrozy

and locals, and rich and poor alike all count as audience. For *Arrow Factory Grotto*, several artists from the collective[13] worked in shifts to cover the exhibition space's three walls and ceiling with personalized vignettes in black and white, a format modeled after the cave chapels. On the central facing wall, the founders of Arrow Factory were painted as astronauts in full gear, mid-spacewalk, their location corresponding to that of the central Buddha and attendants in the caves.[14] This placement was the only pre-meditated design aspect for the decorative program in the "grotto," a symbolic gesture to the curators' work in sustaining Arrow Factory and enabling experimental projects—they are not only saintly, but forward-thinking explorers. Working extemporaneously, the artists covered every available wall surface with their interwoven network of painted meditations on contemporary life to create a space that resembled a secular and contemporary chapel.

11 Arrow Factory, Beijing, October 22, 2011 to January 15, 2012.
12 *Arrow Factory: The Next Four Years*, 2016. See website for details and more photos.
13 A Diao Dui members Chen Xinpeng, Dong Jing, Liang Shuo, Shao Kang, Wang Guangle, Zhang Zhaohong, and Zhou Yi are credited with collaborating on the work.
14 See more photos at the Arrow Factory project page: http://www.arrowfactory.org.cn/?page=diaodui

As a quasi-exercise in non-attachment and reminder of the ephemerality of urban spaces, three months later the work was dismantled.

Appropriated Spaces

As one of the founding members of Arrow Factory, Wang Wei (b. 1972) employs architecture as both a medium and theme. His works have been described as "mindful appropriations of existing spaces,"[15] sometimes translating actual sites into exhibition contexts. Other times he abstractly invokes the built environment through the materials of everyday architecture, such as in his now canonized work *Temporary Space* (2003). Here he hired farmers to construct, and then dismantle a brick room within the gallery space; they used bricks reclaimed from demolition sites in Beijing and worked over the three weeks of the exhibition. For *Historic Residence* (2009),[16] he used appropriation and manipulation of scale to critically examine history, legacy, and extravagance. In this installation Wang Wei created an analog reproduction of two private washrooms built for Mao Zedong and his wife Jiang Qing in Hunan province in 1966. Although he resided there for only eleven days in 1966, this "home" of Mao Zedong has been carefully maintained as a historic residence ever since. While translating these rooms into the gallery, he subjects their floor plans to dramatic spatial expansion, creating two exaggeratedly large washrooms—the sinks several meters from the toilet, the tubs isolated in a sea of period floor tiles. Wang Wei overwhelms the entire gallery space with his mimetic and dramatic recreation, faithful to the original in all but scale.

Historic Residence (2009).
Image courtesy of Wang Wei

The effect was both disorienting and decentering. At first glance the gesture of spatial manipulation appears as a pointless squandering of resources, yet analogies can be found in historical and current political reality. The luxury of the original "residence" in its day is reflected in the two private washrooms, built to the highest possible standards in the 1960s, but antithetical in a time of political turmoil when frugality was highly praised. Wang Wei's spatial distortion inflates the two washrooms to a scale reflecting the historic importance now assigned them. The work also conjures fascination for the private luxuries that might be afforded to the global political elite of today. Entering the work, crossing the tiled floors

---

15 Pauline J. Yao, "Wang Wei: Borrowing from Reality" Source: *ArtTime*, July 2012
16 *Historic Residence*, Space Station, Beijing, September 26–November 7, 2009.

in the absurdly palatial washroom, we seem to be walking in slow motion, only to arrive at the most mundane landmarks: a sink, bathtub, or toilet. In this sense, *Historic Residence* achieves what Bernard Tschumi has described as "spatial torture" or "space violating bodies."[17] Although the artwork has been captured in images, the viewing experience is obligatory to engage with the work at this ontological level, and Wang Wei successfully instrumentalizes an architectural ready-made, prolonging the audiences' experience in the space and giving us pause to consider metaphorical readings of these seemingly mundane and outrageous toilets.

The Value of Empty Space

The relative freedom in Beijing's exhibition spaces can also derive from their generous size, a byproduct of their often post-industrial nature, and locations often removed from the density of urban centers. Michael Lin (b. 1964) often uses building materials and engages existing structures to create artworks as environments both performative and collaborative in nature, but always best experienced onsite. For *Place Libre* (2013)[18] he treated the gallery's space as an invisible commodity, and exploited the gallery's central location within Beijing's 798 Art Zone. In a dramatic gesture on the value of empty space, he erased the artist's hand by camouflaging the gallery's interior as a parking lot, creating a stage that turned the viewer's attention inside out and brought the socioeconomic activities of the surrounding gallery district into play. It was a simple and audacious strategy—Lin's structural manipulations included removing a large section of the gallery's wall adjacent to the road thereby creating an entrance to the interior of the exhibition space. The artwork was effectively invisible, with the gallery's interior disguised as its would-be surroundings. Lin's intervention consisted of thirteen painted white lines on the floor demarcating parking spots and walls painted in a manner customary to commercial parking lots. More than mere formalism, the parking spaces were open to the public during gallery hours and free. Music from a local radio station filled the space, and hourly photographs documented the non-choreographed movement of the autos within.[19]

The repurposed commercial gallery not only provided a stage for visitors to become artistic collaborators but harnessed its post-industrial shell as an architectural ready-made, and further imbricated the creative industries-zoned area as a socioeconomic reality for artists in Beijing. *Place Libre* resonated on multiple levels, as architectural design and allegorical art, and fulfilled functions ranging from a pragmatic need to a practical joke. For drivers entering through the "garage" door, the exhibition was a boon; for art flâneurs entering through the gallery's main door, encountering a parking lot where *objets d'art* are to be expected is a shocking lack of aestheticized or individualized content. The non-materialized art only strengthened one's impression of the everyday aesthetics

---

17   Bernard Tschumi, "Architecture and Violence," *Artforum International Magazine*, September 1981, 44-47.
18   *Place Libre*, Tang Contemporary Art, Beijing, September 14–Oct 30, 2013.
19   Michael Lin, *Place Libre* (London, Black Dog Publishing, 2014).

co-opted for the painted walls, the lines, and the ordinary cars in the extraordinary space. Lin's inversion of artistic content interrogates the role of the gallery's walls in defining art. If art can be discovered within the quotidian, why must it be relegated to "zones" like a caged animal?[20] By disappearing any actual artworks, and delivering instead an experience approximating the everyday, he pushes art's potential function beyond aesthetic imperatives and undermines the invisible values and systems that define "contemporary art."

Ephemerality and Contingencies

One of the most striking features of China's megacities is the ubiquity of construction and demolition present in the urban landscape. This structural ephemerality has been translated to the exhibition context by these artists exploiting the low cost of materials and labor as well as the relative structural flexibility and mutability of gallery environments. A lack of building restrictions and codes allows for creative freedom, especially in regards to the ways the visitors' bodies interact and experience the space. The adaptable potential of the gallery space enables artists to approach their practices in different ways. Liang Shuo (b. 1976) often pushes spatial and material potentiality to extremes, employing not only the architectural shell or surrounding context, but cultivating a practice of spontaneous creativity that is contingent on the situations and materials found onsite. This was the case for *Temple of Candour* (2016),[21] an installation created entirely using materials found onsite at the gallery—shipping crates, rolls of packing foam, drywall, paper, and so on. Without altering the walls or installation design remaining from the previous exhibition, the artist spent nearly four weeks transforming the space.

Using these raw materials, Liang actualized his interpretation of an eighteenth-century, dilapidated (long disappeared) monastery known today only through textual accounts. The audience was afforded only one option to experience the artwork—climb through an entry hole carved through the wall next to the gallery's main entrance. Inside, one follows a path that leads through an

Place Libre (2013).
Image courtesy of Michael Lin

---

20   See art historian Yin Jinan's prescient article on 798, "798 *shi wenhua dongwuyuan ma?* [Is 798 a cultural petting zoo?]", 2004.

21   *Temple of Candour*, Beijing Commune, March 8–April 30, 2016.

installation replete with painted vistas, a steel bamboo forest, the temple (now resurrected in cardboard), and the West Lake rendered in polystyrene wrapping. But to reach each lushly crafted and recycled scene, we must climb over piles of crates and through walls while progressing along the designed path. The different moods and material textures along the way recall the experience of reading a traditional ink landscape painting—in two dimensions the eyes move over a painting's surface, but here, we traverse a three-dimensional landscape whose vignettes are revealed as the body moves through space. The artwork fully exploits multiple layers of time and space within the modernist "white cube" gallery space.

Temple of Candour draws you through its rabbit hole and into a time-bending wonderland ambitiously realized in disposable mediums; it resists material worth. Instead, the artist's time investment in creating a thoroughly convincing world becomes the most valuable dimension of the artwork. We absorb the views of mountaintops inked onto cardboard panels, contemplate time passed in the crumbling eaves of a cardboard temple, and reflect over polystyrene waters. The effect of claustrophobic release is palpable as we emerge from the darkened bamboo forest onto a rickety elevated platform overlooking the dramatically tranquil packing foam lake. Thus the visitor's somatic reading, not the material artifact, is true receipt of "seeing" the work. Liang's *Temple of Candour* entangles two contrasting temporalities and materialities by recreating a fabled past through the material lens of the low-budget contemporary. With the gallery space as palimpsest, the artwork's materiality self-reflexively anticipates its future state of ruin and reflects a contemporary structural reality in megacities today. At the end of the exhibition, the artwork disappears, like the temple from which it takes its name. Its material frankness and extemporaneous creation are enabled by the liberties afforded the artist to interact freely with the space.

Temple of Candour (2016).
Image courtesy of Liang Shuo

Contemporary Histories of Spatial Engagement

Responding to both local contexts and global expectations, the artists discussed here demonstrate only a few strategies by which art intersects with architecture, and how the raw materials of the city are translated into the artists' reflections of contemporary reality. There are many other artists working in similar modes. Despite having a unique historical trajectory, these works can still be called installation art in accordance with

Bishop's definition, although some practitioners are pushing it further. The Chinese art historical context for artworks engaging social and physical spaces of architecture can be traced to exhibition practices in the 1980s and '90s. Historical antecedents can be found in what Gao Minglu theorizes as "Apartment Art,"[22] and in what Wu Hung simply refers as "experimental exhibitions."[23] In the 1990s, expanding urban areas continued to develop alongside experimental art practices, such as in Guangzhou, where exhibitions of the Big Tail Elephant (*Daweixiang*) working group achieved nearly total integration into the high-speed urbanization occurring there.[24] Entirely contingent upon their architectural contexts and borrowing heavily from the raw materials of architecture and the built environment, works from the Big Tail Elephant were situational, fleeting, and exist now in documentary photographs alone.

In 1999, curators Qiu Zhijie and Wu Meichun organized the exhibition *Post-Sense Sensibility: Alien Bodies and Delusion*,[25] whose curatorial premise encouraged a sense of unfamiliarity and decentering encounters in art. It should come as little surprise, then, that the feelings of disorientation or displacement are still associated with the density of an Asian megacity. No longer relegated to underground spaces or impermanent exhibitions within urban folds in the art capitals of Shanghai, Beijing, and Guangzhou, ambitious artists have a range of dedicated art spaces in which to exhibit their works and a larger, more cosmopolitan audience with whom to engage. As Beijing's art infrastructure evolved into the complex machine it is today, and art works liberated itself from the urban landscape and filled pristine gallery spaces and zones, art also became less visually aggressive, adopting the aesthetic of the everyday. In a political culture where highly legible, easily decipherable messages are the enterprise of the state, it is unsurprising that artists have continuously distanced themselves from similar operations through tactics of disorientation and decentering. Whether it produces shocking images in an apartment complex basement or transplants the everyday into the hallowed context of the exhibition space, these artworks do not demand autonomy from their architectural or social environments. Instead, they cultivate a heighten sense of displacement upon encounter.

When an ethos of fast development and structural impermanence is the reality, the intuitive knowledge of the self becomes the primary constant and a yardstick for understanding the world around us. Each of the examples here relied not only on surrounding social and physical spaces and was conceived amidst situational contingencies that fed into the content of the work. In many cases, the most substantive interpretation is derived from experiencing them in person—here, the semiotics embedded in the *tiyan*,

22 Gao Minglu, "Apartment Art Activities in the 90s," in *Total Modernity and the Avant-garde in Twentieth-century Chinese Art*, (Cambridge, Mass.: MIT Press; London: in association with China Art Foundation, 2011), 284-308.
23 See note 5 above.
24 Members Liang Juhui, Chen Shaoxiong, Lin Yilin, Xu Tan. See *Big Tail Elephant* (Bern, Switzerland, Kunsthalle Bern, 1998)
25 The exhibition took place in the basement of a Beijing apartment complex, and included Wang Wei.

or experience, allow for a more emic perspective on how knowledge of the body may be embedded within art practices. Documentation and preservation of these ephemeral works pose problems and challenges. How can works contingent on architectural and other contexts be integrated into art history, the larger critical discourse, or future institutional strategies? Relegated to flat, two-dimensional images, the crucial embodied experiential aspects of such works are being eclipsed by discussions of aesthetics. With afterlives composed of primarily photographic evidence, the physical experience of navigating through these environments and the knowledge gleaned from that process are obscured in the digital artifact. This is a shame, because as we know, not all spaces are created equal.

POLITICAL AND PUBLIC COMMITMENT TO SUSTAINABILITY

JOAN LEUNG LYE

China offers us multiple ways to think about the futures of cities and architecture. Specific strategies are being developed to address some of the negative consequences of rapid urban development, globalization, and environmental problems in China's post-industrial and post-Cultural Revolution eras. Numerous architectural projects give evidence to Chinese cities that have transformed in a blink of an eye. The projects and their protagonists present many promises hand-in-hand with an apprehension about the future of China. The conscientious architect is in the position to invite a continual dialogue and critical thinking about such a future. The discourse and thoughtful review of the projects in, and issues surrounding, China would shed light on cities around the world that are similarly forced by rapid economic and urban development. Critical thinking becomes all the more urgent when architects and non-architects alike are faced with important cultural, social, and environmental questions about the city, especially given the flattening of the globe and the breadth and frequency of regional and global migration. The nature of such sustained and geographically specific forms of migration in recent Chinese history would necessitate a consistent inquiry in contemporary approaches in architecture for these specific locales. These are useful vantage points to initiate questions concerning the specific conditions that support the formation of critical architectural and urban practices, such that architecture can be contextualized in an environment increasingly overwhelmed by iconic and imported architecture.

Awareness of Place and Culture

The regime of economic reform in China had steered architecture towards a different pursuit. Under the ideology of communism and the Cultural Revolution, architecture participated as a specific form of production towards subsistence. Only the essential buildings were produced, and the activity of design had a deliberate commitment against beauty and the realms of the visual and spiritual. Curiously, the abandoned industrial aesthetics of the Shougang Steel Mill and the blast furnaces in Beijing has an unconscious form of beauty. This enormous man-made landscape more than measures up to the canonic and beautiful landscapes of nature around China. Its anticipated conversion into a designated park recalls the similarly industrial abattoirs and food production facilities and markets of Parc de la Villette in Paris. However, there ought to be a concern that the intended interventions would mute the robust history of the place with a park space that exists in a vacuum. The comparable physical potential of the steel mill at the periphery of a great city has intense historical heritage, generated out of purely functional, economic, and political needs. Here is an opportunity to create an unprecedented sense of place, with a careful and thoughtful architectural engagement. Architecture can reframe the public perception of the park as a transformation from the polluter to the green lungs of Beijing. The architecture can be a formless supplementation of the deficiency of the steel mill, putting aside the iconography of conventional representations that would burden this preservation exercise. This site allows for a truly honest relationship between the subject of industrialization and the object of the steel mills through an exciting journey in time. The project holds much promise and anxiety at the same time. It can be a model project on the many levels of a new society that is ecological, technological, historical, political, and economic.

A younger generation of Chinese architects have stepped up to explore the multiple positions and debates on the future of architecture and the city of China. Through several materialized projects, they instilled a desire for a better understanding of the cultural context and identity of architectural forms. They deal directly with emergent social issues that are at once relevant and innovative. The Beijing No.4 High School Fangshan Campus by Open Architecture appears to be an unconscious design in this regard. The building stretches on the terrain, draws movement through it, and choreographs a natural engagement with the diverse activities of the school. The school was structured like a miniature city, but it did not appear contrived. There is a strong anticipation of a natural extension of the social lives of children towards their families in Beijing. In another instance, the projects and essays captured in a book compilation entitled *Homecoming* by the Department of Architecture of the University of Hong Kong also begs the question of the need for national identity in the new Chinese society. The selected works of Hsieh Ying-chun, Liu Jiakun, Hua Li, Meng Yan, Tong Ming, Wang Weijen, and Zhang Ke were the protagonists in the search for a unique ideology amongst Chinese architects who were educated and groomed outside China. They were looking for opportunities in their homeland to demonstrate their critical thinking through their work. One of the contributors of the book Cole Roskam concluded, "you will never go home again," adding a poignancy or a further emphasis on the wider relevance of the debate.

There is an emergence of alternative design approaches in China, especially visible in projects that engage local references, materials, and construction techniques. They were designed to enrich the lives of the local community as much as the visitors to the city. The Red Brick Museum by Dong Yugan is truly inspirational in this sense. The architectural forms of the museum present themselves as "natural" objects of cultural significance. Deeply passionate about his cultural heritage, Dong takes up the position to enhance the rich historical and cultural legacy through an intensive form of experimentation. The patronage of such a project helps to develop healthy roots for society, even though its criticality is still in its infancy. In such projects, the very basis of its context became the design and construction methodologies, and they form the simplest and most sustainable approaches in architecture. The simple choice of material resolves much of the environmental and energy concerns in a delightful construction. Rather than complex technological constructs, a simple and clear solution would ultimately address the global energy and climate problems.

The discourse and thoughtful review of the projects in, and issues surrounding, China would shed light on cities around the world that are similarly forced by rapid economic and urban development.

Redefining Obsolescence in Cultural and Ecological Terms

Beijing has all the features that are traditionally associated with a great city. There are impressive public squares, parks, and boulevards of trees. Magnificent religious buildings and state monuments demonstrating the power of its civilization in terms of its history, art, knowledge, and culture. Beijing's intriguing courtyard residences is distinct from the nineteenth-century residential architecture of Paris, London, New York, and San Francisco. Today, these courtyard districts assume a rather distorted existence. The conservation of memory in the form of a replication of historical architectural features is confusing. What are the lessons in China that will guide the conservation of tomorrow? I read with interest William Lim's reference to Rem Koolhaas in an alternative model of conservation for Beijing. In the book *Preservation Is Overtaking Us?*, Koolhaas clarified that "preservation is for us, a type of refuge" to escape from star architecture. He was speaking in the wake of the subprime mortgage crisis in 2008. He asserted that the global economy's three frothy decades between the early 1980s and the late 2000s were the root of the transformation of serious and necessary architecture of the 1970s into star architecture today. He was concerned with substituting architecture with its own likeness, only slightly improved. The urgency of his retreat to a research about preservation shows a comprehension of the practice of architecture with the purpose of sustaining cultural significance.

In the *hutong*s of Beijing, there were new substitutions of walls, windows, doors, column, column capitals, roofs, or exact copies of entire buildings from foreign cultures. The wholesale replicas of entire buildings from a neoclassical tradition speak to a social and functional dislocation. Driven by aggressive neoliberal capitalism in the last few decades, massive destruction, eviction, displacement and dispossession of traditional urban communities persist in disorienting scale. Like other East Asian cities, Beijing witnessed the disrupting dominance of the rich, powerful, and privileged, and the increased erosion of globalization in the centers of development in relation to activities, cultural aspirations, demographics, and opportunities. The lack of constraint in the production of wealth, backed by unequal legislation, has contributed to an environment that is "out of control." Whether in developing or developed countries, cities seem to be faced with the difficult choice between conservation of traditional value and the adoption of a postmodern reality. In Beijing, the dilemma is between a distinct local Chinese identity or a surrender to globalization and Western influence. Whilst the preservation of architectural heritage is receiving more attention, the emphasis still remains on the hardware. The narratives

Lecture by William Lim at Space-E6, Urbanus, Beijing. Image courtesy of Jeremy Chia, 2015

that gave the buildings life and vitality in the first place tend to be ignored. In a closer examination of the preserved areas in Beijing, there are questions about the essence of the existence of the *hutong*s apart from its current touristic value. In his 1987 book *Mirages and Miracles: The Crises of Global Fordism*, Alain Lipietz said, "this is a time for doubts and questions, a time when schemes fall apart, and when every apostasy can be justified." He was referring to the decline of socialism in the Third World, but almost thirty years later, surrounded by wealth, the future of cities and architecture in China continues to invite doubts and questions.

Interaction between Technology, and the Biological and Ecological Worlds

Technologies in architecture and cities must interact with the biological and ecological world to form a total dynamic system. Tunney Lee, professor at the Massachusetts Institute of Technology, was excited over the sustainable cycle in the once thriving silk production in China. There was an intimate integration with fish farming, where the waste from the silkworm would feed the fish in the pond under the mulberry trees, and waste from the fish would in turn nourish the soil for the trees. Similarly, Neri Oxman, a designer and architect who heads the Mediated Matter research group at the Massachusetts Institute of Technology Media Lab, is researching ways in which digital fabrication technologies can interact with the biological world. Also observing the miraculous life cycle of silk worms, Oxman is working at the intersection of computational design, additive manufacturing, materials engineering, and synthetic biology. Her lab is pioneering a new age of symbiosis between microorganisms and buildings, an innovation that promises harmonious architectural and urban development with ecological life.

Architects must balance their innovative engagement in the hardware of building design and the conditions under which people would actually live responsibly, had they not been overwhelmed by the aggression of a consumerist society. In the context of new technological approaches in sustainable architecture, a direct confrontation with the polarized needs of polluting industries can be dangerous; that is to say, the mere production of new architectural products and the removal of undesirable by-products from industry. There is a polarity brought about by a narrow focus on technological products that merely claims to reduce energy consumption per item. These technological products tend to have a reciprocal effect of encouraging an overly liberal usage, leading to a postponement of a necessary political and public commitment to instigate change. The solution for a sustainable environment must equate a sustainable way of life. As a consequence, the society must be forced to confront one of the most difficult problems of mankind—namely, to tame the desire for easy comfort and excessive consumption. To succeed, architects would need the collaboration of the community far beyond the profession. Architects must acknowledge that one of the most urgent tasks is to overcome the limited definition of obsolescence, and aspire towards a form of sustainability that has cultural and ecological relevance.

In all past forms of socialist thought, the rationalization of production, private ownership, and education had the most profound effect on architecture and the instrumentality of form. While the entire globe seems to have accepted that the path to prosperity is to engage in peaceful trade and consumerism, it is still important to observe how the social form is continually being invoked by different regimes in very different ways. Advancing with greater civility from the days of civil war, colonialism, and new forms of global imperialism, the process of social rationalization is being applied to education in the architectural and urban disciplines. In fact, the contributors of this chapter are deeply involved in the design of architectural pedagogy in schools of architecture in China and elsewhere. Architectural education favors social issues so vehemently, only for students to graduate into a world of disempowered architects, called to comply to the clients in a service industry. Disaffected students of the built environment cannot connect the socially-attuned lessons in school with the real world of rampant profiteering in an uncritical professional service and a distorted urban economy.

A traditional cluster of buildings in Beijing with the coal factory in the background. Image courtesy of Budi Lim, 2015

08
RATIONALIZING

AN AUTOBIOGRAPHICAL NOTE ON HISTORY AND IDENTITY

LIU KECHENG

I am the youngest of my four siblings, who, other than me, were all born in the 1950s. One can tell by comparing the photographs in my family albums that life was happier in the 1950s than in the 1960s. In the few family portraits that I have of the 1960s, my parents seemed tired and disheartened. It was partly due to the Three Years of Natural Disasters, as described by the government at the beginning of the 1960s, but more importantly it was shaped by the unstable political situation of the Great Leap Forward. My mother got into trouble with the authorities before the Cultural Revolution, and my father was also put in jail during the Revolution. Without my parents around, I grew up under the care of my older siblings. Having been born in the 1950s, they experienced a deep contrast between a period of peace and a period of darkness that followed. It forced them to mature at a young age, with a yearning to return order to society. Having been born into a world of chaos, I never experienced a society with order. Hence, order always seems unreal to me, and I would sometimes have a tendency to break up orderliness that creeps into my life. Different from the generation of the 1950s, I am always on the periphery observing the regime of the mainstream, even though I may appear to be part of the mainstream.

The 1980s was China's golden decade and a time of great impact. Everything seemed wonderful at the beginning. All of a sudden, everyone had the opportunity to go to school. The doors to the world were wide open, and everything seemed possible. The nation, the workplace, and the individuals all seemed full of zeal. In the field of architecture, modernist theories of the twentieth century arrived in China like a noble prince from Utopia, virtuous and impeccable. I thought China's future would be how the Western world was at the time. Unfortunately, postmodernism shattered that dream. As followers of the Modern Movement, we were confounded by its fall and betrayal. At the same time, the debate between the "blue civilization" of the West and the "yellow civilization" of the East during the late 1980s also made us realize that China was in a chaotic situation. China needs to find a way out on its own.

Cultural Bearings

After graduation, I was immersed in various "new" Western architectural discourses and theories. Naturally, at the beginning, I embraced them diligently, but they did not make a great impact on me. What I read were translated works, and I was not fluent enough in English to read the originals. There was also no one around me who had a better understanding of the theories. However, there were a few things that left a mark on me. The first were the books I had read before 1989. The professional architectural books at that time were unattractive to me. Besides, there were not many projects, as the market economy has not yet matured. Instead, I had a lot of spare time to read books such as the *Walking Towards the Future* series edited by Jing Guantao, and *Culture: China and the World* series edited by Gan Yang. The work of these prominent cultural activists and intellectuals had a major impact on me. With an open mind, everyone came together to discuss the abstract and long-term issues of the China. In fact, many of my thoughts can be traced back to the readings and discussions I had during that period. They inspired me to think more deeply about the theoretical framework of our culture, beyond a straightforward acceptance or rejection.

The second was the study of urban planning. I used to think logically and rationally. But in time it became unproductive, especially when I discovered that there were fundamental issues with my underlying assumptions of the problems. Ever since then, whenever I discover the same problems, I would work backwards to tried to brainwash myself to disrupt the completeness of my reasoning. In this respect, Han Yi really inspired me. After meeting him at my graduation review, I worked for him at the planning department. During the meetings, he would only discuss a single problem and a single solution, yet he would make the most poignant comments. "If you have a good card, play it. If you try to wait for a hand full of good cards, you will ruin the whole game," he once said. This can also be applied to design—one good aspect is enough to make a project good. Because of this advice, I started to be selective of what I did, instead of pursuing everything. Literature had a bigger influence on me than academic works. The work of Chinese novelist Mo Yan resonated with me. He

> There must be perseverance when urban heritage needs to be protected, and innovation when keeping up with the times in the face of renewal. In fact, conservation itself requires creativity and wisdom.

is capable of expressing his thoughts succinctly in a few words. I really admire his way of telling short stories. Stories such as "My Mother and I" and "My Neighbor and I" were allegories of his own life experiences, but he was able to state the origins and purpose of these narratives, along with clear opinions about the historical period and its social values. Everything came from his daily experiences, and no one can argue with that. In the field of architecture, some architects like to talk about things in a very abstract way, which only overcomplicate matters.

Maturity and Modernity

I did not like the city of Xi'an when I first arrived in the 1980s. After studying, working, and living in it for the past three decades, I slowly got used to its culture and fell in love with the city. Xi'an is an ancient city that knows where it stands in relation to its own history and culture. It is like a mature adult or an elderly full of wisdom and experience. It does not follow any trend, but it remains inclusive. Despite being physically in Xi'an, the knowledge I have of the city in the 1980s was merely from textbooks, which wrongly argued for the architecture of Xi'an to be torn down because they were antiquated and impractical. I started to gain a proper understanding of the city through the Beiyuanmen neighborhood renovation project from the early 1990s onwards. As I grew older, I knew the city better and began paying more respect to it. This was an important personal change. As an architect and an educator, such an attitude was needed to demonstrate care for a mature city.

A lane in the old city of Xi'an. Image courtesy of Lam Lai Shun, 2015

Having moved on from the past, Xi'an today has adopted a modern position. It has a distinctive character and development plan that is more practical and sustainable compared to other cities. In fact, if Xi'an were already as strong as the coastal cities economically, the local government would not have tried as hard to develop the city. After all, the competition between two countries is not as intense as the competition between two cities. Generations of urban planners and governments have promoted the consistent belief that the history and culture of Xi'an should be protected and revealed. At times the ideas were too extreme, such as the notion of "reconstructing the kingdom." But the intent was the same. Certain mistakes were made during the period of experimentation, and we cannot deny that the Xi'an that we know of today remains a result of trial and error. Much of the thought behind the urban development of Xi'an can be discussed through the series of works by Zhang Jinqiu spanning four decades. As a Fellow of the Chinese Academy of Engineering, Zhang was a student of Liang Sicheng. She devoted herself to the study, conservation, and renewal of heritage buildings of the city. She made great contributions to the city, designing many of the works in it, such as the Drum and Bell Tower Plaza, the Provincial History Museum, and the Tang Garden. All of these projects received widespread approval from both the government and the general public alike. Architects of our generation must first inherit the history and culture of Xi'an handed down from our predecessors. Then we ought to develop the same persistent belief, and continue working on studying and conserving the city, whilst improving with modern techniques.

Girl bikes along the Old City Wall of Xi'an, with an expanse of new high-rises beyond.
Image courtesy of Lam Lai Shun, 2015

History and Identity

Chinese cities today are faced with two problems—namely, the weight of its history and the process of rapid modernization. There is a larger underlying question of how a city grows—whether it was naturally born, gradually grown, or artificially manufactured. Facing the impact of modernization, we are not yet fully prepared in terms of our thinking towards a balanced form of urban development. We are lacking in confidence. We try all the time to change, to revamp, and to resist our past; but in the process, we lose the identities of our cities. To change or not to change—that has always been the question for cities. Certain things will settle as time passes and the heritage of the city consolidates. Others will progress with time. Whether you like it or not, change is always occurring. However, as history shows, change is not equivalent to progress. Change is relative. Cultural heritage is the accumulated artifacts of value that persist amidst long-term urban development, and it belongs to the common memory of its people. It allows its inhabitants to experience the rhythm of eras, and evokes a sense of contentment and progressiveness at the same time. Architects of the city must have the ability to deal with both issues of protection and renewal. There must be perseverance when urban heritage needs to be protected, and innovation when keeping up with the times in the face of renewal. In fact, conservation itself requires creativity and wisdom.

In the age of globalization, it is essential to respect our history and be inclusive at the same time. To be respectful, we first need to respect the right of existence of both tangible and intangible heritage. One cannot be selective as to which ones to keep using one's own judgments or using contemporary values. It is immoral to demolish or recklessly change historical buildings and environments. Any addition of new architecture must fundamentally respect history, and should tactfully intervene by way of a dialogue between the old and contemporary ways. In that respect, we must prevent any reproduction of the past, or a reconstruction of "antiques." Such reproduction falsifies history, and is equally disrespectful to the past. With an immensely rich history, we cannot resist the urge to become modern. Our behavior throughout this era has been hasty and reactionary. Even though China has the second highest gross domestic product in the world now, we still need to rediscover who we are today. One way to do so is to discover and learn to inherit our cultural heritage. Every architect, manager, builder, and participant of our cities must relentlessly figure out their relationships to the distinctive characteristics of their cities in the context of the contemporary world.

This essay is translated and adapted from Liu Kecheng, "Lishi zhongxin yu dili bianyuan de diejia" [The Superimposition of Historic Centrality and Geographic Marginailty], *Time+Architecture*, Issue 129, 2013/1, pp.58-64, and "lishi shi zhiyue yeshi ziyuan" [History as Restriction and Asset], *Urban Environment Design*, Issue 64, 2012/08, p.175.

ARCHITECTURE AND URBAN CULTURE

ROCCO YIM

With my practice rooted in Hong Kong, there is a constant need to respond to the disparate cultural and physical landscapes in which we work. This occurs in equal measure in both in this city and in Mainland China, and in this context, I have been intrigued by the relationship between architecture and the city. Does architecture shape the city? Or does the city shape architecture? Ultimately, this is a question that defies simple answers. In China, many cities are being designed from scratch, and they tend to look towards architecture and urban districts to promote an instantaneous identity. The place may be devoid of a meaningful physical context, yet ingrained in the place are inherent elements of tradition, culture, a way of life, and natural attributes. If architecture rediscovers these abstract and seemingly elusive elements, it can evoke these attributes to create culturally and urbanistically relevant entities. Such architecture could anchor and induce the development of the surrounding urban forms. This would greatly help to shape the future city, at least in theory.

On the other hand, in a highly-developed city like Hong Kong, contemporary urban forces tend to reinforce but sometimes transcend the influence of inherent cultural qualities. The configuration of urban infrastructure, behavioral patterns, circulatory movements, and spatial and structural systems in construction would come together to exert both invisible and tangible tensions in the evolution of architecture. In the same instance, forces in the city would also help to shape architecture. Two of my recently completed works—the Guangdong Museum in Guangzhou and the Tamar Government Headquarters in Hong Kong represent such explorations of these two contrasting scenarios.

Grandeur of Vision

The Guangdong Museum is one of the four cultural landmarks for the Zhujiang New Town in Guangzhou. Architecturally conceived as an *objet d'art* on a monumental scale,

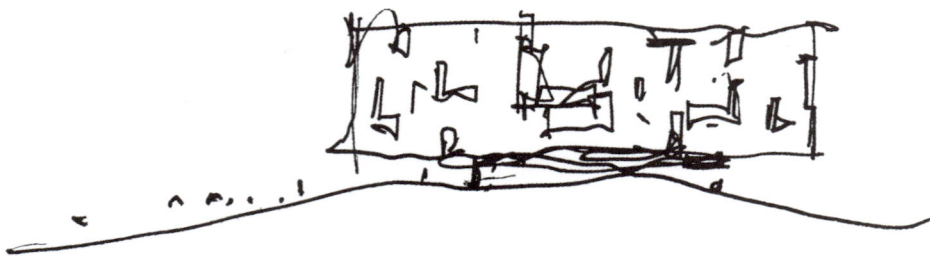

Sketch of Guangdong Museum. Image courtesy of Rocco Yim

it is an allegory of the impeccably and intricately sculpted lacquer box. Such an antique artifact of Chinese origin serves to collect and reflect upon the treasures of the times. The museum is designed to house objects of treasure, and is itself a treasured object of fascination. The spatial arrangement of the museum takes its conceptual reference from the carvings of the legendary Chinese ivory concentric balls. Each carving slices through the museum box and reveals different layers and varying degrees of transparency. Each layer dialogues between the interior halls in an intricate and explorative way, which is then extended and reflected on the design of the external façade. Each elevation is tailored with unique expressions of different geometric voids. These voids are recessed into the building mass to form volumetric patterns that would echo the mystery of the interior spaces.

View of Guangzhou from Guangzhou Tower. Image courtesy of Wellington Kuswanto, 2013

On the urban level, the Guangdong Museum is intended to work together with the other three cultural buildings to create an urban hub where the building forms are in dialogue with one another. In particular, the Guangzhou Opera House by the late Zaha Hadid sits across the central green axis in such a way that there could have been a genuine fusion between the architecture and the public realm, so much so that these buildings and public activities could have contributed to the collective identity of this new district. In the end, however, this intent never quite materialized. The four buildings are interesting pieces of architecture in their own right, but they never really form a meaningful whole because there is a lack of coordination in the spatial flow of the vistas, the movement of the public, and the access they can have to the buildings. Despite the grandeur of the initial vision, the disconnection between architecture and its urban context is sadly too often an occurrence in Chinese cities.

Connectivity and Anti-Object

The Hong Kong Government Headquarter Complex at Tamar, on the other hand, successfully takes its cue from the form of the existing urban district. Conceived as an iconic place rather than an object, the complex contributes to the better working of the city. This new government headquarters embraces the public realm and strengthens the city's connectivity to the harborfront. The centerpiece of the design is a green public connector that brings people from the city to the water. The large complex comprises two interconnected towers for the central government offices. It is flanked on the west by a low and rectangular block for the Chief Executive's office, and on the east by the Legislative Council Complex, which culminates at the northern edge of the Council's Plenary Hall. These groups contrast and complement one another in their architectural form, just as each group in society plays its own role, sometimes in confrontation and sometimes in concert with one another in creation of public policy.

Recalling the city's traditional spirit of open-mindedness and receptiveness, the architecture of the new headquarters takes the form of an overt gesture, a metaphor of an "open door." The openness also reads as a gateway to Victoria Harbor, and a frame for the city rising behind it. At the same time, on an urban level, it is a genuinely humanistic design. Despite its location on a previously isolated site, the doorway now sits over a landscaped carpet of green that knits the city together. It invites the general public to pass through its embrace on their travels from the business district to the waterfront. In this perhaps most important civic complex of the last few decades in Hong Kong, urbanity is chosen over monumentality. Sensitivity regarding security and privacy notwithstanding, the architecture fuses rather than stands aloof from the public realm. It contributes in a deliberately celebratory gesture to the city's famed urban connectivity.

Spontaneity and Openness

In this concept of openness, something unexpected occurred towards the end of 2014, as the people of Hong Kong took to the streets to seek reform in the Hong Kong electoral system. We thought the park would be a public space for people to use, not as a protest site, but for celebrations. The idea was that whatever happens on the park, towards the waterfront, can be seen by all those who are inside the building.

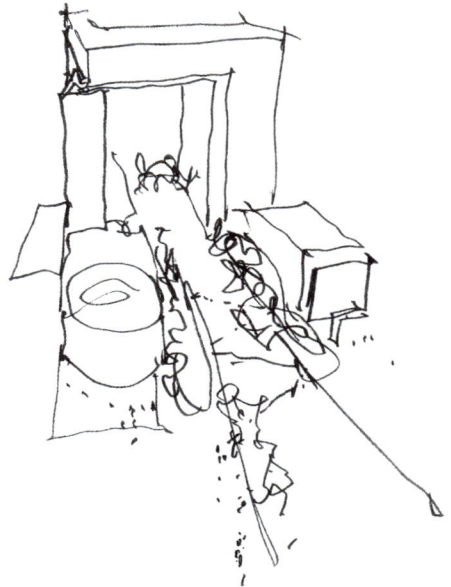

Sketch of the overhead view of HKSAR Government Headquarters. Image courtesy of Rocco Yim

Instead, the Occupy Movement used the whole area in a different way. Hong Kong is such a congested city, I always thought it needs more public spaces—places where exchange of ideas could happen spontaneously, without planning. It was stimulating to see the "Lennon Wall" become what it did. In fact, it would be interesting to see that wall serving this purpose even without the Occupy Movement around it. I see that wall as having its own life—I did not before, but I do now. It would be very stimulating for it to go on being what it was, especially if it happens spontaneously—but that might be too much to hope for. As I walked through the occupied zones towards Central, which felt so much less congested and cleaner, I thought, do we really need so many roads? Can we do something to persuade people to use their cars less, and pedestrianize this area at least occasionally, if not permanently? If we could experiment with fewer roads—not just for protesters, but as a civic space—it would have a very positive effect for the city.

The configuration of urban infrastructure, behavioral patterns, circulatory movements, and spatial and structural systems in construction would come together to exert both invisible and tangible tensions in the evolution of architecture.

These two projects provide food for thought for a socially and culturally sensitive architect. I have come to believe that in the twenty-first century, the city precedes architecture. How to bring about architecture that is intellectually provocative like the Guangdong Museum, but at the same time contributes as significantly to the city as the Tamar Complex? Even if the fences, as a sign of deteriorating trust on all sides, were going up around the government buildings during a period of social unrest, there is still hope that it is not a permanent thing. Not any one side should bear the sole blame, as it is a reflection of this conflict, and of mistrust. If a fence goes up, it can come down too. This is the biggest challenge facing architecture and the city today.

Part of this essay is adapted from an interview with Rocco Yim by Ilaria Maria Sala, "Hong Kong Government Office Architect Reflects on 'Occupy' Movement," *The Wall Street Journal* (online), February 23, 2015, https://blogs.wsj.com/chinarealtime/2015/02/23/hong-kong-government-office-architect-reflects-on-occupy-movement/ Accessed Jun 7, 2016.

MEGABLOCK URBANISM

JEFFREY JOHNSON

The world continues to urbanize in many regions at an astonishing pace. For the first time in history, the world is more urban than rural. Architects, urban designers, and planners must find ways to intervene in this metamorphosis of urban forms. Existing cities are expanding and new ones are being formed without any historical precedent. There is huge consequence in this continual process of urbanization. In many ways, the contemporary Chinese city can provide us with multiple portals to look into how the world's future urban landscape might be formed. An understanding of this phenomena is critical to an architect, urban designer, and planner's ability to participate in the future urbanization of the world. New ways of thinking about cities must be invented to continually adapt. To be truly agile, even the most recently developed theories and strategies may have to be discarded.

China has a total population of almost 1.4 billion, with over half living in cities, equaling about 700 million urban inhabitants. This compares to an urban population of eighty percent in the United States, totaling only 250 million. In the past thirty-five years, China's urban population has ballooned from roughly 150 million in 1978 to nearly 700 million today. This growth was chiefly due to the booming economy since Deng Xiaoping's policy of economic reform and openness in 1978. With an average annual increase in gross domestic product of about eight percent, and with double-digit growth up until the recent few years, millions of migrant workers have left the countryside for more gainful employment opportunities in cities and industrial regions. Never before has the world experienced such rapid urbanization at this scale and sustained pace. It took the United States an entire century to accomplish what it has taken China a single generation. Since 2001, the growth of urbanization in China has been equivalent to the building of a new Chicago each month.

Even more striking is that this trend is expected to continue. The goal of the government's modernization plan is to fully integrate seventy percent of the country's population, or roughly 900 million people, into the city by 2025. This translates into moving 200 to 250 million rural residents into newly constructed towns and cities over

International Historic Examples of Blocks

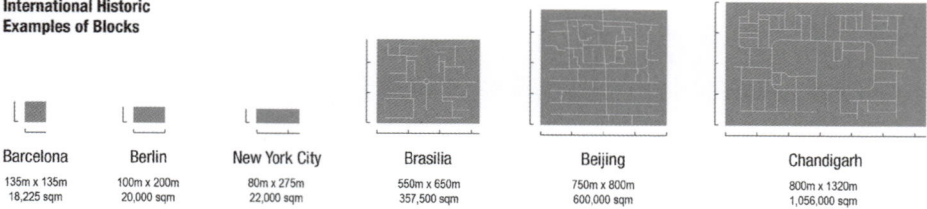

Barcelona	Berlin	New York City	Brasilia	Beijing	Chandigarh
135m x 135m	100m x 200m	80m x 275m	550m x 650m	750m x 800m	800m x 1320m
18,225 sqm	20,000 sqm	22,000 sqm	357,500 sqm	600,000 sqm	1,056,000 sqm

Typical Size of Contemporary Superblocks in Chinese Cities

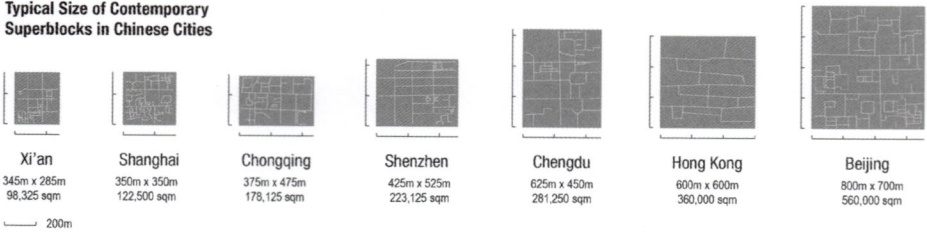

Xi'an	Shanghai	Chongqing	Shenzhen	Chengdu	Hong Kong	Beijing
345m x 285m	350m x 350m	375m x 475m	425m x 525m	625m x 450m	600m x 600m	800m x 700m
98,325 sqm	122,500 sqm	178,125 sqm	223,125 sqm	281,250 sqm	360,000 sqm	560,000 sqm

200m

Urban block scale comparisons worldwide. Image courtesy of Jeffrey Johnson

the next twelve years. This is in part an effort to strengthen the national economy by generating more domestic consumption, which occurs most efficiently in cities by urban inhabitants. According to the 2009 McKinsey Global Institute's *Preparing for China's Urban Billion* Report, this would create more than 220 cities with a million or more population. By comparison, the United States currently has only nine cities of a million or more, and Europe has only thirty-five. As many as 170 new mass-transit systems could be built to support forty billion square meters of new floor space. Fifty thousand buildings could possibly be skyscrapers, equivalent to ten Manhattans. Without dispute, the world has never experienced an urban project of this magnitude. How do existing cities and even new ones confront the pressure of rapid urbanization? Existing cities are transformed almost instantaneously, but what ought to be done with the existing fabric and cores? What socially sustainable solutions can be implemented in order to accommodate such rapid urban growth?

Superblock to Megablock Urbanism

For anyone who has flown into China, what is clear from the air is that the default solution for accommodating the millions of new urban inhabitants is large-scale superblock development. This was a carry-over from the Soviet-era *danwei*-type urban development planning, and the modernist's utilitarian social housing block. Harrison Fraker Jr.'s article, "Unforbidden City," shows grave concerns for superblock developments being constructed and completed at a rate of over ten per day, where housing populations range from the thousands to hundreds of thousands. But these large-scale residential enclaves can now reach sizes of forty hectares and larger according to Kjersti Monson's

2008 analysis of "String Block vs. Superblock Patterns" in China, which would transcend the sizes of superblocks into megablocks. This megablock trend is not only taking over Chinese cities via new developments at the expanding peripheries but also existing city centers via developments whose scales highly contrast that of the historical urban fabric.

Megablocks are spatial instruments with social, cultural, environmental, and economic implications, operating between the scales of architecture and the city. They require new urban laboratories to study its consequences, opportunities, and potential global proliferation. Such a Chinese urban model must be reconsidered through the filters of ecology, economics, and ethics. The megablock is arguably the most critical topic of research in China. There must be new methods to redefine these megablocks, and a form of long-term intervention in the process of urbanization in China. New discoveries of unique and emerging urbanism ought to be deployed in the rapidly urbanizing areas in China. When the Chinese government relinquished its responsibility of providing social housing for its population in 1997, a new commodity-based real estate market was formed. Private developers, first from Hong Kong and Singapore, then from Mainland China, quickly stepped in to fulfill the market demands. The megablock was the perfect model to adopt.

Today, land policies in China would encourage the development of large isolated residential and commercial districts and gated compounds, mainly through a parceling of large tracts of land into a collection of big blocks. These megablocks are then individually auctioned off to a select group of developers. China's central government places much of the burden and responsibilities of urban development in private hands and at the whim of the market economy. The larger the development, the more the developer is responsible for building. In addition to "building" large portions of the contemporary city, private development is also responsible for filling the municipal government's coffers. As part of this decentralization, the central government has pushed the majority of the responsibilities of revenue earning to the local municipalities. Because there is no annual property tax, the municipal governments levy a one-time land sales tax on the developers when they purchase the rights to develop the land. This tax might amount to as much as fifty to seventy-five percent of the municipality's annual revenue, which in turn necessitates a climate of pro-development. Cities need to continually make new land available for development to assist them in raising funds to pay for much-needed infrastructure, schools, security, safety, hospitals, and cultural facilities.

Spatial Consequences: Walled Urban Islands, Mono-functional Enclaves, and *Tabula Rasa*

With rights owned by a single developer, each megablock is designed confidentially as an autonomous enclave. This is usually led by a single design office or design institute. Communication between the developers and designers seldom occur, and no elaborate community or environmental consultation process is mandated or suggested by the government. Often, the master plans seem as though they were designed in a vacuum

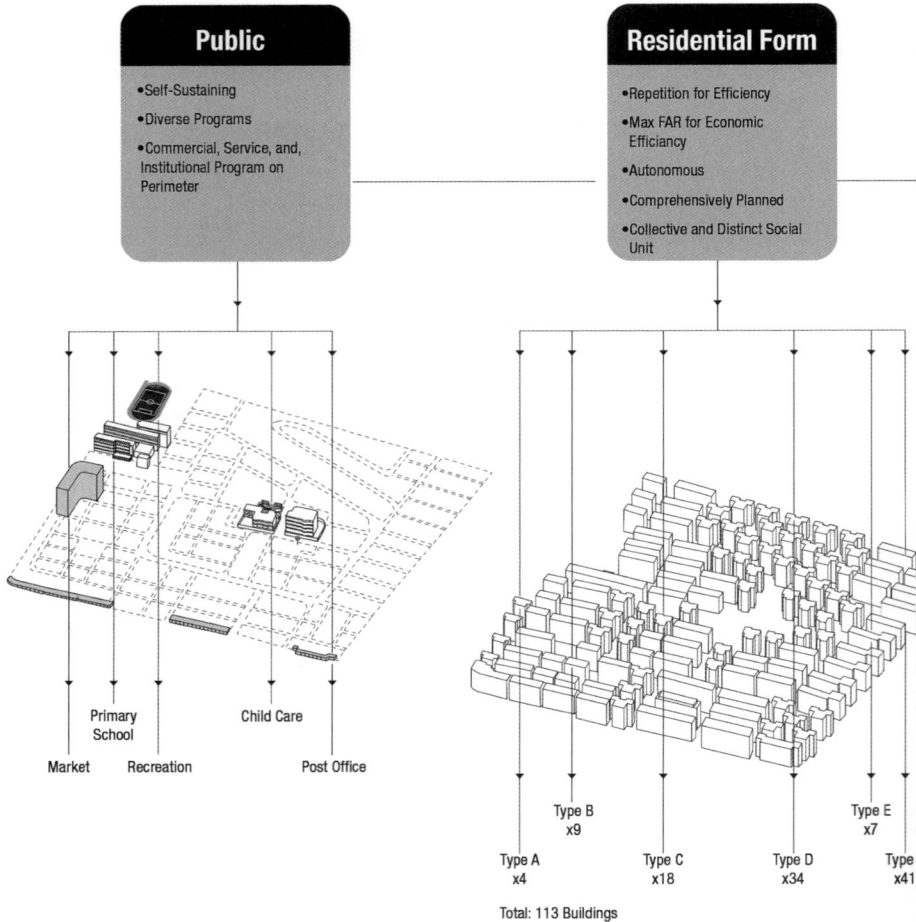

Public
- Self-Sustaining
- Diverse Programs
- Commercial, Service, and, Institutional Program on Perimeter

Residential Form
- Repetition for Efficiency
- Max FAR for Economic Efficiancy
- Autonomous
- Comprehensively Planned
- Collective and Distinct Social Unit

Primary School

Child Care

Market   Recreation   Post Office

Type B
x9

Type E
x7

Type A
x4

Type C
x18

Type D
x34

Type
x41

Total: 113 Buildings

Silver City New Village, Shanghai
31°5'49.81"N, 121°23'38.85"E

Date of completion: 1995
Height: 6 storeys
Population: 12,000
Density: 60000 people/ sqkm
Average Price: 9000 RMB/sqm
source: http://shanghai.fangtoo.com/building/detail_30542/

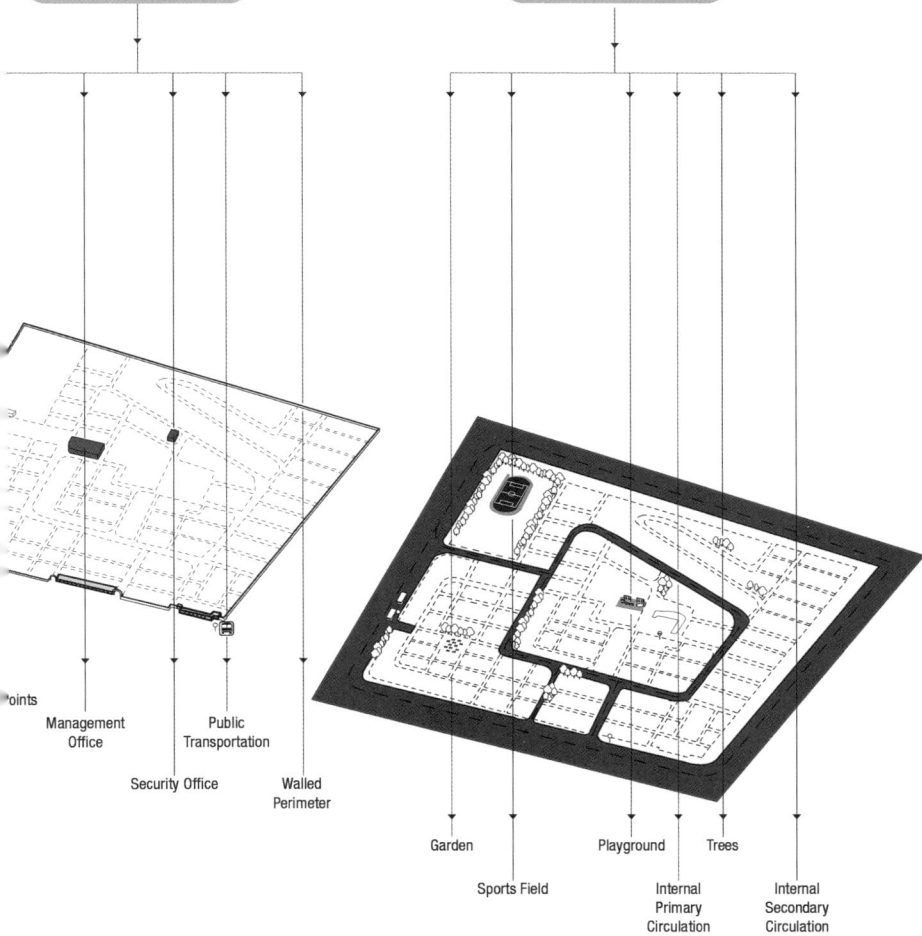

Access

- Disconnected from Adjacent Context
- Impermeable Perimeter
- Controlled Access
- Centralized Security Management

Urban Form

- Centrally Organized
- Introverted
- Requisite Green Area

Points

Management Office

Public Transportation

Security Office

Walled Perimeter

Garden

Sports Field

Playground

Trees

Internal Primary Circulation

Internal Secondary Circulation

What is a Chinese Superblock? Image courtesy of Jeffrey Johnson

with little consideration of the existing or the future contexts. These isolated islands of urban development take no part in an overall urban narrative, turning their backs away from the city around them. Due to China's dominant mandate for the built environment, almost all new megablocks are enclosed by walls with controlled access. New housing developments are designed as self-contained gated communities, placing emphasis on an introspective planning approach. Although this interior-focused strategy can create a localized spatial sense of community, the negative consequence is that it inhibits continuity of public and semi-public spaces between the urban blocks. This creates long expanses of impenetrable street walls unfriendly to the pedestrians, and the urban public as a whole. Additionally, in most cases, very little consideration is given to the self-contained semi-public spaces and building functions that are to form the collective components of the development.

The megablock must be retheorized and replanned to provide an appropriate and positive model.

In regard to functions and building uses, the contemporary megablocks are a far cry from their ideal socialist predecessors. The majority of megablock development is mono-functional, predominantly residential. Whereas with the socialist *danwei* planning, at least in its most ideal form, the urban blocks used to provide all daily functions to its inhabitants within the walls, including employment, housing, recreation, education, dining, and so on. The results of these large-scale developments are "bedroom" communities that lack urban vitality. Making up large sections of the city, these mono-functional communities promote commuting by the automobile. Perhaps the most destructive consequence of megablock development is the clearing of the site to accommodate the new planning. Almost all new megablock projects begin with a *tabula rasa*, seldom incorporating or considering existing urban structures and scales. The megablock is most effective when it is deployed on a flat and cleared site with little or no obstructions. This has obvious social consequences as well. In almost all cases of new development in city centers, whole communities were relocated. Tragically, even the historically significant structures that accommodated them, such as the *hutong* districts in Beijing, were razed to accommodate the new megablock development.

Social Consequences: Housing New China, Real Estate Bubble and Mega Opportunities

For the new elite, the megablock caters to their new lifestyle demands by providing both centrally-located and suburban locations, with exclusive, luxurious, and secure housing estates. The walled and gated megablock is a perfect model to market. Learning much from their recently unified neighbors in Hong Kong, developers and architects found that the megablock could offer their new middle-to-high-income clientele all of the security and luxuries offered to the elite around the globe. The exclusive gated enclave coveted by the newly formed middle- and upper-class residents would now be attained in the form of a megablock in both urban and suburban areas throughout China.

Social Life Activities ■ Informal □ Formal

Chatting Playing Chess
These activities usually take place in the public green space, like gardens and yards.

Casual Dancing
Usually take place at public squares. Especially popular among middle age and seniors.

Walking Walk the Dog Jogging
These activities usually take place at the alley ways with trees aside.

Biking Team Basketball Team Other Sports Teams
These associations usually arrange activities regularly, eg once a week.

Chorus Assoc. Photography Assoc. Other Cultural Assoc.
These associations usually arrange activities regularly, eg once a week.

Educational Lectures, Trainings and Meetings
Usually take place at public classroom or auditorium.

Public Facilities and Services

3 minutes walk to the bank / 3 minutes walk to the post office / 5 minutes walk to the clinic / 3 minutes walk to the bank

Banks, Hospitals, Post Offices Laundry and etc.

10 minutes drive to the cinema / 15 minutes drive to the opera house / 10 minutes walk to Karaoke Bar

Theaters, Opera House and other cultural recreational facilities

Indoor Fitness Center
There is usually one fitness center in the community. Most facilities are designed for middle aged residents.

Outdoor Fitness Playground
It is mostly designed for seniors and children who with their parents.

Retails, Delis, Groceries, Supermarkets, Hair Salons, Restaurants, Bars, Cafe and etc.

Silver City New Village
Shanghai (31°5'49.81"N, 121°23'36.81"E)

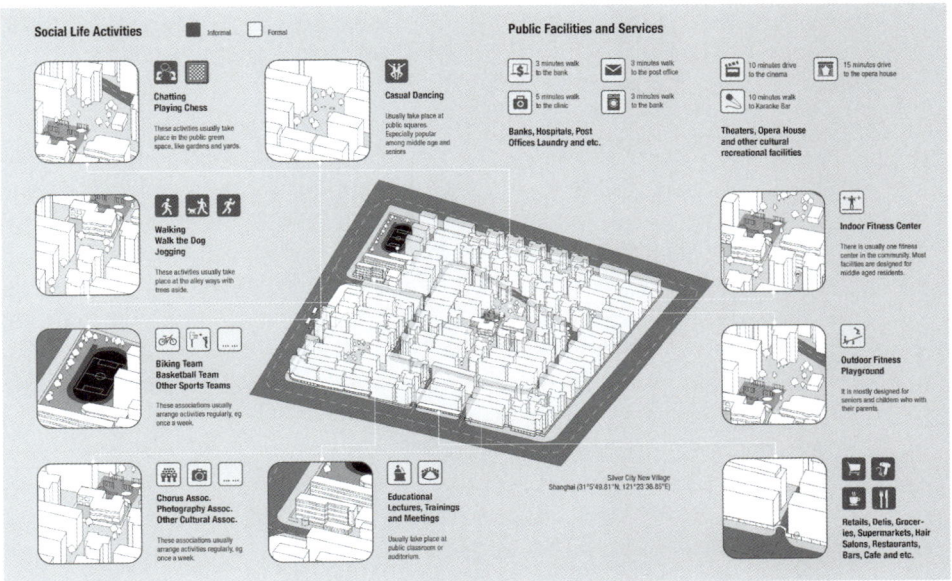

Social activities and public facilities Image courtesy of Jeffrey Johnson

As much as the megablock can respond to the needs and demands of the affluent, it can also expose severe social stratification that has been occurring since the economic reforms of 1978. The megablock proves in many cases to be the perfect scale to enable and maintain this social stratification. This is especially the case for the new migrants from the countryside who have little money for housing. They have little choice than to live in urban villages, or at their place of employment in dormitories, or temporary on-site facilities such as prefabricated trailers. As the middle-class begins to replace the lower-income population in the city centers, the megablocks in the urban perimeter would offer a more livable and hygienic housing environment. Unfortunately, the location at the outer edges of the city would prove to be disconnected from the city center. Many have grown isolated from their original urban home. Generations of families and communities who have spent their entire lives in dense urban centers are being separated. The massive scale and distances of the megablocks make it very difficult for the urban poor to form new communities and support networks.

The commoditization of housing plays a significant role in perpetuating the construction of megablocks. China is experiencing a massive real estate bubble. Due to limited opportunities for investment, real estate became a lucrative investment outlet for the affluent. Until recently, investing in real estate was a sure thing, proving much more reliable than the volatile stock market. Motivated by an insatiable appetite for wealth, this investment craze fueled the construction of thousands of developments that often sit dormant and unoccupied like ghost towns. Yet on paper they are fully "sold-out."

This not only runs the risk of a real estate bubble that could burst at any time, but also escalates property prices. Many cities register double-digit percentage price increments annually. Such an increase makes housing unaffordable for many urban inhabitants, further increasing the gap between the wealthy and the poor.

In the midst of this dominant mandate for the built environment, Chinese cities can still potentially find ways to inject greater social benefits. These self-contained gated communities and housing developments must integrate more daily commerce and urban services. They can also aid in regulating density, localizing infrastructure, and improving governance. The more successful examples of the megablocks can provide a new sense of community for the inhabitants by providing necessary infrastructure, public amenities and facilities. With the ambitious plans to move another 200 to 250 million people into the cities from the countryside by 2025, urban planners and local governments must heed the warnings of such a daunting challenge. In a positive turn, the Chinese government had initiated a campaign to build thirty-six million affordable homes by 2015. The megablock must be retheorized and replanned to provide an appropriate and positive model. Great improvements are needed to make them a truly positive solution for urban development.

NEW RATIONALISM

SUN YIMIN

Architecture is not just about form. Architecture has long been acknowledged as a combination of technology and art. The reality of the present Chinese architectural scene tells another story. We see all kinds of absurd architecture emerging in China, making all sorts of strange statements. They ignore the substance of technology in architecture. Before the existing of architecture as a profession, historical Chinese architectural forms were once reflections of specific materials, construction techniques, lifestyles, aesthetics, and even ethics and morals. As a part of Chinese culture with thousands of years of history, these architectural principles were adequate to be passed on from generation to generation. They constituted the magnificence of Chinese architectural culture and heritage.

In the modern period, with influence from the Industrial Revolution, architecture in China gradually became an academic discipline as well as a profession. Many aspects of China also began to change during this period, including the way of life, building materials, methods of construction, building technology, and craftsmanship. In a mere hundred years, the architecture of the city in China grew into a completely different state compared to the more traditional forms. Many architects are disillusioned by the sheer quantity of construction in China. There is a false sense of achievement when the speed and quantity of construction in China is portrayed as several folds that of Europe. Yet, there is a great suspicion about the fundamental contents of architecture in China and the persistent gap between China and the developed world. In order to pursue personal or corporate fame, many architects, including starchitects, would create contorted and eye-catching forms. Such architecture tends to be constructed from inappropriate materials, illogical in their methods of construction and technology. This trend misleads not only the general public but also the architects and the students of architecture. It reproduces a vicious cycle of desire of a much distorted scale.

Sun Yimin's seminar with William Lim at South China University of Technology.
Image courtesy of Eunice Seng, 2013

Narrow Focus on the Process of Creation

In the field of architecture in China, *jianzhu chuangzuo* describes a condition of creativity in architectural design. The term *chuangzuo* or "create" has taken on a particularly negative Chinese characteristic. Though this term may have origins in both artistic and architectural disciplines, its true meaning was never really absorbed or studied. Architects are given the artistic license to "create" without seriously reflecting on what it means to make, build, or innovate. The "creation" of architecture today commonly means the superficial pursuit of form. The techniques and abilities of architects may have varied from mid-century postmodernism and ornamental architecture to skin or façade architecture today, yet the obsession with formalism has the same genealogy!

The act of "creation" tends to focus on the external appearance of the architecture. Deeply rooted in the core of formalism, architects tend to find a need to render a beautiful story adequate in carrying the form of the architecture. Even foreign architects building in China may feel a strong urge to conjure a deeper meaning in the formal aspects of their architecture. Architects have become cultural snobs obsessed with forums and salons, in efforts to merely theorize their architectural forms. However, when one enters into the construction sites of these architects, one would be overwhelmed by how crude and wasteful their buildings are. Upon a closer inspection of the "famous" buildings around China, one would notice that many of them are totally incompatible with the city!

Shallow Theory and Vague Concepts

There is a lack of deeper philosophical and theoretical thought in the architectural production of China. In the face of a tremendous quantity of building opportunities, the "creative" process in architecture appears to be pale and impotent. Most of the fundamental contents of architectural theory in China originate from textbooks. The most common and reliable way architects produce design theory is to repackage uncontroversial ideas from tradition. They would extract infallible ideas from established books of antiquity, then portentously moralize the old ideas as their own. By switching, attaching, and layering over old theories, many uninspiring architects would narrate their stories from shallow images. This merely fulfills a self-righteous form of theory, allowing the architects to remain "kings in their own house."

Sustainable development and green architecture are the newest trends in our field. As we are facing a time when architectural requirements are increasingly complex, and construction techniques are increasingly advanced, we would require rationalism of a new kind. We have to learn about newly invented technologies and innovative building materials every day. However, if we have a weak foundation in rational thought, these new materials and technologies would only lead to new forms of misuse and even abuse. Therefore, the first thing we should emphasize in Chinese architecture is rational thinking in order to improve the current state of architecture. In the education of an architect, there ought to be an earnest training of the mind, including two aspects of rationalism—namely, urban rationalism and technological rationalism. Urban rationalism is based on a fulfillment of a city's requirements by architecture above and beyond the fulfillment of a building's own functional requirements. To put it differently, when constructing a building, we are also obligated to complete a city! In a healthy era in society, great architecture ought to lead to a city of splendor. When architectural thought is infested with self-serving problems, the city would enter into a state of disorder. The problems of Chinese architecture and urbanism come from within. The lack of pertinent urban theoretical education in China form an emptiness in intellectual thought, and this problem is fully manifested in our architectural production today.

In architectural design competitions, Chinese juries are often criticized for being favorable towards foreign architects. If we forgo our parochialist and nationalist bias and carefully study the competition winning projects, it would be evident that Chinese juries prefer projects that are strong in conceptual representation, or projects that have an elegant narrative. Conversely, entries with rational urban visions and technically sound principles are often not considered appealing. A good example would be the National Center for the Performing Arts in Beijing, which is a piece of public architecture that does not fulfill its responsibility as public space. Technological rationalism is based on the understanding of architecture. Buildings are required to fulfill the functional requirements of materiality. But to a certain amount, buildings must serve functions of spirituality, as achieved through engineering and technical methods. To accomplish such an architectural goal, strict and appropriate engineering and technical means are the first things that need be considered, and they should be carried throughout the entire process. The architecture industry requires Chinese architects to consider the technical problems in architecture more seriously. Local technical methods and skills ought to be put into context, when learning from the experience of developed countries.

The problems that are occurring in China are precisely manifested in two areas. Firstly, architectural designs tend to ignore the fundamental rationalization of structure and material selections, only emphasizing the superficial novelty of form. This would only lead to excessiveness and waste. The Beijing "Bird's Nest" National Stadium and the CCTV Headquarters are good examples of this wastefulness. Both projects consume the greatest amount of steel among these buildings types, and the stadium ranked first in its construction cost among all international construction projects in China. The CCTV Headquarters was supposed to be an auxiliary facility for the Olympics, but it could only be completed four years after the Olympics. Secondly, there is gross negligence of sustainability principles. For instance, the Beijing National Aquatic Center, known colloquially as the Water Cube, has a façade that requires high maintenance and constant energy consumption. The parametric design and technology used in the new terminal of the Shenzhen Bao'an International Airport have delivered a crude-looking façade and a roof that leaks. Locally designed architecture are often facing similar issues. For example, the train stations of the high-profile high-speed railway system were not designed with energy consumption as a yardstick in mind.

To become more rational, the education of an architect in China must first be planned with a scientific and rational pedagogy, where an existing core knowledge of architecture is supplemented with knowledge about cities and urban design during the formative years. The concept of urban design is not only a basic necessity for architects, but also a source for the constant innovation of design logic. Additionally, there is an urgent need to redefine the boundaries of architectural education, in order to include greater in-depth studies of structure, craftsmanship, building materials, and construction technology, and to view them as the foundational knowledge situated alongside the philosophy of pragmatism, economics, and aesthetics. Only when young architects are refreshed with these new principles of architecture would rationalism become fully embedded within their architectural thought.

Utility, Economy, and Total Aesthetics

Pragmatism has an unfortunate association with the minimum and lowly standards of construction in architecture. Taking the design of sports facilities as an example, due to a lack of thorough analysis of recent programmatic requirements, many Chinese sports facilities were unware of new standards in design, such as expanded sizes in basketball courts and a radical increase of headroom of volleyball courts. Such trends have negative effects on many national sports facilities. In spite of the changes in economic conditions and agility of technological changes today, actual research on our understanding of functionality in architecture has regressed. Research conducted on sports buildings in China in the 1980s were not developed further in the 1990s. During the boom time during this period, architects were under heavy duress in their daily production tasks and the ceaseless amount of work.

Even though large investments were made in large national-scale projects, such as the Guangdong Olympic Stadium design by yet another foreign starchitect, the lack of rigorous research and design studies cripple the usability of the facility. Not only sporting functions found the facility limiting; even routine large-scale concerts could not be considered because the roof structure was not designed to withstand the load of equipment expected for performances. The attention-seeking National Center for the Performing Arts in Beijing is also a problematic example, where an impractical metal cladding was added over the top of a functional performance space. The suggestion of sleekness in its expensive cladding materials could not mask the building's lack in practical utility. Even its acoustic quality was compromised.

As China progresses, its society would require an architect to bear a comprehensive responsibility towards the resources given to the project, beyond the routine assessment of a given budget or the economic context of the client and users. It is important to develop this understanding at an early stage of planning in a project. Even in this early phase, the understanding of economics must also go beyond the selection of construction materials and standards of equipment. In the initial conception of an architectural configuration, the architect must peer into the future to consider its long-term usage in order to grasp the investment constraints suitable for a client. At the same time, such a comprehensive economic assessment would imply that an architect can

The concept of urban design is not only a basic necessity for architects, but also a source for the constant innovation of design logic.

have control over a reasonable consumption of resources available to the project. Such an economic view of architecture ought to be the basis of a sustainable development. Accurate positioning of the built fabric on any given site or urban context must be tested rigorously during the early stage of planning. There must be a methodical consideration of the costs associated with different optimum structural forms, appropriate program allocation, and flexible functionality.

In conclusion, it is important not to underestimate the overall impact an architect can have on society. The overall aesthetics of a building or an urban space would also come naturally under the consideration by an architect. A lack of basic understanding of urban design tends to lead an architect to turn a complex design activity into mere formalism. Chinese architects suffer from this problem very much in the same way as foreign architects. The aforementioned examples of the buildings designed for the Beijing Olympics, such as the Beijing National Stadium, or other large-scale interventions, such as the National Center for the Performing Arts, may not be the sole error of architectural design itself. A lack of an urban design research framework in a highly problematic urban site meant that the criteria of design was reduced to an object-making exercise in free space. In considering the overall project and its aesthetics, juries in such architectural competitions would be misled, or they would have an incomplete set of criteria in their assessment. This often resulted in indecisiveness during the judging process, and the winning proposals tend to be widely censured by mass media and the alienated public.

This essay is translated from Sun Yimin, "Zhongguo jianzhu xuyao bushang lixing de ke" [A Rational Lesson for Chinese Architecture], *Journal of Art Observation*, Issue 2014/09, pp.18-19.

CIVIC IDENTITY IN A SHARED CITY

CUI KAI

After thirty years of rapid urbanization, the constantly changing cities in China are still gearing up for the trendiest appearances. While the Chinese are proud of their modern urban landscapes, coupled with tremendous economic growth, Chinese cities have grown banal and too similar to one another. The regional features of Chinese cities had disappeared, because the vernacular architecture and urban fabric are being treated as archaic and unfitting of a modern metropolis. The rush to modernize meant that the old were removed too quickly, like toys to a child, losing their appeal and swiftly discarded. Architecture in the city had failed in its role to become civic landmarks and symbols of hope for the public. After calming down from the exhilarating urban growth, the Chinese have fallen into a sense of incapacity and loss.

By the Eighteenth Party Congress in 2012, the central leaders have issued a new mandate to local governments to identify the distinctive character of their cities. City governments had to reevaluate and determine an architectural style for their cities within a short span of time. With added pressure from the general public, they had to conjure an urban character for their cities. Many sought to reconstruct a historic street or build a scenic promenade along the river. These reawakened aspirations and new approaches towards the design of cities were relatively proactive and feasible. While the general direction of urban transformation is positive, cities must avoid being short-sighted as they had been in the past.

Consolidation and the Character of a City

The character of a city must be consolidated over time and not be achieved by a hasty cosmetic surgery. The truly valuable characteristics of a city are not determined solely by external forms. There are layers of history and everyday cultural practices that add value to one's understanding of a city. The emotional attachment and sense of respect one has for a city are accrued from encounters with the sophistication and civility of its inhabitants as well. The friendliness and elegance of urban life must also be matched by an even more important sense of harmony in its natural and ecological environments. These aspects would go beyond the few outstanding architectural landmarks in the city. Obviously, this cannot be achieved in days or years, but every single correct decision, every small amount of investment, and every sincere effort is an important step. In order to achieve this, the Chinese government needs to wean off its bad habits of changing directions with every change of its leadership. They must pay consistent attention to detail and avoid a singular focus on the building of infrastructure while addressing issues at the management and operation levels. In short, a change in the Chinese government's approach and value system would yield a great influence on the character of Chinese cities. In other words, the character of a city is a good reflection of the competency of its decision-makers.

Forum at Space E-6, Urbanus.
Image courtesy of Andrew Lee, 2015

Cities are organic. They grow and improve constantly. During this process, cities would rise and fall, and many of these cities are beautiful, while others turned out unattractive. With the advance and decline of cities, there are marks left on the urban fabric, contributing to their character. Cities must be encouraged to carefully employ such resources, for the process of protection and regeneration. Cities must be discouraged from destroying or concealing them. A dynamic and imperfect city is far more real and charming than one that is falsely branded and pretentious. One must forbid shallow reasons of international branding, which would only lead to the construction of a superficial image of a city. For the amateur city governments and managers, it is crucial to find workable solutions that are tailored to their cities. In recent years, more scholars, professors, and urban planners are contributing to the debate of this issue, and their research and practices have gained positive results. There are excellent case studies around the world, but one must avoid mimicking only the formal aspects of the results. Cities must strive to maintain their differences in character, in order to celebrate the distinctiveness between various regions and cities.

Responsibility of Architecture: Alienation and Resentment

"Boiled egg," "bird's nest," "big pants," and "long johns." These are the well-understood nicknames of the most iconic megastructures in China. Obviously, it has become customary for urbanites to describe their buildings by their nicknames. While the informal nicknames are provocative, fun, and easy to remember, this syndrome would be of grave concern to an architect. It is unjust that the tremendous amount of fortune, time, and energy spent by the government, architects, and builders would become ridiculed. This lack of appreciation of architecture as an art form is detrimental. It raises urgent questions about the level of architectural and cultural literacy in the contemporary society, and something must be done to improve it.

By the same token, these nicknames show a wisdom of the folk language, and to an extent is a broad cultural tradition. From the youthful and affectionate nicknames of old classmates, to the pseudonyms given to literary heroes such as the protagonists in Shi Nai'an's *Water Margin*. The names represent a particular quality of the subject, revealing the sentiments behind the multitude of narratives associated with them. Especially with the advent of a networked society and a rise of internet-specific language, the nicknaming of a building is usually a reference to its formal qualities. The descriptions are metaphorical and pictorial. The Sydney Opera House is portrayed as an open seashell, the Burj Al Arab Hotel in Dubai is likened to the sail of a ship, and the Louvre in Paris is known as a glass pyramid. Some of them even have more than one nickname, for example, the Chapel of Notre Dame du Haut in Ronchamp has been described as "the ears of god," "the praying hands," and "the white dove." Journalists and historians alike have written about its allegorical forms.

Symbolism has long been part of the discourse of architectural theory. Architectural forms achieve a certain aura by the use of familiar forms that would trigger one's imagination. The hope is that it will resonate with its audience and evoke certain emotions. Architecture tends to desire to convey a sense of nobility, elegance, or even astonishment. Yet ambiguity is the art of the symbolism in architecture. A symbol that is too figurative is usually considered vulgar, but one that is too abstract is not easily recognizable. In the social development of China, it is instead more important to be more moderate—pursuing a responsible combination of architectural space, function, and a positive use of technology.

The situation in China is quite different, however. The buildings were not designed with the kind of symbolism associated with them. It was society at large who had projected the symbolism onto the buildings by their association with the shapes they bore a resemblance to. The nicknames were created through mass media and social media. It reveals certain emotions the society has towards the realities of China, specifically the social polarization created by buildings built by the powerful or built for a highly alienating purpose. The unusual-looking high-rises seemed to represent wealth and power, and they were appearing increasingly aloof to the general society. These buildings naturally aroused public resentment, and therefore attracted unpleasant nicknames. As this phenomenon becomes ever more common, commercial

Cities must strive to maintain their differences in character, in order to celebrate the distinctiveness between various regions and cities.

developers are growing concerned about the effects of the built form. They would request architects to avoid creating forms that will trigger negative connotations, or create forms with a clearly articulated rationalization that is flattering or complimentary, such that the general society would not be encouraged to misread them. This over-emphasis of the built form has misled the society's understanding of the responsibility of architecture.

The Guangzhou Opera House, or the "big bird," located in a newly developed district of Guangzhou.
Image courtesy of Victor Su. 2013

What Should We Share with the City?

Society has an innate capacity to share the good things they are endowed with. This spontaneous capacity was what led to the formation of a city. Marketplaces are a kind of natural social formation, where people can trade and share information, and by the same token, cities are built so that their inhabitants can find safety and common good. People from outside of the city would find it attractive enough to move into one, in order to share its public resources. Such social and urban formations would expand to become the center of politics, economy, and culture. The sharing of urban resources would become a natural right of the people. Conversely, citizens of a city ought to ask what they can offer to the well-being of a city. In other words, while the abundance of urban resources is being shared, should society not continue to find new ways to contribute to the development of a city?

Chinese cities are currently undergoing a period of positive adjustment in its urban development. Local governments are focusing on three key aspect of redevelopment—namely, a reorganization of urban functions, an organic form of regeneration, and an urban rehabilitation in areas of decay. The emphasis on urban design is becoming part of the required official planning process. This means that design professionals will have a new focus in leading the transformation and deployment of existing urban resources. They would also be responsible for improvements of public spaces in the city, and a greater protection of public rights. The capacity to share in the city would hopefully enhance the quality of urban life, and become the driving force behind all design efforts in the future.

There are numerous ways of addressing the question of generosity in the city. A larger proportion of undeveloped land can be allocated for public green area. There can be a strengthening of civic functions and an enlargement of open spaces required in all new development, and new additions in sites undergoing alteration. Gated residential compounds can be transformed into open and freely accessible urban blocks. There can be an enhanced coordination between the different government agencies involved in the management of the city, so that the quality of public space and infrastructure can be elevated. If the notion of "what to share with the city?" can be used as a driving force, or even a slogan to renew and design a city, there will be a betterment in society and life in the city. Everyone has the capacity to share more.

NOTES ON AN ONTOLOGICAL ARCHITECTURE

YUNG HO CHANG

Students of architecture are confused about the definition of architecture as a field. Students may not think of architecture as a field about the making of a building. How is architecture defined today? The contemporary definitions of architecture have been broadened to such extent that architecture could be defined as an abstract intellectual discourse contributive to political activism. It seems as though some aspects of the discipline have been disproportionately emphasized. Subsequent to this distortion, architecture may be understood in one of the following three ways: firstly, as a primarily scholarly or intellectual endeavor, such that it becomes highly abstract—a Peter Eisenman legacy with a dose of Jacques Derrida and poststructuralism, with Eisenman famously declaring that practice is the realization of a theory; secondly, as an artistic exercise, with Frank Gehry as one of the leading figures; or thirdly, as a political act, as epitomized by Hsia Chu-Joe.

Creativity and the Crisis of Architectural Education

After five to eight years of study in an architectural program in countries such as China or the United States, a graduate is very often ill prepared to enter the field. For examples, Chinese students may be familiar with the images of starchitecture, but they do not know the basics of structure. They tend to put an eight-by-eight-meter reinforced concrete frame grid in any of their designs. American students are more likely to be better at making arguments about political and economic issues than at making drawings. It is as if Chinese students have been learning from magazines and Americans from newspapers.

Creativity is often perceived exclusively as a conceptual and artistic endeavor focusing on exterior form-making. It treats architecture as an object or sculpture. Presently, it is a widely-held belief that creativity can and should be taught. Yet, could an English teacher set the goal of producing a Shakespeare in the class with a particular pedagogy? On the other hand, should the English teacher only teach grammar but not inspire the students to be Shakespeare? Or can she achieve both at the same time? An in-depth debate is needed for the questions raised. Can creativity be taught?

Dealing with Big Issues

The way in which global concerns are discussed in architectural classes, especially in the studio, calls to mind one of the great debates of the twentieth century—"Architecture or Revolution?" as initiated by Le Corbusier. Only this time around, more people seem to think that architecture can be revolution. How much does the pressure of political correctness play a role in this tendency? In countries like the United States, such tendency has yet to be analyzed. The five common macro topics in architecture are, in chronological order of influence:

Only when architectural education offers a clearly defined body of knowledge and skills can it provide a base for design as a field of study.

Culture. Architecture is, of course, cultural. But architecture is first of all a part of material culture. A broad theoretical exploration in cultural fields outside of architecture gained momentum during the period of postmodernism. Such interest has inspired, and is still inspiring, a diverse range of interdisciplinary research, such as film and architecture.

City. Research on cities typically focus on abstract socioeconomic and statistical aspects of urbanization. The study of urban form and urban spatial structures have not drawn enough attention.

Technology. For an architect, this term mainly refers to parametric design, or simply the computer as a tool for generating certain forms. It has failed to draw references to technologies in building science, such as structural engineering or daylight design.

Environment. Special design studios designated to energy, pollution, ecology, and sustainability are omnipresent. Architecture degree programs seem to fail to realize that an everyday architectural operation ought to cover fundamental environmental issues in passive design.

Society. Social concerns tend to privilege only certain social groups and extraordinary events. While it is commendable to stress the importance of organized and pro bono design effort in times of disasters to serve the underprivileged, the average middle class who can afford market housing are often left out of the social discussion. The middle class are assumed to have access to better design, but they are not.

These global issues are extremely important; thus it is politically correct to address them. However, if they are discussed or debated too much and too soon in the curriculum, they would become a distraction to the study of architecture. It is not unusual to position a number of big issues in the beginning of a studio and then leap to form-making as a solution. The phenomenon is epitomized with the architectural thesis project, such as final projects submitted prior to graduating from a Master of Architecture degree. For example, the Massachusetts Institute of Technology requires every student, regardless of discipline, to produce a thesis in order to receive a degree. The result of such requirement for architecture students is a project of two parts: one pursuing scholarship, the other pursuing design. The two pursuits are often disconnected. Diagramming, including visual analyses using diagrams, graphs, matrices, and the like, sometimes makes a caricature of this routine. Diagramming is meant to be a conceptual operation, but it often becomes the direct generation of the physical building form. Because of such irreconcilable problems and an incompleteness of architectural education, a highly integrated architectural project ought to be considered in place of a thesis project.

Meeting with Chang Yung Ho in Beijing. Images courtesy of Kee Wei Hui, 2015

Language of Instruction and the Missing Links

The language used in the studios in certain schools tends to be abstract. Some instructors appear to be reluctant to talk about the making of buildings. Even the word "building" could hardly be mentioned, as if they fear they are not being theoretical enough. If this tendency persists, the making of buildings may one day become a secret body of knowledge.

There is a core agenda of architecture that is totally absent from the educational program today. Such agendas have not changed since the making of buildings came into existence. They include, material, structure, construction and craft (from carpentry to digital fabrication), space, function (from use, program, lifestyle, and life to spatial and temporal experience), site, form and aesthetics (from plastic figure and space to light and other form-givers), and other building technologies (from air and water to electricity). If the agendas and subjects above are the foundations of architecture, architectural education should be based on them. If they constitute some of the essential knowledge of the making of buildings, they should not be disregarded as being too pragmatic to be part of the theoretical framework of architecture.

Relationships Reconsidered

Is architecture the art of making buildings? Perhaps there needs to be a reconsideration of the definition of "architecture" by revisiting the original premise of making architecture? The definition of an "architect" can hark back to a builder who can think, or a thinker who can build. It would be someone who uses both the hands and brain. If creativity is based on the core agenda and knowledge, as well as the skills of architecture, it can be about any or all aspects of a building design—space, structure, construction, craft, sustainability, or programs. It would not only pertain to exterior form alone. For example, students can be taught to be creative with passive design, and to treat the orientation of a building and its natural ventilation as opportunities to achieve sustainability.

Architectural inventions may be based on an analysis of new situations and conventions, which are not absolute truths but points of view. This is called rational creativity. Understanding where conventions come from is the first step to going beyond them. This exercise should set architecture apart from fine art. It is important to be aware of the "big issues," but it should be understood that some of the "big issues" may or may not affect design directly. These issues are more about constructing a broad context for practice rather than for individual projects. This marks a necessary return to an ontological architecture.

Remodeling the Core

Only when architectural education offers a clearly defined body of knowledge and skills can it provide a base for design as a field of study. From the vantage point of an architectural education, the more a student comprehends architecture as the set of fundamental concerns, knowledge, and methodologies, the more likely the student will be prepared to venture into other design fields. This is based on the assumption that architecture is more complex than other design studies. From the point of view of other design disciplines, one should study architecture in the first year of school before choosing one or more of the other design professions, including interior design, stage set (scenography) design, furniture design, product design, clothing design, jewelry design, and graphic design (including interactive and digital design).

Basic Skills and Tool Training. Drafting and drawing should be combined, not separated. The curriculum at the Cooper Union serves as a good reference, because it has a long tradition of teaching various approaches to visual thinking. For example, the learning of physical model making could be treated as a departure point to learn about techniques in building construction.

Studio. The studio environment integrates ideas, technology, and the process of making into one. As a foremost material and structural discipline, engineering must be brought into design from the very beginning. Experienced practitioners and engineers should be invited to teach in such studio settings. For example, the old Architectural Association model would have two instructors in one studio. While one focuses more on the conceptual aspect of design, the other helps students to develop the technical proficiency in the projects. The only challenge is that it takes considerable resources to double up studio teachers.

Design Curricular Sequence. Studio projects are typically sequenced from smaller scales and simpler programs to large and complex ones. Can there be a stronger logic in the sequence of learning other than the order of size and programmatic complexity? In a more traditional craft-oriented pedagogy, a sequence based on the study of a material tends to be used. For example, during Mies van der Rohe's tenure as the director of the Department of Architecture at the Illinois Institute of Technology, studios were organized according to materials, followed by a study of structural systems particular or inherent to these materials. This is still a highly relevant approach, setting up a sequence of teaching starting with masonry, concrete, wood, steel, glass, and finally end up with more recently developed materials, such as fiber-reinforced polymer. These materials will serve as generators of different structural forms. Towards the latter part of such a program, studios would be able to integrate other necessary disciplines. This sequencing is crucial in preventing students from spending three to five years floundering at merely the schematic design stage throughout their architectural education.

Construction. For students of architecture to learn about the processes of building, they must have the opportunity to visit construction sites. Ideally, this can take place once or twice every studio or semester in order for them to witness the various stages of construction, as well as gain an exposure to different methods of construction. Hands-on exercises would be valuable, but it could be demanding on the school's resources. For example, the Rural Studio at Auburn University is able to combine teaching and practice with design-build projects. This program exposes students to actual construction processes in order to touch on the "big issues" of social change through design.

General Education and Seminars. There is a critical role for an architectural education to prepare students for independent thinking and an enhancement of their cultural sophistication. General education is important for offering general knowledge and a deep curiosity for a great range of topics. Seminars would be the best platform for students to cover "big issues" and interdisciplinary topics, because they provide a more liberal space for intellectual and political debate.

Art Education. The emphasis of this aspect of an architecture student's education would be an appreciation and familiarization of art. It would be a training in analytical appreciation, not necessarily in drawing or other technical skills. It can sometimes include workshops for students to learn to use their minds and hands at the same time. The typical workshops for making are woodwork, metal work, ceramics, film, computational programming, and others. For instance, the Bauhaus had educated the first generations of modern architects and designers through a training in craft.

Design Culture. An architectural education should provide the physical context and cultural environment to nurture discussions, events, and intellectual activities, and to help stimulate the students' imagination. Cafés or spaces for discourse can be located at the center of the school, alongside well-curated spaces with film programs that reflect on contemporary culture. Architectural education, as a whole, has to position itself as the bedrock for nurturing creativity and imagination.

This essay is not a comprehensive pedagogy but fragments of a new vision of architectural education. It sets out a foundation for architectural education as not only a discipline but a common knowledge. While architectural education remains in a crisis, it is still possible to dream of architecture becoming part of general education one day. Like mathematics and history in college education, architecture ought to be for everyone. The learning of architecture makes one a better human being.

09
AESTHETICIZING

Architecture is often deployed for symbolic functions, and this is where it can suffer the most. Most architects and professionals of the built environment are articulate about their ambitions in the making of architecture, but their work is not always intelligible to the users of their works. Most architects are not as nimble in negotiating and observing the social relations of space, which means they may be less aware or in control of the way their architecture or designs may include or exclude users. This ultimately points to an awareness of a kind of citizenship that is being controlled by space. The choice given to the general consuming public who looks to architecture for solutions can sometimes become a false choice, because there is no participation for end users in this process of rapid urban development. When it comes to the reinvoking of tradition in the search for aesthetics, the meanings ascribed to the Communist Chinese countryside was lost on the ancient Chinese countryside designed for self-cultivation, and enjoyment by the literati and aristocratic class. It is therefore important to realize the intellectual baggage that comes with contemporary explorations of the highly charged genres of landscape and "nature" in China.

Detailing of Guangzhou Opera House by Zaha Hadid.
Image courtesy of Elaine Thian, 2013

AESTHETICS CULTURE AND HABITATION

WU LIANGYONG

The ideological and cultural foundations of the human settlement and habitation in China can be traced back to the early Qin dynasty. These ancient principles proliferated rapidly over the course of the Qin and Han dynasties, evolving into a complex framework. The Sui and Tang dynasties inherited this framework, as well as the accomplishments of the Wei and Jin dynasties. Massive advancements in the realm of art and culture accumulated over time had led to the formation of a complex artistic and aesthetic framework. This may be identified as the second most significant framework. By integrating with the first aspects of politics, economy, and society, one arrives at a more holistic system of understanding. The Chinese human settlement has been continuously enriched and improved under these two frameworks.

According to Qian Mu, the great historian of twentieth-century China, the multifarious planning ideals of the politics and society of the Han dynasty and the intricate refinements in art and literature of the Tang dynasty were the two great foundations of the cultural history of China. Chinese scholarship remains indebted to these two foundations till this day. At present, the Chinese human settlement is facing challenges of new transformations and restructuring. From the historical point of view, this is once again an important revolution in the history of the Chinese human settlement. Without a doubt, a new framework has to be constructed on top of the two great foundations of the Chinese civilization. This new framework is currently in the midst of evolving and structuring.

Habitat as Cultural Construct

The habitat is both a physical and cultural construct. The purpose such construct is to meet the spiritual needs of the people, such that through the development of various cultural fields, the capacity of the society as a whole would be raised. Constructing a "cultural superpower" implies neither a mere construction of technical facilities nor a building of cultural industries. Instead, at the core is the promotion of a Chinese cultural spirit—the propagation of Chinese wisdom and the embodiment of a national sentiment. The development of the Chinese human settlement has always been founded on the basis of its own innate cultural tradition, while constantly absorbing new external knowledge and enriching oneself, evolving and renewing over the course of time. It is indeed timeless, vital, and rich in tradition. While the contemporary civilization is busy absorbing advanced scientific technology and creating a cutting-edge global culture, it must not fail to maintain a heightened awareness of its local culture—an attitude of cultural pride and a spirit of cultural self-reliance. It is imperative to stand together in anticipation of a great Chinese cultural renaissance!

The culture of aesthetics is an ideology that possesses certain aesthetic principles and values, imbued with artistic culture at its core. It is a constituent of the total human culture. The Frankfurt School was the first to put forward such a concept. They advocated the idea of constructing an aesthetic culture and rebuilding an aestheticized and artistic world based on the law of beauty. Hence, one would be able to realize a sublimation of the spirit and

City plan of Fuzhou, Qing Dynasty

transcend the mundane present-day reality through an elevated perspective of aesthetic culture. China embarked on such an investigation and discourse of aesthetic culture only towards the end of the twentieth century. The human settlement in ancient China had attained brilliance in its artistic accomplishments. Its supreme beauty is revealed at the sites of archaeological excavations, places of historical heritage significance, as well as in paintings and poetry by prominent artists. The divinity of the land and ancient rivers had formed countless cities, towns, market places, thoroughfares, and human settlements, embodying a spectacular and infinitely rich aesthetic culture.

The integrated beauty of *Yiwen*

Beauty is life. Since the ancient times, the Chinese have been passionate about the pursuit of an aesthetic quality in an earthly life. Throughout Chinese history, the human settlement has always been centered on the fulfilment of life in an aesthetic and artistic manner. The beauty of the human settlement can be integrated into various forms of art, including calligraphy, literature, painting, sculpture, arts and crafts, and, of course, architecture.

For example, consider how the forms of calligraphy and painting are juxtaposed against the interiors of furniture and other elegant furnishings—namely, the execution of fluid and minimal lines and spaces of Ming-style furniture. Consider also the lintel

Eastern Han pictorial brick rubbing of a courtyard community (left) and
an agricultural production scene (right)

plaque that monumentalizes the main hall, the couplet scrolls that frame the transition
between the indoor and outdoor spaces, the ever subtle change in the light and shadow
brought about by the whispering willows in the courtyard, or the brilliant composition
of rocks that simulate the grandeur of the mountains. There is a consistency in change
and a richness in voids that serve to bring about intrigue. It is only through such deep
appreciation that one would be able to fully comprehend the integral and fluid kind of
beauty. Such an integration could be adequately summed up by the term *yiwen*, or the
arts and culture of ancient China.

Chinese historical records and local chronicles were often compiled from literature
and documents of their times into single volumes called *Yiwenzhi*. The earliest *Yiwenzhi*
was found in *Hanshu,* also known as the *History of the Former Han*. *Yiwenzhi* would
always be the integrated product of various artistic disciplines of that particular era.
Lu Xun compared *yiwen* favorably to the scientific chronicles of *Kexueshi Jiaopian,* also
known as a form of classics—the *Lessons from the History of Science*. He stated that the
greatest achievements in science by the Greeks and the Romans are not inferior to *yiwen*.
The concept of *yiwen* stands for all art forms related to the humanities, and centered on
art and culture. *Yiwen* gradually became the blanket term for various artistic categories,
including but not limited to fine art, literature, technical arts, music and, calligraphy.

Calligraphy is a unique artistic category in China. An architecture of stature is always
framed by an elaborate inscription plaque with the most elegant calligraphy. For example,
located on the central axis, the first key pavilion of the Nanjing Zhongshan Cemetery
has twenty-four Yan-gilt character inscriptions, "The Prime Minister of the Chinese
Nationalist Party Mr. Sun was buried here on the first of June, in the eighteenth year of

the Republic of China." Written by renowned calligrapher Tan Yankai, the grandeur of the place continues to resonate with the generations after. In the making of architecture of such magnitude, every literati would seize the opportunity to express themselves in the calligraphic form. Further examples could be cited, for instance, in the Hangzhou *Guanhaiting* (Pavilion with an Ocean View), the calligraphic inscription writes, "the Tower gazes at the vastness of the horizon sea; the door fronts the tides of Zhejiang River."

Sculptures can also play the lead role in the making of the Chinese habitat, taking command over the entire space. Great examples can be seen in the seated Giant Buddha statue at Leshan, the Fengxian Temple Buddha statue at Luoyang Longmen Grottoes, the lying Buddha at Dazu Mount Baoding Rock, the Big Buddha at Dunhuang Mogao Grottoes, the Guanyin statue at Jixian Guanyin Ge, and many others. Though the sizes of some of these sculptures may be relatively modest, they still possess an enchantment over the entire built environment. Even the smallest of embellishments is capable of enhancing the quality and stature of the habitat. Paintings have been an important form of documentation of the Chinese ancient habitat. The *Xingxiang Handai Shi* stone relief from the Han dynasty has long been hailed as the representative artistic and cultural image of its era. A plethora of great works have been produced as a result of the vital development in painting as an art form by subsequent generations of artists.

Elevated Aesthetics and Theoretical Revelation

It is indisputable that the contemporary city has become increasingly homogenous. It is imperative to embrace the integration of *yiwen* so that a broader scope for creativity can occur, such that there can be a coherent development from content to form. The key to unlocking such potential is found in the *jingjie*—the realm where a soul may shine upon a fully lived life in a meaningful world. Wang Guowei states, "Poetry is the highest form in the realm of *jingjie*, and with *jingjie* it would lead to the cultivation of an honorable character." This does not merely apply to literature; *jingjie* is also the highest pursuit of a cultivation of the individual, alongside the creation of art and other virtuous pursuits as a Chinese. It has deep implications upon the human spirit. There is a requisite need of the habitat to extend itself beyond its physical construct into a cultural one.

To achieve an elevated aesthetic formulation of *jingjie*, the construction of habitation must encompass both spaces of the physical and spiritual. In 1932, Lin Huiyin and Liang Sicheng created a following based on the premise that good architecture will elicit strong human emotions. They coined the term *jianzhuyi* to mean the poetics of architecture, following the poetics of painting and literature in *huayi* and s*hiyi* respectively. Through the passage of time, the beauty of natural materials and the intellect behind the process of making would arrive at a unique synthesis of art, history, and sense of place. In the 1970s, Norwegian architect and theorist Christian Norberg-Schulz referred to a similar concept of *genius loci*, where there is a structured way to describe the phenomenology of architecture. A habitation should be conducive towards the creation of a deeper meaning and spirit of a place. The long-lasting adoration of historical sites such as the Shaoxinglan

Pavilion, Wuhan Yellow Crane Tower, and Hunan Yueyang Tower are not merely indebted to the physicality of the architecture itself. Its holistic *jingjie* coalesces around how the architecture resided in the landscape, how poetry and literature were created around such sites, culminating in a deep form of human appreciation. Since they are capable of evoking emotions over the centuries, one may say that they possess a vitality and charm that has the capacity to withstand the test of time and space. Lamentably, such fine details often escape a casual observer.

Breakfast meeting at Professor Wu's residence.
Image courtesy of Chan Hui Min, 2015

Architects must take on the great responsibility of this era. The quest to pursue beauty in life demands that the creation of the human settlement must be carried out with a heightened sense of self-awareness. The rules of first volume of *Yuan Ye*—the *Records of the Craft of Gardens*—state, "three points craftsman, seven points master," which means this responsibility falls on the shoulders of architects and those who have been empowered. An evaluation of the achievement of an administrator should not be limited to the time in office. A leader must not neglect the golden lesson that "a leader's great deeds benefit the generations to come, and his love is remembered among the people."

Society as a whole must strengthen its cultivation of *yiwen*—including high culture and popular culture—consciously pushing the boundaries and elevating the disciplines, thereby creating new trends for the coming generations. In practical work, the more critical the question at hand, the more controversies may arise throughout the decision-making process. From the processes of formation and creation, there would be a necessary passage of time before a consensus can be reached. This calls for a united effort from the various disciplines of the arts, and a shared passion and charisma. It would also require an exquisite form of artistic wisdom and a noble spirit of collaboration, devoid of prejudices and obstinacies, such that a comprehensive aesthetic culture can emerge from a state of uncertainty.

This essay is translated and adapted from a speech entitled "Renju huanjing yu shenmei wenhua" [Habitation and Aesthetics Culture] by Wu Liangyong at the 2012 Annual Meeting of the Architectural Society of China.

STRUCTURAL WEIGHT OF COLLECTIVE MEMORY

LIU YICHUN

On a rainy day, seated in the corner of my office, I glanced at the crown of the phoenix tree through my window. Set against the gradually darkening Shanghai sky, the words of Luigi Moretti from the year 1936 resonated in me. He described a poetic and indescribable depth of being surrounded by nature.[1] The message came from an interview of Moretti by Italian journalist Luigi Diemoz. Just the day before, I had read two other Moretti essays, "Structure as Form" and "Ideal Structures in the Baroque and in the Architecture of Michelangelo." These essays made me feel both excited and disheartened at the same

Office of Atelier Deshaus, West Bund Shanghai.
Image courtesy of Chen Hao / Atelier Deshaus

time. I was excited because my thoughts on structure have a similar nature to that of Moretti's. But I was disheartened because there was no way I could have experienced the structures of those Ancient Roman and Renaissance buildings discussed in his writings. However, as I connect to these concepts within the space offered by the text, from the era of Ancient Rome to the Renaissance, and from pre-war Italy to my Shanghai window-side desk, the preoccupation with structure seems to transcend time and space without ever growing old.

---

1   Luigi Diemoz, "Artist's Intensions: Luigi Moretti, Architect," in Federico Bucci and Marco Mulazzani, eds., *Luigi Moretti: Works and Writings* (New York: Princeton Architectural Press, 2002), p.158.

Conceptual diagram of the Shanghai Urban Space Art Season held at
Laobaidu Wharf Coal Warehouse in 2015. Image courtesy of Atelier Deshaus

Materiality, Place, and Reinvention of the Future

There is a relationship between the materiality or structure of a building, and its connection to the specificity of the place or the region. This conjures a form of collective memory, which is a way in which society looks back to the specificity of the place. If our society can recount the memory of a place and a specific period during which a particular generation had produced a highly specific material culture, we will be able to understand or distinguish what have been accomplished. Whether it is the notion of looking back at our material past or looking forward to a utopia, the purpose is to define where we are now—our contemporary existence. For example, if the structure and materials of a construction area no longer connected to the local characteristics of a place, then there will be a disconnected reality. Architects are always involved in the production and reproduction of an existing structural type. This reverence for a structural type is not nostalgia. Only in the constant working and reworking of structure can we begin to invent the future.

As the multiple layers of meaning of structure or its increasing abstraction begin to obscure our understanding of architecture, I feel excited that Moretti's extremely sensitive text can conjure a fuller impression of architecture in our minds. Oftentimes I find myself unable to relate to the contemporary conditions of speed and transience in China. Apart from external production conditions such as shorter design and construction phases, shorter occupation time, and a limited budget, there are no new and compelling questions of time that could alter the more persistent and practical values in architecture. Quite the contrary, the short lifespan of an architectural project in China provides a direct means for me to express the ways in which architecture can resist time and achieve permanence. Architecture is a straightforward way of communicating my conviction that structure itself embodies the innate possibility of connecting to time and the human body, and to the function and topography.

Connection of Time and the Human Body

Our quest to transform an industrial ruin into an exhibition venue in a little over a month would be a great way to discuss this question of time and structure. In collaboration with the Shanghai Urban Space Art Season in 2015, the Laobaidu Wharf Coal Warehouse was used temporarily as the venue for an exhibition entitled *Reloading*. It was part of a demonstration of adaptive reuse studies of Shanghai industrial buildings. The coal warehouse is part of a long-abandoned coal loading dock on the east side of Huangpu River, and the history of this pier can be traced back to the Emperor Guangxu years of the Qing dynasty. In 1995, the annual throughput at the Laobaidu Wharf had reached 9.35 million tons. After nearly twenty years of industrial development in Shanghai, the wharf had to be hastily relocated due to urgent urban renewal efforts. The site was turned into a riverside green park, and the reuse of these industrial structures became a hot topic for a fresh round of urban renewal discussions in Shanghai.

Two years prior to the art exhibition, this coal loading dock was refurbished once. The original plan to add a new building nearly led to the demolition of the dock. In fact, all the roof and walls partitions had been totally demolished, leaving only the reinforced concrete skeleton. Jacques Derrida evokes the relationship between the city and nature, as he wrote that "the relief and design of structures appears more clearly when content, which is the living energy of meaning, is neutralized, somewhat like the architecture of an uninhabited or deserted city, reduced to its skeleton by some catastrophe of nature or art. A city no longer inhabited, not simply left behind, but haunted by meaning and culture, this state of being haunted, which keeps the city from returning to nature." The city's return to nature is predicated on the ongoing processes of decline and renewal, just like the existing coal warehouse was left due to an incomplete demolition and abandonment. The few times I was able to visit the site in its original state of ruin, I felt as though I was entering into nature. The surfaces of the exposed structural skeleton were rapidly weathering, and the concrete was decaying from within.

In his essay "Structure and Form," Moretti expounded on the state of function and form after they have been concealed by the structure. He wrote, "The history of architecture testifies to the existence in every work of the three categories of form and, therefore, to the density and the tension particular to every point of the architectonic space. These points would have a very different density and tension were they in a solely structural, formal, or functional space." [2] Taking the coal warehouse as an example, built with a specific function for the storage and transportation of coal, the structure now reveals an inexplicable tension due to the loss of this function. As I stood on top of the warehouse, I could observe the dilapidated columns that had failed to protect the steel reinforcement bars protruding at its ends. With the backdrop of ships cruising by the meandering Huangpu River, I started to imagine the abandoned warehouse as a natural park.

Building of Production: Production of Building

There is a rational and heroic strength associated with industrial buildings, while they are involved in a direct and utilitarian process of production. When these buildings are adopted into the context of everyday life, there is an inherent tension. This contradiction also engenders an agitation within an experiential space that our bodies can relate to. The delicate awareness of such spaces of production in the context of urban Shanghai can bring value to architecture as a discipline.[3] The curator Feng Lu was able to identify an unfamiliar value within such everyday spaces. The spatial construction of *Reloading* within the temporality of the Laobaidu Coal Warehouse was an attempt to address the inherent connection between structure and form. All that was needed for the redemption of meaning in our understanding of the structure was the addition of two small exhibition halls at the top of the structural frame. The experience of the sequence of spaces turned solemn, like that of a church, when it culminated at these two exhibition halls, which were designed with pitched-roof forms in the likeness of a house form. The columns on the two sides constituted a simple enclosure, creating an unusual monumentality. This gave rise to a classical aura. This experimental intervention of a new function and new forms bestowed new meaning to the structure, even though it had become neutralized due to the loss of its original function.

The rooftop of the warehouse with the Huangpu River in the background. Image courtesy of Atelier Deshaus

A fixed circulation and sequence of exhibition was designed based on the opportunities inherent in the existing structure. Visitors would first ascend to the platform on the fifth floor through a giant steel staircase made of recycled material from the original conveyor belt for coal. The platform was the first spatial climax of the sequence, as this was the best location to view the Huangpu River. A sleek steel sheltered corridor would then direct visitors into the introduction exhibition hall. Two rows of

---

2   Luigi Moretti, "Structure and Form", in Bucci and Mulazzani, eds., *Luigi Moretti: Works and Writings*, p.176.
3   Feng Lu, *Reloading Exhibition: Urban Renewal in Practice of Laobaidu Wharf*, Shanghai Urban Space Arts Season, 2015, p.8.

metal pipes were installed as a "tapping device" for a sound installation inside the funnel of the coal warehouse. This allowed the passage of sound to follow the channeling functions of the coal funnels, and reinforcing the character of the spatial configurations. Descending from the intro-duction hall, visitors would pass by an open plan space. They would experience the documentary film projection hall on the fourth floor before reaching the themed exhibition hall and temporary auditorium on the third floor. The skylight high above the themed exhibition hall took advantage of the openings of the original structure, as the enclosure punctured through the fourth floor and was revealed on the top floor. This gave way to the spatial volume of the new exhibition space, and would continue to guide visitors on a downward journey. The second floor was the most important exhibition hall of the entire show, but it was the most constricted space with a low ceiling.

The display area for building models was situated in the gaps of the coal funnels, where the tapered concrete planes served as the projection surfaces for videos. It had the effect of a layering of time. With eight exhibition case studies, eight models, eight videos, and eight audio sequences, the sound artist turned the roughness of the

The sunken hall beneath the eight coal funnels, before and after revitalization. Image courtesy of Atelier Deshaus

existing space into a concert hall. The music was difficult to forget. The space began to resonate with a discernible and unique characteristic of sound. From the second floor of the exhibition hall to the first was a large, sunken hall that was covered by eight coal funnels. Through each funnel, one would be immersed in the specially recorded sounds of the underwater motor, the subway passing by, or pieces of coal tumbling down the funnel. The funnels had become a new container for sound. As these sounds had made an impression on the visitors through the metal pipes in the earlier sequence, the visitors arriving at this hall would have harmonized in their minds the disparate sounds and spaces into a holistic experience.

Unexpected Kind of Dignity

The reorganized exhibition space capitalized on every element of the existing structure. The new spatial interventions consisted only of the two house-forms made with the simplest of structures—lightweight steel studs encased in laminated gypsum boards. The circular skylight in the introduction hall carefully avoided the skeleton frame, yet inadvertently, one or two framing members are visible through the circular skylight. At the center of the main entrance, one of the structural steel studs was intentionally exposed to reveal an honesty about the state of construction of the black box. The surface of the

black box was covered in exposed polymer-modified bituminous sheets with a smooth texture, softly reflecting light like a horse's mane. This was a material rarely used in such a raw and exposed way; hence, the bituminous sheet cladding stood out in stark contrast against the concrete ruins. The various smaller scale interventions provided interpretive ways of understanding the ruinous structure, giving it an unexpected kind of dignity.

"A work of architecture is consumed according to the visible expression of its surfaces, its skin, independent of how these forms are internally connected to structures of concrete reality, weight and materials, and tensions. The degree of correspondence or interdependence between the structure to be consumed, the visible structure, or simply architecture, and the real structure can vary from exact identification, to slight alternation, to complete divergence with the real structure. Of the two extremes, absolute divergence belongs to the realm of scenography. One need only think of the commemorative mechanisms of the Baroque. The other extreme is in the field of engineering, deaf and devoid of spirituality and therefore outside the world of architecture. Or instead, the absolute divergence can touch the very pinnacles of this art."[4]

Moretti argued for the contemporary relevance of the ideal structures in Baroque architecture and the architecture of Michelangelo. An internal structure and an external scenography would come together to construct the meaning of architecture. Yet architecture in China today have grown accustomed to an obfuscating of the structure. There are unbearable aesthetic demands on the exterior of architecture, and architects have forgone the inherent expression of the structure. I believe that for architecture, both aspects are equally important. I found a diary entry written on the day the structural frame of our new office building had just been completed. "I have just been thinking about that mass of air, which may become intricately intertwined with the unknown, the tangible and the intangible. All aspects are wrapped up in a shell, forming darkness and light, tenseness and relief, but they remain reticent. The house at this moment has a sense of ruin as though it is far from the worldly and abandoned by the secular. Yet I know full well that this moment is ephemeral—then, it will be advancing into the world."[5] I recall now the moment the scaffoldings of the Long Museum had just been dismantled. It proved that even though the final structure was giving way to the scenography of the site and to the secularism of its use, the inherent structure is still rightfully the evidence of architecture's existence. The structure possesses an eternal value in the river of time.

This essay is translated from Liu Yichun, "Neizai de jiegou yu waizai de fengjing" [Structuring with Mindscape and Landscapes], *Time+Architecture*, Issue 148, 2016/2.

---

4   Luigi Moretti, "Ideal Structures in the Baroque and in the Architecture of Michelangelo", in Bucci and Mulazzani, eds., *Luigi Moretti: Works and Writings*, p.192.
5   Liu Yichun, "What is Structure?" *The Architect Journal*, No. 174, 2015, p.47.

ARCH-SCENARIOS IN RUINS

HE JIANXIANG

Urban sprawl of an uncommon kind in the Pearl River Delta (PRD) has transformed the former urban-rural dichotomy into a mega geographical collage. The juxtaposition of numerous theme park-like new low-density residential developments, golf courses, urban villages, new towns, new central business districts suggest that this form of indiscriminate sprawl can be described as pan-urbanism. They are all bounded by a continuously growing super highway system, which injects immense fluidity into the mega city. Such cities have become ephemeral. Along with the brand-new material development of the city is the parallel decay of urban space, especially the industrial fabric that formed the first wave of urbanization in the PRD. This low-density fabric has been decaying rapidly since major industries migrated from the PRD towards inland China. The large number of abandoned factories formed the hollow urban infills of PRD's pan-urbanism. Production escaped and factory sites soon turned into a state of ruin. The Chinese city is expected to continue to grow both outwards towards the margins and inwards towards these ruins. The destiny of industrial ruins would be an eventual elimination, and in its place, another familiar wave of large urban redevelopment and urban spectacles. Thus, it is apt to name these industrial remains as "ephemeral ruins."

Establishing *Fengjing*: Tectonic Interventions in an Ephemeral Landscape

The main theme in traditional Chinese literature and architecture can be described in the concept of *fengjing*. While the notion of landscape is routinely translated as such, this term is not a represented objective like the Western term of "landscape." Instead, *fengjing* ought to be better translated into a specific and subjective impression or expression of external objects and scenography. Hence, the coined term "arch-scenario" may instead be a more adequate term in articulating a spatial interpretation of the Chinese *fengjing*. To establish an arch-scenario is to construct a new proxemics—to design a new tectonic intervention that resides within an existing site and space, and mediates between the new and the old, the present and the memory, and architecture and the user's body. This interaction between time, space, and the human body becomes the actual component of the new architecture that we have to build for. In other words, to build in China is to build in the *mise en scène* of the pan-urban.

This new type of architectural space would be similar Michel Foucault's description of "heterotopia." It is a new place that we can perceive the real time-space of a city; hence, it resists and withholds further growth of the pan-urban morphology and even redirects ongoing urbanization in a specific manner. The abandoned industrial ruin becomes the perfect spatial laboratory for an architectural experiment in arch-scenario. The exercise in these ruins is an architectural operation with both real and surreal aspects. Architecture is making a return to its origin. An implanted arch-scenario is composed of three dimensions—namely, the subjective object, the layers of time, and the *tékhn*. Exhibiting the requisite techniques and craft of the building, the *tékhn* reminds us of the suffix of *arkh-tékhnē*, as in the architecture in Greek, which stands for the attendant skill, art, craft, and trade. By this means, there is a hope that we are able to reconnect contemporary Chinese architecture with our cultural tradition, and architects could again redeem their social roles and imagination in an urban complex.

> **We need to learn to view our urban ruins in a different way. They are valuable lessons—old and new—for both architects and the broader society.**

Transforming the Honghua Ruins

The factory complex occupies eight hectares and finds itself in the mountains of near the coast of east Shenzhen. Completed in 1982, it witnessed the heyday of the garment manufacturing industry in the PRD region. Following the decline of the industry, Honghua finally bankrupted in 2003. To compensate for the debt, all the machines were removed, and almost all metallic parts of the buildings were dismantled and sold as scrap. Only concrete and masonry remained on site. The fading of human activity gave way to the flourishing of nature that surrounded it. Indeed, nature would accelerate the ruination of this modern construction. Bearing the traces of industrial production and the invasion from nature, the workshop building's triangular plan and double-roof shell had the appearance of a new kind of post-industrial temple. Our intervention started from this observation. The specificity and layers of time and space led us to attempt to preserve the symbiotic relationship between the man-made structure and the immersive nature.

The first built project in Honghua was the Z Gallery, a reconversion of the former rinsing workshop into a reception center for the iD Town Art District. It also served as seven individual artist studios. The new intervention was offset from the ruin-shell of the existing building, so as to instigate a clear spatial dialogue with the site's historic past. By maintaining this physical distance between the new and the old, the interweaving of artificial and natural forces became legible as a strong contextual presence. The Z Gallery was a linear black steel box floating on the ground level of this industrial relic. An exhibition space, a café, meeting rooms, and a small reception were organized within the box. In order to cope with summer heat and humidity of South China, the black box's façade was equipped with a series of wall-sized pivoting doors and sliding glass doors. The design helped to maintain the low energy cost for air-conditioning. These movable wall and door panels also responded to the diverse demands on the space, allowing for different degrees of openness for different events and seasons.

In conjunction with the former loading entrance, the packing workshop of Honghua was the second to be altered. This would become the museum of iD Town. It was concep-

tualized as a restructuring of the spatial narratives of the vacant building. The new architecture was independently implanted onto the original interior ground slab of the old workshop. The industrial ruin was regarded as a large open concrete pavilion, in order to establish the new multi-layered time-space logic into it. The core space of the gallery—the main exhibition hall—was lifted up as a black steel box in the center of the old building. Its special double-roof skylight gave a gentle diffused lighting effect to the exhibition space. The enclosed exhibition box con-nected to the ground floor via two semi-glass halls. Several free-standing functional blocks supported the elevated main hall, and defined the ground space and functions.

Art exhibition at the museum of iD Town. Image courtesy of Likyfoto / O-Office

These included an entry showroom, auditorium, art shop, and flexible multifunctional spaces. The ground floor is open in all directions to the original ground of the factory, as well as to the surrounding natural landscape.

The third was an intervention of the original dormitory housing for the first batch of migrant workers. Located on the north hillside of the valley, this four-story masonry-concrete building was transformed to the Youth Hotel of iD Town. Considering the tight budget for the project, it was critical to minimize additions. The original fabric of the building was maintained in as many aspects as possible. Inside the old structure, the only intervention was the installation of the building's mechanical system along the internal corridor, including vertical shafts and horizontal ducts covered by new ceilings. The only interventions on the façade were the black steel apertures added to the original openings. Guest rooms were upgraded with air-conditioning units, and the exterior compressors were housed in the same black steel apertures. With these projected apertures, each room drew a little closer to the huge crowns of the banyan trees, which practically covered the façade of the dormitory. The original dormitory rooms on the ground floor were recombined into larger spaces for public functions through subtle alterations of the original structures. Each opening was again marked by the projected black steel aperture windows, but the public nature of the first floor allowed for more colorful trapezoidal forms.

The main entrance of iD Town was the former loading entrance of the factory. The top slab of the loading deck was a meter and a half higher than the level of the access road, and the outer limit of docking deck was a vehicular ramp connecting the deck with the road. This fourth intervention was composed as multiple conditions of entry, preparing visitors for a series of immersive arch-scenario experiences. The first was a continuous zig-zagged and gently sloping plaza, defined by a sequence of fair-faced concrete walls that guides visitors from the roadside plaza up to the open space on the deck level. This path gave way to vehicular traffic when needed. The second was a light but sophisticated straight steel bridge that connected directly between the two levels. The third approach experience stemmed from the industrial water treatment tank, which was converted to a landscaped pool. Before arriving at the entry pavilion of the museum, Visitors would be welcomed into the site through steel bridges and a glass-floor stage above the tank and be offered an uncanny experience of the previous usage of water. The multiple approaches spoke of a cultivation of arch-scenarios, using the industrial ruin to reweave the relationship between the artificial and natural.

A woman and her child play behind the Z Gallery.
Image courtesy of Likyfoto / O-Office

From Building Production to Spectacles

We are living in a state where architecture is reduced to the pure repetition of typical units and floors in favor of quick profit. As a profession, architecture has become a mere servant in the chain of building production, building economics, or spectacles in our cities. In the face of the rapid growth of pan-urbanism, the urban fabric is doomed to become future ruins. We are surrounded by ruins, but architects are paid and trained to ignore them, or to cleanse and replace them with generic and fast building solutions. We need to learn to view our urban ruins in a different way. They are valuable lessons—old and new—for both architects and the broader society. Christopher Woodward once suggested, "When we contemplate ruins, we contemplate our own future." These lessons can open new doors to ancient Chinese views of our contemporary landscape, and our arch-scenarios.

TRUTH IN LANDSCAPE

DONG YUGAN

In my book *Minimalism* written in 2003, there were a number of reflections on how alienated humanity had become during the times of industrialization, and the formation of cities for production. The lineage in the questioning of authenticity in architecture were based on the moral values behind the Western religion and its architectural tradition. It endeavored to express the originality and performativity of each aspect of architecture as clearly as possible—the load-bearing structure is designed as a demonstration of strength, the roof is designed as light as possible so it is not a loading liability, and so on. There is a paradox. If everything is self-evident, it means that architecture would only be limited to an expression of structure. Yet architecture is not just a technical field, and there are a multitude of responsibilities it has to come to terms with. Louis Kahn had his faith in Judaism, and in China, it is paramount for a fuller expression of architecture that treats its own beliefs more seriously.

Faith, Authenticity, and a System of Practice

In the decades of teaching architecture, students would read the works of literati Li Yu from the late-Ming dynasty to come to terms with the discourse of truth in architecture. The capacity to distinguish between the multiple realities of truth and authenticity would be extremely helpful in the protection of cultural relics in China. These truths, however, are not easy to establish in design practices. Li was well known for his creative prowess, and he famously transformed the traditional window into the framing of a landscape with likeness to a well-proportioned Chinese scroll painting. However, Li's first criteria for window design was its firmness and structural integrity. Beyond its structural integrity, the windows must have other reasons for being; otherwise, it becomes sheer pragmatic economics rather than architecture. There are many dominant principles of architecture that had withstood the test of time, but there must be a role for contemporary architects to continue to ensure that these traditional principles are not the only ones defining architecture today. To illustrate, over the course of my practice, I have developed a set of clear formal strategies, where the tectonics of a building requires a contiguous expression from the ground to the walls and even the ceilings, whose surfaces were required to be lined in bricks. The reality of the tectonic expression overrides the traditional expectation or structural truth of a ceiling being a light-weight material. It turned out that the construction of a masonry ceiling was relatively achievable, without the bricks falling off by gravity. In this instance, the authenticity of the construction was emphasized by a higher tectonic truth; yet in another instance, the choice of bricks may prove inauthentic.

The brick ceiling of the Red Brick Museum.
Image courtesy of Budi Lim, 2015

There is no deliberateness in creating architecture that is ironic, nor is my interest to challenge the existing truths in construction and architecture? A pursuit of architecture does not need to be centered on overturning all the traditional truths of construction and practice as a show of strength or integrity. When it comes to the advent of minimalism or an overt position of truth and simplicity in architecture, one needs to look no further than Mies van der Rohe. The reason why architects admire Mies is because some of his principles in design had formed the basis of architectural education around the world, including China. Architects' belief in the clarity of structure is staunch—of extreme, mythical proportions. Mies subscribed to Thomas Aquinas' moral philosophy of order and truth to such an extreme that he argued that a true expression of structural order would bring one closer to God. What are the values in our architectural beliefs in China today? With a shallow understanding of the morality and belief system of these canonical works, and without the pedagogical bearings of specific forms of architectural education, the works Mies may be inaccessible to the majority.

History and Knowledge in Cultural Exchanges

By the same token, without a strong background of Chinese history and architectural knowledge, can the Suzhou gardens be recognized by the uninitiated as the epitome of Chinese culture? Is there a disciplinary field that comes with the study and appreciation of Chinese architecture and landscapes? This may lead to an undesirable form of freedom in an absolute democracy, where everyone has the right to impose a new reading, or a possible misreading, of architecture. There is a longstanding interest in the appreciation of the Chinese landscape. But one has to realize that what such interests are always predicated on one's foreknowledge of the culture of China. To give an example, Wang Shu once brought me to examine a beautiful landscaped wall in the Hangzhou Wenlan Court built during the reign of Emperor Qianlong in the Qing dynasty in 1782. The moss covered and naturally overgrown ferns on the wall appeared like a real-life Northern Song dynasty landscape painting. Wang Shu intimated that the famous Jacques Herzog had also shown appreciation for the artistic beauty of the wall. But it is likely that these were two very different kinds of appreciation of the same phenomenon.

In any cultural exchange, there has to a shared platform. This is why it is important to recognize that one's understanding of Chinese architecture and landscape is necessarily niche, if not elitist. It is likely that a small group of like-minded thinkers with an informed understanding of a theme would instigate the common comprehension of the topic. While everyone is entitled to their own explanation, such explanations may be very esoteric. A common platform would facilitate effective communication across different cultures. There is big role for education to play in the formation of such commonality and shared platforms. In contemporary China, architects seem familiar with the shared platform and discourses around Western architecture, but they are paradoxically less familiar with the discourses undergirding their own Chinese architecture. There has to be a conscious looking back at the traditions of Chinese architecture, in order to appreciate the presence of such common platforms. This is why like-minded architects such as Li Xinggang would persist in seeking me out in advancing the discourse of Chinese gardens. Such contemporary consciousness is particularly important, because there is no clear road map to such cultural formations. This awareness is an incredible stimulus in the interrogation of China's cultural specificity.

There is one branch of thought that suggests that the Chinese literati would make landscape the focus of their discourse, while buildings are in the domain of craftsmen, merely accommodated by the broader environment. Conversely, Western architecture has a strong focus on object of buildings. Interestingly, the problem facing China right now is the loss of traditional craftsmen and the necessary skills in the making of good architecture. On the one hand, there is an urgent need for architects to learn the core knowledge of the Chinese literati—the managing of a harmonious relationship between the architecture and the surroundings. On the other hand, there is a need to learn what the literati did not have to master—the making of architecture. For example, it would be unsatisfactory to merely adopt a traditional perspective if one has to give form to a pagoda-like structure within a certain landscape. Considering the complex situation of China's scarcity of resources, massive population, and inadequate land and policies, is the study of Chinese gardens a luxury? This rhetorical question is no different from asking why the Westerners continue to hang on to their religions or beliefs.

There has to be a conscious looking back at the traditions of Chinese architecture, in order to appreciate the presence of such common platforms.

In traditional Chinese living environments, every important piece of architecture would have its own specific garden, whether they are palaces, temples, government houses, residential buildings, or tombs. The gardens may well represent the heavens in traditional Chinese culture. Unlike other cultures, heaven is a place where you can enter only after death and purification. The heavens in China exist in daily lives, from certain landscape territories of the Han and Tang dynasties to the mountains at the end of the

Ming dynasty. Nowadays, the decrease of habitable space is similar to the decrease of space from the Han and Tang dynasties to the Ming and Qing dynasties. There are gardens in Japan that are only two-thirds of a square meter, yet huge backyards can be found in many contemporary Chinese houses. Most of the landscapes that accompany Chinese real estate developments get their inspiration from the French gardens. This shows that traditions from other cultures can enter our everyday life; hence, it is certainly possible to bring some aspects of the Chinese traditional garden design into the cities of China today.

The outdoor spaces at the Red Brick Museum. Images courtesy of Budi Lim, 2015

Experimentation and Value Systems

Given its place in antiquity, it is difficult to see the study of Chinese gardens as the beginning of a new concept of architectural design. Such scholarship falls into two different categories, one involving a deep and extensive study of the different fields in broader Chinese culture, and the other a simpler yet equally rigorous process of design experimentation and interpretation of the well-honed concepts. The study of Chinese gardens has received considerable attention in recent years, with faithful forums to discuss the lifestyle and traditions of the Chinese literati, as well as advertisements of mainstream real estate developments showcasing the elegance of Chinese landscapes. One of these advertisements located along the Fourth Ring Road of Beijing read, "From the Norwegian forest and the Vancouver woods to Tang-dynasty Chinese gardens." This represents the free market's "dream" of the Tang dynasty, awkwardly legitimizing the historic Suzhou gardens for a Beijing context. It would have been easy to follow this trend, but because there is such a vastness in this scholarship, there is no legitimate way to approach this subject despite years of study. It is no use ignoring or belittling the impetus from the consumerist tendencies of the general public. Yet it is not a stable trend that one can seriously depend on.

This awareness came from my thesis study over a decade ago, when I came to terms with an overreliance on the Western theories of landscape and architecture, and I realized that my knowledge of Chinese gardens can only compete with that of a tour guide. The dominant knowledge of Chinese gardens today is mainly focused on the formal expressions. Even in the replication of traditional Chinese gardens for real estate developments in China, most Chinese designers could only give instructions with precise measurements, but not offer them something deeper. "The changing of a scene as one ambulates through the landscape" was a term to describe the experiences in Chinese gardens, according to Yang Hongxun in his 1982 treatise on the classical gardens of China. He also argues that this narrated experience can also be used on any other kinds of landscape design as well. A deeper understanding of how movement is conjured, and how the scenery changes, would be necessary. It is like the study of proportions in design—the awareness that cutting away of any object would be a process of manipulating proportions, but one needs a greater understanding of a value system of what constitutes good proportions.

This essay is translated and adapted from Dong Yugan, "Tingyuan, jianzhu liuyi—Shenghuo yu zaoxing" [Six Issues on the Courtyard and Architecture: Life and Modelling], *Architectural Journal*, Issue 534, 2013/02, and "Qidian, zhongdian, xiulian" [Inspiration, Completion, and Experience], *Designer and Designing*, Issue 45, 2010/02.

CULTURAL TRANSLATIONS

MARIO GANDELSONAS

During the twentieth century, the practice of architecture became increasingly global in scope. This tendency saw a dramatic acceleration, in particular, due to the development of the global economy, the Internet, personal computers, and mobile devices. Parallel to the processes of globalization, the speed of urbanization was extreme to the point where over half of the world's population are living in cities. The challenges for architectural and urban design in the twenty-first century would take place within this increasingly new and dynamic context. Cities all over the world would continue to grow and modernize at an unprecedented pace. When I first proposed the China Studio at Princeton University in 1993, it had never been more urgent for architecture students to gain an international experience and for Chinese students to be more cognizant of the imminent transformations taking place in China. Nowhere were these new realities more apparent than in the rapidly growing cities of China. The China Studio was established two years later in 1995, and it developed up until 2012 as a cross-cultural exchange between Princeton University and Tongji University. In its earlier iterations, it included the University of Hong Kong. The program not only exposed western students to Chinese culture undergoing a unique process of transformation, but it also enabled educational exchanges and opportunities for Chinese students and faculty.

The China Studio was a constant source of creativity, generating new design ideas, and new ways of looking at the city of the twenty-first century. Every Fall semester between 1995 and 2012, students from the China Studio would travel primarily to Shanghai and Suzhou to examine specific urban sites and the challenging problems that grew from modernization in China. In some years, the studio would also travel to Beijing, Hangzhou, Shenzhen, and Hong Kong. These select groups of graduate students would engage firsthand with the unique architecture, landscape, and urbanism of the region and participate in design workshops primarily held at the College of Architecture and Urban Planning at Tongji University. American and Chinese students would work together to present their work to a panel of world-class architectural experts. It was this combination of on-site learning, cultural exchange, and thoughtful design challenges that made the

China Studio a unique architectural pedagogy and a model for international programs in schools throughout the United States and around the world.

Pedagogical Experiment in Interdisciplinary Translations

It is impossible to overstate the importance of first-hand exposure to the sites and cities that were the subject of the students' design work. For most of these Princeton students, the China Studio represented their first opportunity to travel to China and, for some of

the American students, their first significant educational experience abroad. While in China students were not only experiencing the city directly—gathering site information and photographs necessary for their design work—they were also working closely with their counterparts from Tongji University. Travel to China would offer Princeton students exposure to a unique mix of urgent issues associated with modernization, urbanization, and globalization, while at the same time introduce them to China's rich cultural history. Indeed, the Chinese students would also gain a new awareness of their own Chinese culture and history, in the context of the complex mix of history and modernity that made up the total experience of China.

The structure of the China Studio reflected this double goal of introducing the students to Chinese classical culture as well as exposing them to the processes of urban modernization. Located in the ancient imperial city of Suzhou, three important gardens became the intellectual and cultural site for the first part of the studio. They included the Wangshi Yuan Garden (Master of the Net Garden), the Zhuo Zheng Yuan Garden (Garden of the Humble Administrator), and the Liu Yuan Garden

Project by Garret R. Ricciardi on Shanghai, c. 2001. Image courtesy of Princeton SoA The China Studio

(Lingering Garden). The program for the first part consisted of a "reading" these three remarkable gardens. The urban site for the second part of the studio was always the site for a real project that had a particular relevance in the process of modernization of Chinese cities. Shanghai offered numerous sites during the 1990s and the early 2000s, and in the seven iterations of the program between 2004 and 2010, Suzhou itself offered different sites as a unique urban laboratory. Studio sites were also found in Beijing in 1997 and Hangzhou in 2000 and 2002. The program for the second part of the studio would include the design of new urban districts, infrastructure and urban nodes. The entry point into China tended to occur via Suzhou and Shanghai, scheduled during the Fall term break at the end of October. There would be a joint presentation of the student projects at

Tongji University in Shanghai, followed by a discussion of the different architectural and pedagogical approaches to the program.

Suzhou was the center of culture for hundreds of years, known for the beauty of its gardens. It was the subject of poetry, an inspiration for painters, and the site for unique works of landscape and architecture. Built by King Helü in 514 BC, the city was crisscrossed by canals that run alongside streets and alleys. The city gained its unique character in the countless number of small bridges across the canals, framed by the white walls of houses with roofs of dark gray tiles. As an old saying goes, "Up in the sky there is paradise, down on earth there are Suzhou and Hangzhou." Suzhou is the city famous for its gardens, and Hangzhou for its West Lake, and the saying aptly describe the lofty place that Suzhou occupies in Chinese culture. A metropolis of industry and commerce in the southeastern coast of China since ancient times, Suzhou was always a hub for merchants. Continuing this tradition, Suzhou was officially declared part of "the coastal economic open zone of the Yangtze Delta." Major industrial developments coupled with a tremendous expansion in foreign trade transformed Suzhou into one of the economic engines of China. Two new industrial cities were developed, the China-Singapore Suzhou Industrial Park to the east of the historical city built in 1994, and the Suzhou New District to the west built in 1992. These sites were the subject of the final five years of the China Studio from 2006 to 2010, with a focus on the different aspects of urban infrastructure.

Reading and Writing the Chinese Garden

The "reading" of the Chinese Gardens in Suzhou became the distinctive feature of the China Studio, and it ended up defining its pedagogical identity. The Chinese garden was the site of articulation of many cultural practices. It provided a unique opportunity to approach Chinese culture, since the design of the Chinese garden resulted from the collaboration between scholars, gardeners, painters, architects, poets, and calligraphers.

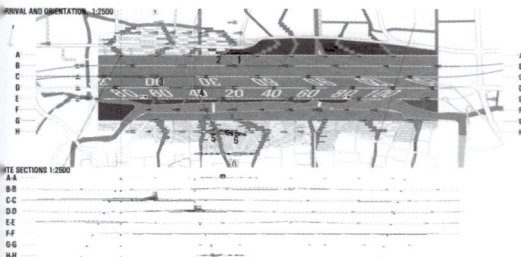

Project by Chris Hillyard on Suzhou, c.2007.
Image courtesy of Princeton SoA The China Studio

Chinese gardens could be seen as complex compositions of courtyards or as continuous sequences linking landscapes of different sizes. A water element, a pond or lake is usually the heart of the garden where pavilions, libraries, and study rooms would offer moments of repose and reflection. The experience of the garden would take place essentially in a temporal dimension through controlled visual and relational trajectories impossible to figure out from a plan view. These long viewing trajectories would be compressed in the spaces of relatively small gardens by means of zigzagging or meandering paths and bridges. These dynamic paths would constantly position and reposition the viewer, while walls and buildings would also be employed to reframe the views.

One could imagine the designer of the Chinese garden as a group that would possess different artistic disciplines. The client was usually a scholar who would include himself in the process of design alongside a painter, an architect-builder, a poet, and a gardener. Since everybody in the group would have the foreknowledge of the formal structures and elements of a typical garden and their relationships to one another, the challenge for the group would be to develop an idea throughout the design process. And because the design would have been partaken by an interdisciplinary entity, including multiple authors instead of a single creative author, the genealogical or authorial aspect would be diminished. Instead, the focus would be upon the work and its development through a number of "translations" of the idea from one art form to another and from theory to practice. An imaginary description of the process could start with a poem suggesting scenes that the painter would render in two dimensions, from the verbal to the non-verbal. At that point, the architect and the gardener could introduce the third dimension of space and the dimension of time through alternating moments of movement and stasis. This interplay would suggest pavilions and paths, giving material form to the scenes first suggested by the poem. From that point, a feedback loop would start a never-ending process of change and redesign that would continue for hundreds of years. During this time, the materials that made the garden, the different plants, shrubs, and, in particular, the trees would continue to grow, receive pruning, and change.

The circulation of the idea from one art form to another in the creation of the Chinese garden could be seen as a complex process of translation and, to some extent, transformation. The idea expressed through the words of the poetic language were not equivalent to the images that translated them into the painter's two-dimensional field. The same could be applied to the architect's translation,

> There were important lessons to be learned from this transformation of the Chinese garden from a private world of an elitist model of refinement into an urban public space open to everybody.

who could expand and develop the idea in the built structure, in order to suggest, among other things, transparency and opacity, openings and closures, and multiple framings of a single view. And the gardener who created the landscapes would set the stage for the materialization of the idea. The Chinese garden could be seen as the combined effect of multiple translations. The process of design would articulate a multiplicity of artistic disciplines, and it would in turn be articulated by the different disciplines. The garden resulted from the coexistence of multiple texts that would develop in time, like a visual score that included the choreography of the visitor's bodies in motion, constantly framed, fragmented, and reflected.

The "writing" of the Chinese garden may be a never-ending process of translation—a condensing of energies of the interdisciplinary group that co-designed it. Then for the students of the China Studio, the process of design would open up new questions and new

Project by Gavri E. Slasky on Suzhou, c.2007. Image courtesy of Princeton SoA The China Studio

developments that could release the potential and latent relationships contained in the condensed energy of the garden. One obvious and recurring question was the distance in time, language, and culture that separated the students from the garden. The China Studio dealt with this question by proposing two moments in the development of the project. In the first moment, before traveling to China, the students would study the formal representation of the Suzhou Gardens, their plans and sections, and the trajectories and key viewpoints, as they attempted to unpack the multiplicity of disciplines and discourses. On the basis of this initial research, they would develop a thesis "at a distance" without having visited the garden. In the second moment, upon visiting the garden, the students would allow the actual physical garden to evoke new narratives, dictate the trajectories, and suggest new viewing vantage points other than the ones they had analyzed. By comparing the result of the research initiated at Princeton against the actual garden, the students would complete a final iteration of their project. The "rewritten" garden would become the source of inspiration for their final architectural and urban projects.

The process of "reading" was central to the China Studio's exploration of the Chinese garden. It was concerned not just with the "text"—the garden as it existed as the result of historical formal transformations—but also with the garden as a reflection of sociopolitical and cultural contexts. While the Chinese garden as "text" was altered throughout the centuries, the user as "reader" would change over time as well. Created originally as private gardens for enjoyment by a wealthy individual, a scholar, or a government official,

the gardens were restored to its original splendor. After many years of neglect, the walled gardens were opened to the general public only around the 1950s. For students arriving from Princeton, where public space historically carried a negative connotation, there were important lessons to be learned from this transformation of the Chinese garden from a private world of an elitist model of refinement into an urban public space open to everybody. This issue resonated with the millennial students who grew up with the openness of the internet in an increasingly urbanized world. This represented the best outcome of the confluence of civic and artistic spheres that the Chinese students could be proud of. But more importantly, this knowledge could be redeployed for contemporary endeavors in architecture. The Princeton students took back with them worthy lessons of the Chinese gardens as newly understood roles as centers of cultural thought and oases of calm in contrast to the ever increasing speed of accelerated urbanization. This new public sphere is even more poignant in the context of the radical changes that had affected China in the last twenty-five years. In the heart of expanding twenty-first-century Chinese megalopolises, the Chinese gardens provided Princeton and Chinese students the unique opportunity to interact with history and culture.

COMMON AND TIMELESS SPACES

ZHU XIAOFENG

Chinese contemporary architecture used to have two major directions to choose from—one that combined with tradition, with critical regionalism as its main theoretical basis, and another that blended with globalization, with the neoliberal economy as its harbinger. Today, these two directions are not mutually exclusive, and they are advancing in parallel. Instead, the architectural disciplines ought to be anchored by two even more decisive foundations—one is to serve the needs of society, from economic and spatial responsibilities to spiritual or emotional ones; and another would be the advancement within the discipline of architecture itself. When these two entities combine as one and overlap to a large degree, the development of architecture would be healthy. Conversely, if the two are broken apart, architecture would fail. The greatest source of influence in the twentieth century is modernism, which originated from the West. It was an ongoing process of systematizing and universalizing architectural innovation. When this system spread along with the economic and political systems around the world, it came into conflict with other regional cultures and politics. The latter half of the last century saw the process of modernism grafting itself onto China, and the two foundations became fractured. Projecting forward, the well-being of China's architectural development would depend on whether the innovation of architecture and the society it serves can have the possibility of reconciliation.

Inheritance of Tradition

The inheritance of tradition is extremely necessary, but it is not possible for every single building to accomplish this mission. If society does not respond to its memories of events and its living habits through architecture, then it is simply throwing away its accumulation of wisdom. Many Chinese architects of the last century have put tremendous effort in extending the role of tradition in architecture, such as Chen Chi-Kwan, Wang Dahong, and Feng Jizhong. However, due to the specific problems of that era, architecture was able to undertake a systematic process of inheritance and transformation. It is regrettable that the influences of these pioneers have not become mainstream in the architectural profession in China. There is a profound need to continue along the lines of exploring the needs of society, with an impetus to innovate. There are substantial lessons from the works of the pioneering architects, where the next generation of Chinese architects could inherit their wisdom and perhaps pick up the common threads. Critics argue that the construction industry in China has failed the Chinese society it serves. The extent of this destructive force is much more than what most had come to realize. China relies on a land development model that prioritizes the cheap procurement of new land, and the development of physical buildings. This had led to a surge in highly repetitive architecture in new Chinese cities, especially the sprawling new towns. The primary concern of the government is how to parcel and sell land, and the point of departure from the planning phase is its marketability. Next would be the planning of the municipal urban systems, especially the transportation system, and the last would be the everyday needs of the people. This prevailing system of the past twenty years must be reformed, because the future of China cannot be bolstered by the economy of land sales alone.

The specificity of a Chinese trait in urban development is debated and speculated about in highly-stimulated discussions in China, and with little dispute, the Chinese *xiaoqu* or residential district is one such urban form with a tangible Chinese quality. In all large and medium cities across China, these residential compounds tend to be circumscribed as gated developments by Chinese developers, as they have quickly evolved into a ubiquitous mode of living for the urban population. In the "long river of history" of the past twenty years, several well-tempered *xiaoqu* typologies have transformed into the gold standards for urban living. Additional elements have been attached to the *xiaoqu* to add value and give form to a standardized package, such as *xiaoqu* greening, *xiaoqu* security, *xiaoqu* property management, and of course, the *xiaoqu* common space. The common space in a *xiaoqu* is essentially the communal space, or a form of public space, for its residents. While it appears to be a generous offering from the developer and architects to the residents, in reality they are the required open spaces separating one building from another. The pursuit of maximum economic returns from the built-up area by

> **Architecture has the duty to offer a kind of experience that would radically transform society. The goal is to create experiential architecture through a reorganization of space and time.**

a developer, coupled with code-required daylight hours that dictate the orientation of residential buildings and market-determined housing unit types, would ensure that the open communal spaces are distorted into some form of awkward residual spaces. The slightly cynical Chinese urban inhabitant would describe such spaces as the *chicken ribs* of Chinese high-rise residential architecture—a Chinese term for something that is too tasteless to be consumed but a pity to throw out. The greening, park benches, and outdoor exercise equipment are tantamount to the breading and sweet-and-sour sauce that garnish the meatless chicken rib. China has long been obsessed with being more economical with its land resources. While it is undeniable that the external spaces between the *xiaoqu* residential buildings are designed to allow each housing unit to enjoy sufficient sunlight, ventilation, and a good amount of privacy, they cannot afford to be left as passive and default open communal spaces. There is simply insufficient good quantity communal and public spaces around the housing districts, especially when the high-cost of such developments are taken into consideration.

To compound the problem, these *xiaoqu* open spaces are surrounded by gates and walls, isolated, and unrelated urbanistically with the street life of the city. Internally, as a shared space amongst the residents, there is often a limited sense of identity or sense of belonging due to the bland spatial qualities. Apart from visual attractiveness, there tends to be insufficient community functions in the *xiaoqu* common spaces to instigate energetic or meaningful interactions for residents. Most of the middle-class *xiaoqu* residents are gainfully employed white-collar office workers. They would leave their homes early and come home late at night, socializing away from their homes even during weekends, and the dominant common or public spaces they encounter are around their offices, restaurants, shopping malls, karaokes, and cafés. The main users of the *xiaoqu* common spaces are perhaps the elderly who have morning exercise routines or children who would need a safe play space after school. It

A generic *xiaoqu* neighborhood in Guangzhou. Image courtesy of Takeo Muraji, 2013

is ironic that these active user groups are precisely the ones without a voice in pushing for a better common environment. The *xiaoqu* common spaces are pastured, neat, clean, and convenient, yet somehow lethargic. On the one hand, they can be elaborately adorned by the developers and architects; on the other hand, they tend to be underused and underappreciated. This *xiaoqu* typology is only an example of the Chinese Dream, where the yearning for an idyllic ideal rapidly turns into a kind of inertia and acquiescence. In the age of an instant economy and urbanity, the *xiaoqu* is a close approximation of the contemporary model of Chinese living.

Space for Exchange

The courtyard is another distinct space in Chinese architecture. It is not only a traditional space but also a social space for exchange. Over the centuries, Chinese society has maintained family cohesion through the courtyard by enhancing interactions among relatives and friends, creating a sense that the Heavens and the Earth are within reach of one another, and establishing a connection with nature. For the urbanites living in the metropolitan conditions today, all these aspects are considered a luxury. In any conception of architecture, it is important to allow a built form to have a dual relationship with the ground floor and courtyard space in order to bring about a fluid interconnection between the indoors and outdoors. Anticipating the potential of such a traditional form, one of our completed projects, the East China Normal University Affiliated Bilingual Kindergarten,

The courtyard space at East China Normal University Affiliated Bilingual Kindergarten.
Image courtesy of Scenic Architecture

experimented with an interplay of courtyards. Located in the town of Anting, at the northwest area of Shanghai bordering Huaqiao, Suzhou, this is one of three schools in the community. It was the first public architecture by Anting Motor City in collaboration with Dulwich College. Centered on a courtyard for the school children, this low-rise kindergarten is 6,600 square meters in area, and accommodates fifteen classrooms and all sorts of outdoor activities. The courtyard offers the children and teachers, who would eventually become a social group, both a connection to nature and opportunities for interactions. The courtyard offers them the emotions and memories associated with the traditional courtyard lifestyle, and helps them learn about their surroundings. With a relatively undefined space, they exercise their own creativity with the kinds of furniture they bring to the courtyard, the relationships to the interior spaces of the classrooms, and the inventive activities they teach themselves to play. There is a greater curiosity and sensitivity to the activities taking place in the courtyards, as the mysterious scenery unfolds before the children, oscillating between different courtyards and interior spaces. As a series of interior and courtyard spaces are strung along the pathway, the children would have frequent opportunities to interact with small doses of nature and society. These experiences of exploration and interactions would eventually become a crucial part of the children's memories.

In approximately seventy percent of the projects in China, architects would have no avenue to interact with the future users of the buildings they design. In this alternate reading of "exchange," this critical space for a more socially-grounded transmission of ideas is absent in most Chinese projects. Amongst the clients that Chinese architects serve today, the majority are not the real users of the buildings but local governments and developers who hold the rights to develop the land. The former tends to prioritize the public appearance of the architecture rather than its function, while the latter tends to pursue architecture through market research that predetermines the most marketable floor plans and readymade consumer product. The pervasiveness of this problem in China means there is little care for the ordinary users of these buildings. Even if architects voluntarily consider the needs of the unknown users with the noblest of intentions, their efforts would be speculative at best. Because of the rarity and exclusivity of a more direct connection between clients and architects, such clients would grow to become the most respected ones in the portfolio of architects in China. Given the potential for greater mutual respect and a marked improvement in the quality of the work, the practice of architecture in China must aim to promote and create a mainstream interest in this space of exchange between client-users and architects.

Architecture is always a form of media that is situated between man and the environment, and between man and the spaces beyond the self in an intensely social sense. Architecture also possesses other content. In the present Chinese society, there is a massive importance ascribed to the role of architecture, and the architect has the privileged role as its organizer. Apart from the design of private living environments, the most urgent roles for architecture would be to invite an exploration of nature, as well as to enhance social interaction in the public realms. The modest courtyard in traditional housing was the first hint of a kind of social architecture, and the design of other kinds of civic or public buildings should really do much more towards the fundamental needs of society, from airports and train stations to buildings of consumption and culture and many others. Architecture has the duty to offer a kind of experience that would radically transform society. The goal is to create experiential architecture through a reorganization of space and time. The discipline of architecture has always privileged spatial concepts over time, but in China, it has to realize the increasing importance of the organization of time. The focus on time would signal not only a new kind of interaction with the past but also an awareness of the highly nuanced contemporary. Because it heeds to the wisdom of the past, it can lead to vast and stimulating possibilities of the future.

This essay is translated and adapted from Zhu Xiaofeng, "Yongheng de jianzhu" [Timeless Architecture], *Interior Design and Construction*, Issue 2013/12, pp.100-101, and "Ganga de 'xiaoqu shi gonggong kongjian' " [Awkward Public Spaces in Gated Communities], *Time+Architecture*, Issue 93, 2007/1, pp.45-46.

Discussion session at the Tianzi Pier along the Pearl River, Guangzhou. Image courtesy of Wellington Kuswanto, 2013

BIOGRAPHIES

Robert Adams is Associate Professor at the University of Michigan. Read at Southern California Institute of Architecture (SCI-Arc), Adams is interested in the intersection of architecture, civic infrastructure, and disability culture, and his work has been published internationally. He has also participated in multiple exhibitions, such as "Ruralopolitan Maneuvers: Beijing's Urban and Rural Villages" which he collaborated with Robert Mangurian and Mary-Ann Ray for *China In Flux: Mapping The Middle Zone* in Shanghai, and "Reyner Banham Loves Beijing" for the *Third Architectural Biennial Beijing*.

Lee Ambrozy is a PhD candidate at the Institute of Fine Arts, New York University. She was the editor and translator of Ai Weiwei's blog with MIT Press in 2011 and has taught at the Central Academy of Fine Arts, China (CAFA). The former editor of *Artforum*'s Chinese language website, her articles and reviews have appeared *in Artforum, Yishu,* and *ArtAsiaPacific*. Her current research examines intertextuality in painting and material culture of the late Tang through the Song dynasties.

Chang Yung Ho is the founder of Atelier FCJZ and a professor at Tongji University and Massachusetts Institute of Technology (MIT). Originally from Beijing, he read at the University of California at Berkeley, has been practicing in China since 1992 and established his office in 1993. Chang has taught at various architecture schools in the USA and China, and served as the head of the Department of Architecture of MIT from 2005 to 2010 and founded the Peking University Graduate Center for Architecture in 1999.

Chen Ling is the co-founder and principal designer of WSP Architects, Beijing, which was established in 1999. He graduated from Wuhan University of Technology in 1990, and later continued his study at Université Paris 1 Panthéon-Sorbonne. Chen specializes in architecture, urban planning, and interior design. Chen was elected as one of the "Ten Greatest Architects in China" in 2005 and obtained numerous honors including the Bauwelt Prize in 2005 and Chicago Athenaeum International Architecture Award in 2009.

Jeremy Chia is an architectural designer at Ong&Ong and a researcher at the Asian Urban Lab (AUL) and AA Asia. Graduated from National University of Singapore, Chia's research interests include methods of production and potentialities in architecture, and the morphology and use of public spaces. He has organized several workshops and conferences for AUL and AA Asia, as well as edited publications such as *Incomplete Urbanism: A Critical Urban Strategy for Emerging Economies* (2011), *Public Space in Urban Asia* (2014), *Incubations: A Guidebook To Procuring Innovative Architecture* (2014), and *Singapore Dreaming: Managing Utopia*, co-edited with H. Koon Wee (2016).

Cui Kai is the Vice President and Chief Architect of China Architecture Design & Research Group. After graduating from Tianjin University in the early 1980s, he spent four years in Shenzhen and Hong Kong. With over two decades of professional practice, Cui has won multiple awards and honors, including China Architecture Design Master in 2000 and Liang Sicheng Award in 2007. At present, he is among other positions the Vice President of the Architectural Society of China, Co-Director of UIA Competitions Commission, and a part-time professor of Tianjin University. In recent years, he had organized several gathering architects' projects, among which includes the ongoing project of Yujiapu CBD in Tianjin Binhai New Area.

Dong Gong is the founder of Vector Architects, established in 2008, and a design tutor at the School of Architecture of Tsinghua University. Dong read at Tsinghua University, University of Illinois, and the Technical University of Munich. He has been invited as a guest speaker by universities including Tianjin University and Southeast University. His projects have been published by multiple journals including *A+U, Architectural Review, Domus, Area, Mark, C3, T+A, Architecture Journal*, and *World Architecture.*

Dong Yugan is a teacher at the Graduate Centre of Architecture, Peking University. His general education course, Analysis of Modern/Contemporary Architecture, started eight years ago and remains one of the most popular courses of the university. He has written more than seventy essays, which were published in various magazines, and five small books, three of which were reprinted within half a year. His buildings, most notably the Red Brick Art Museum, has been widely published and exhibited in China and abroad. His design works related to the garden have been collected continuously into the *Annual Book of China's Architecture Art.*

Mario Gandelsonas has been Professor at the School of Architecture at Princeton University since 1991, as both a practice architect and theorist whose specializations include urbanism and semiotics. He is the director of Center for Architecture, Urbanism and Infrastructure and the Principal Researcher of the project "Twenty First Century Infrastructure". Gandelsonas is a frequent contributor to architectural journals and has published extensively, including *Shanghai Reflections: Architecture, Urbanism, and the Search for an Alternative Modernity, X-Urbanism: Architecture and the American City, The Urban Text,* and *Agrest and Gandelsonas, Architects.*

Han Tao is a lecturer as well as a PhD candidate at the Department of Architecture at CAFA from 2006. Han is also the founder of Thanlab, an office established in 2003 which explores the future potential of temporary construction for new art spaces and alternative structural forms for adaptation of dilapidating industrial buildings. Han received his BArch in Architecture from Tongji University and continued his design study at CAFA.

He Jianxiang is a co-founder of O-office Architects, a practice based in Guangzhou established in 2007 with Ying Jiang, and a guest professor at Guangzhou Academy of Fine Arts. He was born in Xinhui, China, and received his BArch from South China University of Technology in 1996. In 2000, he received his MArch from the Katholieke Universiteit Leuven, Belgium. He has lectured in several universities in China and abroad.

Hua Li is the founder of Trace Architecture Office (TAO) and a visiting professor at Tsinghua University, from which he graduated. He read at Yale University and practiced in New York and Beijing before founding TAO in 2009. He has also been a guest critic at the University of Hong Kong (HKU), CAFA, and Universität der Künste Berlin. Hua and TAO has won important worldwide architectural awards, and was listed in Design Vanguard 2012 by *Architectural Record Magazine.*

Huang Weiwen chairs the Shenzhen Centre for Public Art, Shenzhen Centre for Design, and the Shenzhen Biennale of Urbanism\Architecture Organizing Committee Office. He is a former official of the Urban Planning and Land Resources Commission of Shenzhen's municipal government and. Huang was a 2010 Loeb Fellow at Harvard University's Graduate School of Design (GSD). He has actively participated as the main organizer of the Hong Kong-Shenzhen Bi-city Biennale of Urbanism/Architecture (HKSZ UABB).

Huang Wenjing co-founded OPEN Architecture with Li Hu in New York in 2006, with a project office in New Delhi, India. After graduating from Tsinghua University and Princeton University, Huang worked for six years in New York-based Pei Cobb Freed and Partners (formerly I.M. Pei Architects), where she was a senior designer and an associate. She is a licensed architect in the New York State and a member of AIA. Besides practice, Huang is also a visiting assistant professor at HKU and Tsinghua University. She was also a senior editor for *World Architecture Magazine.*

Jiang Jun is Associate Professor in Guangzhou Academy of Fine Art. Professionally trained as an architect at Tongji University and Tsinghua University, Jiang is passionate about archive-editing and free-lance-writing. His work has been featured in in three museums in New York, Los Angeles, and Chicago and is the first Chinese magazine being exhibited overseas in traveling solo exhibitions. He is formerly a visiting fellow at the ESRC Centre on Migration Policy and Society of Oxford University and a project director at Strelka School of Architecture, Design, and Media in Moscow.

Jeffrey Johnson is a founding director as well as a core teaching member of China Megacities Lab at Columbia University. He is also a co-founding principal of SLAB, an architecture and urbanism studio based in New York City, organizing collaborative international China Megacities Lab/Columbia University design studios and workshops in China, and has organized and participated in a number of international forums and exhibitions. Johnson was an executive curator for the 2011 HKSZ UABB.

Michael Kokora is a partner at Object Territories, an architecture, landscape, and urban design practice with offices in Hong Kong and New York. He is an assistant professor at HKU and teaches in the MArch and MLA programs. Prior to founding his own office, he was with OMA. Kokora holds a BA from the University of Minnesota and a MArch from Yale University.

Kengo Kuma is Professor at the Graduate School of Architecture, University of Tokyo and founder of Kengo Kuma & Associates established 1990. Kuma completed his master's degree at the University of Tokyo in 1979 and continued to study at Columbia University as a Visiting Scholar. His current office is founded after experimenting with a small studio named Spatial Design Studio in 1987. Emphasizing on natural materials and technological advancement, Kuma reinvents and reinterprets traditional Japanese construction theories and elements with practice and prolific writings. His recent work in China reveals his sensitivity to put forward a close relationship with vernacular materials and site surroundings.

Andrew Lee is a director of Ong&Ong. Graduated from the National University of Singapore, Lee is involved in various infrastructure and railway-related projects in Singapore, including the MRT Stations of Bedok Reservoir, Bedok Town Park, Tan Kah Kee, and Upper Changi. Apart from practice, he also co-edited *Incubations: A Guidebook to Procuring Innovative Architecture*, the previous AA Asia Monograph, with Jeremy Chia on 2014.

Joan Leung Lye is the co-founder of Lotus Architects Ltd, established in 1987 with her late husband, Professor Eric Lye. Leung Lye graduated from MIT and was a professor of the Department of Architecture at HKU before she founded her company. Her Clubhouse at the Arch won the Grand Award of Quality Building Award for 2008. She is a member of the West Kowloon Cultural District Advisory Committee and the Heritage and Conservation Committee, and publishes papers on architecture education, interior architecture, and green building.

Li Han and Hu Yan are founding members of Drawing Architecture Studio. Their studio offers a creative platform integrating architecture, art, design, urban study, pop culture, and aiming to explore the new models for the creation of contemporary urban culture. Li studied architecture at CAFA and RMIT University. As well as a National Class 1 Registered Architect in China, he had worked as senior architect in China Architecture and Research Group in Beijing for seven years before establishing DAS. His current practice includes architecture design, urban research, and publication. Hu received her BFA from Concordia University in Montreal, Canada. She has years of experiences in branding and product design. Their studio won the second place at 2016 RIBA Journal Eye Line Drawing Competition, an annual international event hosted by RIBA Journal. The three winning drawings are *Qilou Old Street*, *Tuan Jie Hu*, and *Dashilar*.

Li Hu is the principal of OPEN Architecture, founded since 2011, and is visiting professor at Columbia University and HKU. Li read at Tsinghua University and Rice University. He was a partner in the Beijing office of Steven Holl Architects (SHA), leading some of the office's most ambitious and successful projects including Linked Hybrid, Vanke Center, Nanjing Museum for Architecture, and Chengdu Raffles City. Together with Steven Holl and Chang Yung Ho, Li co-founded the architectural journal *32 Beijing/New York* in 2002. In addition to practice, he is also the director of Columbia University GSAPP's Studio-X Beijing, a global network of advanced research laboratories.

Li Shiqiao, PhD is Weedon Professor of Asian Architecture at the University of Virginia. He practiced architecture in London and Hong Kong after his completion of study at Tsinghua University, AA School of Architecture, and Birkbeck College, University of London. He initiated design proposals which were published and exhibited in journals and international exhibitions such as *Bauwelt*, *Domus China*, *World Architecture*, *Cultural Politics*, *Theory Culture & Society*, *Cultural Studies*, and *Architectural Theory Review*. His books include *Understanding the Chinese City*, *Architecture and Modernization,* and *Power and Virtue*, *Architecture and Intellectual Change in England 1650–1730.*

Nartano Lim is the Head of Design for Selangor Properties Berhad based in Kuala Lumpur. Lim studied graphic communications management and fine arts at New York University and architecture at Syracuse University. He worked in New York City with Robert A.M. Stern and Arakawa + Gins, as well as Singapore, Shanghai, and Kuala Lumpur with DP Architects as an Associate Director. Lim was previously an Assistant Professor at Syracuse University and an invited critic at Yale University. In 2012, he authored *Sand to Spectacle: The Dubai Mall* and has been published in *IKEAgrams: Project on the Waterfront* by Benjamin Pell and T.L. Brown.

William S.W. Lim, DArch *honoris causa,* graduated from the Architectural Association (AA) London and continued his graduate study at Harvard University. His professional work involves architecture, planning, and development economics. Lim founded Design Partnership (presently DP Architects) in 1967 and William Lim Associates in 1981. He is president of AA Asia and chairman of AUL. He was the first president of the Singapore Heritage Society from 1988-1997, and of the Singapore Planning and Research Group (SPUR) from 1966-1968. Lim was conferred a DArch *honoris causa* by RMIT University in 2002 and Honorary Professor of LaSalle-SIA College of the Arts, Singapore, in 2005. Currently, Lim writes and lectures on a wide range of subjects relating to architecture, urbanism and culture in Asia as well as on current issues relating to the postmodern, glocality, and social justice. His latest publication is *Incomplete Urbanism: A Critical Urban Strategy for Emerging Economics* in 2012.

Liu Jiakun founded Jiakun Architects in 1999, a multidisciplinary office based in Chengdu which specializes in contemporary architectural issues inspired by folk wisdom. Liu received several domestic and international awards in architectural field, such as the Honor Prize of the 7th ARCASIA, Chinese Architecture & Art Prize in 2003, and Architectural Record Magazine China Awards. His work has been widely published and recognized by prestigious architectural magazines such as *A+U, AV, Area,* and *Made in China.* He has been invited to give lectures at MIT, Royal Academy of Arts, Palais de Chaillot in Paris, Bauhaus in Dessau and many top universities in China.

Liu Kecheng is dean of School of Architecture of Xi'an University of Architecture and Technology, his alma mater, chair of DOCOMOMO China, director of Conservation Center of Monuments and Site of Shaanxi Province, and director of Xi'an Research Institute of Urban Heritage. His research and practice focuses mainly on the preservation of cultural heritage and museum design. He has received National Expert with Extraordinary Contributions Award in 1994, National Expert of the New Millennium Award in 2006 and 100 Contemporary Architects in China in 2012.

Liu Yichun is the co-founder of Atelier Deshaus in Shanghai, established in 2001 with Chen Yifeng and Zhuang Shen. Graduated at Tongji University, Liu had an immense success under the bloom of municipal projects in Shanghai set up by the Central Government at that time. Soon after leaving the commercial practice, he served as Chief Architect of the Architectural Design Institute of Tongji University from 1997. His ambitions of reviving Chinese tradition is based on his reinterpretation of ancient Chinese philosophy into a new meanings of Chinese architecture.

Long Ying, PhD is Associate Professor at Tsinghua University. With a background of environmental engineering and city planning, Long's research focuses on quantitative urban studies and applied urban modeling. He had worked for Beijing Institute of City Planning as a senior planner for eleven years. Familiar with planning practices in China and versed in the international literature, Long's academic studies creatively integrates international methods and experiences with local planning practices. He is also the founder of Beijing City Lab, an open research network for quantitative urban studies.

Ma Qingyun is founder of MADA s.p.a.m., established 1996, and the dean of the School of Architecture at the University of Southern California (USC). Ma studied at Tsinghua University and the University of Pennsylvania and acquired a keen business sense centered on design intelligence. As the dean since 2007, Ma has started up new programs and established the USC American Academy in China for visiting scholars to facilitate their research and foster academic exchange. He is also a frequent speaker and juror at events such as the 2008 Beijing Olympics, the prestigious Rome Prize, and the 2010 Shanghai World Expo.

Meng Yan is an architect licensed in the New York State and the co-founder of Urbanus with Liu Xiaodu and Wang Hui. Meng studied architecture at Tsinghua University and Miami University. Meng leaded Urbanus in numerous projects in China, such as Dafen Art Museum, Tulou Collective Housing, OCT Art & Design Gallery and Loft Renovation, and Maillen Hotel & Apartment, winning international reputation for the firm. He was appointed chief curator of the Shenzhen Pavilion in the 2010 Shanghai Expo and has been an academic committee member of the HKSZ UABB.

Ou Ning is Adjunct Assistant Professor at Columbia University GSAPP. Graduated from Shenzhen University, he is an artist, filmmaker, writer, and editor. Ou has directed documentaries on the urban, including *San Yuan Li* (2003) and *Meishi Street* (2006), and curated multiple biennales in China, including the *2009 HKSZ UABB* and *2011 Chengdu Biennale*. He is also known for his seminal books *New Sound of Beijing* (1997), *Odyssey: Architecture and Literature* (2011), *The Chinese Thinking: Rem Koolhaas and Hans Ulrich Obrist Interviewed China's Leading Figures* (2012), and *South of Southern: Space, Geography, History and the Biennale* (2013).

Mary-Ann Ray is the Taubman Centennial Professor of Practice in Architecture at the University of Michigan and Urban Planning and Adjunct Faculty Member at SCI-Arc. She has also held numerous visiting chair at Yale University and Rice University. Ray is the principal of Studio Works Architects in Los Angeles and the co-Founder and Director of B.A.S.E. Beijing and B.A.S.E. Mumbai. She was a recipient of the Rome Prize in 1987-1988. Among her published books are *Pamphlet Architecture No. 20: Partly Underground Rooms and Buildings for Water, Ice and Midgets*; *Wrapper or 40 Possible City Surfaces for the Museum of Jurassic Technology*; and the recent *Caochangdi: Beijing Inside Out*.

Daan Roggeveen is the co-founder and director of MORE Architecture, a research-based office based in Shanghai. He studied architecture at Delft University of Technology and worked with NL Architects and MADA s.p.a.m. He was also the curator at the Shanghai Study Centre of HKU, organizing the public lecture series "Follow the Money" and the exhibitions *Olympic Cities*, *The Future of the Museum*, and *Monument to Progress*. His multidisciplinary research studio Go West Project, with journalist Michiel Hulshof, launched *How the City Moved to Mr Sun – China's New Megacities*, an acclaimed book on the transformation on Chinese cities in 2011. His most recent publication is *Progress & Prosperity: The New Chinese City as Global Urban Model*.

Ruan Hao is the founding principal of LYCS Architecture. Ruan studied architecture at Tsinghua University and Princeton University, and is one of the youngest architectural awardee of China's "Recruitment Program of Global Experts," and the very first architect selected for Forbes China 30-under-30. He was also recognized by IMAGE 50 Under 50: Innovators of the 21st Century, 2013 China Top 10 Interior Designers, Goldman Sachs Global Leaders, and Asia Society Asia 21 Leaders. He was the youngest visiting fellow at Harvard University GSD, where he later taught a design studio with Wang Shu. Currently, Ruan is a lecturer at the China Academy of Art School of Architecture.

Eunice Seng, PhD is Chair of the Departmental Research Postgraduate Committee (PhD) for Architecture and Associate Professor at the Faculty of Architecture, HKU. She is also the founding principal of SKEW Collaborative. Her research interests include the histories and theories of modernity, housing in the metropolis, politics of power and post-colonialism, as well as utopias, artifacts and their cultural representations. Current research projects include "Inventing the Public: The Colonial Complex and Modern Collective Housing in Singapore, 1936-1976," and "Building Housing Experiments: A Comparative Analysis of Modern Housing in Hong Kong, Singapore and London, 1950s." She is a member of the Affordable Housing Research Network and Asian Urban Lab.

Shi Jian is a scholar, curator, and publisher, as well as the co-founder of POSITION with Zhu Tao and Zhao Leilian, which promotes architectural tourism in China and other parts of the world. He believes that tourism is an effective medium for public to get a deeper glimpse and perspective of what architecture really is. His architecture criticisms have been covered extensively in *Time+Architecture* and occasionally presented in other architectural periodicals including *Architect, New Architecture,* and *World Architecture.*

Sun Yimin, PhD graduated from Harbin Institute of Technology with BEng, MArch, and PhD degrees. He was selected as national culturist of the project of talent selection by Guangdong government and was candidate for the national Outstanding Youth Foundation. Being the first Doctor of Physical Architecture graduated in China, Sun enjoys a national prime position in physical architectural research. As member of the National Physical Architecture Committee, Sun has participated in judging, feasibility study, and project

argumentation of several national stadium construction projects.

Victor Su is a managing partner at SHCC Architects. He studied architecture at Parson School of Design and the University of Pennsylvania. Su's work is mainly based in Taiwan and is socially active in promoting the local culture, organizing lectures and activities that promote public involvement in architecture. He received a nomination at the World Architecture Festival Award 2011 and a prize at the Internazionale Marmi e Macchine Carrara SpA Marble Architectural Award East Asia. His work was also exhibited in *11th International Architecture Exhibition* at La Biennale di Venezia.

Wang Fei is the founder of FWStudio, an interdisciplinary studio in China and the USA. Wang read at McGill University, Virginia Tech, and Tongji University. He is a guest editor of *Time+Architecture* and *Urban Flux.* His books include the co-edited *Inter-Views: Trends of Architectural and Urbanism Institutions in North America and Europe* (2010) and *Poetics of Construction, The Discourse of Tectonics in Contemporary China* (2014). An architect, educator, and critic, Wang has lectured at numerous design and art institutions including HKU, Tongji University, University of Michigan, the Architectural Association, and China Academy of Art.

Wang Shu is dean and professor of Architecture School of China Academy of Art in Hangzhou and an honorary professor at HKU. Born in 1963 in Urumqi, Xinjiang, Wang studied architecture at the Nanjing Institute of Technology. He co-founded Amateur Architecture Studio with his wife Lu Wenyu in 1997, focusing on experimental building tactics based on intensive research and a traditional understanding of construction. He became the first Chinese Kenzo Tange Visiting Professor at the Harvard University GSD in 2011, and the first Chinese Pritzker Prize Winner in 2012.

Shirley Woo is an architectural designer of the Shanghai branch of Kengo Kuma & Associates, where she has been working on multiple China-based projects since 2013. Woo studied architecture at the University of Hong Kong. With a continued interest in Japanese architecture, Woo worked at several firms in Japan. Her graduate thesis, Fading Coastline, explores the potential of a resilient maritime community in Sendai, Japan, and it was published in *Taiwan Architecture.*

Wu Gang is a principal designer and general manager in WSP Beijing from 1999. Before he worked as a partner in WSP Architects and Engineers Munich, Germany, Wu studied landscape architecture at Tongji University and architecture at Technical University of Karlsruhe. He also serves as associate professor at Chinese University of Hong Kong and visiting professor at Nanjing University and Southeast University. Wu's work have been widely published and exhibited in Dutch Design Week 2008, Architectural Biennial in Beijing 2004, China Modern Construction Exhibition in Düsseldorf, Germany 2003, and WA Chinese Architecture Award in 2002. A member of AA Asia, he was also elected as one of the "Ten Greatest Architects in China" in 2005, and one of the "100 Most Influential Chinese Architects" in 2004.

Wu Liangyong is Professor at Tsinghua University. Born in Nanjing in 1922, Wu studied architecture at National Central University, Chongqing, and Cranbrook Academy of Art, and worked with Professor Liang Sicheng in founding the Department of Architecture of Tsinghua University in 1946. Wu has held multiple leading positions of academic societies, such as the Urban Planning Society of China, the Architectural Society of China, and the China Society of Urban Studies. Since 1987, Wu has taken change of a research project of Beijing Ju'er Hutong New Courtyard House and won a few of awards in the national level.

Xu Tiantian is the founding principal of the Design and Architecture Beijing (DnA Beijing). She read architecture at Tsinghua University and Harvard University, specializing in urban design. Prior to establishing DnA Beijing, she worked at the United States and with OMA in the Netherlands. Her extensively researched on the Rural Construction Movement, Zhejiang Province, collaborating with local villagers and workers with over a dozen of projects built or under construction. She has also initiated "Field Work Station" in Songyang as an open platform for artists and designers to exchange with rural culture.

Rocco Yim, DSocSc *honoris causa*, is the founder of Rocco Design Architects. Born and educated in Hong Kong, Yim's works have consistently been awarded both in Hong Kong and overseas since winning the First Prize Award for the L'Opéra de la Bastille international competition in 1983. Yim is a regular invited speaker in local and international symposia. His works have been exhibited four times in the Venice Biennale over the last decade, and widely published, notably in *The City in Architecture* (2003), *Being Chinese in Architecture* (2004), *Presence* (2012), and his monograph, *Reconnecting Cultures* (2013).

Yu Kongjian, DDes, is the founder of Turenscape and dean of the College of Architecture and Landscape of Peking University. Yu received his DDes at Harvard University. His ecological approach to urbanism has been implemented in over 200 cities in China and abroad, and have had significant impact on national policies aiming at improving the environment in China, obtaining the Overseas Chinese Achievement Award and the One Thousand Talents Award. His most recent book, *Designed Ecologies: The Landscape Architecture of Kongjian,* explores Yu's work in eleven essays by noted authors, extensively documenting 22 selected projects.

Zhang Ke is the founder of standardarchitecture, a leading new generation design firm engaged in practices of planning, architecture, landscape, and product design. Based on a wide range of realized buildings and landscapes in the past ten years, the studio has emerged as one of the most critical and realistic practice among the youngest generation of Chinese architects and designers, winning various awards in China and abroad. Zhang Ke studied at Tsinghua University and Harvard University.

Zhan Yuan is a partner of LYCS Architecture and is an instructor at the China Academy of Art School of Architecture. He graduated from Harvard University and Tianjin University, where he studied under Danish architect Biarke Ingels and Swiss architect Christian Kerez. Prior to joining LYCS, Zhan worked at Kengo Kuma and Associates. At LYCS, he led a number of award-winning projects, including the Tiantai No.2 Primary School. Zhan was invited to speak at various events Harvard, Zhejiang, and Tianjin University, and was also invited to join the 2013 Harvard Asia Business Forum as a main speaker.

Zhao Liang, PhD is a director at Taikang Community, a subsidiary of the Chinese insurance company Taikang Life. Zhao studied architecture at Tsinghua University, and his PhD from Harvard University specializing in urbanism. Subsequently, Zhao was lecturer at MIT's Department of Urban Studies and Planning, where he collaborated with his Harvard professor Alex Krieger in urban design projects for Shanghai, winning the UNESCO Gold Medal at the UIA. Zhao returned to China in 2008 and worked in Vanke Group prior to his current position.

Darren Zhou is Design Principal at SKEW Collaborative, Shanghai and Hong Kong, and Adjunct Assistant Professor at the Shanghai Study Center of HKU. A LEED accredited profession, Zhou is from Singapore and received his BA at Columbia University and MArch at Princeton University. He has won awards from Blueprint, LEAF, Green-Dot, and WIN, and in 2016 he was awarded 40 Under 40 in Architecture from Perspective. Zhou is also the program director of Cities in Asia, a summer program of HKU.

Zhou Yi is a curator of the Inside-Out Museum and CAFA. Born in 1972 in China, Zhou moved to America in 1991, where he studied at Cooper Union and the Tyler School of Art. Zhou is active in curating and collaborating with artists, musicians, as well as in participating in community work, pioneering a drawing competition for children with autism in China. He also served as a project director of the Miniature Museum with Thomas Tsang. In 2010, he was invited as a guest speaker at the Department of Architecture at HKU.

Zhu Tao, PhD is Associate Professor at HKU. Zhu studied at Chongqing University and Columbia University, practices in China, and writes on contemporary Chinese architecture and urbanism, including a chapter entitled "Architecture in China in the Reform Era 1978-2010" for *A Critical History of Contemporary Architecture 1960-2010* (2012). His latest book, *Liang Sicheng and His Time* (2014), traces Liang's complex relationship with the changing regime of Chinese government and explored spatial vision dominated by political factors.

Zhu Xiaofeng is the design principal and founder of Scenic Architecture, as well as Visiting Professor at Tongji University and HKU. Zhu read at Shenzhen University and Harvard University, and has received several awards for his work, including the 40 under 40 Award from Perspective for Young Asian Design Pioneers. His office participated in international exhibitions including *China Contemporary* at NAI Rotterdam, *China Design Now* at the Victoria & Albert Museum in London, *New Trends of Architecture in Europe and Asia-Pacific* in Tokyo, and the *2010 Venice Architecture Biennale*.

ACKNOWLEDGEMENTS

This research and interlocution with academics, theorists, critics, and practitioners from China would have been impossible without the consistent support of non-profit organization AA Asia. Financial support for this publication, including a number of forums, seminars and study trips were provided by a grant from AA Asia. Founded by William S.W. Lim, AA Asia was formally set up as a society in 1993 after a group of Architectural Association graduates from Asia came together for informal dialogues. AA Asia has since been steadfast in promoting the study and research of architecture in Asian cities. It has supported research, symposia, lectures, study trips, and discussion series at countless Asian cities to better grasp the deep historical and social bearings of each Asian culture. Most notably, AA Asia organized the *Non-West Modernist Past Conference* in 2011 on the historiography of modern architecture outside Western canons, as well as the *Asian Design Culture Conference* in 2008 on the unique identities of different Asian creative cultures. I would like to thank Sonny Chan, Chan Hui Min, and Tan Szue Hann, who have served AA Asia sacrificially in the past few years. AA Asia has also benefited from advice from academics and practitioners from a variety of cities, including Leon van Schaik, Tan Dan Feng, Karan Grover, Budi Lim, Takeo Muraji, Lim Teng Ngiom, Lilian Chee, Randy Chan, Liao Weili, Duangrit Bunnag, and Robert Powell. By its sheer size, China had to be covered by a number of research, lectures, and study trips in a multi-year project. It returns full circle to the same social themes covered in the very first AA Asia China symposium *Contemporary Vernacular: Conceptions and Perceptions* in 1997, which culminated in a book edited by Christopher Lee. Co-organized by Tsinghua University, there were four key sections of "history," "culture," "social tectonics," and "tectonics." I would like to extend my sincerest thanks to Professor Wu Liangyong for not only hosting the initial 1997 symposium, but also contributing an essay to this volume. It was the pioneering work of Lim, Wu and their generation of academics and architects who have set the tone for a humanist agenda in the study of Asia on its own historical, social and architectural terms. This is the same juncture where one encounters this particular study of China's architecture and its social battleground.

In addition to the fifty-seven authors who had contributed their intellectual enterprises to this volume, I would like to recognize the research, editorial, and translation assistance given to me by Chu Lai Jing, Nicole Li, Christina Kong, Alex Yuen, Aaron Liu, and Susan Wang from HKU, SCI-Arc, and SKEW Collaborative. The ideas behind the social project of architecture were honed during the decade-long teaching and practice with loyal collaborators Eunice Seng, Darren Zhou, and Lam Lai Shun. The formulating of new research and teaching materials, and the theorizing of this incredible Chinese condition occurred at HKU, with allies such as Zhu Tao, Dorothy Tang, Zhi Wenjun, Li Shiqiao, Austin Williams, and Ma Qingyun who were generous in engaging in productive debates about this topic in Hong Kong, Shanghai, and Los Angeles. The editors of journals cited in this volume also deserve special gratitude. Many forums, debates, seminars and discussions took place in different cities in China, and they would not have been possible without the comradeship and hospitality of many. Sun Yimin, Zhang Zhenhui, and Song Gang hosted a lively lecture series and forum at the South China University of Technology. Yungho Chang, and Lu Lijia anchored a highly engaging evening discussion session in Beijing. Liu Xiaodu, Meng Yan, and Wang Hui generously opened their Space-E6 for two fiercely debated forums in Shenzhen and Beijing. Huang Wenjing, Li Hu, and Shi Jian gave their time to host two discussion sessions at the Beijing No.4 High School and the Linked Hybrid. Weng Ling hosted a productive session at the Beijing Center for the Arts. Han Tao supported in a special seminar at the Chinese Academy of Oil Painting. Xu Tiantian generously offered her time in our session at the Songzhuang Art Museum, despite having to juggle motherhood and work. Wu Gang hosted the most fascinating discussion at the Baidu Headquarters. Hua Li was liberal in his time and engagement with us in a dialogue at the Tree Clubhouse. Laurence Loh and Takeo Muraji were part of a lecture series at the HKU Shanghai Study Center. Giel Groothuis engaged us in a discussion at the Dutch Design Workspace. Interlocuters during the three-year project includes Wang Weijen, Tat Lam, Zhu Pei, Liang Jingyu, Shean Chien, Mark Hemel, Jennifer Lee and Pablo Castro, Daan Ooievaar, Ma Yansong, Simon Yu, Lu Wenyu, Cherry Cheung, Yuan Ling, and Lu Xiaoxuan. Assistants from various Chinese architectural practices rendered timely help during the manuscript preparations, including Gao Lezhou, Renee Xue, Zhang Yun, and Chen Tianle.

This book has also drawn upon the ideas expounded in the seminars, lectures, meals, and study trips to China taken together with colleagues from different parts of Asia. In particular, I had the benefit of learning from Angelene Chan, Theodore Chan, Jeremy Chan, Benjamin Chew, James Goh, Wellington Kuswanto, Nartano Lim, Poon Yew Wai, Quek Leng Leng, Arjun Rosha, Victor Su, Xavier Tan, and Elaine Thian during a study trip to Shenzhen and Guangzhou undertaken from October 26 to 30 in 2013. In addition, precious insights were gained from Joan Leung Lye, Stephen Cairns, Budi Lim, Dika Terra Lim, Wong Xue Nie, Alvin Arre, Gene Dulig Arre, Jeremy Chia, Desmond Chua, Brian Suarez Erick, Kee Wei Hui, Andrew Lee, Low Yee Von, Jessa Lyni, Yutaro Muraji, Quay Say Yeow, Quek Kiok Seng, Frank Quek, Jesse Lyn Salvatus, Sia Teong Heng, Tan Szue Hann, Yap Weng Seng, Paul Yoo, Felicia Youh, and Nasir Nassar Zain during a study trip to Beijing from March 5 to 10 in 2015. Lena Lim, Koh Tai Ann, Charles Lee, and Qiu Wen Hao shared their critical thoughts with me during both study trips.

GLOSSARY

baihuawen 白话文

bao'an 保安

baojie 保洁

baomu 保姆

beipiao 北漂

cailiao 材料

canjiren 残疾人

canlan 灿烂

chaiqian 拆迁

chengshi 城市

chengzhongcun 城中村

chi guojia 吃国家

congyezhe 从业者

dadao 大道

danwei 单位

dashou xiaofang 大收小放

datong 大同

di 地

dikuai 地块

dingzihu 钉子户

fazhi 法治

fengjing 风景

fengturenqing 风土人情

gengdu 耕读

gewu zhizhi 格物致知

gongshe 公社

gongzheng 公正

guankan 观看

guxiang 故乡

haipiao 海漂

huayi 画意

hukou 户口

hutong 胡同

jiajian gouzhu 加建构筑

jianzhu 建筑

jianzhuyi 建筑意

jingjie 境界

kan 看

kongxincun 空心村

li 礼

liulang 流浪

liumang 流氓

liuxuesheng 留学生

matouqiang 马头墙

pingdeng 平等

qigong 气功

qiguai 奇怪

ren 仁

sanmianguang 三面光

shanzhai 山寨

shangceng jianzhu 上层建筑

shehui zhuyi hao 社会主义好

shiyi 诗意

shuzu 鼠族

siheyuan 四合院

tiyan 体验

tui'erjinsan 退二进三

tulou 土楼

wuliao 物料

wuxing 物性

xiangbalao 乡巴佬

xiaodao 小道

xiaojie 小姐

xiaokang 小康

xiaoqu 小区

xiaoshangfan 小商贩

xiaotou 小偷

xin 信

yi 义

yiguo liangzhi 一国两制

yindizhiyi 因地制宜

yiwen 艺文

yizhu 蚁族

youtiao 油条

zhi 智

zhuangzhi yishu 装置艺术

ziyou 自由

INDEX